ALSO BY HENRY LOUIS GATES, JR.

Finding Your Roots, Season 2: The Official Companion to the PBS Series
Finding Your Roots, Season 1: The Official Companion to the PBS Series
The Henry Louis Gates, Jr. Reader
Life Upon These Shores
Black in Latin America
Tradition and the Black Atlantic
Faces of America
In Search of Our Roots
Lincoln on Race and Slavery
Finding Oprah's Roots
America Behind the Color Line: Dialogues with African Americans
The Trials of Phillis Wheatley
Little Known Black History Facts
Wonders of the African World
Thirteen Ways of Looking at a Black Man
Colored People
Loose Canons
Figures in Black
The Signifying Monkey

WITH EMMANUEL K. AKYEAMPONG

The Dictionary of African Biography

WITH KWAME ANTHONY APPIAH

Encyclopedia of Africa
The Dictionary of Global Culture
Africana: The Encyclopedia of the African and African American Experience
Encarta Africana

100
Amazing Facts
About the
Negro

100
Amazing Facts
About the
Negro

HENRY LOUIS GATES, JR.

PANTHEON BOOKS / NEW YORK

Portions of this work originally appeared, in different form,
in *The Root* (www.theroot.com).

Library of Congress Cataloging-in-Publication Data
Name: Gates, Henry Louis, Jr., author.
Title: 100 amazing facts about the Negro / Henry Louis Gates, Jr.
Description: New York : Pantheon Books [2017]. Includes index.
Identifiers: LCCN 2016024453 (print). LCCN 2016024539 (ebook).
ISBN 9780307908711 (hardcover). ISBN 9780307908728 (ebook).
Subjects: LCSH: Blacks—History—Miscellanea.
African Americans—History—Miscellanea.
Classification: LCC CB235.G39 2017 (print). LCC CB235 (ebook).
DDC 973/.0496073—dc23
LC record available at lccn.loc.gov/2016024453

www.pantheonbooks.com

Jacket images: (top, left to right, details) *Thomas-Alexandre Dumas* by Olivier
Pichat, akg-images; map of Spanish Florida and Jackie Robinson, both Library
of Congress, Washington, D.C.; (bottom, left to right) *The Redemption of Ham*
by Modesto Brocos y Gómez, akg-images; Malcolm X, Keystone Pictures
USA/Alamy; Madam C. J. Walker, Library of Congress, Washington, D.C.

Jacket design by Oliver Munday

Printed in China
First Edition
2 4 6 8 9 7 5 3 1

To Marial Iglesias Utset

Contents

100
Amazing Facts
About the
Negro

1

Which journalist was among the first to bring black history facts to the masses?

FOR BLACK FAMILIES in the middle of the twentieth century, "Mr. Rogers" was a columnist for the legendary *Pittsburgh Courier,* and his pithy and always intriguing tidbits of African and African-American history armed them with facts about the black experience that seemed more like fantasies. Since students weren't being taught anything about black people at school, Joel A. Rogers was just about the only source of black history that a few generations had.

The first edition of his now legendary *100 Amazing Facts About the Negro with Complete Proof,* published in 1957, was billed as "A Negro 'Believe It or Not,'" signifying on Robert Ripley's brain-bending series that had premiered in the *New York Globe* in October 1919.[1] Rogers's little book was priceless because he was delivering enlightenment and pride, steeped in historical research, to a people too long starved on the lie that they were worth nothing because their ancestors had *contributed* nothing to world civilization. Deep in his bones, Rogers knew what a lie that was, and he used every ounce of creative energy he had to expose the twin fallacies on which it was based: racial purity and white supremacy. For African Americans of the Jim Crow era, Rogers was their first black history teacher. And he wrote to educate, with the black everyman and everywoman foremost in his mind.

Did he sometimes embellish what he had found? Yes; he wasn't above shock journalism. Did he miss key details? Absolutely. His style was brief and to the point, using a minimum of words and ambiguity so that the "facts" could speak for themselves.

Critics skeptical of Rogers's style dismissed him as a "vindicationist" for an aggrieved race, as Thabiti Asukile notes.[2] And many of the subsequent ninety-nine chapters in this book will put Rogers's amazing facts to the test. Although he didn't bat a thousand, he consistently and tantalizingly raised questions about history that stimulated others to dig deeper. But he was as serious a researcher as they come, as serious as W.E.B. Du Bois and Carter G. Woodson. And when you study his life, you realize he wasn't just an aficionado of amazing facts. He *was* one of those facts.

Joel Augustus Rogers was born in Negril, Jamaica, on September 6, 1880, to Samuel and Emily (Johnstone) Rogers. When university study was precluded in the Caribbean, Rogers served for four years in the Royal Garrison Artillery.

A heart murmur may have kept him from serving overseas but not from traveling. As for looks, he was told he could pass for Cuban, but when he emigrated to the United States in 1906, it became clear that under the old one-drop rule, he was black. Thus he was relegated to the hard-luck side of the color line, a fact made all too clear when he was dissed at a restaurant in New York's Times Square.[3]

Joel Augustus Rogers in 1936, soon after he began work on *100 Amazing Facts About the Negro*.

After visiting Boston, Rogers made his way westward to Chicago, where the University of Chicago denied him admission because, in Asukile's words, "he did not possess a high school diploma." From then on, Rogers knew that whatever he accomplished in life as a man of letters would have to be done without degrees.

Rogers was especially devoted to debunking the false religion of racial purity then being expounded in such racist texts as Thomas Dixon's 1905 novel *The Clansman,* later adapted for the screen by D. W. Griffith in 1915's *Birth of a Nation.* The whole legal apparatus of segregation hinged on the illusion that whites and blacks could easily be identified, then rigidly categorized, so that any advantages in life were doled out only to those free of any (obvious) "drops" of African blood.

Rogers's game plan was simple: proudly claim for the black race any man, woman, or child, including gods and goddesses, in the pages and paintings of history who manifested traces of African or "Negroid" ancestry. Textbook examples were the Russian novelist Alexander Pushkin and Alessandro de' Medici, as well as Gen. Thomas-Alexandre Dumas and Alexandre Dumas. Rogers poked as much as he prodded, while restoring to greatness lost heroes of the black experience, among them Saint Maurice, Benjamin Banneker, Toussaint Louverture, Paul Cuffee, Cetshwayo, and various Congressional Medal of Honor recipients.

Rogers waged his battle against Jim Crow on three broad fronts: history, genealogy, and genetics, as the historian W. Burghardt Turner pointed out in 1975.[4] Rogers didn't need yet-to-be-discovered DNA science to tell him that sex between the races had been going on since time immemorial. If anything, Turner explained, Rogers detected "a seemingly mystical attraction of the light to the dark" (not the other way around) and tried proving it in his mini-exposés of famous world leaders.

Rogers did all this virtually by himself. No mainstream publisher would touch his books, so he released them through his own imprint: the J. A. Rogers Historical Research Society. Making matters more difficult, he had no grants or foundation support to speak of and no lectureships or professorships to sustain him. Except for a three-hundred-dollar infusion from journalist H. L. Mencken, he paid his own way.

The black press (effectively, the nation's first black studies departments) gave Rogers his day job reporting the news, first for the *Chicago Enterprise* and then, when he moved back to New York in 1921, for fellow Jamaican Marcus Garvey's *Daily Negro Times.* From there, his rise was quick. Of particular help was the noted black essayist George Schuyler, who networked Rogers to A. Philip Randolph's socialist *Messenger* magazine before they became colleagues at the *Pittsburgh Courier.* It was for the *Courier* and the *New York Amsterdam News* that Rogers made two critical trips abroad in the 1920s.

The world was suddenly different after the war. Some European powers had fallen, and the future of others was in doubt, while a nascent Pan-Africanism, encouraged by Du Bois, was on the rise. In the thick of it, Rogers traveled across Britain, North Africa, Italy, and Spain, absorbing everything he could. He made Paris his home base and there became a proselytizer of jazz. He even had his essay "Jazz at Home" anthologized in the founding document of the Harlem Renaissance, Alain Locke's *The New Negro: An Interpretation.*[5]

In his spare time, Rogers hunted for whatever lost or buried information from the black past he could find. He was just as fascinated by the written word as he was by the visual arts. (It helped that he spoke several languages.) For his efforts, as Asukile writes, Rogers was elected to the Paris Society of Anthropology.[6] And when he returned home to Depression-era New York, he was a library of one, like his Harlem neighbor Arthur Schomburg.

With encouragement from Schuyler and a green light from Robert Vann, his editor at the *Courier,* Rogers launched his popular "Your History" column as a weekly vehicle for communicating the treasure trove of amazing facts he had brought back. Rogers's series ran from 1934 all the way to 1966 (though from 1962 on it was called "Facts About the Negro").

Rogers died doing what he loved: researching black history. After having a stroke on an expedition to Washington, D.C., he passed away at St. Clare's Hospital in New York on March 26, 1966, at eighty-five. He was buried at Ferncliff Cemetery in Westchester County, New York. His widow, Helga Rogers-Andrews, a former translator in the German government whom Rogers had married in 1957, heroically kept the story of this very private man, and his many books, alive until her own death in 2013. Generations of scholars, teachers, and students are the beneficiaries of Joel A. Rogers's remarkable historical discoveries.

The best way to honor him, I think, is to follow his example by taking nothing we are taught for granted; to be ever curious, open, and alive; and to take ourselves to task for being too easily impressed by what is handed to us. This book, *100 Amazing Facts About the Negro,* is an homage to Rogers's work. Thank you, Joel A. Rogers. Because of you, the field of black history has never been stronger.

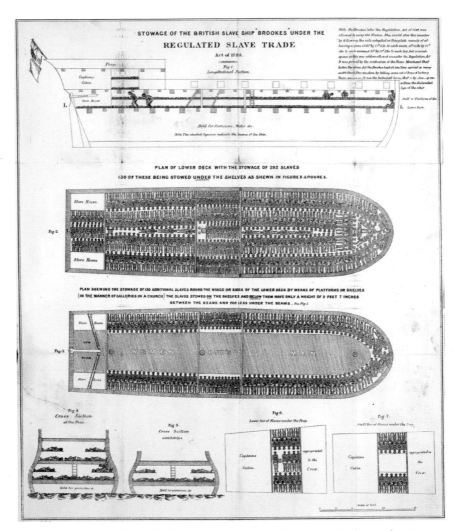

Stowage of the British Slave Ship Brookes *under the Regulated Slave Trade Act of 1788.*
Broadside, ca. 1788.

2

How many Africans were taken to the United States during the entire history of the slave trade?

THE MOST COMPREHENSIVE ANALYSIS of shipping records over the course of the slave trade is the Trans-Atlantic Slave Trade Database.[1] While the editors are careful to say that all their figures are estimates, they are the proverbial gold standard in the study of the slave trade. According to the database, between 1525 and 1866, 12.5 million Africans were shipped to the New World. Some 10.7 million survived the dreaded Middle Passage, disembarking in North America, the Caribbean, and South America.

And how many of these 10.7 million Africans were shipped directly to North America? Only about 388,000.

In fact, the overwhelming majority of the African slaves were shipped directly to the Caribbean and South America; Brazil alone received 4.86 million. Some scholars estimate that another 60,000 to 70,000 ended up in the United States after touching down in the Caribbean first, so that would bring the total to approximately 450,000 Africans who arrived in the United States over the course of the slave trade. Most of the 42 million members of the current African-American community descend from this tiny group of less than half a million Africans.

3

Who was the first African to arrive in America?

THE FIRST AFRICANS to arrive in what is now the United States were *not* the "twenty and odd" who arrived as slaves in Jamestown, Virginia, from what is now Angola, in 1619.[1] As a matter of fact, Africans arrived in North America more than a *century* before the *Mayflower* landed at Plymouth Rock in 1620. The first documented African to arrive wasn't even a slave.

Juan Garrido was born in West Africa around 1480. His notarized *probanza* (his curriculum vitae, more or less), dated 1538, says he moved from Africa to Lisbon, Portugal, stayed in Spain for seven years, and then, seeking his fortune and perhaps a bit of fame, joined the earliest conquistadors to the New World. All the sworn witnesses to this document affirm that Garrido was *horro,* or free, when he arrived in Spain. Sailing from Seville around 1503, he arrived on the island of La Española, which is today called Hispaniola, the island on which the Dominican Republic and Haiti reside. He later settled in San Juan, Puerto Rico.[2]

Garrido was the first black conquistador. And like the other conquistadors, he soon succumbed to the lure of wealth and fame in the New World. He joined Diego Velázquez de Cuéllar and the legendary Juan Ponce de León in the colonizations of Cuba and Puerto Rico, respectively. Then, in 1513, he joined de León's well-known expedition to Florida in search of the Fountain of Youth, which would bring him to America.

In his *probanza,* Garrido claimed to have been "the first to plant and harvest wheat" in the New World. But like the other conquistadors, he was no saint: he participated in Hernán Cortés's destruction of the Aztec empire, along with 100,000 Tlaxcalan allies. He settled in Mexico City in

Juan Garrido, as he appears in a manuscript written by Diego Durán, *Historia de las Indias de Nueva España e Islas de la Tierra Firme,* 1581. Madrid, Biblioteca Nacional.

1524 for four years, then began a gold-mining operation with slave labor. He joined Cortés in the 1530s for an expedition into lower California in search of the mythic Black Amazons. He was rewarded for his services to Cortés with land and paid positions. He spent his final years as a Spanish subject back in Mexico City, where he died in the late 1540s.

4

Who was the first black saint?

A THIRD-CENTURY ROMAN LEGIONARY who was born in Thebes in Upper Egypt, Maurice was martyred in what is today Switzerland for refusing to massacre Christians for the Roman Empire. He was canonized by the early church, long before the pope vested authority over the processes of canonization and beatification exclusively in the Holy See in 1634.

In the late fourth century Theodore, the bishop of Octudurum, had a vision in which he saw the martyrdom of Maurice and his fellow soldiers at Agaunum. Soon after, the cult of Maurice was established and a church was built on the site. Then, in the early sixth century (ca. 515), devotees established an abbey there on land donated by King Sigismund of Burgundy. The abbey is still an active monastery and pilgrimage site, and the tomb of Saint Maurice has been excavated. His feast day is September 22.

Many early depictions of Maurice misrepresented him as a white man. The first time he was portrayed as black was in about CE 1240, in a magnificent stone statue, standing next to the grave of Otto I, Holy Roman emperor, in the Magdeburg Cathedral in central Germany.

Scholars believe depictions of Maurice as a dark-skinned African started appearing at this time because the Holy Roman emperor Frederick II Barbarossa had ambitions to match the span of the pope's spiritual dominion and rule the entire world. Supporting this theory is the fact that Frederick had black Africans at his court and in his retinue. Magdeburg, where the first image of Maurice as a black African appeared, was on the frontiers of the empire and was a region of military expansion.

The black Saint Maurice became the subject of some of the greatest works of art created during the late Middle Ages and the Renaissance. His cult became important in many places across Germany through the sixteenth century, and hundreds of images of him stand in European churches. He is the patron saint of soldiers, swordsmiths, armies, infantrymen, weavers, and dyers and of several towns in Europe, including Manresa, Spain, and Piedmont, Italy.

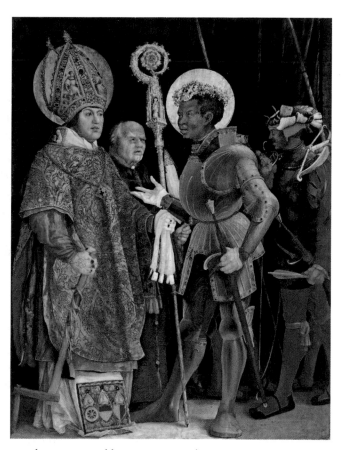

Matthias Grünewald. *St. Erasmus and St. Maurice.* Ca. 1520–24. Oil on panel. Halle, Germany, Collegiate Church.

5

Who was the first black president in North America?

VICENTE GUERRERO BECAME the second president of the Republic of Mexico in 1829, fifty-four years before Abraham Lincoln signed the Emancipation Proclamation, making him the first black president in North America.

Disparagingly nicknamed "el Negro Guerrero" by his political enemies, Guerrero would in the United States have been classified as a mulatto. According to his biographer Theodore G. Vincent, Guerrero was of mixed African, Spanish, and Native American ancestry. His father, Juan Pedro, "was in the almost entirely Afro-Mexican profession of mule driver."[1] Scholars speculate that his paternal grandfather was either a slave or a descendant of African slaves.

Guerrero was born in 1783 in a town near Acapulco called Tixtla, which is now located in the state that bears his name. He joined the fight for Mexico's independence from Spain in 1810, under the leadership of another black man, also a mulatto, Gen. José María Morelos y Pavón, a Catholic priest who played the dominant leadership role in the war until he was killed in combat in 1815. Morelos, like Guerrero, is one of Mexico's greatest heroes. (His face graces the fifty-peso bill, and a Mexican state is also named for him.) Within a year of Morelos's death, Guerrero became general of the rebels, fighting guerrilla skirmishes until Mexico was granted its independence in 1821.

Guerrero ran twice for president, once in 1824 and again in 1828, both times unsuccessfully. Claiming foul play, he and his supporters rebelled and toppled the new government; he became president on April 1, 1829.

On September 16, 1829—Mexico's Independence Day—he abolished slavery throughout the country (this was one reason that Texans would fight to secede from Mexico a few years later, in 1836). Unfortunately, Guerrero was driven out of office for it. Two years later he joined the rebel forces fighting the new government. Betrayed by one of his friends, he was executed in February 1831.

Anacleto Escutia. *Vicente Guerrero*. 1850. Oil on canvas. Mexico City, Museo Nacional de Historia, Castillo de Chapultepec.

6

Who were Africa's first ambassadors
to Europe?

MANY PEOPLE ASSUME that the flow of human beings, ideas, trade, and information between Europe and Africa was one-way, and that Africans were a "primitive" people outside time, living in ignorance and isolation until Portuguese navigators "discovered" them sometime in the fifteenth century, then forced them into slavery.

But long before English settlers arrived at Jamestown in 1607, African kingdoms were a lot more sophisticated and highly organized, and those kingdoms' relations to European visitors and to their monarchs back home much more complicated, than we have been led to believe. The flow of contact between Europe and Africa went in both directions.

African kingdoms established formal diplomatic relations with European kingdoms as equal parties. Some independent African kingdoms actually sent their own ambassadors to their European counterparts, and they were accorded all the rights and privileges of other nations' ambassadors.

As the historians Linda Heywood and John Thornton discovered, the king of Kongo (in today's Angola) sent an ambassador named Chrachanfusus to the court of the king of Portugal as early as 1488.[1] He presented the king with many splendid gifts, including ivory that was "marvelously white and shone," according to a report by Portuguese chronicler Rui de Pina. Chrachanfusus was baptized and given the name João da Silva. He is the first African ambassador to Europe of whom we have records.

Antonio Manuel was born in a province of the kingdom of Kongo circa 1570. As Heywood and Thornton tell us, he was educated there and became a *mestre de escola* (teacher). His first official position was to oversee the Church of the Holy Trinity in Soyo. (The king of Kongo, Nzinga a Nkuwu, willingly converted to Roman Catholicism in 1491, and his son and successor, Afonso, strengthened the role and status of the Catholic Church during his reign. Kongo was a Catholic kingdom thereafter.)

The Kongo king Alvaro II appointed Antonio Manuel ambassador to Rome in 1604. The king sent him there to complain to the pope about the behavior of the Portuguese man who had been sent to Kongo as the bishop in 1596.

Manuel traveled to Rome by sailing first to Brazil. Though it seems counterintuitive, it was quicker to travel to Europe from Angola this way, because of the flow of currents and the direction of the winds. He also wanted to go to Brazil to attempt to free a Kongo nobleman who had been wrongly enslaved. Manuel demonstrated considerable diplomatic skills in successfully negotiating this man's release, but the remainder of his travels turned harrowing.

Dutch pirates intercepted his vessel while he was en route to Portugal and stole most of his money and possessions. When he finally arrived in Lisbon, he sought the aid of some of his fellow Kongos who were living there but was denied. So he turned to the church.

Various clergy in the Carmelite Order in Lisbon and in Madrid gave Manuel shelter, support, and encouragement. He spent the next several years writing to various high-placed ecclesiastical officials, attempting to complete his mission. When he finally made it to Rome, he was seriously ill and nearly destitute.

At the Vatican, Manuel was housed in a wing of the papal residences. When the pope heard that he was near death, he visited him and personally gave him last rites. Francesco Caporale created a bust of him, and it adorns a side of the chapel in Santa Maria Maggiore in Rome.

Francesco Caporale. Funerary bust of *Antonio Manuel, Marquis of Ne Vunda.* 1629. Colored stone. Rome, S. Maria Maggiore.

7

Who was the first black explorer of the North American Southwest?

THE FIRST ENSLAVED AFRICAN to arrive in Florida whom we can document by name was a man named Esteban. Long before the explorers Lewis and Clark crossed the continent, he traversed the land that would later become the United States, through the Southwest, to the Pacific Ocean.

Esteban was born in West Africa and sold into slavery in a Portuguese town on Morocco's Atlantic coast. According to the historian Robert Goodwin, he was shipped to Spain as a slave from the town of Azemmour, in Morocco, in 1522. Andrés Dorantes de Carranza purchased him and brought him to Florida in April 1528.[1]

Under attack by the Native American residents where they landed, the expedition sailed on rafts across the Gulf of Mexico to what is today Galveston, Texas. There a storm sank three of the five rafts. Esteban, his master, and fourteen others survived both the storm and the harsh conditions during the winter of 1528.

When the party decided to travel inland, they were captured and enslaved for five years by the Karankawa Indians. In 1534 Esteban and the four remaining survivors escaped and were befriended by other Native Americans, who regarded the tiny band of strangers as healers and medicine men. Esteban, according to an eyewitness account, was a gifted linguist and quickly mastered different Native American languages, so he served as translator.

The men traveled through what is now Texas, Arizona, New Mexico, and northern Mexico—ultimately, a total of fifteen thousand miles.[2]

Esteban's luck eventually ran out, though: in May 1539, the Zuni Indians of Hawikuh in New Mexico executed him, regarding him as a harbinger of more unwanted and dangerous visitors. But by the time of his death, Esteban and his three companions had seen more of the North American Southwest than any other non–Native American.

Estevanico the Moor with Cortés, entering Mexico in 1519. *Codex Azcatitlan.* Ca. 1550–1600. Paris, Bibliothèque nationale.

8

Which slave literally wrote his way to freedom?

OVER THE COURSE of slavery in the United States between 1513 and 1865, tens of thousands of people managed to escape. First, before 1763, they went *south* from the Carolinas and Georgia to the haven afforded by Spanish Florida; later, they headed *north* from the southern colonies and states across the Mason-Dixon Line.

The oddest story of a slave escape is that of Ayuba, who *wrote* his way out of slavery. The man who came to be known in England as "Job ben Solomon" was born Ayuba Suleiman Jallo (in French, Diallo) into a prominent family in Bundu, an independent precolonial country located in current Senegal. Bundu, a strictly Muslim country, was situated where the Falémé River meets the Senegal River.

Ayuba was a member of the Fulbe ethnic group. As his biographer Allan Austin tells us, Ayuba was a highly learned man, adept at both Koranic and Arabic studies.[1] And, as the historian John Thornton explains, "he was a religious cleric who, like so many other Africans at the time, sold people as slaves, along with [selling] other things, as a way of participating in the international economy of his day, as an incidental element of his life."[2]

Sometime in February 1730, he left his home on a two-week journey to purchase paper and other goods in exchange for two slaves. Mandingo slave traders captured and sold him to an English captain whom he had angered over the terms of sale of those two slaves. Ayuba survived the Middle Passage on board the slave ship *Arabella* (voyage 75094 in the Trans-Atlantic Slave Database) and ended up enslaved on a tobacco plantation on Kent Island, near Annapolis, Maryland.

William Hoare of Bath.
Job ben Solomon.
1733. Oil on canvas.
Doha, Qatar Museums Authority.
The pouch around his neck
contains a copy of the Qur'an.

Renamed Simon by his master, Ayuba managed to run away, only to be recaptured and imprisoned. He was visited by a lawyer named Thomas Bluett, who was fascinated by this man's insistence on praying, by his refusal to eat pork or consume alcohol, and most of all, by the phenomenon of an African man writing on the wall of his prison cell in some unknown language.

And then one day Ayuba sat down and wrote a letter, in Arabic, imploring his father back in Senegal to come to America and rescue him from slavery.

Ayuba gave the letter to his master, Alexander Tolsey, who in turn gave it to Vachel Denton, who sent it by boat to Henry Hunt, an English merchant in London for whom Denton was a factor or agent. Hunt worked with Captain Pyke, the man who had sold Ayuba into slavery in the first place. (It was a very small world.) Pyke in turn showed the letter to Gen. James Oglethorpe, the founder of the colony of Georgia. Oglethorpe contacted his friend in the Royal African Company, Sir Bibye Lake, who sent it to John Gagnier, a professor who held the Laudian Chair of Arabic at the University of Oxford, asking him to translate it. And what the letter revealed astonished them.

Amazed that an African was literate and well educated, and obviously very intelligent and of noble lineage, Oglethorpe got the Royal African

Company (which possessed a monopoly on the slave trade) to purchase Ayuba and ship him from Annapolis to London.

Dressed in his native garb, as in his portrait by William Hoare, Ayuba was the toast of London. Called Job ben Solomon, he befriended a host of English notables, including the physician to the king, Sir Hans Sloane; the antiquarian Joseph Ames; and the Duke of Montagu, who would become one of his many patrons. Ayuba had an audience with King George II and Queen Caroline and was even made an honorary member of the Spalding Gentlemen's Society, of which Isaac Newton and Alexander Pope were members. These friends raised the funds to purchase his freedom from the Royal African Company, allowing him to return home.

In the final twist in a most ironic life, Ayuba did indeed return to Senegal, arriving on August 8, 1734, on board the *Dolphin Snow,* but now as an employee of the Royal African Company. He assisted the company in its bid to compete with the French commercial presence in Senegambia, including, presumably, the slave trade. One of the first things he did after he landed was to trade some of the gifts his English patrons had given him to purchase two horses and, incredibly, a female slave.

Ayuba died in Gambia in 1773, the same year that the Boston slave Phillis Wheatley, who wrote fondly of "pleasing Gambia" as her own native land, became the first person of African descent to publish a volume of poetry in English.

9

What was the first black town in North America?

BY 1570 THE COLONY OF New Spain (as Mexico was then called) "had received an estimated 36,500 Africans, of which 20,000 had survived," the historian Herman Bennett tells us. By 1600 the number of Africans "collectively rivaled, if not outnumbered, Spaniards throughout New Spain." And at Vera Cruz, "persons of African descent constituted 63 percent of the nonindigenous population."[1]

It was near Vera Cruz that the first black-ruled town was granted status as a self-governing municipality by Spain in 1609, eleven years before the *Mayflower* landed on Plymouth Rock. It is called Yanga, and a large statue of its founder graces the town square today.

The town is named for Mexico's most famous runaway slave, Gaspar Yanga, who was, as the historian Jane Landers tells us, "an enslaved West African of the Bran nation." In 1570 or so, Yanga escaped from his enslavement near Vera Cruz and formed a *palenque* (a community of runaway slaves, or maroons) in the nearby mountains at Cofre de Perote. Yanga's *palenque* survived illegally for almost forty years, "[raiding] Spanish convoys along the Camino Real [Royal Road] and nearby haciendas for items they could not produce themselves."[2]

By 1609, the Spanish authorities had had enough. The viceroy, Luís de Velasco II, mounted a major assault on the settlement, but to no avail. Under the leadership of an Angolan named Francisco de la Matosa, Yanga and his compatriots successfully defended themselves and then negotiated a settlement with the Spanish.

They had eleven demands, which included freedom for all of the run-

Erasmo Vásquez Lendechy.
Gaspar Yanga monument, erected
in the town now named after him
near Veracruz, Mexico. Bronze.
1970s.

away slaves who had lived in the settlement before 1608; official recognition of the town's sovereignty, including the right of Yanga and his heirs to become governors; exclusion of the Spanish, except on market days; and a Roman Catholic church administered by Franciscan monks. In return, Yanga agreed to pay tribute to the Spanish and to serve the king militarily when asked. He also agreed to return future fugitive slaves, if paid for returning them, but subsequent complaints from the Spanish suggest that the town continued to be a haven for runaways.

Yanga and his followers established the town of San Lorenzo de los Negros (also called San Lorenzo de Cerralvo) in 1609; it was formally recognized by the Spanish in 1618. Now called Yanga, the town exists to this day in the state of Veracruz.

10

Who was George Washington's runaway slave?

OF OUR FIRST FIVE PRESIDENTS, four owned slaves. The biggest slave owner among them was the father of our country, George Washington, who, together with his wife, Martha, owned about two hundred slaves at the beginning of the Revolution. Two of them became quite famous, for very different reasons.

William "Billy" Lee, Washington's personal servant, was the only slave whom Washington freed outright upon his death. In John Trumbull's famous 1780 painting of the president, Lee is depicted looking adoringly at his master and standing faithfully by his side.

At the other extreme of attitudes toward the master of Mount Vernon was a fascinating rebel named Harry, whose dogged determination to be free suggests that not all of Washington's slaves found him to be the benevolent master whom historians have depicted. Harry's first escape from Mount Vernon occurred on July 29, 1771. Washington was not amused: he "paid one pound and sixteen shillings to advertise for the recovery of his property," the historian Cassandra Pybus tells us.[1] Harry was returned a few weeks later. Undaunted and determined to be free, Harry awaited a second chance.

That would come in the early years of the Revolution, on November 14, 1775, when John Murray, the fourth Earl of Dunmore and the royal governor of the colony of Virginia, issued an astonishing proclamation that freed any slaves who were willing to bear arms for the British Crown. They ran away in droves.

Pybus estimates that between twenty and thirty thousand defected to the British side during the war—a stunningly high figure, since historians estimate that about five thousand black men served in the Continental Army. Washington privately admitted that slave defections would gain momentum "like a snow ball in rolling."[2]

The general was right: Harry seized his opportunity and ran away in 1776, as did three white indentured servants. And they were not the last to do so. As late as April 1781, eighteen slaves fled the plantation. Though the war was raging, Washington was determined to retrieve his property and hired a slave catcher, who managed to return seven but not Harry.

Harry served nobly in Dunmore's all-black loyalist regiment called the Black Pioneers. Rising to the rank of corporal, he participated in the invasion of South Carolina and the siege of Charleston, in charge of "a

John Trumbull. *George Washington and his servant Billy Lee.* 1780. Oil on canvas. New York, The Metropolitan Museum of Art.

company of Black Pioneers attached to the Royal Artillery Department in Charleston in 1781."[3]

At war's end, with the British defeat, Harry was part of a black community consisting of some four thousand people who found safe haven in the British zone in New York, nervously awaiting their fate, since the victorious Americans insisted in the peace treaty that all runaway slaves be returned. Washington, despite the victory over British tyranny, remained ever determined to regain his escaped property. He instructed his army contractor, Daniel Parker, to do his best to find his slaves.

But the British kept their word. In July 1783, on board a ship named *L'Abondance,* a forty-three-year-old Harry set sail with his wife, Jenny, and 405 other black men, women, and children for Nova Scotia and freedom, in a settlement they named Birchtown.

11

Who was the first black person in the United States to lead a "back to Africa" effort?

THE PERSON WHO SPEARHEADED "the first, black initiated 'back to Africa' effort in U.S. history," according to the historian Donald R. Wright, was Paul Cuffee (or Cuffe), a sea captain and entrepreneur who was perhaps the wealthiest black American of his time.[1] Cuffee was born on Cuttyhunk Island, off the southern coast of Massachusetts, one of ten children of a freed slave, a farmer named Kofi Slocum. In 1766 Kofi purchased a 116-acre farm in Dartmouth, on Buzzards Bay, which he left upon his death in 1772 to Paul and his brother, John. When his father died, Paul changed his surname from Slocum to Cuffee and began what would prove to be an extraordinarily successful life at sea.

Starting as a whaler, then moving into maritime trading, Paul Cuffee eventually "bought and built ships, developing his own maritime enterprise that involved trading the length of the U.S. Atlantic coast, with trips to the Caribbean and Europe," according to Wright. But he was also politically engaged.

Cuffee's dream was that free African Americans and freed slaves "could establish a prosperous colony in Africa," one based on emigration and trade. As Wright puts it, "Cuffee hoped to send at least one vessel each year to Sierra Leone, transporting African-American settlers and goods to the colony and returning with marketable African products." Sierra Leone was already populated in part by former American slaves who had received their freedom by running away from their masters and joining the Brit-

Chester Harding. *Sea Captain Paul Cuffe*. Early nineteenth century. Oil on canvas. Boston, New England Historic Genealogical Society.

ish as loyalists in the Revolutionary War. The British had also founded a settlement in Sierra Leone for London's Committee of the Black Poor; it was called the Province of Freedom in 1787. Then Freetown was founded as a settlement for freed slaves in 1792, the year the black loyalists (including George Washington's former slave Harry Washington) were relocated from Nova Scotia, where conditions had proved too harsh.

Cuffee wanted to distinguish his plan from British and American efforts, which essentially used colonization as a way of removing the threat that free African Americans posed to the continuation of slavery. So in 1811 he founded the Friendly Society of Sierra Leone, a cooperative black group intended to encourage "the Black Settlers of Sierra Leone, and the Natives of Africa generally, in the Cultivation of their Soil, by the Sale of their Produce." He made two trips to the colony that year.

In 1812 Cuffee traveled to Baltimore, Philadelphia, and New York to form an African-American version of the British "black poor" organization. Named the African Institution, it had self-contained branches in each city and was charged with mounting a coordinated, black-directed emigration movement.

On December 10, 1815, Cuffee made history by transporting thirty-eight African Americans (including twenty children), ranging in age from six months to sixty years, from the United States to Sierra Leone on his brig, the *Traveller,* at a cost of $5,000. When they arrived on February 3,

1816, Cuffee's passengers became the first African Americans who willingly returned to Africa through an African-American initiative.

Cuffee's dream of a wholesale African-American return to the continent, however, soon lost support from the free African-American community. As black abolitionist and businessman James Forten sadly reported in a letter to Cuffee dated January 25, 1817, several thousand black men had met at Richard Allen's Bethel African Methodist Episcopal Church to discuss the merits of Cuffee's colonization program and the work of the African Institution. The news was devastating: "Three thousand at least attended, and there was not one soul that was in favor of going to Africa. They think that the slaveholders want to get rid of them so as to make their property more secure." And then in August, Forten co-authored a statement that declared, "The plan of colonizing is not asked for by us. We renounce and disclaim any connection with it."

The cause of black emigration would, however, be taken up by a future succession of black leaders, including Henry Highland Garnet, Bishop James T. Holly, Martin R. Delany, Bishop Henry McNeal Turner, and of course Marcus Mosiah Garvey.

12

Who was the first black person
to see the baby Jesus?

THE FIRST BLACK MAN to see the baby Jesus is thought to have been the wise man known as Balthasar. The Bible tells us that soon after Jesus was born, wise men from the East—"Magi"—came to his birthplace to pay homage with great and wondrous gifts: "After Jesus was born in Bethlehem in Judea, during the time of King Herod, Magi from the East came to Jerusalem and asked, 'Where is the one who has been born king of the Jews? We saw his star when it rose and have come to worship him'" (Matthew 2:1). Directed by the diabolical King Herod to Bethlehem, upon the advice of his "chief priests and teachers of the law," "they went on their way" (Matthew 2:9), "and the star they had seen when it rose went ahead of them until it stopped over the place where the child was." Upon entering the house, "they saw the child with his mother Mary, and they bowed down and worshipped him. Then they opened their treasures and presented him with gifts of gold, frankincense, and myrrh" (Matthew 2:11).

Since the Bible makes no reference to the color or race of the wise men, how, when, and why did Balthasar come to be portrayed as black? Like the story of the transformation of the Egyptian soldier and martyr Saint Maurice, the story of Balthasar's changing racial representation has been traced in great detail by the art historian Paul Kaplan.[1]

By the eighth century, Kaplan tells us, the Three Kings had become associated with the continents of Asia, Africa, and Europe, whose peoples were thought to be descended from the three sons of Noah. By the late tenth or early eleventh century, Balthasar was clearly described as a black

Nicolas Poussin. *Adoration of the Magi.* 1633. Oil on canvas. Dresden, Gemäldegalerie Alte Meister.

man: "Patizara [Balthasar], dark black, fully bearded, having a red tunic and short white cloak, and dressed in green slippers."

The first depictions of Balthasar as a black African appeared in Germany—coincidentally, also the source for the transformation of Saint Maurice, the Egyptian martyr and first black saint. A black man began to appear in German heraldic depictions of the coats of arms of the Three Kings in 1370, and in 1437 Balthasar was clearly represented in a work of art as a black man in Hans Multscher's Wurzach Altarpiece.

By the 1400s, the identity of one of the Magi as a black African had become widely accepted throughout Christendom, in part because of the increasing contact between Europeans and Africans in the latter half of the fifteenth century, especially due to the growth of the slave trade. As Kaplan puts it, "By 1500, the story of the Magi in art constituted the preeminent means of integrating the inhabitants of the non-European world into the Western Christian universe. Still associated with Prester John [legendary king of the Ethiopians and discoverer of the Fountain of Youth], the black King was too useful to be discarded. The black Magus/King was a predominantly positive character entwined in a web of attitudes which could damage as well as support the position of black people in European society."

13

Where was the first black town in what is now the United States?

IN THE LATE 1600S, Spanish Florida exercised a powerful draw on the collective imagination of slaves to the north in Carolina. It was their first Promised Land. At least since 1687, if slaves made it down to Florida and professed belief in "the True Faith"—Roman Catholicism—they were declared to be free. News of this haven spread through the slave grapevine.

Sometime between March and November 1738, Spanish settlers in Florida formed a town named Gracia Real de Santa Teresa de Mose, two miles to the north of St. Augustine. Initially, it consisted of thirty-eight men, all fugitive slaves who had fled enslavement in the Carolinas and Georgia to seek sanctuary and freedom in Florida. Fort Mose, as it came to be known, deserves to be remembered as the site of the first all-black town in what is now the United States. It was manned entirely by armed black men under the leadership of Francisco Menéndez, who became leader of the black militia there in 1726. Fort Mose was also the first line of defense between the Spanish settlers in Florida and their enemies, the English colonists to the north in Carolina.

The historian John Huxtable Elliott observes that "as news of the foundation of Mose spread through the South Carolina plantations, groups of slaves broke loose and tried to make for Florida."[1] In November 1738, twenty-three men, women, and children escaped from Port Royal, South Carolina, and fled to St. Augustine. Florida's governor Manuel Montiano refused to return them to their supposed "owners," just as his predecessors had done since 1687. In March 1739 four more slaves and an Irish servant made their escape to St. Augustine using stolen horses.[2]

All this was prelude to the famous Stono Rebellion, the most violent uprising of African-American slaves in the eighteenth century. On Sunday, September 9, 1739, at Stono Bridge, south of Charleston, about twenty slaves, hailing from Angola, killed two store attendants and stole arms and ammunition. As they marched south toward Florida, their ranks swelled to about one hundred, and they continued to burn plantations and kill white settlers. A ferocious battle with the colonial militia left a field of death, including twenty of the colonists and forty slaves. Slaves who fled were later captured and beheaded. But not even this unfortunate outcome deterred other slaves in the region from seeking their freedom: in June 1740 about 150 slaves rebelled near the Ashley River, just outside Charleston. Fifty were captured and hanged.

Outraged by the actions of the slaves at Stono, and fearful of more rebellions from slaves seeking to escape to Florida, the English countered with a siege of Florida between 1739 and 1740 that culminated in the destruction of Fort Mose.

Francisco Menéndez was captured and sold as a slave, but by 1759 he was free and once again in command at Mose, which the Spanish reconstructed

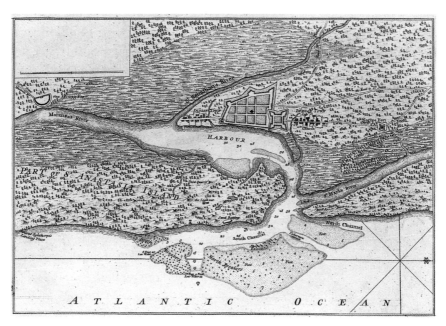

Fort Mose, labeled "Negroe Fort," as recorded on a map of Saint Augustine by Thomas Jefferys, 1763.

in 1752. In 1763, under the terms of the Treaty of Paris, the Spanish were forced to abandon Florida but gained Cuba in return. In August, Menéndez led forty-eight men, women, and children onto the schooner *Nuestra Señora de los Dolores* (Our Lady of Sorrows) and sailed to Cuba, where they settled in Regla, a town near Havana.

14

What happened to the "forty acres and a mule" that former slaves were promised?

THE "FORTY ACRES AND A MULE" promised to newly freed slaves was the federal government's first systematic attempt to provide reparations. Proto-socialist in its implications, the plan proposed a massive confiscation of private property—some 400,000 acres—formerly owned by Confederates, and its methodical redistribution to former black slaves. It would be radical in any country today.

The history of race relations in the United States would have been profoundly different if this policy had been implemented and enforced; if the former slaves had actually had access to ownership of land, of property; if they had had a chance to become self-sufficient economically, and to build, accrue, and pass on wealth. After all, one of the principal promises of America was the possibility of average people being able to own land and enjoy all that landownership entailed. Of course, this promise was not to be realized for the overwhelming majority of the nation's former slaves.

The source of the policy of "forty acres and a mule" was Union general William T. Sherman's Special Field Order No. 15, issued on January 16, 1865. (Actually, Sherman's order prescribed the forty acres but not the mule, which would come later.)

By this order, 400,000 acres of land—"a strip of coastline stretching from Charleston, South Carolina, to the St. John's River in Florida, including Georgia's Sea Islands and the mainland thirty miles in from the coast," as the historian Barton Myers reports—was to be redistributed to the newly freed slaves.[1]

This idea for massive land redistribution was actually the result of a discussion that Sherman and Secretary of War Edwin M. Stanton held four days before Sherman issued the order, with twenty leaders of the black community in Savannah, Georgia, where Sherman was headquartered following his famous March to the Sea. Stanton had suggested to Sherman that they gather "the leaders of the local Negro community" and ask them something no one else had apparently thought to ask: "What do you want for your own people" following the war?[2] Stanton and Sherman met with the black ministers on January 12, on the second floor of Charles Green's mansion on Savannah's Macon Street.

The abolitionists Charles Sumner and Thaddeus Stevens and other Radical Republicans had been advocating land redistribution "to break the back of Southern slaveholders' power," as Myers observes. But Sherman's plan took shape only after the ministers' meeting. In its broadest strokes, "forty acres and a mule" was *their* idea.

Their chosen leader and spokesman, Garrison Frazier, told Sherman and Stanton that the Negro wanted land. "The way we can best take care

Rev. Ulysses L. Houston. *"He was a friend to all."* 1890. Lithograph. W. & M. publishers, Savannah, Georgia.

of ourselves," Reverend Frazier began, "is to have land, and turn it and till it by our own labor . . . and we can soon maintain ourselves and have something to spare . . . We want to be placed on land until we are able to buy it and make it our own." And when asked where the freed slaves "would rather live—whether scattered among the whites or in colonies by yourselves," Brother Frazier replied, without missing a beat, "I would prefer to live by ourselves, for there is a prejudice against us in the South that will take years to get over." When polled individually around the table, all but one—James Lynch, twenty-six, who had moved south from Baltimore—said that they agreed with Frazier. Four days later Sherman issued Special Field Order No. 15, after President Lincoln approved it.

The effect throughout the South was electric. As the historian Eric Foner explains, "the freedmen hastened to take advantage of the Order." Baptist minister Ulysses L. Houston, a member of the group that had met with Sherman, led one thousand blacks to Skidaway Island, Georgia, where they established a self-governing community with Houston as the "black governor." And by June, "40,000 freedmen had been settled on 400,000 acres of 'Sherman Land.' "[3] Sherman later ordered that the army could lend the new settlers mules; hence the phrase "forty acres and a mule."

And what happened to this astonishingly visionary program, which would have fundamentally altered the course of American race relations? In the fall of 1865, Andrew Johnson, Lincoln's successor and a southern sympathizer, overturned the order and, as Myers sadly concludes, "returned the land along the South Carolina, Georgia and Florida coasts to the planters who had originally owned it"—to the very people who had declared war on the United States of America.

15

Were slaves actually eaten by dogs?

THREE THINGS ABOUT Quentin Tarantino's 2012 film *Django Unchained* fascinated me as a scholar of slave narratives. The first was its claims about slaves and their access to horses; the second, the use of bloodhounds not merely to track slaves, but to devour them; and third, sadistic rituals of wrestling to the death, which Tarantino calls "Mandingo fighting." Several times during the film, characters purport to be shocked to see a black man riding a horse. Django (played by Jamie Foxx) says, "They ain't never seen a nigger on no horse," while the ultimate house servant, Stephen (played by Samuel L. Jackson), wonders incredulously, "Who dat nigger on a horse?" And a few times a white character, outraged, demands, "What's that nigger doing on that nag?"

The truth, though, is that slaves rode horses, and some famously so. The contrast between slaves on foot and free men riding in horse-drawn carriages was a narrative device that Frederick Douglass himself used as one of the key binary oppositions to demonstrate the distinctions between a slave and her or his master. In the first chapter of his autobiography, Douglass says that he saw his mother only "four or five times," and only at night, because she was a slave for a Mr. Stewart, who lived about twelve miles away. He stresses that she was relegated to "travelling the whole distance on foot, after the performance of her day's work. She was a field hand."[1]

By contrast, Douglass's master—whom he suspects to be his father—seems to have had something of a horse fetish, his "riding equipage" consisting of "three splendid coaches, three or four gigs, besides dearborns and barouches of the most fashionable style." And "in nothing," Douglass

Richard Ansdell. *The Hunted Slaves*. 1861. Oil on canvas. Liverpool, International Slavery Museum.

stresses, was his master "more particular than in the management of his horses." Nevertheless, the care and feeding of the horses—including, presumably, their exercise—was the responsibility of "old Barney and young Barney," two slaves, father and son. And of course, the Barneys would have ridden the horses, just as countless other attendants to their masters' horses would have. The care, feeding, and exercising of horses was part and parcel of plantation life.

The most famous black horseman in the Revolutionary period was William "Billy" Lee, George Washington's slave and personal attendant, the only slave whom Washington freed upon his death. Billy Lee was, by all accounts, a superb horseman and rode just behind his master.

Slaves also rode horses professionally. From colonial times, slaves served as jockeys, as the historian Lisa K. Winkler writes, long before black men dominated the first decades of the Kentucky Derby (in the first Derby in 1875, thirteen of fifteen jockeys were black): "When President Andrew Jackson moved into the White House in 1829, he brought along his best Thoroughbreds and his black jockeys. Because racing was tremendously popular in the South, it is not surprising that the first black jockeys were slaves. They cleaned the stables and handled the grooming and training of some of the country's most valuable horseflesh," they "were allowed to travel the racing circuit," and "they competed alongside whites."[2] So, as effective as the trope may be in *Django* in distinguishing a free Negro from a slave, it is not historically accurate.

Professional slave catchers used dogs to chase and capture fugitive slaves. As the historian David Doddington writes, "it was the use of trained dogs that appears to have most concerned" the slaves.[3] Former slaves accused masters, patrollers, and professional slave catchers of using "savage dogs, trained to hunt and follow the track of the poor colored fugitive," according to the 1857 slave narrative of William J. Anderson.[4]

But tracking slaves is one thing; devouring them, as happens in *Django,* is quite another. Did this happen—could this have happened—given the fact that the ultimate goal of a master was to exploit his human chattel for maximum profit, and that destroying property might not be the best business decision?

Apparently, it sometimes did happen. A slaveholder from Louisiana named Bennett H. Barrow "kept a detailed diary," says Doddington, "and frequently mentioned the importance of dogs in capturing runaways, as well as the terrible violence they could inflict: 'hunting Ruffins Boy Henry, came across Williams runaway caught him dogs nearly et his legs off, near killing him.'"

The most horrendous—and systematic—use of man-eating dogs occurred not in the United States but during the Haitian Revolution, in the former slaves' war with Napoléon's army on Saint-Domingue (the French name for the colony that became the nation of Haiti). As the historian Philippe Girard notes, "France's use of man-hunting dogs during the Haitian Revolution was the most disturbing crime in this singularly cruel conflict and is still vividly remembered in Haiti today."[5] These dogs not only hunted but *ate* their captives, and the use of dogs as agents of "execution regularly took place . . . in front of the government house in Cap [an important city now known as Cap-Haïtien], much to the annoyance of local residents who complained about the noise."

The pitting of two slaves fighting to the death in the arena happened only in Hollywood films such as *Mandingo* and *Drum,* as the journalist Aisha Harris observes. Aside from the immorality of it, slaves were too valuable as investments to kill capriciously in this way. Destroying one's property was not the smartest business strategy.[6] But "battles royale" (boxing contests, during which young black men beat each other senseless for the pleasure of drunken white gawkers, who sometimes paid for admission), as depicted in Ralph Ellison's classic novel *Invisible Man,* were a less savage version of the fighting matches depicted in these feature films.

16

Where was the first Underground Railroad?

STORIES ABOUND OF SLAVES escaping from the harsh life of southern plantations and finding their freedom in the North by "following the North Star" across the Mason-Dixon Line, frequently guided by that courageous conductor on the Underground Railroad Harriet Tubman.

After 1830 slaves in the southern states fled *north* to gain their freedom, following the metaphorical "drinking gourd" (as the Big Dipper was called). But this hadn't always been true. The very first slaves in what is now the United States fled to their freedom by running *south*, not north.

The reason has to do with the early colonial rivalry between Spain and England for territory, manpower, and resources. As the historian Jane Landers outlines, that drama unfolded in the late 1600s and early 1700s among Charleston, South Carolina, Savannah, Georgia, and St. Augustine, Florida.[1]

The first African slaves came to what is now the United States to help found San Miguel de Gualdape, a settlement near Sapelo Sound, Georgia, in 1526. A few decades later, in 1565, the Spanish founded St. Augustine, bringing with them perhaps some fifty African slaves. Just over a century later, Barbadian planters of English descent founded Charleston, which was "but 10 days journey" from St. Augustine. The New World rivalry between colonial Spain and England was on.

Unlike the English settlement at Charleston, the Spanish settlement at St. Augustine included some free blacks and mulattoes. Incredibly, the Spanish governor, Juan Márquez Cabrera, armed them to fight, forming a black militia in the settlement in 1683. In 1686 this militia formed part of a Spanish force that began to raid Carolina territory. The presence of black soldiers

Map illustrating territory traversed by slaves escaping to
Spanish Florida. *Tabula Mexicae et Floridae* . . . (detail).
Amsterdam, Peter Schenck. Ca. 1710.

among the Spanish forces must have astonished the Carolina slaves. Only
a year later the first documented group of black slaves—eight men, two
women, and a nursing child—managed to escape south from Charleston to
St. Augustine, covering the 277 miles or so in a stolen canoe. The Spanish
refused to return them to the English and granted them their freedom.

From this point on, Spain would deploy black fugitive slaves in raids
against English settlements to the north, and grant freedom to escaping
slaves on religious grounds. But the truth was that Spain was also seeking to weaken the colonies of their British rivals.

Just six years later, in 1693, the Spanish king, Charles II, attempting
to systematically undermine the economy of the Carolinas, decreed that
Florida would be a religious sanctuary for fugitive slaves seeking "the
true faith"; his royal proclamation declared that he was "giving liberty
to all . . . the men as well as the women . . . so that by their example and
by my liberality others will do the same." Virtually overnight this new
and unprecedented route to freedom was established. We can think of it
as the first metaphorical "underground railroad"—the slaves' first route to
freedom—and it ran *south.*

17

What was the second Middle Passage?

THANKS TO the Trans-Atlantic Slave Trade Database, we know that about 388,000 Africans were transported directly to the United States over the course of the slave trade, which ended officially in 1808. This brutally cruel and disruptive phase is known as the Middle Passage.

But the *second* phase of forced migration, known as the domestic, or internal, slave trade, involved two and a half times the number of black people who were taken from Africa to the United States: "In the seven decades between the ratification of the Constitution [starting in 1787] and the Civil War [1861]," the historian Walter Johnson tells us, "approximately one million enslaved people were relocated from the upper South to the lower South . . . two thirds of these through . . . the domestic slave trade."[1]

The enormity of the second Middle Passage was due to the unprecedented growth of the cotton industry. Until Eli Whitney invented the cotton gin and had it patented in 1794, cotton harvesting was extremely labor-intensive. The cotton gin is deceptively simple: it just separates cotton fibers, or "lint," from the seeds. Before the cotton gin, one person could clean about a pound of cotton a day, but using the cotton gin, one person could clean fifty pounds a day. The effects were immediate and dramatic: in 1790 the United States produced 1.5 million pounds of cotton, but in 1800 it produced *35 million* pounds.[2] By 1830 that figure had grown to *331 million*, and by 1860, on the eve of the Civil War, cotton production had grown to *2,275 million* pounds.

As profits from cotton production soared, slaves became extremely valuable commodities since the slave trade from Africa had ended in 1808. Owners in the Upper South, whose tobacco plantations were no longer sufficiently profitable, sold them south in droves. As the historian Ira Berlin observes, "The internal slave trade became the largest enterprise in the South outside of the plantation itself, and probably the most advanced in its employment of modern transportation, finance and publicity."[3]

The result of this migration, Berlin tells us, was that "the slave populations of Alabama, Mississippi, Arkansas, and Texas swelled beyond recognition. The territory of Mississippi—which encompassed lands that would eventually be part of Mississippi, Alabama, and Florida—contained some 3,000 slaves at the beginning of the nineteenth century. In 1860, well over 400,000 slaves lived in Mississippi alone."[4] In turn, the value of slaves continued to soar. As the historian Steven Deyle points out, "Southern slave prices more than tripled," rising from $500 in New Orleans in 1800 to $1,800 by 1860 (the equivalent of $30,000 in 2005).[5]

Of the 3.2 million slaves working in the fifteen slave states in 1850, *1.8 million* worked in cotton. Cotton produced by slave labor was so profitable that it would take a costly civil war, and the loss of more than 600,000 lives, to end it.

William L. Sheppard. *The First Cotton Gin.* Wood engraving, *Harper's Weekly,* December 18, 1869.

18

How much did the cotton industry shape American history and the lives of enslaved Africans?

THE PHRASE MOST COMMONLY USED to describe the growth of the American economy in the 1830s and '40s was "Cotton Is King." This slogan refers to the plantation economy of the slavery states in the Deep South, which led to the creation of the second Middle Passage. But the economic importance of cotton was not simply a southern phenomenon. Cotton was one of the world's first luxury commodities, after sugar and tobacco.

Cotton production was extraordinarily profitable, and the cotton plantations, the northern banking industry, the New England textile factories, and a huge proportion of the economy of Great Britain were all interconnected and overlapping. Given this arrangement, it was something of a miracle that slavery was finally abolished in this country at all.

The economic value of the slave population was staggering. Steven Deyle shows that in 1860, the total value of all U.S. slaves was "roughly three times greater than the total amount of all capital, North and South combined, invested in manufacturing" and was "equal to about seven times the total value of all currency in circulation in the country, three times the value of the entire livestock population, twelve times the value of all American farm implements and machinery, twelve times the value of the entire U.S. cotton crop and forty-eight times the total expenditure of the federal government that year."[1] As we have seen, the invention of the cotton gin greatly increased the productivity of cotton harvesting by slaves. This resulted in dramatically higher profits for planters, which in

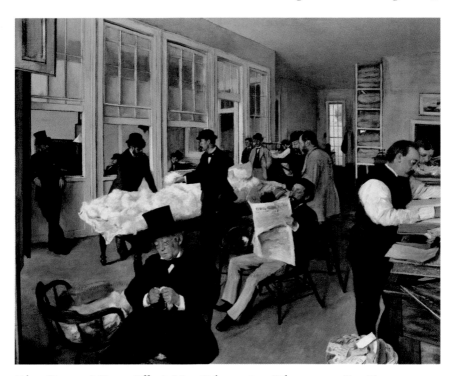

Edgar Degas. *A Cotton Office in New Orleans.* 1873. Oil on canvas. Pau, France, Musée des Beaux-Arts.

turn led to a seemingly insatiable rise in demand for ever more slaves, in a savage, brutal, and vicious cycle.

Slave-produced cotton "brought commercial ascendancy to New York City, was the driving force for territorial expansion in the Old Southwest and fostered trade between Europe and the United States," according to the historian Gene Dattel.[2] Further: "Britain, the most powerful nation in the world, relied on slave-produced American cotton for over 80 percent of its essential industrial raw material. English textile mills accounted for 40 percent of Britain's exports. One-fifth of Britain's twenty-two million people were directly or indirectly involved with cotton textiles."[3]

Cotton fed the textile revolution in the United States. "In 1860," notes the historian Ronald Bailey, "New England had 52 percent of the man-ufacturing establishments and 75 percent of the 5.14 million spindles in operation." The same went for looms. In fact, Massachusetts "alone had 30 percent of all spindles, and Rhode Island added another 18 percent." Most impressively of all, "New England mills consumed 283.7 million pounds of cotton, or 67 percent of the 422.6 million pounds of cotton used by U.S. mills in 1860." In other words, on the eve of the Civil War, New England's economy, so fundamentally dependent upon the textile industry, was inextricably intertwined with "the labor of black people working as slaves in the U.S. South."[4]

If there was one ultimate cause of the Civil War, it was black-slave-grown cotton—"the most important determinant of American history in the nineteenth century," says Dattel. "Cotton prolonged America's most serious social tragedy, slavery, and slave-produced cotton caused the American Civil War."

19

How much African ancestry does the average African American have?

MANY OF THE DNA TESTS that we use today didn't exist even a decade ago. These newer tests use a type of DNA called autosomal DNA to estimate how much of a person's ancestry traces to each of the world's ancestral populations via an "admixture test." This type of test can also be used to identify long stretches of identical DNA that two individuals share, thereby establishing the fact that they are related genetically even more recently and thus are cousins. In other words, if we could produce an ideal family tree for two individuals who share a significant stretch of autosomal DNA, one person would appear by name on *both* of their family trees. Analyzing your autosomal DNA allows you to find your "lost" ancestors by connecting you to these genetic relatives.

What exactly is genetic admixture? I asked a few prominent geneticists to define it. Dr. George Church, a professor at Harvard Medical School and a pioneer in the mapping of the human genome, defines it as "the breeding between two or more previously isolated populations." Dr. Joanna Mountain, the senior director of research for 23andMe.com, adds, "Every one of us has the story of our ancestry hidden in our DNA. Any section of DNA—say, one piece of chromosome 3—can be linked with people who lived in a particular geographic location thousands of years ago. By adding up the fractions of DNA from each location, we can determine the percentage of a person's ancestors who lived in each location."

She also stresses the importance of using regional or geographic categories in genetic ancestry tracing, rather than the standard four or five so-called racial divisions that have been employed in the West since the eighteenth century, which is one reason why her company now uses thirty-one categories of "ancestry composition."

Dr. Nathan Pearson, the principal genome scientist at Ingenuity, tells us that "interbreeding has occurred throughout history, and notably leaves telltale traces in our genomes that hint strongly at who came together, and when. The ingredients in your genome track which regional populations mingle in your family tree, and in what proportions," revealing "the mix of recent continental origins among your ancestors." Think of admixture, he says, "as gene mingling."

Exactly how "black" are black Americans, then? According to 23andMe .com, the average African American is 73.2 percent sub-Saharan African, 24 percent European, and only 0.8 percent Native American.

Modesto Brocos y Gómez. *The Redemption of Ham.* 1895. Oil on canvas. Rio de Janeiro, Brazil, Museu Nacional de Belas Artes.

For African-American males, still another astonishing fact has been revealed about their paternal ancestry—their father's father's father's line—through their Y-DNA: a whopping 35 percent of all African-American men descend from a *white male ancestor* who fathered a mulatto child sometime in the slavery era, probably from rape or a coerced sexual act.

Two things about these results are particularly fascinating. First of all, it is extremely rare for African Americans tested by these DNA companies to receive a result of 100 percent sub-Saharan African ancestry, although each company has analyzed Africans and African immigrants who *did* test 100 percent sub-Saharan in origin. Ranges, of course, vary from individual to individual. Spencer Wells, director of *National Geographic*'s Genographic Project, explained to me that the African Americans they've tested range from 53 percent to 95 percent sub-Saharan African, 3 percent to 46 percent European, and 0 percent to 3 percent Native American. So there is a lot of genetic variation within our ethnic group, as is obvious to anyone even casually glancing at black people just walking down the street.

Clearly even the most phenotypically "African" (or what used to be called "Negroid") African Americans have significant levels of European ancestry. This finding is important because it deconstructs the notion of biologically fixed races that our society inherited from the racist pseudo-science of the eighteenth century and that it drew upon to justify slavery and the property rights of masters who fathered children with their slaves.

The bottom line, judging from these DNA test results, is that black and white Americans are inextricably interconnected at the level of their genomes, and African Americans are a profoundly mixed people, far more so than anyone thought possible before these tests were invented. And no matter what your features are—your shade of brown, your hair texture, the shape of your lips and nose—if you are an African American reading this book, you are likely mixed as well, even if you don't think you look that way.

As fascinating as admixture results are, it is important to remember that identity can be constructed in various and deeply nuanced ways. As George Church notes, "Two people with a certain cancer-causing allele have potentially much more in common than two people with the same admixture." In other words, while "race" is socially constructed, alleles or genetic mutations are not. Biology matters. The challenge for us is to understand how it does and does not matter, especially in a society that has historically called upon science to justify an oppressive social order.

20

Who originated the concept of the "talented tenth" black leadership class?

ONE OF THE MOST IMPORTANT CONCEPTS of the many that W.E.B. Du Bois defined was "the talented tenth." "The Negro race, like all races, is going to be saved by its exceptional men. The problem of education, then, among Negroes must first of all deal with the Talented Tenth; it is the problem of developing the Best of this race that they may guide the Mass away from the contamination and death of the Worst, in their own and other races."[1]

These sentences effectively challenged Booker T. Washington's strident advocacy of industrial training as the ideal curriculum for the daughters and sons of the former slaves, rather than a classical liberal arts education, the sort of education that Du Bois had received at Fisk and then at Harvard.

But Du Bois was not the author of this concept. As Evelyn Brooks Higginbotham first noted, the term was actually invented by a white man, Henry Lyman Morehouse (the man for whom the great Morehouse College was named), seven years before Du Bois popularized it.[2] In an essay by that very title published in 1896, Morehouse coined the term and defined it in this way: "In the discussion concerning Negro education we should not forget the talented tenth man. An ordinary education may answer for the nine men of mediocrity; but if this is all we offer the talented tenth man, we make a prodigious mistake." Why? Because, Morehouse continues, "the tenth man, with superior natural endowments, symmetrically trained and highly developed, may become a mightier influence, a greater inspiration to others than all the other nine, or nine times nine like them."[3]

Evangelists. Henry Lyman Morehouse (at bottom), as he appears with other prominent church leaders of his time. 1877. Composite print.

EVANGELISTS.

It is no accident that Morehouse published this essay just a few months after Booker T. Washington's address at the Cotton States and International Exposition in Atlanta the previous September, less than a year before the infamous *Plessy v. Ferguson* Supreme Court decision was handed down on May 18, 1896, cementing "separate but equal" as the law of the land for the next half century. In this widely heralded speech, which Du Bois mockingly dubbed the "Atlanta Compromise," Washington stressed, among other things, the importance of industrial or vocational curricula over a college education for black people.

Morehouse, without naming Washington, challenged his position:

I repeat that not to make proper provision for the high education of the talented tenth man of the colored people is a prodigious mistake. It is to dwarf the tree that has in it the potency of a grand oak. Industrial education is good for the nine; the common English branches are good for the nine; but that tenth man ought to have the best opportunities for making the most of himself for humanity and for God.

Morehouse didn't name Du Bois but was clearly thinking of him; Washington, he hinted, was actually a prime example of those " 'self-made' men, so-called, whose best powers were evoked by rare opportunities."

Fascinatingly, Morehouse's and Du Bois's concept of a supposedly elite 10 percent of "the race" accords almost exactly with the size of the Free Negro population in the 1860 census. On the eve of the Civil War, 11 percent of the African-American community was composed of Free Negroes, and quite surprisingly far more of them lived in the South (258,346) than in the Northeast (155,983). And it was this group of freed persons to whom President Abraham Lincoln was referring when he announced, in the last speech of his life, that he advocated giving "the elective franchise" to "the very intelligent [colored man], and on those who serve our cause as soldiers," who numbered about 200,000.[4]

Adding the number of free black men to the number of black soldiers, it's easy to see that Abraham Lincoln effectively introduced the notion of a privileged "talented tenth" within the race who would be accorded more rights than the remaining nine-tenths, the 3.95 million slaves who would really be freed only by the ratification of the Thirteenth Amendment in December 1865. So perhaps we should give Lincoln the credit for inventing the concept.

Despite its narrow scope and elitism, Lincoln's proposal was a fairly radical idea in an America that had just suffered massive losses from a civil war that undeniably was fought to end black slavery. Standing on the grounds of the White House listening to the president's speech that day, April 11, 1865, was a man named John Wilkes Booth. When he heard Lincoln say that he wanted to give even some black men the right to vote, Booth was heard to remark, "That means nigger citizenship. That is the last speech he will ever make."[5] Four days later, Booth assassinated Lincoln. The Fifteenth Amendment to the Constitution, which extended to all black men the right to vote, would be ratified on February 3, 1870, five years after Lincoln's death.

21

Who was the first African-American fighter pilot?

EUGENE JACQUES BULLARD BECAME the first African-American combat pilot, seeing active duty during World War I. Born in Columbus, Georgia, Bullard was one of ten children. When he was eleven, he ran away from home and, according to Caroline Fannin, worked as a jockey in the South, "liv[ing] for a time with a band of [English-born] gypsies, who taught him to ride racehorses."[1] In 1912 he ended up in Norfolk, Virginia, where, according to William Chivalette, he "stowed away on a German ship bound for Aberdeen, Scotland."[2] In Liverpool, he joined a group of traveling minstrel performers called Freedman's Pickaninnies. After touring in Russia, Berlin, and elsewhere in Europe, Bullard and the Pickaninnies ended up in Paris, where he would remain for much of the rest of his life.

With the outbreak of war in 1914, Bullard, at nineteen, enlisted in the French Foreign Legion. He served in the Moroccan Division of the Third Marching Regiment, first as a machine gunner "in some of the bitterest fighting on the Western front," Fannin tells us, including at the Somme front, where, Chivalette writes, "300,000 Frenchmen were lost by the end of November." Then, in 1915, Bullard was transferred to the 170th Infantry of the French army, from which he earned his nickname, "the Black Swallow of Death."

The combat Bullard saw was incredibly dangerous. In a battle of the Champagne Offensive, according to Chivalette, "five hundred men began the battle, but . . . only 31 remained—a 94 percent casualty rate." Bullard, who said he received "a little head wound" in the fighting, was one of the few survivors.

His unit faced its most dangerous combat at Verdun, which the Germans "code named Verdun Operation Execution Place." Chivalette says that "in the 10 months of Verdun more than 250,000 died, 100,000 were missing, and 300,000 had been gassed or wounded." Bullard later remarked, "I thought I had seen fighting in other battles but no one has ever seen anything like Verdun—not ever before or ever since." It was hell. For a "crippling thigh wound" received at Verdun on March 5, 1916, he was awarded the prestigious Croix de Guerre and the Médaille militaire.[3]

Now unable to return to the field, he "transferred to aviation gunnery," according to Fannin. And on May 5, 1917, he earned his pilot's license, giving Eugene Jacques Bullard the historical distinction of becoming, in Chivalette's words, "the very first black fighter pilot in history." He was trained for advanced flight and combat and was assigned to Squadron 93 of the legendary Lafayette Escadrille, or "Flying Corps"—young American volunteers who flew for France. In SPAD S.VII and Nieuport biplane fighter aircraft, Bullard flew, Fannin tells us, "at least twenty missions over the Verdun sector" and claimed to have shot down two German fighters.

After the United States entered the war, Bullard was abruptly transferred back to the 170th Infantry, probably because the United States wouldn't accept the presence of a black pilot, a policy that would not change until the ban was lifted in 1940. Bullard applied to transfer to the U.S. Air Force, but despite his proven record of superior combat skills, his "application was ignored for the duration of the war," Chivalette writes.

Following the war, Bullard joined a jazz combo as a drummer, then became the manager of Le Grand Duc, one of the most popular of the early jazz clubs in Paris, famous as an initial venue for Ada "Bricktop" Smith. He used his experiences there to start his own jazz club, Club L'Escadrille, named after his unit in the air corps. In 1923 he married a wealthy French woman, Marcelle Straumann, and they had three children.

When World War II broke out, Bullard attempted to rejoin his old infantry unit, the 170th. When that proved impossible, Bullard—now aged forty-five or so—joined the 51st Infantry at Orléans. In June, Chivalette tells us, he was "badly wounded" for the second time in combat with the Germans, while "his dozen or so compatriots were killed." Bullard made his way to Spain, fleeing certain death at the hands of the occupying Nazis, and was evacuated to New York, where he recovered. After the war, he was employed as an elevator operator in Rockefeller Center for the rest of his working life.

Eugene Jacques Bullard photographed
while in the 170th French Infantry
Regiment, ca. 1918. He wears
the military decoration of the
Croix de Guerre on his chest.

In 1954 Bullard received one of the greatest honors that any veteran
could receive. "The French government requested his presence to help
relight the Eternal Flame of the Tomb of the Unknown French Soldier
at the Arc de Triomphe in Paris," writes Chivalette. Five years later, the
French government honored his heroism by naming him a Chevalier of
the Legion of Honor.

Bullard died in 1961 and is buried in the French War Veterans section
of the Flushing Cemetery in Queens, New York. According to Fannin,
Bullard received a total of fifteen medals for his military service from the
French government. In 1992, after years of official neglect, the Smithsonian's National Air and Space Museum installed his bust. And at long last,
the U.S. Air Force posthumously commissioned him as a second lieutenant
in 1994.

22

Did black people own slaves?
If so, why?

ONE OF THE MOST VEXING PARADOXES in African-American history is that free black people in this country bought and sold other black people starting at least in 1654, and they continued to do so through the Civil War. Some fascinating questions must be asked about black slave owners: How many black "masters" were involved, how many slaves did they own, and *why* did they own them?

Historians have been arguing for some time over whether free blacks purchased family members as slaves in order to protect them—motivated by benevolence and philanthropy, as historian Carter G. Woodson put it—or whether they purchased other black people primarily to exploit their free labor for profit, just as white slave owners did. The evidence shows that, unfortunately, both reasons are true. The great African-American historian John Hope Franklin states this clearly: "The majority of Negro owners of slaves had some personal interest in their property." But, he admits, "there were instances . . . in which free Negroes had a real economic interest in the institution of slavery and held slaves in order to improve their economic status."[1]

So what do the actual numbers of black slave owners and their slaves tell us? In 1830 about 13.7 percent (319,599) of the black population was free. Of these free Negroes, 3,776 owned 12,907 slaves, out of a total of 2,009,043 slaves owned in the entire United States. So the numbers of slaves owned by black people overall was quite small by comparison with the number owned by white people. The historian Thomas J. Pressly, using Woodson's statistics, calculates that 54 (or about 1 percent) of these black slave own-

Big House, Melrose Plantation, Natchitoches Parish, Louisiana. Begun in 1833 by Louis Metoyer.

ers in 1830 owned between 20 and 84 slaves; 172 (about 4 percent) owned between 10 and 19 slaves; and 3,550 (about 94 percent) each owned between 1 and 9 slaves. Crucially, 42 percent owned just 1 slave.[2]

Pressly also shows that in several states the percentage of free black slave owners as the total number of free black heads of families was quite high, namely 43 percent in South Carolina, 40 percent in Louisiana, 26 percent in Mississippi, 25 percent in Alabama, and 20 percent in Georgia.

It is reasonable to assume that the 42 percent of free black slave owners who owned just one slave probably owned a family member to protect that person, as did many of the other black slave owners who owned only a few more slaves. As Woodson put it:

> The census records show that the majority of the Negro owners of slaves were such from the point of view of philanthropy. In many instances the husband purchased the wife or vice versa . . . Slaves of Negroes were in some cases the children of a free father who had purchased his wife. If he did not thereafter emancipate the mother, as so many such husbands failed to do, his own children were born his slaves and were thus reported by the enumerators.[3]

Moreover, Woodson explained, "Benevolent Negroes often purchased slaves to make their lot easier by granting them their freedom for a nominal sum, or by permitting them to work it out on liberal terms." In other words, these black slave owners, the clear majority, cleverly used the system of slavery to protect their loved ones.

But not all did. The historian Richard Halliburton, Jr., concludes, after examining the evidence, that "it would be a serious mistake to automatically assume that free blacks owned their spouse or children only for benevolent purposes."[4] Woodson himself noted that a "small number of slaves . . . does not always signify benevolence on the part of the owner." And John Hope Franklin noted that in North Carolina, "without doubt, there were those who possessed slaves for the purpose of advancing their [own] well-being . . . these Negro slaveholders were more interested in making their farms or carpenter-shops 'pay' than they were in treating their slaves humanely." These black slaveholders, he concluded, made "some effort to conform to the pattern established by the dominant slaveholding group within the State in the effort to elevate themselves to a position of respect and privilege."[5] In other words, most black slave owners probably owned family members to protect them, but many turned to slavery to exploit the labor of other black people for profit.

WHO WERE THESE BLACK SLAVE OWNERS?

John Carruthers Stanly—born a slave in Craven County, North Carolina, the son of an Igbo mother and her master, John Wright Stanly—became an extraordinarily successful barber and real estate speculator in New Bern. By the early 1820s, Stanly owned three plantations and 163 slaves and even hired three *white* overseers to manage his property.[6] He fathered six children with a slave woman named Kitty and eventually freed them.

William Ellison was born a slave in 1790, on a plantation in the Fairfield District of South Carolina, far upcountry from Charleston. In 1816, at the age of twenty-six, he bought his own freedom and soon bought his wife and their child. In 1822 he opened his own cotton gin and became quite wealthy. By the time he died in December 1861, not long after the Civil War began, he owned nine hundred acres of land and sixty-three slaves. He was wealthier than nine out of ten white people in South Carolina. Not one of his slaves was allowed to purchase his or her own freedom.[7]

Black slaveholders were not only men. The wealthiest black person in

Charleston in 1860 was Maria Weston, who owned fourteen slaves and property valued at more than $40,000, at a time when the average white man earned about $100 a year. The historian Larry Koger tells us that, at least for a time, "in Charleston City, [South Carolina,] the female heads of black families dominated the black slaveholding community. In 1850, the number of black women who owned slaves was reported at 123 by the federal census."[8] Greed is gender blind.

Why They Owned Slaves

These men and women were among the largest free Negro slaveholders, and their motivations were neither benevolent nor philanthropic. One would be hard pressed to account for their ownership of so many slaves except as avaricious, rapacious, acquisitive, and predatory.

But lest we romanticize all of those small black slave owners who ostensibly purchased family members only for humanitarian reasons, even in these cases the evidence can be problematic. Halliburton presents some hair-raising challenges to the idea that black people who owned their own family members always treated them well:

> A free black in Trimble County, Kentucky, "sold his own son and daughter South, one for $1,000, the other for $1,200." . . . A Maryland father sold his slave children in order to purchase his wife. A Columbus, Georgia, black woman—Dilsey Pope—owned her husband. "He offended her in some way and she sold him." Fanny Canady of Louisville, Kentucky, owned her husband Jim—a drunken cobbler—whom she threatened to "sell down the river." At New Bern, North Carolina, a free black wife and son purchased their slave husband-father. When the newly bought father criticized his son—the son sold him to a slave trader. The son boasted afterward that "the old man had gone to the corn fields about New Orleans where they might learn him some manners."[9]

Carter Woodson, too, tells us that some of the husbands who purchased their spouses "were not anxious to liberate their wives immediately. They considered it advisable to put them on probation for a few years, and if they did not find them satisfactory they would sell their wives as other slave holders disposed of Negroes." He then relates the example of a black man, a shoemaker in Charleston, South Carolina, who purchased his wife for

$700. But "on finding her hard to please, he sold her a few months thereafter for $750, gaining $50 by the transaction."

Given the long history of class divisions in the black community and given the role of African elites in the long history of the transatlantic slave trade, perhaps we should not be surprised that we can find examples throughout black history of just about every sort of human behavior, from the most noble to the most heinous, as we can in any other people's history.

23

How did Harriet Tubman become a legend?

HER NAME AT BIRTH was Araminta Ross. While the radical abolitionist John Brown called her "General" and claimed that her strength was "Most of a Man," she was known far and wide as "the Moses of her people." We know her today as Harriet Tubman. She took her mother's name, Harriet, around 1844, when she married a free black man, John Tubman. How a twenty-seven-year-old fugitive slave became what one of her biographers, Milton C. Sernett, calls "the all-comprehending black hero of our time" is one of the most fascinating sagas in all of African-American history.[1]

Separating fact from fiction and history from myth in the life and times of Mrs. Tubman does nothing to diminish her stature as one of the truly great heroines of African-American history. Fortunately, a few dogged historians have uncovered the facts, including the biographers Sernett, Catherine Clinton,[2] Jean M. Humez,[3] and especially Kate Larson, whose masterly biography was published in 2004.

While today we celebrate Harriet Tubman as one of the greatest foes of slavery (and the future face of the U.S. twenty-dollar bill), she did not spend her final years in comfort or even with the full recognition that she deserved. She finally was awarded a widow's pension in 1895 in recognition of the Civil War service of her second husband, who was twenty years her junior. But it wasn't until 1899 that Tubman finally received a pension for her own military service: twelve dollars per month. "She was not a soldier, officially," Larson writes, "and her on-again, off-again role as a scout and a spy made consistent payment for her services unlikely. . . . She was never paid as a Union nurse, which may have been an additional source of irrita-

Harriet Tubman (1823–1913) nurse, spy and scout. Studio photograph by Harvey B. Lindsley, Auburn, New York. Ca. 1870s–80s.

tion for Tubman. Like the black troops, Tubman was performing her jobs as well as her white counterparts, but still was not treated equally."[4]

Tragically, she spent her final decade in a desperate search for financial support. By 1901, Tubman's luster had faded, and she was deeply in debt. It was then that Robert W. Taylor, the financial secretary of the Tuskegee Institute, stepped in to help with his book about her, *Harriet Tubman: The Heroine in Ebony*.[5] Taylor hoped that sales of the book, with its introduction by Booker T. Washington himself, would attenuate her destitution.

Taylor wrote that Tubman "stands without a parallel in history— solitary, majestic, sun kissed." Nevertheless, "the hand of affliction has rested heavily upon her for more than a year," making her "dependent almost entirely on what may be handed her by occasional callers and the scant earnings of her brother, several years her senior." Tubman, he concluded, was "bowed down with infirmity," her gait "unsteady, her eye is dim; the sun of her life ere long must set." The appeal yielded a total of seventy-seven dollars. As a newspaper article dated June 3, 1911, related, "Harriet Tubman, the aged negress, known as the 'Moses of her people,' was last Thursday taken to the Harriet Tubman home, penniless, to end her days." She spent the last two years of her life in the home and died in 1913.

Sarah Bradford, Tubman's first biographer, initiated the mythmaking about her exploits. In *Scenes in the Life of Harriet Tubman* (1869) she wrote that Tubman had rescued three hundred people and made nineteen trips back to the South.[6]

W.E.B. Du Bois gave Bradford's exaggerated figure legs when he dramatically boosted the number of people she'd rescued:

> "Moses," as Mrs. Tubman was called by her own people, was a most remarkable black woman, unlettered and very negrine but with a great degree of intelligence and perceptive insight, amazing courage and a simple steadfastness of devotion which lifts her career into the ranks of heroism. Herself a fugitive slave, she devoted her life after her own freedom was won, to the work of aiding others to escape. First and last Harriet brought out several thousand slaves.[7]

Du Bois is also a source of a claim that the reward on Tubman's head was ten thousand dollars.

No new images of Tubman appeared until the Great Depression and World War II, when three African Americans—Aaron Douglass, Jacob Lawrence, and Mary McLeod Bethune, all of whom Du Bois would also have found "negrine," perhaps—lionized her in different ways. First, the artist Aaron Douglass resurrected her nobly in what Sernett describes as his "powerfully evocative mural" entitled *Spirits Rising*, painted in 1930–31. Yet it was the young artist Jacob Lawrence's famous thirty-one-panel mural, *The Life of Harriet Tubman*, completed in 1940, that would do the most to enshrine Tubman's image in art and lore.

Lawrence's magnificent narrative series is a masterpiece of modern art, and its effect was immediate. In 1943 the first serious Tubman biography, by Earl Conrad, was published.[8] It prompted the popular journalist Walter Winchell to write that Tubman was "history's greatest Negro woman" and, even more astonishing, that she was "one of America's two or three foremost women" regardless of race.[9]

Within a year Tubman would reach unprecedented stature: at the height of World War II, her name would be affixed to a U.S. cargo ship. Incredibly, Mary McLeod Bethune and her National Council of Negro Women achieved the impossible by waging a successful effort to have one of the Liberty ships, commissioned by the U.S. Maritime Commission, named in her honor. The SS *Harriet Tubman* was christened and launched on June 3, 1944, complete with blessings from First Lady Eleanor Roosevelt, who could not attend herself. Jeanetta Welch Brown, executive secretary of the National Council of Negro Women, put it thusly that day: "It has been a long time since the name of Harriet Tubman, one of America's immortals, has been used widely in this land. But she is back with us." Bethune's organization used the launching of the ship "to inaugurate a national war-bond drive to raise two million dollars, the approximate cost of the ship."[10]

Writers suddenly interested in Tubman turned to that seemingly reliable source, Sarah Bradford, and perpetuated her myths. "In many respects," Sernett says, "the Tubman revitalization of the second half of the twentieth century was merely a reinvigoration of the Tubman myth crafted by her admirers [especially Bradford] and fueled by highly fictionalized versions of her life."

Even some of the most respected historians stubbornly cling to Bradford's "300 rescued souls in 19 trips," but the facts do not support that claim. Larson has finally set the record straight: "In total, she made approximately thirteen trips, spiriting away roughly seventy to eighty slaves, in addition to perhaps fifty or sixty more to whom she gave detailed instructions, nearly all from Dorchester and Caroline Counties in Maryland." Sarah Bradford, Larson tells us, "flagrantly exaggerated those numbers."[11]

The historian David Blight notes that "Tubman had long been a malleable icon of America's antislavery past."[12] Of our many heroines and heroes of the black past, few deserve this curious form of canonization more than does Harriet Tubman, the counterintuitive slave who was perhaps the first African American to demonstrate that the Underground Railroad ran in two directions, not merely from South to North. However, none of her contemporaries could have imagined the degree to which she has been canonized today, the curious way in which we have been able to use her myth to reflect our own aspirations, desires, and ideological agendas across a wide and varying set of perspectives.

24

When did black literature begin to address African-American sexuality?

SEX WAS A TABOO SUBJECT throughout much of the history of African-American literature. Black authors, male and female, traditionally were prudish, avoiding black sexuality in their texts like the plague. (Cases of rape, seen as a sign of the brutality and psychosis of white oppression, were an exception.)

In a speech delivered at the NAACP's Chicago convention in June 1926, W.E.B. Du Bois addressed the vexing subject of the depiction of sex in African-American literature: "The young and slowly growing black public still wants its prophets almost equally unfree. We are bound by all sorts of customs that have come down as second-hand soul clothes of white patrons. We are ashamed of sex and we lower our eyes when people will talk of it." And why was this true? Du Bois explained that "our worst side has been so shamelessly emphasized that we are denying we have or ever had a worst side. In all sorts of ways we are hemmed in and our new young artists have got to fight their way to freedom."

Zora Neale Hurston was the first black novelist to heed Du Bois's call for an explicitly full and celebratory representation of black sexuality—and she did so through a female protagonist. In her masterpiece, *Their Eyes Were Watching God* (1937), Janie Starks is comfortable with and celebrates her own sensuality. She insists on her right to choose her own lovers in spite of the strictures of the black community.

For creating this portrait, Hurston got into serious trouble with contemporary black male authors. The great novelist Richard Wright wrote a heated and vitriolic review. He was deeply troubled that her black female character not only has healthy sexual fantasies but also goes through two marriages to black men whom she realizes that she doesn't love, black men who abuse her in one way or another, one of whom she leaves and the other of whom she metaphorically "kills" by disparaging his manhood in public. For the first time in African-American literary history, sexual politics met literary politics.

What most bothered Wright, however, was that "her novel is not addressed to the Negro, but to a white audience whose chauvinistic tastes she knows how to *satisfy*" (emphasis added). He charged her with pandering to the lurid tastes and fantasies of white males. Her prose, he says, "is cloaked in that facile sensuality that has dogged Negro expression since the days of Phillis Wheatley." He accused her of "voluntarily continu[ing] in her novel the tradition which was forced upon the Negro in the theater, that is, the minstrel technique that makes 'the white folks' laugh."[1]

A year later Hurston retaliated. In a review of Wright's four interrelated novellas, *Uncle Tom's Children,* she charged that Wright wasn't concerned with "understanding and sympathy"; rather, it was "a book about hatreds," composed of "stories [that] are so grim that the Dismal Swamp of race hatred must be where they live." And the only role of sex, she said, was as a motivation for murder: the "hero gets the white man most Negro men rail against—the white man who possesses a Negro woman. He gets several of them while he is about the business of choosing to die in a hurricane of bullets and fire because his woman has had a white man. There is lavish killing here, perhaps enough to satisfy all *male* black readers."[2]

What lay at the core of this dispute? Wright accused Hurston of using "highly charged language" to titillate white readers, especially white males. Hurston felt, on the contrary, that it was Wright who pandered to white readers, especially to white males, by writing about black male violence against white racists.

Wright included three sex scenes in his great novel, *Native Son* (1940), two of which he allowed to be cut when it was chosen to be the first Book of the Month Club selection by a black author. Each of these scenes is troublesome in a different way, and none of them even remotely began to fulfill the challenge that Du Bois issued, or to speak to the concerns that James

Zora Neale Hurston, *Their Eyes Were Watching God* (Philadelphia: J. B. Lippincott, 1937). Dust jacket of first edition.

Baldwin would later express. In one of the cut scenes, Bigger masturbates in a movie theater ("I'm polishing my night stick," he tells the boy sitting next to him, who is masturbating as well) while watching a newsreel detailing the latest exploits of Mary Dalton, the pretty daughter of his new employer.

In the second excised passage, Bigger kisses this same Mary as he carries her, drunk, up the stairs to her bedroom, feeling "her body moving strongly" and "the sharp bones of her hips move in a hard and veritable grind." And then when Mary's blind mother walks into the bedroom, Bigger smothers Mary to death to avoid detection.

Bigger does have a sexual relationship with his black girlfriend, Bessie, but it, too, is deeply problematic. After Bessie joins him in his hiding place following Mary's murder, Bigger rapes her. And what does he do afterward? He murders her, just as he did Mary. Sex, for Bigger, is inextricably intertwined with what he hates, the system he finds emasculating and castrating and to which he wishes to do violence. From rape to murder seems like a natural progression for Bigger, fueled as his desire and sexuality are by anger.

James Baldwin once said of Wright and his fellow black male writers that "in most of the novels written by Negroes until today . . . there is a great space where sex ought to be; and what usually fills this space is violence. This violence, as in so much of Wright's work, is gratuitous and compulsive . . . because the root of the violence is never examined."[3]

In 1975 Marilyn Nelson Waniek wrote a pioneering essay that elaborated on Baldwin's insight. Far too many black writers—especially male writers, including Wright—traditionally substituted the figure of white men (as the embodiment of an all-encompassing and all-determining anti-black racism) precisely in the place in their texts where a reader might expect to find the development of healthy sexual relations between black characters. "Many critics have complained of a scarcity of fulfilling heterosexual relationships in novels by Black American authors," she wrote, and this "would include most of the novels written by black men in this country," novels that lack "a lasting sexual relationship between the Black protagonist and a woman."[4]

Instead, "the most completely developed relationships [in the novels of black males] are those between the Black protagonists and their white male friends, who tend to be older than the protagonists. All of the protagonists are finally alone, left to build their own identities out of the division within their psyches and in America. And in the space where sex should be is instead the awful confrontation of Black self with white self, and Black self with white society."

Fortunately, the representation of both black heterosexuality and homosexuality has been a fundamental part of both the gay and black women's literary movements over the past few decades. But perhaps this tendency in earlier African-American literature written by men helps to explain the crisis in black male-female relations that has been such a deeply troubling aspect of contemporary African-American culture.

25

Is most of what we believe about the Underground Railroad true?

WHEN STUDENTS TALK ABOUT the Underground Railroad, they seem to be under the impression that it was akin to a black, southern Grand Central Terminal, with regularly scheduled routes that hundreds of thousands of slave "passengers" used to escape from southern plantations, aided by that irrepressible, stealthy double agent Harriet Tubman. Many also seem to believe that thousands of benign, incognito white "conductors" routinely hid the slaves in secret rooms concealed in attics or basements, or behind the staircases of numerous "safe houses," the locations of which were coded in "freedom quilts" sewn by the slaves and hung in their windows as guide-posts for fugitives on the run.

It was the editor of the *Weekly News* of Oberlin, Ohio, in 1885, who first made the Underground Railroad sound like a massive rail operation, for a piece on his town's pivotal role in aiding fugitives to escape. The "rail-road," according to legends that grew up around it, was composed of "a chain of stations leading from the Southern states to Canada," as Wilbur H. Siebert put it in his massive pioneering (and often wildly romantic) 1898 study.[1] Others imagined it as "a series of hundreds of interlocking 'lines'" that ran from Alabama or Mississippi northward through the South, all the way across the Ohio River and the Mason-Dixon Line, as the histo-rian David Blight summarizes the fanciful notions.[2] Fleeing slaves, often entire families, were allegedly guided at night in their desperate quest for freedom by the proverbial "Drinking Gourd," the slaves' code name for the North Star.

Charles T. Webber. *The Underground Railroad*. 1893. Oil on canvas. The Cincinnati Art Museum. Among those rescuing runaway slaves in this wintry scene are abolitionists Levi Coffin and his wife, Catherine.

Larry Gara,[3] David Blight, and others have worked diligently to address some of the most common myths about the Underground Railroad.

1. *Well-intentioned white abolitionists, many of whom were Quakers, ran it.* The genuinely interracial coalition between the Underground Railroad and the abolition movement was perhaps the first such instance in American history, and the role of the Quakers in its success cannot be gainsaid. It was, nevertheless, predominantly run by free northern African Americans, especially in its earliest years, most notably the great Philadelphian William Still. He operated with the assistance of white abolitionists, many of whom were Quakers. "Much of what we call the Underground Railroad," Blight writes, "was actually operated clandestinely by African Americans themselves through urban vigilance committees and rescue squads that were often led by free blacks."

White and black activists such as Levi Coffin, Thomas Garrett, Calvin Fairbank, Charles Torrey, Harriet Tubman, and Still were genuine heroes of the Underground Railroad. William Still himself recorded the rescue of 649 fugitives sheltered in Philadelphia, including 16 who arrived on one day alone, June 1, 1855.[4]

2. *The Underground Railroad operated throughout the South.* The Railroad's expansion did not occur until after the passage of the Fugitive Slave Act in 1850. But very few people, relatively speaking, engaged in its activities. After all, it was *illegal* to assist slaves escaping to their freedom. Violating the 1850 act could lead to charges of "constructive treason." Being an abolitionist or a conductor on the Underground Railroad, according to the historian Donald Yacovone, "was about as popular and as dangerous as being a member of the Communist Party in 1955."[5]

3. *Most fugitive slaves who made it to the North found sanctuary along the way in secret rooms concealed in attics or cellars, and many escaped through tunnels.* Most fugitive slaves spirited themselves out of towns under the cover of darkness, not through tunnels, the construction of which would have been huge undertakings and quite costly. And few homes in the North had secret passageways or hidden rooms in which slaves could be concealed.

4. *Slaves created freedom quilts and hung them at the windows of their homes to alert escaping fugitives to the location of safe houses and secure routes north.* This is one of the oddest myths propagated in all of African-American history. If a slave family had the wherewithal to make a quilt, they used it to protect themselves against the cold, not to send messages about supposed routes on the Underground Railroad. On occasion, messages were given out at black church gatherings and prayer meetings, but not about the day and time that Harriet Tubman would be coming to town. The risk of betraying individual escapes and collective rebellions was far too great for escape plans to be widely shared.

5. *The Underground Railroad was a large-scale activity that enabled hundreds of thousands of people to escape bondage.* No one knows for sure how many slaves actually escaped to a new life in the North, Canada, Florida, or Mexico. Some scholars estimate between 25,000 and 40,000, while others top that figure at 50,000. Elizabeth Pierce, an official at the National Underground Railroad Freedom Center in Cincinnati, says the number could be as high as 100,000.

We can put these estimates in perspective by remembering that in 1850 there were 434,495 free Negroes (more than half of whom were still living in the South), while in 1860 there were still only 488,070. The difference would include those fugitives who had made it to the North on the Underground Railroad, plus natural increase. So we can see that unfortunately only a few fugitive slaves actually made it to the North during this decade.

Astonishingly, more than 50,000 slaves ran away not to the North but "within the South" annually by the 1850s, according to John Hope Franklin and Loren Schweninger.[6] But few of them made it to freedom.

It should not come as a surprise to us that very few slaves escaped from slavery. The Underground Railroad was a marvelously improvised, metaphorical construct run by courageous heroes, most of whom were black.

6. *Entire families commonly escaped together.* According to Franklin and Schweninger, as Blight summarizes, "80 percent of these fugitives were young males in their teens and twenties who generally absconded alone. Indeed, [between 1838 and 1860] 95 percent fled alone. Young slave women were much less likely to run away because of their family and child-rearing responsibilities. Entire families with children did attempt flight to freedom, but such instances were rare."

The Underground Railroad was not the nineteenth century's equivalent of Grand Central Terminal. "Running away," as Blight summarizes, "was a frightening and dangerous proposition for slaves, and the overall numbers who risked it, or for that matter succeeded in reaching freedom, were 'not large.'" It did succeed in aiding thousands of brave slaves, each of whom we should remember as a hero of African-American history, but not nearly as many as we commonly imagine—and most certainly not enough.

26

Did Russia's Peter the Great adopt
an African man as his son?

JOEL ROGERS, in *100 Amazing Facts About the Negro,* described a great black general who served in the court of Peter the Great: "Abraham Hannibal, captured as a slave in Africa, was adopted by Peter the Great as his son and taught military engineering. Later Hannibal became tutor to the heir of the throne, and commander in chief of the Russian army. He died in 1782 at the age of 90, owning vast estates and 2000 white slaves."

It turns out that Abram Gannibal (Rogers anglicized his name as Abraham Hannibal) was indeed a member of Peter the Great's court, but Peter was his godfather, not his adoptive father. And amazingly, Alexander Pushkin, "the father of Russian literature," was Gannibal's great-grandson.

Since Russia, unlike the other imperial powers, had no African colonies, a black person was a rarity, even as late as the 1980s. Three centuries earlier, when Gannibal arrived, a black person would have been an odd sight indeed.

Gannibal was born in Logone (now Logone-Birni, in present-day Cameroon) around 1697. According to the historians Catharine Theimer Nepomnyashchy and Ludmilla A. Trigos, he was enslaved following a military battle and taken to Tripoli, then to Constantinople. A Russian spy transported him to St. Petersburg "as a gift to Tsar Peter the Great, who was known for his love of the exotic and the odd."[1]

Peter, "the ruler of the largest contiguous empire on earth," took Gannibal as his godson, standing over his baptism in 1705.[2] The two became quite close: Gannibal traveled with Peter to Europe, in 1716 visiting the Netherlands and in 1717 Paris, where he studied military engineering at

Gustav von Mardefeld. *Peter the Great with a Black Page*.
Ca. 1720. Watercolor miniature on vellum. London,
Victoria & Albert Museum.

the artillery school at La Fère. When he returned to Russia in 1722, he
became Peter's personal secretary and then engineer-lieutenant in the Pre-
obrazhensky Regiment, where he taught mathematics and wrote a two-
volume textbook on geometry and fortifications.

After Peter suddenly died, Gannibal had the good fortune to be named
the tutor of the future Peter II during the two-year reign of Peter's wife,
Catherine I. But when Catherine died, Gannibal "found himself at the
mercy of the powerful Prince Menshikov against whom he had plotted,
and was sent to Siberia, ostensibly to design and oversee the building of
fortifications in the remote town of Selenginsk."[3] After three years of
effective exile in Siberia, Gannibal returned to St. Petersburg.

In 1731 he married Evdokia Dioper, the daughter of a Greek captain.
The marriage deteriorated when Evdokia gave birth to a white baby girl.
Gannibal did not believe that she could be his daughter and charged his

wife with adultery. He used extreme measures in attempts to force her to confess: "The legal documents include allegations that Gannibal set up a private torture chamber in his home to force his wife into testifying as he wished and that, for her part, Evdokia engaged in multiple infidelities and even plotted with one of her lovers to poison her husband."[4]

Long before their divorce was final (the proceedings would take twenty-one years), Gannibal began a relationship with a Swedish noblewoman, Christina Regina von Schöberg. The two had seven children and enjoyed a happy marriage until their deaths, just months apart.

When Peter's daughter, Elizabeth I, became empress in 1741, Gannibal was promoted to major-general and governor-general of the city of Revel, in Estonia. He was given an estate at Mikhailovskoe, which, Nepomnyashchy and Trigos tell us, nearly a century later "would become so important to his great-grandson's life and work."[5] A gift from the Empress Elizabeth, the estate was "populated by—according to the census of 1744—806 serfs," explains the Pushkin biographer T. J. Binyon.[6]

In 1759 Gannibal was promoted to the rank of general and a year later was awarded the Order of Saint Alexander Nevsky, which, when "presented by the empress in person," the historian N. K. Teletova writes, "was the pinnacle of his career."[7] Gannibal retired to the estate of Suida outside of St. Petersburg, where he dictated his reminiscences, a copy of which his great-grandson would own.

Gannibal died in 1781, during the American Revolution. Voltaire himself incredibly called Gannibal "the dark star of the Enlightenment." At a time when most persons of African descent were enslaved throughout the New World, Gannibal, a black African, was accorded all of the rights and privileges of Russian nobility.

27

Were Alexander Pushkin's African roots important to him?

ALEXANDER PUSHKIN IS WIDELY REGARDED as "the father of Russian literature," the Shakespeare of the Russian literary tradition. As described in Amazing Fact no. 26, Pushkin was also the great-grandson of a Cameroon-born general, Abram Petrovich Gannibal, a godson of the Russian monarch.

Pushkin was born on June 6, 1799, eighteen years after his great-grandfather Gannibal's death.[1] He was an indifferent student at the lyceum outside St. Petersburg, preoccupied as he was with writing poetry. He graduated in 1817 and took a position at the Collegium of Foreign Affairs in St. Petersburg, where over the next three years he associated with members of the radical movement who in 1825 would be responsible for the Decembrist Uprising, a plot to overthrow Nicholas I and place the emperor's brother on the throne.

Pushkin circulated a series of radical poems unofficially, one of which, "Ode to Liberty," would be found among the papers of the major Decembrist conspirators. By this time, Pushkin had been exiled to his mother's estate in northern Russia, so he escaped punishment, although the five ringleaders were sentenced to death.

Forgiven by Nicholas I in 1826, Pushkin began an extraordinary period of creativity, completing over the next five years two of his masterpieces, *Eugene Onegin* and *Boris Godunov,* and four tragedies, including *Mozart and Salieri.* During this period, he also began a novel about his great-grandfather, *The Moor of Peter the Great,* which he never completed.

In 1831 Pushkin married Natalia (or Natalya) Goncharova, and like his great-grandfather's first marriage, to Evdokia Dioper, Pushkin's marriage was deeply troubled. It would even have fatal consequences. A French military officer, Georges d'Anthès, pursued his wife, and in 1836, enraged, Pushkin challenged him to a duel. He retracted the challenge when d'Anthès married his wife's sister. But d'Anthès continued his pursuit, so Pushkin challenged him once again. On January 27, 1837, Pushkin was mortally wounded, and he died two days later. All Russia grieved. Virtually overnight, Pushkin was hailed as the indisputable father of Russian literature.

The father of Russian literature identified with his great-grandfather's African heritage as a matter of choice. He wrote about it on several occasions. In an 1824 letter, he even highlighted his relation to black slaves in the United States: "One can think of the fate of the Greeks in the same way as of the fate of my brother Negroes, and one can wish both of them liberation from unendurable slavery."[2]

Vasily Andreevich Tropinin. *Alexander Sergeyevich Pushkin*. 1827. Oil on canvas. St. Petersburg, National Pushkin Museum.

One of Pushkin's favorite possessions, according to Nepomnyashchy and Trigos, was "an inkstand featuring a black man leaning against an anchor and standing in front of two bales of cotton (made to hold ink). Accompanying it was a note [from his close friend, Pavel Nashchokin] stating: 'I am sending you your ancestor with inkwells that open and that reveal him to be a farsighted person.' Pushkin was extremely pleased with the gift, which he kept on his desk to the end of his days."[3] The note and the gift were clever puns, as Marial Iglesias Utset explains: "It is based on a pun with 'ink' (*chernila,* in Russian) and 'black' (*cherni,* in Russian)."[4] As Nepomnyashchy and Trigos show, the inkstand "holds the ink (*chernila,* literally, the 'black stuff') for Pushkin to ply his trade and thus attests to the creativity of its owner."

Because the word for *ink* in Russian has the same root as the word *black,* that inkstand, we might say, was Pushkin's signifier of his black ancestry, centrally placed on his desk as a visible testament to the irony that a man of recent African descent was playing such a seminal role in the creation of Russia's national literary tradition.

Racism accosted Pushkin in death as it did during his life. One of his classmates noted after his passing that "in him was manifested all the ardor and sensuality of his African blood," while another noted that he was frequently "flaring up into a fury, with unbridled African passions (such was his mother's ancestry), eternally absent-minded, eternally absorbed in his poetic dreams."[5] And some Russian commentators have done their best to erase the significance of his blackness, or to claim that he had no interest in it at all, or that it was irrelevant to his genius.

But they couldn't be further from the truth. Pushkin would fight with his pen to protect his great-grandfather's honor. When a literary rival, Faddei Bulgarin, cast aspersions on Gannibal's status as a slave "bought . . . for a bottle of rum," Pushkin responded that "the blackamoor purchased cheaply grew up diligent, unpurchasable, a confidant to the tsar, and not a slave."[6]

Fyodor Dostoevsky perhaps defined Pushkin's unique status best, referring to what today we might call his cultural hybridity: "I state categorically that there has never been a poet with such universal responsiveness as Pushkin. It is not only a matter of responsiveness but also of its amazing depth, the reincarnation in his spirit of the spirit of foreign peoples, a reincarnation that is almost total and is therefore miraculous." Pushkin's literary legacy shines brightly, nearly two centuries after his tragic death, "under the sky of my Africa," as he once put it so lyrically himself.[7]

On February 11, 1847, on the tenth anniversary of Pushkin's death at the age of thirty-eight following a duel, the abolitionist and poet John Greenleaf Whittier wrote an article about Gannibal's famous great-grandson for the *National Era*, an American abolitionist newspaper. "The poet of Russia," Whittier exclaimed, "the favorite alike of Emperor and people," it turns out, was a black man: "Can it be possible that this man, so wonderfully gifted, so honored, so lamented, was a colored man—a negro? Such, it seems, is the fact. Incredible as it may appear to the American reader."

Pushkin's life, he concluded, exposed "the utter folly and Injustice of the common prejudice against the colored race in this country. It is a prejudice wholly incompatible with enlightened republicanism and true Christianity . . . With our feet on the neck of the black man, we have taunted him with his inferiority; shutting him out from school and college, we have denied his capacity for Intellectual progress; spurning him from the meeting-house and church communion, we have reproached him as vicious, and incapable of moral elevation."

For American abolitionists just three years before the passage of the Fugitive Slave Act, Pushkin was a grand and irresistible symbol: "Do not . . . Pushkin's songs of a great nation waken within all hearts the sympathies of a common [human] nature?"[8]

28

Was Jackie Robinson court-martialed?

ON APRIL 15, 1947, at Ebbets Field in Brooklyn, New York, Jack Roosevelt Robinson, at the age of twenty-eight, became the first African American to play for a Major League baseball team since the 1884 season, when Moses Fleetwood "Fleet" Walker played for the Toledo Blue Stockings. Before a crowd of 26,623 spectators (of whom approximately 14,000 are thought to have been black), Robinson scored a run to contribute to the Dodgers' 5–3 victory over the Boston Braves.

During a relatively short career spanning only ten seasons, Robinson was Rookie of the Year in 1947 and Most Valuable Player in 1949. He took his team to the World Series six times (including one World Championship in 1955) and made the All-Star Team six times. He was inducted into the Hall of Fame in 1962, and in an unprecedented gesture to his enormous historical significance and prowess as an athlete, Major League Baseball retired his number, 42, in 1997, the first time this has been done for any athlete in any sport.

What many people don't know is that Lt. Jack Roosevelt Robinson was actually court-martialed in 1944. Had he been found guilty, the whole course of black participation in professional baseball and every other professional sport, as well as the modern civil rights movement, would have been profoundly affected.

As Arnold Rampersad details in his masterful biography, on July 6, 1944, Robinson "became entangled in a dispute that threatened to end his military service in disgrace." While riding on a military bus returning to a

Comic book cover, "Special!
Inside the Dodger Training Camp!
Read Rookie on Trial!"
Jackie Robinson, No. 5, 1951.

hospital from "the colored officers club," he sat down next to Virginia Jones, the wife of one of his fellow officers. Jones looked white, at least to the white bus driver. After a few blocks, the driver abruptly ordered Robinson "to move to the back of the bus."[1] Robinson, justifiably outraged, refused. He had read that segregation was no longer allowed on military buses and proceeded to engage in a form of protest prefiguring a similar action by Rosa Parks eleven years later.

Robinson described what happened next:

> The bus driver asked me for my identification card. I refused to give it to him. He then went to the Dispatcher and told him something. What he told him I don't know. He then comes back and tells the people that this nigger is making trouble. I told the driver to stop fuckin with me, so he gets the rest of the men around there and starts blowing his top and someone calls the MP's.

Robinson was placed under "arrest in quarters," which meant that "he would be considered under arrest at the hospital, although without a guard. Robinson was then taken to the hospital in a police pickup truck." A white officer would recall that Robinson "was handcuffed, and there were shackles on his legs. Robinson's face was angry, the muscles on his face tight, his eyes half closed."

On July 24 Robinson was transferred to the 758th Tank Battalion, "where the commander signed orders to prosecute him." On that day, he was arrested. His fate was in the hands of nine men, eight of them white.

Robinson faced two charges: "The first, a violation of Article of War No. 63, accused him of 'behaving with disrespect toward Capt. Gerald M. Bear, CMP, his superior officer' . . . The second charge was a violation of Article No. 64, in this case 'willful disobedience of lawful command of Gerald M. Bear, CMP, his superior.'" Robinson had fought to defend himself bravely on the evening of the incident, including reportedly saying quite heroically, "Look here, you son-of-a-bitch, don't you call me no nigger!" After a four-hour trial, he was exonerated: "Robinson secured at least the four votes (secret and written) needed for his acquittal. He was found 'not guilty of all specifications and charges.'"

As the philosopher Cornel West has put it, "More even than either Abraham Lincoln and the Civil War, or Martin Luther King, Jr., and the civil rights movement, Jackie Robinson graphically symbolized and personified the challenge to the vicious legacy and ideology of white supremacy in American history"—a challenge, West says, that "remains incomplete, unfinished."[2]

Baseball was America's "national pastime" and was also, accordingly, the ultimate bastion of white male dominance. If professional sports—let alone the larger society—were to be desegregated, the effort had to commence on the baseball field. To understand the broad social and political impact of Robinson's actions on the field, we need only consider the chain reaction of crucial episodes in the history of the civil rights movement that unfolded almost immediately after his first season with the Dodgers.

On July 26, 1948, just over a year after Robinson faced his first pitcher at Ebbets Field, President Harry Truman issued Executive Order 9982, abolishing racial discrimination in the armed forces. Truman's timing may well have been informed by Robinson's successful integration of professional baseball. Truman's desegregation of the military no doubt informed the Supreme Court's *Brown v. Board of Education* decision desegregating public schools in 1954, which in turn informed the actions of Rosa Parks on her bus, leading to the Montgomery Bus Boycott. Out of the Montgomery Bus Boycott emerged the leadership role of the young Martin Luther King, Jr.

Jackie Robinson alone did not set off this chain of events, but his courage and bravery played a major role in the history of integration, both on the field and throughout American society. No history of the civil rights movement would be complete without noting Robinson's major role and according him a place of honor and immortality in African-American history.

29

What were the largest slave rebellions in America?

1. STONO REBELLION, 1739

The Stono Rebellion was the largest slave revolt to be staged in the thirteen colonies.[1] On Sunday, September 9, 1739, a day free of labor, about twenty slaves under the leadership of a man named Jemmy provided whites with a painful lesson on the African desire for liberty. Many members of the group were seasoned soldiers, either from the Yamasee War or from their experience in their homes in Angola, where they were captured and sold, and they had been trained in the use of weapons.

They gathered at the Stono River and raided a warehouse-like store, Hutchenson's, executing the white owners and placing their victims' heads on the store's front steps for all to see. They moved on to other houses in the area, killing the occupants and burning the structures, marching through the colony toward St. Augustine, Florida, where under Spanish law they would be free.

Many more were drawn to the march, and the insurrectionists soon numbered about one hundred. The slaves fought off the English for more than a week before the colonists rallied and killed most of the rebels, although some very likely reached Fort Mose.

2. THE NEW YORK CITY CONSPIRACY OF 1741

About 1,700 blacks lived in a city of some 7,000 whites who appeared determined to grind every person of African descent under their heel. Some form of revenge seemed inevitable. In early 1741 Fort George in New York burned to the ground. Fires erupted elsewhere in the city—four in one day—and others in New Jersey and on Long Island. Several white people claimed they had heard slaves bragging about setting the fires and threatening worse. They concluded that a revolt had been planned by secret black societies and gangs, inspired by a conspiracy of priests and their Catholic minions—white, black, brown, free, and slave.

A sixteen-year-old Irish indentured servant, under arrest for theft, claimed knowledge of a plot by the city's slaves to kill white men, seize white women, and incinerate the city. In the investigation that followed, thirty black men, two white men, and two white women were executed. Seventy people of African descent were exiled to far-flung places like Newfoundland, Madeira, Saint-Domingue, and Curaçao. Before the end of the summer of 1741, seventeen blacks would be hanged and thirteen more sent to the stake.

3. Gabriel's Conspiracy, 1800

In 1776 a slave named Gabriel was born on the Prosser plantation, just six miles north of Richmond, Virginia, and home to fifty-three slaves. A skilled blacksmith, he cut an imposing figure, standing more than six feet tall, and when he was away from the forge, he dressed in fine clothes. But what most distinguished him was his ability to read and write: only 5 percent of southern slaves were literate.

Inspired by the French and Saint-Domingue revolutions of 1789, Gabriel imbibed the political fervor of the era and concluded, albeit erroneously, that the ideology of Jeffersonian democracy encompassed the interests of black slaves and white workingmen alike, and that united, they could oppose the oppressive Federalist merchant class.

Gabriel began to formulate a plan, enlisting his brother Solomon and another servant on the Prosser plantation to fight for freedom. Word quickly spread to Richmond, nearby towns and plantations, and well beyond to Petersburg and Norfolk, via free and enslaved blacks who worked the waterways. Letting so many black people learn of his plans exposed Gabriel to the possibility of betrayal.

But he persevered, aiming to rally at least a thousand slaves to his banner of "Death or Liberty," an inversion of the famed cry of the slave-holding revolutionary Patrick Henry. With incredible daring, Gabriel determined to march to Richmond, take the armory, and hold Governor

James Monroe hostage until the merchant class bent to the rebels' demands of equal rights for all. He announced that his uprising would take place on August 30.

As luck would have it, on that day one of the worst thunderstorms in recent memory pummeled Virginia, washing away roads and making travel all but impossible. Undeterred, Gabriel believed that only a small band was necessary to carry out the plan. But many of his followers lost faith, and he was betrayed by a slave named Pharoah, who feared retribution if the plot failed.

The rebellion was barely under way when the state captured Gabriel and several co-conspirators. Twenty-five African Americans were hanged together before Gabriel went to the gallows and was executed, alone.

4. German Coast Uprising, 1811

In 1811, about forty miles north of New Orleans, Charles Deslondes, a mulatto slave driver on the Andry sugar plantation in the German Coast area of Louisiana, also took inspiration from the Haitian Revolution that ended seven years prior. He would go on to lead the largest and most sophisticated slave revolt in U.S. history.[2] (The Stono Rebellion occurred during the colonial period, before America won its independence from Great Britain.) Deslondes communicated his intentions to slaves on the Andry plantation and in nearby areas, and on the rainy evening of January 8, he and about twenty-five other slaves rose up and attacked the plantation's owner and family. They hacked to death one of the owner's sons but carelessly allowed the master to escape.

The Andry plantation, as a warehouse for the local militia, was well outfitted—Deslondes and his men had chosen it wisely as the place to begin their revolt. They ransacked the stores and seized uniforms, guns, and ammunition. As they moved toward New Orleans, intending to capture the city, dozens more men and women joined the cause, singing Creole protest songs while pillaging plantations and murdering whites. Some estimated that the force ultimately swelled to 300, but it is unlikely that Deslondes's army exceeded 124.

Wade Hampton, a South Carolina congressman, slave master, and Indian fighter, was assigned the task of suppressing the insurrection. With a small force of regular U.S. Army soldiers and militia, Hampton took two days to stop the rebels. The pitched battle ended only when the slaves ran out of ammunition, about twenty miles from New Orleans. In the slaughter that followed, the slaves' lack of military experience was evident: the whites suffered no casualties. On the other hand, more than one hundred insurgents were killed, with whites severing the heads of many of their victims and placing them along the road to New Orleans.

5. Nat Turner's Rebellion, 1831

Born on October 2, 1800, in Southampton County, Virginia, the week before Gabriel was hanged, Nat Turner impressed his family and friends with an unusual sense of purpose. On August 22, 1831, driven by prophetic visions and joined by a host of followers—about seventy armed slaves and free blacks—he set off to slaughter the white neighbors who enslaved them.

"The Discovery of Nat Turner" by Benjamin Phipps, October 30, 1831. Wood engraving by William Henry Shelton for Alexander H. Stephens, *A Comprehensive and Popular History of the United States* (Chattanooga, Tenn., 1882).

In the early morning hours, they bludgeoned Turner's master and his master's wife and children with axes. By the end of the next day, the rebels had attacked about fifteen homes and killed between fifty-five and sixty whites as they moved toward the county seat of Jerusalem, Virginia. White militia began to attack Turner's men, and other slaves who had planned to join the rebellion suddenly turned against it, undoubtedly concluding that it was bound to fail. Most of the rebels were captured quickly, but Turner eluded authorities for more than a month.

On Sunday, October 30, a local white man stumbled upon Turner's hideout and seized him. A special Virginia court tried him on November 5 and sentenced him to hang six days later. A barbaric scene followed his execution. Enraged whites took his body, skinned it, and distributed parts as souvenirs. They rendered his remains into grease. His head was removed and for a time sat in the biology department of Wooster College in Ohio. (In fact, pieces of his body—including his skull and a purse made from his skin—have been preserved and are likely still hidden in storage somewhere.)

Of his fellow rebels, twenty-one went to the gallows, and another sixteen were sold away from the region. As the state reacted by passing harsher laws controlling black people, many free blacks fled Virginia for good. Turner remains a legendary figure, remembered for the bloody path he forged in his personal war against slavery, and for the grisly and garish way he was treated in death.

30

What were the biggest acts of betrayal within the enslaved community?

IN A SPEECH DELIVERED to Student Nonviolent Coordinating Committee workers in Selma, Alabama, on February 4, 1965, Malcolm X, in one of his most memorable, humorous, and devastatingly effective rhetorical performances, defined the difference between the "house Negro" and the "field Negro," thereby historicizing black self-loathing and betrayal. "If the master's house caught on fire," Malcolm said, "the house Negro would fight harder to put the blaze out than the master would. . . . He identified himself with his master more than his master identified with himself." The field Negro, on the other hand, "hated his master" and was willing to flee at the first opportunity.

Was Malcolm X right about his black-and-white depiction of the "politics," as it were, between house and field? Were "house Negroes" responsible for the biggest acts of betrayal within the slave community? With all due respect to Malcolm, the answer is: not really, though there are always exceptions.

The historical record is full of masters expressing their fears that their house servants were trying to poison them. As the historian Deborah Gray White explains, "As early as 1755 a Charleston slave woman was burned at the stake for poisoning her master, and in 1769 a special issue of the *South Carolina Gazette* carried the story of a slave woman who had poisoned her master's infant child."[1]

Among many other alleged poisonings, in 1785 in New Orleans "a slave named Julia . . . was said to have confessed to putting ground glass in her mistress's food," according to the historian Ned Sublette. She was given two hundred lashes and placed in the stocks "for two hours a day for eight days."[2]

Historically, as Frederick Douglass eloquently pointed out, the slave who had access to literacy found the urge to achieve *physical* freedom, to run away, well-nigh irresistible. Such a slave was far more likely to have been a house slave than a field slave, to use Malcolm's formulation. Once slaves were literate, they understood even more fundamentally than when illiterate that they were intellectual equals, by *nature,* with their masters, and that the deprivation of the right to learn to read and write was another form of slavery—*metaphysical slavery.* And so these literate slaves—whether living in the house or in the field, or in the house *and* then in the field, as Douglass did—spent a lot of time plotting their escape.

Some house servants, however, did conform to Malcolm's harsh generalization about them. Henry Bibb, in his slave narrative of 1849, charges house slaves with a penchant for duplicity: "Domestic slaves are often found to be traitors to their own people, for the purpose of gaining favor with their masters; and they are encouraged and trained up by them to

The house slave Stephen, played by Samuel L. Jackson, confronts his master Calvin J. Candie (Leonardo DiCaprio) in *Django Unchained* (Columbia Pictures, 2012).

report every plot they know of being formed about stealing any thing or running away, or any thing of the kind; and for which they are paid."[3] Still, Bibb's characterization was not typical of house slaves, since we know today the evidence is much more mixed.

Yet not all slaves sought freedom when given the opportunity, and some even betrayed the attempts of their fellow slaves to stage rebellions. And here Malcolm's hyperbolic allegory has some basis in historical fact. We can think of this small group of slaves as the ancestors of Samuel L. Jackson's character, Stephen, in the 2012 film *Django Unchained,* and we even know some of their names, and the rewards they received for their acts of betrayal, thanks to the research of several scholars.[4]

Historians trace the first major slave conspiracy in Colonial America to Gloucester County, Virginia, in 1663. This early attempt to strike a blow for freedom was "a conspiracy of slaves and indentured servants who planned 'to destroy their masters and afterwards to set up for themselves,'" as the historian Mary Miley Theobald writes.[5]

The plot was unsuccessful, however, because "as would happen again and again, [it] was betrayed from inside." An indentured servant named Berkenhead foiled the plot, for which he "received a reward of five thousand pounds of tobacco plus his freedom. Several bloody heads dangled from local chimney tops as a gruesome warning to others." We don't know if Berkenhead was white or black, but the historian Herbert Aptheker says that "he was probably a white indentured servant."[6]

Unfortunately, there were several betrayals that we can definitely attribute to black people. A rebellion of African-Americans slaves planned for Easter Sunday 1710 in Virginia, Theobald tells us, was betrayed by a slave named Will, who "got his freedom" in return, while his master, "Robert Ruffin, was reimbursed for his value with £40 of public money." The two black leaders of the plot were tried, convicted, and executed.

In June 1740, according to Rory T. Cornish, a slave named Peter "betrayed a serious plot that involved possibly 150 to 200 slaves who planned to capture and burn Charleston itself."[7] Sixty of the conspirators were tried, and fifty were executed.[8] That same year, up in Prince George's County, Vincent Harding tells us, "Maryland courts received depositions from several African Americans," which, the court recorded, were "relating to a most wicked and dangerous Conspiracy having been formed by them to destroy his Majesty's Subjects within the Province, and to possess themselves of the Whole Country."⁹

As we learned in Amazing Fact no. 29, in 1800 Gabriel Prosser had planned to lead a major rebellion in Richmond, Virginia. Delayed by a torrential rain, the plan fell apart when several slaves, one aptly named Pharoah, exposed it. Although Gabriel escaped, a slave named Billy later betrayed him again, seeking the $300 reward that had been placed on Gabriel's head. Gabriel, along with twenty-three of his co-conspirators and his two brothers, Solomon and Martin, was hanged for his role in the plot. Billy received $50.[10]

Denmark Vesey, who won $1,500 in a lottery in Charleston, South Carolina, in 1799, used the money to purchase his freedom. By 1822 he had formed the plans for a large rebellion of slaves to unfold on Bastille Day, July 14. Vesey's plot was betrayed by two slaves, Peter Prioleau and George Wilson, and a free person of color named William Penceel.

Frederick Douglass's early attempt to escape his enslavement on the Freeland Farm in Maryland in 1836 was betrayed, most probably by a slave named Sandy.[11] Douglass and his four co-conspirators, the great fugitive slave wrote in his 1845 *Narrative,* were "sent off to the jail at Easton."[12]

One of the largest groups of slaves to attempt to flee their enslavement did so in Washington, D.C., in 1848. Seventy-seven slaves tried to escape on board the ship *The Pearl* but were captured on Chesapeake Bay. They were betrayed by a man named Judson Diggs, after one of the participants refused to pay him for taking him to the dock. Diggs had been a slave until gaining his freedom in 1845, just three years before the attempted escape on *The Pearl.*

"Fate," as the historian John Paynter put it,

which occasionally plays such strange and cruel tricks in the lives of men, presented in this instance a Machiavellian combination of opposing forces, that was disastrous to the enterprise of the fugitives. Judson Diggs, one of their own people, a man who in all reason might have been expected to sympathize with their effort, took upon himself the role of Judas. Judson was a drayman and had hauled some packages to the wharf for one of the slaves, who was without funds to pay the charge, and although he was solemnly promised that the money should be sent to him, he proceeded at once to wreak vengeance through a betrayal of the entire party.[13]

The former slave Isaac Johnson, in his narrative of 1901, related a horrific outcome of a slave betrayed. "While working for John Madinglay," as Harry Thomas summarizes the incident,

> Johnson befriends Bob, a free Canadian engineer who was wrongfully arrested during a trip to New Orleans and sold into slavery. Bob tells Johnson about free life in Canada and eventually the two conspire to run away. Unfortunately, Bob is betrayed by a fellow slave, and both he and Johnson are eventually recaptured. Madinglay blames Bob for inciting the escape attempt, and Bob is whipped and then burned with hot coals before his throat is cut "just enough so he would die gradually."[14]

Perhaps the ultimate betrayal of one black person by other black people, ironically, was the brutal and tragic assassination of Malcolm X himself. Incredibly, just seventeen days after delivering his speech in Selma, he was shot to death by a group of men he might reasonably have identified as a mixture of house and field Negroes, from within the Nation of Islam, including Thomas Hagan (also known as Talmadge Hayer) and a squad of five other thugs, according to Malcolm's Pulitzer Prize–winning biographer, Manning Marable.[15] The political differences between "house" and "field"—never truly a black-and-white dichotomy, even in slavery—most certainly are not that simple today.

31

What is one of the most novel ways a slave devised to escape bondage?

HENRY BROWN WAS BORN into slavery around 1815 on a plantation called the Hermitage in Louisa County, Virginia, fairly close to Charlottesville, where Thomas Jefferson was still living at Monticello. Upon his master's death, when Brown was fifteen, he was sent to work for his late owner's son, William, in his tobacco factory in Richmond. In about 1836 he married another slave (curiously, with their owners' consent), a woman named Nancy, who was owned by a bank clerk. Brown was able to rent a house for them. Together they had three children.

Over time Nancy was sold twice. Her third owner, Samuel Cottrell, actually charged Brown fifty dollars a year to keep her from being sold. But in August 1848, Cottrell sold Nancy anyway, along with Nancy and Henry's children, to a Methodist minister in North Carolina. Brown raced to the jail where his family was being held, but it was too late. As they were shuffled through the streets of Richmond, Brown held Nancy's hand for four miles. Nancy and the three children were marched on foot along with 350 other slaves, in the horrendous second Middle Passage, all the way to North Carolina. At the time, Nancy was pregnant with their fourth child. The two would never see each other again.

Brown writes in his slave narrative that he begged his master to purchase his family, but his master refused: "I went to my *Christian* master . . . but he shoved me away."[1] Devastated and overcome by the most acute sense of his own sheer powerlessness, Brown sought solace and guidance through prayer. "An idea," he reported, "suddenly flashed across my mind."

The Resurrection of Henry Box Brown at Philadelphia, Who escaped from Richmond Va. in a Box 3 feet long 2½ ft. deep and 2 ft. wide. This lithographic print of Brown's astounding feat was self-published in 1850.

"Brown's revelation," as Paul Finkelman and Richard Newman write, "was that he have himself nailed into a wooden box and 'conveyed as dry goods' via the Adams Express Company from slavery in Richmond to freedom in Philadelphia."[2]

How was he to realize such a bold, wild idea? How would he avoid suffocation in this coffinlike encasement? What about claustrophobia? How long could a human being live in a box without becoming dehydrated? Not to mention deal with his bodily functions? Adams Express advertised a one-day trip from Richmond to Philadelphia, a distance of 250 miles— but only if the package encountered no glitches, no delays. If it did, the trip could take much longer.[3]

Though he stood only five feet, eight inches tall, Brown at the time weighed 200 pounds, so finding a box big enough would not be easy. His friend James Caesar Anthony Smith, a free black man who sang with Brown in the choir of First African Baptist Church, introduced Brown to Samuel Alexander Smith, a white shoemaker and gambler, whom Brown paid $86 to help.

Through James Smith's intervention, a black carpenter named John Mattaner built the wooden box—"complete with baize lining, air holes, a container of water and hickory straps"—to fit Brown's rotund frame. Samuel Smith corresponded with James Miller McKim, a Philadelphia abolitionist (and the father of the future famed architect Charles McKim), for guidance. McKim asked Smith to address the package to James Johnson at 131 Arch Street.[4]

As the scholar Hollis Robbins writes, "Smith's correspondence with McKim about the timing of the trip, particularly his attention to the breakup of the ice on the Susquehanna [River], indicates his—and perhaps Brown's—practical understanding of the conditions necessary for the box to arrive swiftly enough for Brown to survive the journey."[5] The entire box measured only 3 feet 1 inch by 2 feet by 2 feet 6 inches. Brown burned his hand with sulphuric acid so he could justify taking the day off without raising suspicion. He took along a few biscuits and a small bladder of water to sustain himself.

With "This Side Up With Care" painted on the container, at four a.m. on March 23, 1849, Brown's friends loaded his boxed self onto a wagon and delivered it to the depot.

Brown nearly died on the harrowing twenty-seven-hour trip. One wrong move, one unguarded sound or smell, would lead to his return to slavery. At one point he was turned upside down, in spite of the label on the box, for several hours. In his slave narrative, he describes the sickening effect of traveling much of the journey upside down. His relief came when two passengers, wanting to talk, tipped the box flat to sit on it. But the box was flipped again when it was loaded onto a train in Washington, D.C. Brown had no choice but to remain silent and immobile, no matter how the box was positioned.

The box traveled by wagon to a depot, where express workers hefted it onto a railcar. It was then loaded onto a steamboat, another wagon, another railcar, a ferry, and still another railcar. Finally, some twenty-four hours after the trip began, the box arrived at the depot in Philadelphia. In a change of plans, arrangements were made for it to be delivered to the Anti-Slavery Committee's office on North Fifth Street, and there it arrived three hours later.[6] No one could know if the cargo was alive or dead. The four waiting abolitionists, including McKim, tapped on the lip of the crate four times, the signal that all was clear.

Finkelman and Newman describe what happened next: "A small, nervous group, including William Still, the African-American conductor of Philadelphia's Underground Railroad, pried open the lid to reveal . . . the disheveled and battered Henry Brown, who arose and promptly fainted," but not before exclaiming, "How do you do, gentlemen!"[7] Revived with a glass of water, Brown sang Psalm 40: "Be pleased, O Lord, to deliver me!" McKim noted that the trip "nearly killed him" and that "nothing saved him from suffocation but the free use of water . . . with which he bathed his face, and the constant fanning of himself" with his hat. He had managed to breathe through the three small holes that Mattaner had bored into the box with a gimlet. Brown called his trip "my resurrection from the grave of slavery."

Henceforth, the word *Box* would become Henry's self-chosen legal middle name, with no quotation marks around it. And his friend James Smith gained a nickname from the adventure too: he became known as James "Boxer" Smith.

Overnight, Brown became a celebrity on the abolitionist lecture circuit. A great storyteller with a gifted voice for song, he toured the North testifying about the evils of slavery and repeating the details of his imaginative mode of escape. The Fugitive Slave Act of 1850 put an end, for a time, to Brown's celebrity, at least on this side of the Atlantic. After being assaulted twice on the streets of Providence, Rhode Island, Brown—like many other prominent fugitive slaves—fled to England in October 1850, to avoid arrest by a slave-catcher. Ever the showman, Brown soon became a most colorful feature on the British lecture circuit, traveling from Liverpool to Manchester.

In 1875, at the age of sixty, Brown returned to the United States, again touring the North and advertising himself as the man "whose escape from slavery in 1849 in a box 3 feet 1 inch long, 2 feet wide, 2 feet 6 inches high, caused such a sensation in the New England States, he having traveled from Richmond, Va. to Philadelphia, a journey of 350 miles, packed as luggage in a box."[8] According to the historian Martha Cutter, Brown and his family moved to Ontario in the early 1880s, and they performed across that province and in western New York. In 1886 Brown moved to Toronto; city tax rolls list him as a "Professor of Animal Magnetism," "Lecturer," or "Traveler." He died there on June 15, 1897.[9]

32

Who was the first black head of state in modern Western history?

BRONZINO'S *Portrait of Duke Alessandro de' Medici* depicts a mulatto who also happened to be a member of one of the most powerful families in history and the first duke of Florence almost five hundred years ago. Joel Rogers listed him both in his *100 Amazing Facts* and in volume 2 of his *The World's Great Men of Color*. His conclusion was startling: "That Alessandro was a despot there is no doubt whatever." It was a remarkably frank assessment from Rogers, who had a tendency to romanticize the achievements of just about every person with the proverbial "one drop" hidden in the shadows of world history.[1]

A PIVOTAL POTENTATE

Like the first black president of Mexico, Vicente Guerrero, and our first black president, Barack Obama, Alessandro de' Medici (1511–37)—the first black head of state in the history of the modern Western world—was a mulatto. He was the son of an African slave and one of two Medici males, either a duke or a future pope. With the latter's blessing, Alessandro served as duke himself—of Florence—from the age of nineteen to his assassination at age twenty-six at the hands of his cousin. The reason the cousin gave: Alessandro was a tyrant out of step with his times, a military ruler in a republican age.

Alessandro was a pivotal change *agent* in Florence's form of government—and not for the better. His promotion to duke was the fateful moment when republican government in Florence came to an end. According to the art historian Paul Kaplan,

> The Medici had risen to power in Florence in the 1430s, but they were not able to obtain an official title to go with their supreme political author-ity in the city until 1529, when the Holy Roman Emperor Charles V of Habsburg promised the Medici Pope, Clement VII, that he would make Alessandro the Duke of Florence. Alessandro actually returned to Florence as ruler in 1531, and in 1532 his hereditary ducal title was con-firmed by the Emperor.[2]

The Medici clan retained this position until 1737.

Alessandro's black African ancestry was captured in various media by contemporary Italian artists, and after his death it was commented upon by those who knew him and by those who hated him. Yet until recently, art museum curators and art historians tended to downplay his blackness, perhaps because many royal families, including the Habsburgs, could trace their bloodlines directly to him. But now, thanks to the research of John K. Brackett, Paul Kaplan, Joaneth Spicer, and Mario de Valdes y Cocom

After Jacopo da Pontormo.
Alessandro de' Medici. Ca. 1550.
Oil on limewood panel. London,
Victoria & Albert Museum.

(hereafter Mario de Valdes), Alessandro's African ancestry has been generally embraced by scholars.

He was nicknamed "the Moor" and "the mule of the Medici," and "the written and pictorial evidence are more than sufficient to prove Alessandro's black African descent," observes Brackett.[3] Mario de Valdes notes further that one person described Alessandro as "brown [with] thick lips, kinky hair."[4]

Between 1494 and 1512, the Medici family was expelled from Florence as part of an ongoing effort to establish a republican form of government there. Alessandro was born in Urbino, Italy, the son of an African woman named Simonetta, a de' Medici household slave. What historians can't decide is whether Alessandro's father was Lorenzo di Piero de' Medici or Giulio de' Medici. Lorenzo was the Duke of Nemours and ruler of Urbino, while Giulio was a cardinal who would go on to become Pope Clement VII in 1523. Most scholars give the nod to Lorenzo, though some seem to savor the titillation of speculating that this black man was the son of a Roman Catholic pope, because Giulio took pains to protect and support Alessandro's troubled and controversial rule, providing fodder for rumors that he was Alessandro's father.

But Lorenzo di Piero de' Medici's bloodline was the more impressive. He was the grandson of Lorenzo "the Magnificent," the ruler to whom Niccolò Machiavelli dedicated his classic work *The Prince* in 1513. Taking the lead in raising Alessandro, Lorenzo freed Simonetta on the promise that she give up her rights to their illegitimate son. (In Florence at the time of Alessandro's birth, the slave status of children followed the father, while in much of the rest of Italy slave status followed the mother, as it did in the United States.) When Lorenzo died, Alessandro was only eight, but his other potential father, the future pope Clement VII, made sure he and his cousin Ippolito had a regent in place to secure their line of the family's claim to future rule.

Medici rule in Florence was the hallmark of monarchy, but a republican movement sought to unseat the family's traditional power base in 1527, the same year that Emperor Charles V sacked Rome. Between 1527 and 1530, the Medici family was expelled from the city during the Siege of Florence.

In 1530, after an eleven-month siege by imperial forces seeking to end republican rule, Florence surrendered, allowing Alessandro's reign to begin. (Florence and other city-states were more like small countries than cities at that time; "Italy" was a geographical description rather than a country, as we use that term today.) A year later, under Clement's order, Alessandro was made hereditary duke and quickly assumed immense political power. In the process, he made a number of powerful enemies, many of whom went into exile to Venice.

Upon the advice of his sponsor, Pope Clement VII, Alessandro, among other things, decreased the number of open government positions in Florence, a move that angered patrician families who depended on such posts for their income and status. He also was charged with removing from the Palazzo della Signoria "the great bell" used to convene *parlamenti* and with confiscating the private arms of citizens. Others accused him of routinely imprisoning his opponents and murdering "two men with his own hands," as Brackett reports. Others accused him of "using his power to sexually exploit the citizenry," Valdes writes, including allegations that he frequented brothels and seduced his subjects' wives and daughters as well as nuns. Alessandro's reputation as a tyrant, like his fate, was sealed.[5]

When his patron, Pope Clement VII, died in 1534, Alessandro found his world beginning its inevitable slide toward self-destruction, set in motion, in part, by his plans to construct a large military base in the middle of Florence (the Fortezza de Basso) to be manned by foreign troops. A year later Alessandro's cousin Ippolito was poisoned, just after being appointed Florence's ambassador to Charles V in hopes of seeking Alessandro's ouster. For this reason, Alessandro was presumed to be the architect of his cousin's assassination.

In 1536 Charles V, however, demonstrated his support for Alessandro by allowing him to marry his illegitimate daughter, Margaret of Austria. (By this time, Alessandro had fathered two children, a son named Giulio and a daughter named Giulia, with his mistress, Taddea Malespina.) But the emperor's support was to no avail: in 1537 Alessandro was assassinated by his cousin, Lorenzaccio ("wicked Lorenzo") de' Medici, who later claimed that he was able to trick Alessandro away from his bodyguards by setting up a sexual trap. In a 1540 publication in which he defended his actions, Lorenzaccio accused Alessandro of tyranny, sexual improprieties, and, incredibly, poisoning his own mother, for which there is no evidence. After fleeing Florence, Lorenzaccio was himself murdered twelve years later.

Alessandro's children Giulio and Giulia were raised by Alessandro's successor, Cosimo de' Medici. Giulia became princess of Ottojano, and Giulio became first admiral of the Knights of San Stefano, founded to fight the Turks. Through their offspring, according to Mario de Valdes, "the greater majority of the noble houses of Italy can today trace their ancestry back to Alessandro de' Medici," a black man, and "so can a number of other princely families of Europe," including the Habsburgs.[6]

33

Were there any successful slavery escapes by sea?

ROBERT SMALLS WAS BORN on April 5, 1839, behind his owner's city house at 511 Prince Street in Beaufort, South Carolina. His mother, Lydia, served in the house. She had grown up in the fields on the Sea Islands, where, at the age of nine, she was taken from her own family. It is not clear who Smalls's father was. Some say it was his owner, John McKee; others, McKee's son Henry; still others, the plantation manager, Patrick Smalls. What is clear is that the McKee family favored Robert Smalls over the other slave children, so much so that his mother worried he would reach manhood without grasping the horrors of the institution into which he was born. To educate him, she arranged for him to be sent into the fields to work and watch slaves at "the whipping post."

"The result of this lesson led Robert to defiance," wrote his great-granddaughter Helen Boulware Moore and the historian W. Marvin Dulaney, and he "frequently found himself in the Beaufort jail."[1] If anything, Smalls's mother's plan had worked too well, so that "fear[ing] for her son's safety . . . she asked McKee to allow Smalls to go to Charleston to be rented out to work." Again her wish was granted. By the time Smalls turned nineteen, he had tried his hand at a number of city jobs and was allowed to keep one dollar of his wages a week. (His owner took the rest.) Far more valuable was the education he received on the water; few knew Charleston harbor better than Robert Smalls.

It was where he earned his job on the *Planter*. It was also where he met his wife, Hannah, a slave of the Kingman family working at a Charleston hotel. With their owners' permission, the two moved into an apartment

"Robert Smalls, Captain of the Gun-Boat 'Planter.'" Wood engraving, *Harper's Weekly,* June 14, 1862.

together and had two children: Elizabeth and Robert Jr. Wishing for a permanent union, Smalls asked his wife's owner if he could purchase his family outright. They agreed but at a steep price: $800. Smalls had only $100. "How long would it take [him] to save up another $700?" Moore and Dulaney ask. Unwittingly, Smalls's "look-enough-alike," the *Planter's* captain, C. J. Relyea, gave him his best backup.

By this time, it was 1862, the Civil War was under way, and Union ships were in Charleston harbor, blockading it. To white Confederates, the ships were another example of the North's enslavement of the South; to actual slaves like Robert Smalls, they signaled the tantalizing promise of freedom. Under orders from Navy secretary Gideon Welles in Washington, navy commanders had been accepting runaways as contraband since September 1861. While Smalls couldn't afford to buy his family on shore, he knew he could win their freedom by sea—and so he told his wife to be ready for whenever opportunity dawned.

That opportunity was at hand on the night of May 12, 1862. The white officers came ashore, and Smalls confided his plan to the slaves on board. According to the Naval Affairs Committee report, two chose to stay behind. "The design was hazardous in the extreme," it states. Smalls and his men had no intention of being taken alive; they would either escape or use whatever guns and ammunition they had to fight and, if necessary, sink their ship. "Failure and detection would have been certain death," the navy report makes plain. "Fearful was the venture, but it was made."

At two a.m. on May 13, Smalls donned Captain Relyea's straw hat and ordered the *Planter*'s skeleton crew to put up the boiler and hoist the South Carolina and Confederate flags as decoys. Easing out of the dock, in view of Confederate brigadier general Roswell Ripley's headquarters, they paused at the West Atlantic Wharf to pick up Smalls's wife and children, along with four other women, three men, and another child.

At 3:25 a.m., the *Planter* accelerated "her perilous adventure," the navy report continues. From the pilothouse, Smalls blew the ship's whistle while passing Confederate Fort Johnson and, at 4:15 a.m., Fort Sumter, "as cooly as if General Ripley was on board." Smalls not only knew all the right navy signals to flash; he even folded his arms like Captain Relyea so that, in the shadows of dawn, he convincingly passed for white.

"She was supposed to be the guard boat and allowed to pass without interruption," Confederate aide-de-camp F. G. Ravenel explained defensively in a letter to his commander hours later. Only when the *Planter* passed out of Rebel gun range did the alarm sound—the *Planter* was heading for the Union blockade. Approaching it, Smalls ordered his crew to replace the Palmetto and Rebel flags with a white bedsheet his wife had brought on board. Not seeing it, Acting Volunteer Lt. J. Frederick Nickels of the USS *Onward* ordered his sailors to "open her ports." It was "sunrise," Nickels wrote in a letter the same day, an illuminating fact that may have changed the course of history, at least on board the *Planter*—for now Nickels could see.

The dean of Civil War historians, James McPherson, quotes the following eyewitness account:

> Just as No. 3 port gun was being elevated, someone cried out, "I see something that looks like a white flag"; and true enough there was something flying on the steamer that would have been *white* by application of soap and water. As she neared us, we looked in vain for the face of a white man. When they discovered that we would not fire on them, there was a rush of contrabands out on her deck, some dancing, some singing, whistling, jumping; and others stood looking towards Fort Sumter, and muttering all sorts of maledictions against it, and *"de heart of de Souf,"* generally. As the steamer came near, and under the stern of the *Onward,* one of the Colored men stepped forward, and taking off his hat,

shouted, "Good morning, sir! I've brought you some of the old United States guns, sir!"[2]

That man was Robert Smalls, and he and his family and the entire slave crew of the *Planter* were now free.

After "board[ing] her, haul[ing] down the flag of truce, and hoist[ing] the American ensign" (his words), Lieutenant Nickels transferred the *Planter* to his commander, Capt. E. G. Parrott of the USS *Augusta*. Parrott then forwarded it on to Flag Officer Samuel Francis Du Pont (of the "du Pont" Du Ponts), at Port Royal, Hilton Head Island, with a letter describing Smalls as "very intelligent contraband." Du Pont was similarly impressed, and the next day wrote a letter to Navy secretary Welles, stating, "Robert, the intelligent slave and pilot of the boat, who performed this bold feat so skillfully, informed me of [the capture of the Sumter gun], presuming it would be a matter of interest." He "is superior to any who have come into our lines—intelligent as many of them have been." While Du Pont sent the families to Beaufort, he took care of the *Planter*'s crew personally while having its captured flags mailed to Washington via the Adams Express, the same private carrier that had delivered Box Brown to freedom in 1849.

On May 30, 1862, the U.S. Congress passed a private bill authorizing the navy to appraise the *Planter* and award Smalls and his crew half the proceeds for "rescuing her from the enemies of the Government." Smalls received $1,500 personally, enough to purchase his former owner's house in Beaufort off the tax rolls following the war, though according to the 1883 Naval Affairs Committee report, his pay should have been substantially higher.

In the North, Smalls was feted as a hero and personally lobbied Secretary of War Edwin Stanton to begin enlisting black soldiers. After President Lincoln acted a few months later, Smalls was said to have recruited five thousand soldiers by himself. In October 1862 he returned to the *Planter* as pilot as part of Admiral Du Pont's South Atlantic Blockading Squadron. According to the Naval Affairs Committee report, Smalls engaged in approximately seventeen military actions, including the April 7, 1863, assault on Fort Sumter and the attack at Folly Island Creek, South Carolina, two months later. There he assumed command of the *Planter* when, under "very hot fire," its white captain became so "demoralized" he hid in the "coal-bunker." For his valor, Smalls was promoted to the rank of captain, and from December 1863 on, he earned $150 a month, making him one of the highest-paid black soldiers of the war. Poetically, when the war ended in April 1865, Smalls was on board the *Planter* in a ceremony in Charleston harbor.

Following the war, Smalls continued to push the boundaries of freedom as a first-generation black politician, serving in the South Carolina state assembly and senate and for five nonconsecutive terms in the U.S. House of Representatives (1874–86). Then he had to watch his state roll back Reconstruction in a revised 1895 constitution that stripped blacks of their voting rights. He died in Beaufort on February 22, 1915, in the same house behind which he had been born a slave. He is buried behind a bust at the Tabernacle Baptist Church. Even in the face of the rise of Jim Crow, Smalls stood firm as an unyielding advocate for the political rights of African Americans: "My race needs no special defense, for the past history of them in this country proves them to be equal of any people anywhere. All they need is an equal chance in the battle of life."[3]

34

How was black support enlisted for World War II, when the armed services were segregated?

BLACK LEADERS HAVE HISTORICALLY FELT that African Americans could make the strongest case for freedom and citizenship if they demonstrated their heroism and commitment to the country on the battlefield. Yet by the time the United States was attacked at Pearl Harbor on December 7, 1941, memories of the 200,000 black men who had served during the Civil War (and those who had served in every other American war since) had been, if you will, lost at sea.

Since the 1890s, despite the abolition of slavery and the three Reconstruction amendments to the Constitution, Jim Crow segregation pervaded every aspect of American society. The military was no exception. Following the Japanese sneak attack on Pearl Harbor, black men who volunteered for duty or were drafted were relegated to segregated divisions and combat support roles, such as cook, quartermaster, and grave digger. The military was as segregated as the Deep South.

It was difficult for African Americans not to see the hypocrisy between conditions at home and the noble war aims that President Franklin Roosevelt articulated in his famous "Four Freedoms" speech on January 6, 1941. And because of the gap between the promise and the performance of American freedom when it came to race relations, many black people frankly felt alienated from the war effort.

Despite this discrimination, more than 2.5 million African Americans

The Ink Spots promote the Double V campaign at the Savoy Ballroom, Pittsburgh, Pennsylvania, 1942.

registered for the draft when World War II began; 1 million served. A key voice in the war effort was the *Pittsburgh Courier,* the nation's most widely read African-American newspaper. Two months after the attack on Pearl Harbor, the *Courier* launched a national campaign that urged black people to give their all for the war effort, while at the same time calling on the government to do all it could to make the rhetoric of the Declaration of Independence and the equal rights amendments to the Constitution real for every citizen, regardless of race. In honor of the battle against enemies from without and within, they called it the Double V campaign.

THE CAMPAIGN

When the war broke out, the overwhelming number of black soldiers served in segregated units. Rather than tackle integration of the military head-on, civil rights leaders A. Philip Randolph, Walter White, and others organized a march on Washington to protest discrimination in the defense industry, which, well before Pearl Harbor, was receiving lucrative contracts from Uncle Sam to build up Britain's and the nation's defenses.

Eleanor Roosevelt met with Randolph and White to ask them to call off the march, but they refused; FDR then met with them, and they still refused—unless he signed an executive order banning discrimination in the defense industry. Facing a public relations disaster, FDR came around, and on June 25, 1941, he issued Executive Order 8802, creating the Fair Employment Practices Committee to enforce a new rule—that "there shall be no discrimination in the employment of workers in defense industries or government because of race, creed, color, or national origin."[1]

The march was called off, but it laid the groundwork for Martin Luther King, Jr.'s March on Washington in 1963. And it established the mood within the black community to monitor race relations at home, even amid the war against fascism abroad. One man, deeply concerned about all this, sat down and wrote a letter to the editor of the most widely read and influential black newspaper in the country, with a national circulation well above 200,000.

On January 31, 1942, the *Pittsburgh Courier* published a letter from James G. Thompson of Wichita, Kansas, titled "Should I Sacrifice to Live 'Half American?'" Thompson wrote:

> Being an American of dark complexion and some 26 years, these questions flash through my mind: "Should I sacrifice my life to live half American?" "Will things be better for the next generation in the peace to follow?" "Would it be demanding too much to demand full citizenship rights in exchange for the sacrificing of my life?" "Is the kind of America I know worth defending?" "Will America be a true and pure democracy after this war?" "Will colored Americans suffer still the indignities that have been heaped upon them in the past?" These and other questions need answering.[2]

Then he proposed a new sign, "the double V V for a double victory":

> The V for victory sign is being displayed prominently in all so-called democratic countries which are fighting for victory over aggression, slavery, and tyranny. If this V sign means that to those now engaged in this great conflict, then let we colored Americans adopt the double V V

for a double victory. The first V for victory over our enemies from without, the second V for victory over our enemies from within. For surely
those who perpetrate these ugly prejudices here are seeking to destroy
our democratic form of government just as surely as the Axis forces.

The *Courier* had already run stories protesting the navy's use of black
sailors only as "messmen," and on January 3, 1942, the paper denounced
the American Red Cross's refusal to accept black blood in donor drives.
But nothing could have prepared the editors for the public's enthusiastic
response to Thompson's letter.

A week later, on February 7, 1942, two months to the day after the
Pearl Harbor attack, the *Courier* published on its front page an insignia
announcing "Democracy at Home Abroad."[3] The following week the
paper stated that it had published the insignia "to test the response and
popularity of such a slogan with our readers. The response has been overwhelming." Henceforth "this slogan represents the true battle cry of colored America." As the editors concluded, "we have adopted the Double 'V'
war cry—victory over our enemies on the battlefields abroad. Thus in our
fight for freedom we wage a two-pronged attack against our enslavers at
home and those abroad who would enslave us. WE HAVE A STAKE IN
THIS FIGHT . . . WE ARE AMERICANS TOO!"

The Double V campaign ran weekly into 1943. To promote patriotism,
the *Courier* included an American flag with every subscription and encouraged its readers to buy war bonds. Double V clubs spread around the country. Each week the paper published a photo of a new "Double V Girl,"
frequently lifting two fingers in a V sign. Celebrity and political endorse-
ments followed, including from Lana Turner (pictured with a caption that,
in a bit of cross-promotion, mentioned that her movie *Slightly Dangerous* featured blacks in the cast) and former presidential candidate Wendell Willkie
(shown wearing a Double V pin, which the *Courier* sold for five cents).[4] A
Double V hairstyle called "the Doubler" also became popular, historian
Patrick Washburn recalls, as did Double V gardens and Double V baseball
games. Other black newspapers soon joined the *Courier*'s campaign.[5]

To measure the campaign's impact, the *Courier* ran a survey, asking
readers "Do You Feel that the Negro Should Soft Pedal His Demands
for Complete Freedom and Citizenship and Await the Development of
the Educational Process?" On October 24, 1942, it published the results:
88.7 percent of readers responded no, with only 9.2 percent responding yes.

Needless to say, not everyone was pleased with the Double V campaign: the federal government systematically monitored the black press, including this campaign, during the war. So to avoid charges of disloyalty or aiding and abetting the enemy, the *Courier*'s editorial added a caveat to its poll results: "No one must interpret this . . . as a plot to impede the war effort. Negroes recognize that the first factor in the survival of this nation is the winning of the war. But they feel integration of Negroes into the whole scheme of things 'revitalizes' the U.S. war program."[6]

Still, the *Courier*'s campaign kept the demands of African Americans for equal rights at home front and center during the war abroad.

THE LEGACY OF THE CAMPAIGN

In September 1945 the Double V insignia disappeared from the paper, replaced by a Single V, indicating that more work combating antiblack racism needed to be done at home. But as the historian Clarence Taylor concludes, "Although the *Courier* could not claim any concrete accomplishments, the Double V campaign helped provide a voice to Americans who wanted to protest racial discrimination and contribute to the war effort."[7]

The Double V campaign had at least two important legacies following the war. First, the *Courier*'s sportswriter, Wendell Smith, doggedly used his columns (which would feature prominently in the 2013 film *42*) to denounce segregation in professional sports, contributing without a doubt to the Brooklyn Dodgers' decision to sign Jackie Robinson in 1947, which in turn had a ripple effect. And on July 26, 1948, President Harry Truman issued Executive Order 9981, which ordered the desegregation of the U.S. armed forces. With that action, the Double V campaign at last realized one of its principal goals.

35

How did the Black Sambo memorabilia that is collected today come to be?

THE FIRST QUESTION THAT strikes any student of Sambo art is, Why so many images? Why in the world did anyone think it necessary to produce *tens of thousands,* perhaps hundreds of thousands, of discrete racist images, a set of fixed types or motifs, including those luscious watermelons and irresistible plump chickens, ranging across virtually every conceivable form of American popular culture following the end of Reconstruction and particularly at the turn of the nineteenth century? The explanation is that the ubiquity of these images was used to justify Jim Crow.

After the Thirteenth Amendment abolishing slavery was ratified at the close of the Civil War, the Reconstruction period (1865–77) affirmed that African Americans were inherently equal to white Americans and all other human beings and were capable of voting, serving as jurors, testifying in court, buying and cultivating land, forming stable social and cultural institutions, marrying, having families, raising children, learning to read and write—in short, capable of mastering and exemplifying all of the hallmarks of citizenship that make this republic great. Despite centuries of antiblack racist discourse, in twelve short years the mass of the African-American people (90 percent of whom had still been in bondage in 1860) demonstrated that they were human beings just like everybody else.

But then the genie of freedom and equality was forced back into the bottle of segregation and second-class citizenship. As W.E.B. Du Bois put it, "The slave went free; stood a brief moment in the sun; then moved back again toward slavery."[1] How did it happen? How were the emancipated "moved back again toward slavery" after only a few years "in the sun"?

The assault was double-barreled: a series of Jim Crow laws and court rulings effectively reversed or neutralized the Civil Rights Act of 1875 and the Fourteenth and Fifteenth Amendments (guaranteeing equal protection under the law and outlawing race-based voting discrimination, respectively). At almost the same time, a massive mountain of negative Sambo images were distributed; they were intended to *naturalize* the image of the black person as subhuman and in doing so *justify and subliminally reinforce* the perverted logic of the separate and unequal system of Jim Crow. The assault was brilliantly evil and devastatingly effective.

Following the Civil War, the new technology of chromolithography made it cheap to mass-produce multicolored advertisements. By the 1890s— precisely when Jim Crow was hardening as the law of the land—extremely demeaning and negative images of African Americans were among the most popular with the public. So popular were they, so widespread their distribution and consumption, that virtually anywhere a white person saw an image of an African American, they saw one of these stereotypes of a subhuman, deracinated beastlike being, like a visual mantra reinforcing the negativity of difference.

So when a white person confronted an actual black human being, he or she was "an already read text," to use Barbara Johnson's brilliant definition of a stereotype.[2] It didn't matter what an individual black man or woman said and did, because negative images of *them* in the popular imagination already existed, as if they were "always 'in place,'" as the scholar Homi K. Bhabha puts it, "already known." These images were repeated over and over again, "anxiously . . . as if the essential . . . bestial sexual license of the African [for example] that needs no proof, can never really, in discourse, be proved."[3] The racist stereotype was subconsciously imposed on the face of actual African Americans, the American mask of blackness, and these images justified the rollback of the gains black people had made during Reconstruction.

The fears and anxieties of black people from within the white collective unconscious were projected onto a plethora of everyday, ordinary consumer objects including postcards and trading cards, teapots and tea cozies, children's banks and children's games, napkin holders and pot holders, clocks and ashtrays, sheet music and greeting cards, consumer products

For the Sunny South. An Airship with a "Jim Crow" Trailer. Color halftone print, *Puck,* February 26, 1913.

such as Aunt Jemima pancake mix and Gold Dust washing powder, Nigger Head tobacco and Jolly Nigger Head banks, "Pick the Pickaninny" songs, puzzles and dolls, Valentine's Day cards, and a seemingly endless number of watermelon-devouring and chicken-stealing "coons." A veritable deluge of Sambo imagery spread throughout virtually every form of advertisement for a consumer product.

One motif illustrated evolution by showing the transmutation of a watermelon into a "coon." A subgenre of lynching postcards also became popular, especially "The Dogwood Tree," depicting five black bodies hanging from one tree in Sabine County, Texas, in June 1908. Between 1889 and 1918, according to the NAACP, more than three thousand lynchings took place in the United States, a reflection of the powerful effect these racist images had in enabling otherwise decent people to commit the most horrific crimes.[4]

In this Sambo "art," antiblack racism found its daily existence, drowning out the actual nature and achievements of black people. It explains why so many black thinkers and artists embarked upon the "New Negro" movement between 1900 and 1925, starting with Du Bois's exhibition of photographs of middle-class Negroes at the Paris Exposition of 1900. As Du Bois put it:

> One cannot ignore the extraordinary fact that a world campaign begin-ning with the slave-trade and ending with the refusal to capitalize the word "Negro," leading through a passionate defense of slavery by attrib-uting every bestiality to blacks and finally culminating in the evident modern profit which lies in degrading blacks—all this has unconsciously trained millions of honest, modern men into the belief that black folk are sub-human, . . . a mass of despicable men, inhuman; at best, laugh-able; at worst, the meat of mobs and fury.[5]

Chromolithography and the American marketplace made antiblack rac-ism a commodity, widely consumed in the most unconscious ways, rein-forcing and reflecting the legalization of racism and the delimitations being systematically inflicted upon the rights of black citizens by the courts and southern legislatures. As the historian Thomas Holt concludes in a brilliant analysis of the role of minstrelsy in naturalizing antiblack racism, "It is pre-cisely within the ordinary and everyday that racialization has been most effective, where it *makes* race," a process "that *fixes* the meaning of one's self before one even has had the opportunity to *live* and *make* a self, . . . capable of communicating at a glance accumulated stores of racialized knowledge."[6]

Why should we collect these racist artifacts? Du Bois offers an answer. "In the fight against race prejudice," he explained, "we were facing age-long complexes sunk now largely to unconscious habit and irrational urge."[7] The shadow of these images still haunts every African American's existence within American society, like ghosts of Jim Crow, because "it is at this level that race is reproduced long after its original historical stimulus—the slave trade and slavery—have faded. It is at this level that seemingly rational and ordinary folk commit irrational and extraordinary acts," as Holt writes.

These images are still very much with us, as one can see by examining the horrifically racist images of President Barack Obama collected at the Jim Crow Museum of Racist Memorabilia at Ferris State University in Michigan, founded and curated by David Pilgrim. And we need to study these images in order to deflect the harm that they continue to inflict upon African Americans at the deepest levels of the American unconscious.

36

Who was Plessy in the *Plessy v. Ferguson* Supreme Court case?

ON THE AFTERNOON OF Tuesday, June 7, 1892, Homer Plessy, a thirty-year-old shoemaker in New Orleans, purchased a first-class ticket on the 4:15 East Louisiana local and took his seat on board. Nothing about Plessy stood out in the whites-only car. Had he answered one question negatively, nothing might have.

Instead, when train conductor J. J. Dowling asked Plessy what all conductors had been trained to ask under Louisiana's two-year-old Separate Car Act—"Are you a colored man?"—Plessy answered, "Yes," prompting Dowling to order him to the "colored car."[1] Plessy refused. The engineer abruptly halted the train so that Dowling could dart back to the depot and return with Detective Christopher Cain. When Plessy resisted moving to the Jim Crow car once more, the detective had him removed, by force, and booked at the Fifth Precinct on Elysian Fields Avenue. The charge: "Viol. Sec. 2 Act III, 1890" of the Louisiana Separate Car Act, which, after requiring "all railway companies . . . to provide equal but separate accommodations for the white, and colored races" in Sec. 1, stated that "any passenger insisting on going into a coach or compartment to which by race he does not belong, shall be liable to a fine of twenty-five dollars, or in lieu thereof to imprisonment for a period of not more than twenty days in the parish prison."

It took only twenty minutes for Homer Plessy to get bounced from his train but another four years for him to receive a final decision from the U.S. Supreme Court. He was far from alone in the struggle. The eighteen-member citizens group to which Plessy belonged, the Comité des Citoyens of New Orleans (made up of "civil libertarians, ex–Union soldiers, Republicans, writers, a former Louisiana lieutenant governor, a French Quarter jeweler and other professionals," according to the historian Keith Medley), left little to chance.

In fact, every detail of Plessy's arrest had been plotted in advance with input from one of the most famous white crusaders for black rights in the Jim Crow era: the Civil War veteran, lawyer, Reconstruction judge, and best-selling novelist Albion Winegar Tourgée. Even the East Louisiana Railroad conductor Dowling and Detective Cain were in on the scheme.

Critically important to the legal team was Plessy's color—that he had "seven eighths Caucasian and one eighth African blood," as Supreme Court justice Henry Billings Brown would write in his majority opinion, referring to the uniquely American one-drop rule that a person with any African blood, no matter how little, was considered black.

The Jim Crow era was so devastating in drawing and deepening the color line that upon hearing the case name *Plessy v. Ferguson* (1896), most people today immediately think of the slogan "separate but equal," and, because of it, wrongly assume that the two named parties in this famous court case had to have been, on the one hand, the darkest of black people and the most southern of whites. At the same time, we err in seeing *Plessy* through the prism of the case that undid separate-but-equal a half cen-

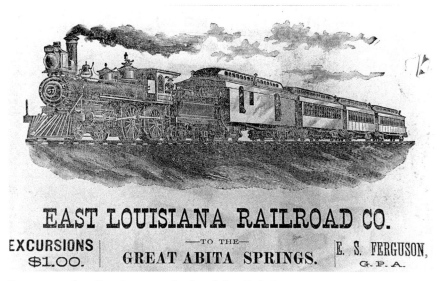

Passenger ticket, East Louisiana Railroad Co., E. S. Ferguson, owner.

tury later, *Brown v. Board of Education* (1954), so that the struggle becomes *only* one of securing civil rights in an integrated society instead of through multiple and sometimes contradictory paths: equality, independence, and racial uplift, to name a few.

Thanks to historians like Kenneth Mack and especially Charles Lofgren, Brook Thomas, Keith Weldon Medley, and Mark Elliott, we know that what is most amazing about *Plessy*'s backstory is how conscious its testers were of the false stereotypes undergirding Jim Crow and the just-as-false binary posed by its laws ("white" and "colored"), without any clear definition among the states of what "white" and "colored" actually meant or how they were to be defined.[2]

As Lofgren shows in his watershed account, the question was, did a man at the time of *Plessy* have to be one-fourth black to be considered "colored," as was the case in Michigan, or one-sixteenth as in North Carolina, or one-eighth as in Georgia? Or were such judgments better left to juries as in South Carolina or, better yet, to train conductors as in Louisiana?

Plessy, Tourgée, and his legal associates knew their climb was uphill; everywhere they turned, it seemed, new theories of racial distinction and separation were being constructed. While today we might call proponents of those theories quacks, people in those days regarded them (for the most part) as leading scientists—men with college degrees and titles who, even in those rare cases when they were sympathetic to black people and their rights, felt strongly that mixing too closely with whites would lead either to black extinction through a race war or to dilution by way of absorption.

Reinforcing their views on race were legislators and judges. The legal history of Jim Crow accelerated in 1883, when the Supreme Court struck down the federal Civil Rights Act of 1875 for using the Fourteenth Amendment to root out private (as opposed to state) discrimination. As Justice Joseph Bradley wrote for the majority, "there must be some stage in the process of his elevation when he [a man who 'has emerged from slavery'] takes the rank of a mere citizen and ceases to be the special favorite of the laws."[3]

To say *Plessy* was a long shot on such terrain is an understatement. Yet Tourgée and his legal team were determined to use their test case to dismantle the legal scaffolding propping up Jim Crow. Elated by Homer Plessy's flawless execution of the East Louisiana line plan, the Comité des Citoyens bailed him out before he had to spend a single night in jail.

Five months later, on November 18, 1892, Orleans Parish criminal court judge John Howard Ferguson, a "carpetbagger" descended from a Martha's Vineyard shipping family, became the Ferguson in the case by ruling against Plessy. Ferguson had dismissed an earlier test case because it involved *inter*state travel, where the federal government had exclusive jurisdiction, but in Plessy's all-*in*-state case, the judge ruled that the Separate Car Act constituted a reasonable use of Louisiana's "police power." "There is no pretense that he [Plessy] was not provided with equal accommodations with the white passengers," Ferguson declared. "He was simply deprived of the liberty of doing as he pleased."

A month later the Louisiana Supreme Court affirmed Ferguson's ruling. Now Plessy's lawyers had what they'd hoped for: an opportunity to argue on a national stage. In the winter of 1893 they took Plessy's case to the U.S. Supreme Court.

Contrary to popular memory, "The gist of our case," they wrote in their brief (as quoted in Lofgren), "is the unconstitutionality of the [Separate Car Act's] assortment; *not* the question of equal accommodation." In other words, if train conductors could be authorized to classify men and women by race, according to visible and, in Plessy's case, invisible cues, where would the line-drawing stop? "Why may it [the state] not require all red-headed people to ride in a separate car? Why not require all colored people to walk on one side of the street and the whites on the other?"

One of Tourgée et al.'s main arguments focused on the indeterminacy of race and the reputational risks (and rewards) posed to those who couldn't (and could) pass for white. As they expressed in *Plessy*'s brief:

> How much would it be *worth* to a young man entering upon the practice of law, to be regarded as a *white* man rather than a colored one? Six-sevenths of the population are white. Nineteen-twentieths of the property of the country is owned by white people. Ninety-nine hundredths of the business opportunities are in the control of white people . . . Indeed, is [reputation] not the most valuable sort of property, being the master-key that unlocks the golden door of opportunity?

A majority of the Supreme Court's then-serving justices decided against opening the door to the Plessy team's arguments. In his opinion for the Court, handed down on May 18, 1896, Justice Henry Billings Brown explained that, as a technical matter, he didn't have to address Homer Plessy's particular "mixture of colored blood," because the appeal his lawyers had filed challenged only the constitutionality of Louisiana's Separate Car Act, not how it had been applied to the actual sorting of Plessy or any other man. At the same time, for the sake of argument, Brown wrote, even if one's color was critical to his reputation (and thus constituted a property right), he and the Court were "unable to see how [the Louisiana] statute deprives him of, or in any way affects his right to, such property." As a result, the Court held, Louisiana's Separate Car Act passed constitutional muster as a "reasonable" use of the state's "police power." As far as "separate but equal" went, Jim Crow had seven justices' blessings.

Perhaps what is most amazing about *Plessy v. Ferguson* is how un-amazing it was at the time. As Lofgren and others have shown, contemporary newspaper editors were much more concerned about the nation's most recent economic crisis, the Panic of 1893, its overseas forays to the south and west, and the relative power of unions, farmers, immigrants, and factories. For most, *Plessy v. Ferguson* acquired its notoriety only years later as a result of the *Brown* school desegregation cases and of future lawyers like Charles Hamilton Houston and Thurgood Marshall, who found inspiration for their strides against Jim Crow segregation in *Plessy*'s lone dissent by Justice John Marshall Harlan—of all the justices a southerner and a former slaveholder. "Our Constitution is color-blind, and neither knows nor tolerates classes among citizens," Harlan had reminded the *Plessy* majority.

37

What is Juneteenth?

The people of Texas are informed that, in accordance with a proclamation from the Executive of the United States, all slaves are free. This involves an absolute equality of personal rights and rights of property between former masters and slaves, and the connection heretofore existing between them becomes that between employer and hired labor. The freedmen are advised to remain quietly at their present homes and work for wages. They are informed that they will not be allowed to collect at military posts and that they will not be supported in idleness either there or elsewhere.

—*General Orders No. 3, Headquarters District of Texas,*
Galveston, June 19, 1865[1]

WHEN MAJ. GEN. GORDON GRANGER ISSUED the above order, he had no idea that in establishing the Union Army's authority over the people of Texas, he was also establishing the basis for a holiday, Juneteenth (*June* plus *nineteenth*), which would become the most popular annual celebration of emancipation from slavery in the United States. After all, by the time Granger assumed command of the Department of Texas, the Confederate capital in Richmond had fallen; the "Executive" to whom he referred, President Lincoln, was dead; and the Thirteenth Amendment abolishing slavery was well on its way to ratification.

But Granger wasn't just a few months late. The Emancipation Proclamation itself, ending slavery in the Confederacy (at least on paper), had taken effect two and a half years before, and in the interim, close to 200,000 black men had enlisted in the fight.

As Granger and the eighteen hundred bluecoats under him soon found out, news traveled slowly in Texas. Though Gen. Robert E. Lee had surrendered in Virginia, the Army of the Trans-Mississippi had held out until late May, and even with its formal surrender on June 2, a number of ex-rebels in the region took to bushwhacking and plunder.

That wasn't all that plagued the extreme western edge of the former Confederate states. Since the capture of New Orleans in 1862, slave owners in Mississippi, Louisiana, and points east had been migrating to Texas to escape the Union Army's reach. In a hurried reenactment of the original Middle Passage, more than 150,000 slaves were coerced to make the trek west. As one former slave remarked, "It look like everybody in the world was going to Texas."[2]

When Texas fell and Granger dispatched his now-famous Order No. 3, it wasn't exactly instant magic for most of the Lone Star State's 250,000 slaves. On plantations, masters had to decide when and how to announce the news—or wait for a government agent to arrive—and it was not uncommon for them to delay until after the harvest. Even in Galveston

Official Juneteenth Committee, Austin, Texas, June 19, 1900.

city, the ex–Confederate mayor flouted the army by forcing the freed people back to work.[3]

Those who acted on the news did so at their peril. Former slave Susan Merritt recalled, "You could see lots of niggers hangin' to trees in Sabine bottom right after freedom, 'cause they cotch 'em swimmin' 'cross Sabine River and shoot 'em."[4] In one extreme case, according to Elizabeth Hayes Turner, a former slave named Katie Darling continued working for her mistress another six years. (She "whip me after the war jist like she did 'fore," Darling said.)[5]

Hardly the recipe for a celebration—which is what makes the story of Juneteenth all the more remarkable. Defying confusion and delay, terror and violence, the newly "freed" black men and women of Texas, with the aid of the Freedmen's Bureau (itself delayed from arriving until September 1865), now had a date to rally around. In one of the most inspiring grassroots efforts of the post–Civil War period, they transformed June 19 from a day of unheeded military orders into their own annual rite, Juneteenth, beginning one year later in 1866.

For the freed people of Texas, Juneteenth was, from its earliest incarnations, "usable" as an occasion for gathering lost family members, measuring progress toward freedom, and inculcating rising generations with the values of self-improvement and racial uplift. This was accomplished by reading the Emancipation Proclamation, sharing religious sermons and spirituals, and preserving slave food delicacies (always at the center: the almighty barbecue pit), as well as incorporating new games and traditions, from baseball to rodeos and, later, stock car races and overhead flights.

Juneteenth was strengthened as its committee members contested the Jim Crow faithful of Texas, who, in the years following Reconstruction, rallied around their version of history in an effort to glorify (and whitewash) past cruelties and defeats. When whites forbade blacks from using their public spaces, black people gathered near rivers and lakes and eventually raised enough money to buy their own celebration sites, among them Emancipation Park in Houston and Booker T. Washington Park in Mexia.

Further strengthening the holiday's chance for survival was its move across state lines—one person, one family, one carload or train ticket at a time. As Isabel Wilkerson writes in her brilliant book, *The Warmth of Other Suns,* "The people from Texas took Juneteenth Day to Los Angeles, Oakland, Seattle, and other places they went."[6] As it spread, the observance changed, especially in the 1920s, when the consumer age infiltrated black society with advertisements for fancier Juneteenth getups and more elaborate displays of pomp and circumstance.[7]

Juneteenth might have vanished from the calendar (at least outside Texas) had it not been for a remarkable turn of events during the civil rights movement that exposed many of the country's shortcomings about race relations. In 1968 Martin Luther King, Jr., had been planning a return to the site of his famous "I Have a Dream" speech in Washington, this time to lead a Poor People's March emphasizing nagging class inequalities. Following his assassination, it was left to others to carry out the plan, among them his best friend, the Rev. Ralph Abernathy, and his widow, Coretta Scott King. When it became clear that the Poor People's March was falling short of its goals, the organizers decided to cut it short on June 19, 1968, well aware that it was now just over a century since the first Juneteenth celebration in Texas.

As William H. Wiggins, Jr., a scholar of black folklore and cultural traditions, explains, "These delegates for the summer took that idea of the [Juneteenth] celebration back to their respective communities. For example, there was one in Milwaukee." And another in Minnesota. It was, in effect, another great black migration. Since then, Wiggins added, Juneteenth "has taken on a life of its own."[8]

Responding to this new energy, in 1979 Texas became the first state to make Juneteenth an official holiday. Since then, forty-four other states and the District of Columbia have recognized Juneteenth as a state holiday or holiday observance.

38

Who was the first black American woman to be a self-made millionaire?

ON DECEMBER 23, 1867, Sarah Breedlove was born to two former slaves on a plantation in Delta, Louisiana. While the rest of her siblings had been born on the other side of emancipation, Sarah was free. But by the age of seven she was an orphan toiling in those same cotton fields. To escape her abusive brother-in-law's household, she married at fourteen, and together she and Moses McWilliams had one daughter, Lelia (later A'Lelia Walker), before Moses mysteriously died.

After Reconstruction, too, was dead in the South, Sarah moved north to St. Louis, where a few of her brothers had taken up as barbers, themselves having left the Delta as "exodusters" some years before. Living on $1.50 a day as a laundress and cook, Sarah struggled to send Lelia to school— and did—while joining the African Methodist Episcopal Church, where she networked with other city dwellers, including those in the fledgling National Association of Colored Women.

In 1894 Sarah tried marrying again, but her second husband, John Davis, was less than reliable and was also unfaithful. At thirty-five, she found that her life remained anything but certain. "I was at my tubs one morning with a heavy wash before me," she later told the *New York Times*. "As I bent over the washboard and looked at my arms buried in soapsuds, I said to myself: 'What are you going to do when you grow old and your back gets stiff? Who is going to take care of your little girl?'"

Adding to Sarah's woes was the fact that she was losing her hair. As her great-granddaughter A'Lelia Bundles explained, "During the early 1900s, when most Americans lacked indoor plumbing and electricity, bathing

Madam C.J. Walker, hair culturalist, entrepreneur, and advocate of black women's financial independence. Studio photograph, early twentieth century.

was a luxury. As a result, Sarah and many other women were going bald because they washed their hair so infrequently, leaving it vulnerable to environmental hazards such as pollution, bacteria and lice."[1]

In the lead-up to the 1904 World's Fair in St. Louis, Sarah's personal and professional fortune began to turn when she discovered the "Wonderful Hair Grower" of Annie Turnbo (later Malone), an Illinois native with a background in chemistry who'd relocated her hair-straightening business to St. Louis. Sarah tried Turnbo's products, and they more than worked. Within a year Sarah went from using them to selling them as a local agent. Perhaps not coincidentally, around the same time, she began dating Charles Joseph (C.J.) Walker, a savvy salesman for the *St. Louis Clarion*.

In turn-of-the-century America, the color line that court cases like *Plessy v. Ferguson* drew excluded blacks from most trade unions and denied them bank capital, trapping them in lives as sharecroppers or menial, low-wage earners. One of the few ways out was to start a business in a market that was segmented by Jim Crow.[2] Hair care and cosmetics fit the bill. The start-up costs were low. Unlike today's big multinationals, white businesses in those days were slow to respond to blacks' specific needs. And there were a slew of remedies to improve upon from well before slavery. Turnbo seized the opportunity and created her Poro brand, one of as many as forty thousand black-owned businesses launched between 1883 and 1913.

In 1905, while she was still a Turnbo agent, Sarah stepped out of her boss's shadow by relocating to Denver, where her sister-in-law's family resided. (Apparently, she'd heard black women's hair suffered in the Rocky Mountains' high but dry air.) C.J. soon followed, and in 1906 the two made it official—marriage number three and a new business start. Sarah officially changed her name to "Madam C.J. Walker."

Around the same time, she awoke from a dream in which, in her words, "a big black man appeared to me and told me what to mix up for my hair. Some of the remedy was grown in Africa, but I sent for it, mixed it, put it on my scalp, and in a few weeks my hair was coming in faster than it had ever fallen out." It was to be called Madam Walker's Wonderful Hair Grower. Her initial investment: $1.25.

Sarah's industry had its critics, among them the leading black institution-builder of the day, Booker T. Washington, who worried (to his credit) that hair straighteners (and, worse, skin-bleaching creams) would lead to the internalization of white concepts of beauty. Perhaps Sarah was mindful of this, for she was deft in communicating that her dream was not emulative of whites but was divinely inspired and, like Turnbo's Poro Method, African in origin. However, she went a step further. The name Poro "came from a West African term for a devotional society, reflecting Turnbo's concern for the welfare and the roots of the women she served," according to a Harvard Business School case study.[3] Whereas Turnbo took her product's *name* from an African word, Madam C.J. claimed that the crucial ingredients for her product were African in origin.

On top of that, the name she gave it was uncomfortably close to Turnbo's Wonderful Hair Grower. It wouldn't be the only permanent sticking point between the two: some claim it was Turnbo, not Walker, who became the first black woman to reach a million bucks. One thing about Walker's start-up was different, however: her brand, with the *Madam* in front, had the advantage of French cachet, defying many white people's tendency to refer to black women by their first names or, worse, as Auntie.

In promoting her Wonderful Hair Grower door-to-door, at churches and club gatherings, then through a mail-order catalog, Walker proved to be a marketing magician. She sold her customers more than mere hair products: she offered them a lifestyle, a concept of total hygiene and beauty that in her mind would bolster them with pride for advancement.

To get the word out, she masterfully leveraged the power of America's burgeoning independent black newspapers. (In some cases, her ads kept them afloat.) It was hard to miss Madam Walker when reading up on the latest news, and in her ad copy, she was a pioneer at using black women—actually, herself—as the faces in both the before *and* the after shots; others had typically reserved the latter for white women only.

In 1911 Walker had the foresight to incorporate, and even when she couldn't attract big-name backers, she invested ten thousand dollars of her own money, making herself sole shareholder of the new Walker Manufacturing Co., headquartered at a state-of-the-art factory and school in Indianapolis, a major distribution hub.

Perhaps most important, Madam Walker transformed her customers into evangelical agents, who, for a handsome commission, multiplied her ability to reach new markets while gaining an avenue out of poverty, much as Turnbo had provided one to her. In short order, Walker's company trained some twenty thousand "Walker Agents" at an ever-expanding number of hair-culture colleges that she founded or set up in established black institutions. There they learned a whole "Walker System," from vegetable shampoos to cold creams, witch hazel, diets, and those controversial hot combs.

Contrary to legend, Madam Walker didn't invent the hot comb. According to A'Lelia Bundles, a Frenchman, Marcel Grateau, popularized it in Europe in the 1870s, and even Sears and Bloomingdale's advertised the hair-straightening styling tool in their catalogs in the 1880s.[4] But Walker improved the hot comb by widening the teeth, and as a result of its popularity, sales sizzled.

Careful to position herself as a "hair culturalist," Walker built a vast network of consumer-agents united by their dreams of looking—and feeling—different, from the heartland of America to the Caribbean and parts of Central America. Whether her business stimulated emulation or empowerment was the debate—and in many ways it still is—one thing was for sure: it was big business. "Open your own shop; secure prosperity and freedom," one of Madam Walker's brochures urged. Those who enrolled in "Lelia College" even received a diploma.

If imitation is the highest form of flattery, Walker had the *Mona Lisa* of black beauty brands. Among the most ridiculous knockoffs was the white-owned "Madam Mamie Hightower" company. To keep her products distinctive, Walker placed a special seal with her likeness on every package. So successful, so quick, was Walker in solidifying her presence in the consumer's mind that when her marriage to C.J. fell apart in 1912, she insisted on keeping his name. After all, she'd made it famous.

Madam Walker succumbed to kidney failure at the age of fifty-one on May 25, 1919. Among her last words: "I want to live to help my race." Among her last actions, according to Bundles, was to make a $5,000 pledge to the NAACP's anti-lynching fund. She revised her will, "directing two-thirds of future net profits of her estate to charity and bequeathing nearly $100,000 to individuals, educational institutions and orphanages." Her obituary in the *New York Times*—bluntly titled "Wealthiest Negress Dead"—estimated her personal fortune at $1 million. In fact, it was between $600,000 and $700,000, which in today's dollars would be nearer to $8 million. (Her company was worth more.)[5]

39

Did black combatants fight in the Battle of Gettysburg?

GETTYSBURG WAS *the* symbolic battle of the American Civil War, and Pickett's Charge was Robert E. Lee's greatest miscalculation, the climax of his second and final northern invasion. While close to 200,000 African Americans served in the Union Army and Navy during the war, those who'd taken up arms by July 1863 were engaged farther west and south. Two weeks later, for example, the Fifty-fourth Massachusetts Infantry Regiment would make its desperate assault on Fort Wagner, South Carolina.

Even before the First Kansas Volunteer Infantry in October 1862, "individual black soldiers had been fighting since the beginning of the war, especially in the west, but not as units," according to the historian Donald Yacovone.[1] At the federal level, the use of black troops had been authorized in July 1862 with the passage of the Second Confiscation and Militia Act, but President Abraham Lincoln didn't take advantage of this power until he added this provision to the final version of the Emancipation Proclamation.

According to John Heiser, Gettysburg National Military Park historian, the evidence that black soldiers fought at the Battle of Gettysburg is "scanty" and "untrustworthy."[2] Allen Guelzo writes of a report from a Union sergeant who recorded that "an American citizen of African descent had taken position, and with a gun and cartridge box, which he took from one of our dead men, was more than piling hot lead into the Graybacks."[3] This man is the only African American on record as a "combatant," Guelzo notes, but he was not a soldier. African Americans primarily served sup-

Samuel Weaver (right) and black workers exhuming Union dead for reburial, Hanover, Pennsylvania, near Gettysburg, February 1864.

port roles: ambulance and supply-wagon drivers, hospital attendants, and teamsters. And hundreds, including on the southern side, served as personal body servants (i.e., slaves) tending to white officers.

But that is not the whole story. Thanks to the invaluable research of Margaret Creighton, we now know that Gettysburg wasn't just a three-day affair but a longer campaign that enveloped an entire region and countless African-American lives.[4]

Two weeks before the Battle of Gettysburg proper (July 1–3, 1863), a brigade of Confederate cavalry led by Gen. Albert Jenkins crossed the Potomac River and headed up the Cumberland Valley into Pennsylvania. These rebel soldiers weren't interested only in conducting reconnaissance, cutting communications lines, or raiding farms for cattle and other food supplies. They sought something more valuable: "contraband." The Confederate invasion offered them a tempting opportunity to reverse the flow of the Underground Railroad, and in the fog of war, they didn't discriminate between runaways, refugees, and free black people born and raised north of the Mason-Dixon Line.

On June 12 Pennsylvania governor Andrew Curtin had warned of the invasion. Black people living along the porous border between slavery and freedom (including under the Fugitive Slave Law) were quick to react: of all the citizens of southern Pennsylvania, they knew what the invasion would mean. Those who could packed up and escaped north to Harrisburg and east to Philadelphia.

Gettysburg itself was home to a "thriving black community," John Heiser explained,[5] numbering close to two hundred in 1860 (approximately 8 percent of the borough's total population, according to Creighton). Most lived in the Third Ward and worked as domestics, tenant farmers, and hired hands; they rented homes and owned lands and businesses. Many attended the powerful African Methodist Episcopal Church in town, which was active on the Underground Railroad. In anticipation of the coming battle, many had fled for safer terrain, among them the confectioner Owen Robinson, an ex-slave who, despite having legal papers, knew better than to take a chance of being sent back. Some were too infirm to make the trip and couldn't leave. Others who stayed faked injury to avoid appearing enticing to slavers. Still others hid, were hidden, or, in extreme cases, were confined by their white employers.

On the night of June 15, Confederate troops swept into Chambersburg and rounded up whomever they could seize and carry back to "Dixie" by horseback or in wagons. They continued, in town after town along the Pennsylvania border, for two weeks leading up to the battle, even during it. The terror was widespread and prolonged, with one white witness likening blacks' furious attempts at an exodus to those of "buffalo before a prairie fire."[6]

It is impossible to identify the exact number of ex-slaves and free blacks taken during the Gettysburg campaign. Estimates range anywhere from thirty to forty to several hundred, based on various first-person accounts. (Confederates didn't keep good records on this subject, and even if they did, many were burned during the fall of Richmond in 1865.)

In a few instances, whites intervened. Blacks resisted, too, by escaping, hiding, and fighting back. One nameless black man succeeded in disarming and shooting his captor; another was mutilated for trying. As Creighton writes, "They slashed his chest and abdomen, cut off his genitals, and poured turpentine on the lacerations. A Vermont soldier saw him as he lay in a barn near the Potomac River, 'grinding his teeth & foaming at the mouth.' "[7]

While blacks were not invited to take up arms on either side, a few had their lands seized and their homes destroyed during the battle, including James Warfield near Seminary Ridge. (Confederate general James Longstreet, aware of the taking of contraband, may have used the Warfield home for his headquarters during the fighting.)[8] The farm of Abraham and Elizabeth Brien, on Cemetery Ridge, ended up in the middle of Pickett's Charge. Some rebels even took cover in the Briens' barn; nearly all were killed or captured.

On the edge of the Brien property was the shack of Margaret Palm, a black laundress, who, having fended off an earlier kidnapping attempt in 1857, had warned her neighbors to flee before being tied up themselves. Another woman, referred to as "Old Liza," "took advantage of the chaos and the crowds of soldiers and civilians and bolted" to the Lutheran Church in town, Creighton writes.[9] Others were forced to cook for Confederate troops who'd offered their white employers protection.

Everywhere, the threat of capture persisted during the battle; while the confusion saved some, another witness, Creighton explains, "saw 'a number of colored people' corralled together and marched away."[10] More than a few blacks of Gettysburg were inspired to join the Union cause as soldiers, among them prominent citizens like Randolph Johnston and teacher Lloyd Watts of the Twenty-fourth U.S. Colored Troops; both became sergeants.

When the fighting at Gettysburg was over, the Rebels' black teamsters, many of them slaves hired out by their white owners, drove the retreat. Sixty-four were captured and taken to Fort McHenry in Baltimore. Not until December 18, 1863, did the U.S. War Department decide how to handle those still there:

> Those who wish to take the oath of allegiance can be discharged, and if they so choose, continue as private servants of officers, or serve the Government as Cooks, Teamsters, Laborers or in any other capacity in which they can be useful. Those who refuse to take the oath of allegiance will be detained as prisoners of war, and will be employed or not, as the Commanding Officers of the Post where they are confined, may deem expedient and proper.[11]

What was clear, based on the events of June and July 1863, was that black lives north of the Mason-Dixon Line were worth more to Confederate kidnappers than to many of the white Union draftees they'd be battling. After Gettysburg, however, they'd also have to contend with a much larger contingent of black soldiers—black soldiers bearing arms.

40

Before Emancipation, didn't most free blacks live in the northern half of America?

BEFORE THE CIVIL WAR, the United States consisted of slave states and free states, divided by the so-called Mason-Dixon Line—actually, a series of lines drawn by "compromising" Congresses throughout the first half of the nineteenth century. Most people believe that slaves must have resided below the line and free black people above it, and that every man, woman, and child in chains was trying to escape to the North as soon as they could.

But in 1974 a book came along—a once-in-a-generation masterpiece of research and analysis—that shook up our constellation of inherited "facts." The author was the great historian Ira Berlin, and his book was *Slaves Without Masters: The Free Negro in the Antebellum South*.[1] More recently, in 2006, Eva Sheppard Wolf's graceful *Race and Liberty in the New Nation* has built on Berlin's magisterial study.[2]

In 1860, that raging year of Lincoln's election and southern secession, a total of 488,070 free blacks lived in the United States, about 10 percent of the entire black population. Of those, 226,152 lived in the North and 261,918 in the South. In the South they lived in fifteen states—Delaware, Kentucky, Maryland, Missouri, North Carolina, Tennessee, Virginia, Alabama, Arkansas, Florida, Georgia, Louisiana, Mississippi, South Carolina, and Texas—plus the District of Columbia. A few months before the Confederacy was born, there were 35,766 more free black people living in the slave-owning South than in the North. And they stayed there during the Civil War.

In 1860, as Berlin illustrates, 100 percent of the African Americans living in the North were free (compared to only 6.2 percent in the South). So

Free blacks at Haxall's Mill, Richmond, Virginia, June 1865. Stereo photograph from image by Alexander Gardner.

why did the majority of free blacks live below the Mason-Dixon Line? At no time before the Civil War (at least not after the first U.S. Census was taken in 1790 and future states were added) did free blacks in the North ever outnumber those in the South. What is the reason?

To understand how the South created—and acquired—its majority of free black people, you would have to travel back in time to the Revolutionary War, when natural rights fever and military necessity (first among the British) stimulated the first major surge of free blacks in America. During the Colonial era, there had been only a scant few. (In 1755, the only English colony to keep track, Maryland, counted 1,817; Virginia had about the same in 1782.) By 1810, there were 108,265, representing "the fastest-growing element in the Southern population," with a dramatic 89.3 percent spike between 1790 and 1800 and another 76.8 percent jump between 1800 and 1810.

Manumissions—formal acts of emancipation by slave owners—were one reason, to be sure, but there were other sources besides. Some free blacks were runaways; others were immigrants. Among the immigrants were those who had fled the West Indies (often with their own slaves) during the 1791 slave revolt against the French in Saint-Domingue, which after thirteen years defeated France and became the independent Republic of Haiti in 1804. In 1803 Napoléon Bonaparte, exhausted and in need of cash from the struggle, sold his country's vast Louisiana territory to the Americans under its slave-owning president, Thomas Jefferson. With the Louisiana Purchase, the United States acquired thousands of "free people of color," many of whom had sprung from sexual unions between French and Spanish colonists and black slaves. The acquisition of these lands, then, caused another important surge in the South's free black population.

Still another group of free people of color (originally from Saint-Domingue) emigrated from Cuba to New Orleans in 1809, during the upheavals of the Napoleonic Wars, doubling the size of the black population there. In nearly every decade leading up to the Civil War, the rate of growth among southern free blacks would slow (it was a mere 10 percent between 1850 and 1860), but by 1810 the South had a free black population that was there to stay.

So who were they?

The short answer is, they lived as far as they could from the *Gone With the Wind* South. As Berlin showed in a demographic profile, free blacks in the South largely resided in cities—the bigger the better, because that was where the jobs were. (In 1860, 72.7 percent of urban free blacks lived in southern cities of 10,000 or more.) They were predominantly female (52.6 percent of free blacks in the South were women in 1860), because, according to Berlin, free black men had a greater tendency to move out of the region. They also were older than the average slave, because they often had had to wait to earn or buy their freedom, or in not uncommon cases, they were "dumped" by their owners as weak or infirm. (In 1860, 20 percent of free blacks were over the age of forty compared to 15 percent of slaves and whites.) Free blacks also were lighter in color (40.8 percent of southern free blacks in 1860 reported mixed racial ancestry versus 10.4 percent of slaves); not surprisingly, slaves with their master's blood were more likely to be favored by him, and as Berlin showed, favored slaves were more likely to be freed.

Just as critical as Berlin's findings about the North and South was his revelation that the South really consisted of "two Souths," an Upper and a Lower, distinguished, among other things, by their histories, geographies, and outlooks.

The Upper South (Delaware, Maryland, Virginia, and North Carolina, and later Kentucky, Missouri, Tennessee, and D.C.) had seen significant manumission following the Revolution; moreover, its soil was increasingly inhospitable, giving it a more negative outlook about slavery's future.

The Lower South (Alabama, Arkansas, Florida, Georgia, Louisiana, Mississippi, South Carolina, and Texas), by contrast, had never embraced manumission fever, and because there was so much money to be made from cotton, it never wavered in its commitment to the slave economy.

Consequently, Berlin writes, southern free blacks fell into two broad groups. The vast majority lived in the Upper South (224,963 versus 36,955 in the Lower South in 1860). They were on average darker-skinned and more rural than their Lower South counterparts. By contrast, free blacks in the Lower South were fewer in number, lighter-skinned, and more urban, creating a much more pronounced three-caste system based on gradations of blackness: mulattoes (those who would be called biracial today), quadroons (those with one black grandparent), and octoroons (those with one black great-grandparent).

According to Berlin, "throughout the South, a light skin was the freeman's distinguishing characteristic," and "the slaveholder's increasingly selective liberation of favored bondsmen and the difficulties slaves had running away or purchasing their liberty meant that free Negroes were generally more skilled, literate, and well connected with whites than the mass of slaves." This was especially true in the Lower South, where some free blacks even owned slaves—like Andrew Durnford of Louisiana, who, says Berlin, had "some seventy-five slaves" working on his sugar.

Repressive laws, especially in the Upper South, reflected whites' suspicion (and very often hatred) of free blacks and helped create a vast free-black underclass that lived along a thin line between slavery and freedom, debt and dependency, poverty and pride. There were repeated attempts to deport them, to register them, to jail them for indolence, to tax and extort the free black wage-earners, and to disenfranchise them altogether from voting or testifying in court against whites. Berlin quotes a saying at the time, that "even the lowest whites [could] threaten free Negroes . . . with 'a good nigger beating.'" Their precarious situation created perverse incentives for free blacks to try to distinguish themselves from slaves, sometimes even to pass as white if they could.

Many of these laws laid the groundwork for the later Jim Crow era. By the 1850s, Berlin reveals, only Delaware, Missouri, and Arkansas still allowed legal manumission of free blacks, and Arkansas, on the eve of secession, threatened its small population of free blacks with an impossible choice: self-deport or be re-enslaved. The result was that across the South in the antebellum period, there were quasi-free blacks who had been illegally freed without papers or prospects. Add to them those who passed as white or were kidnapped back into bondage, and even the clearest of census numbers begins to seem shaky.

41

Why did free black people living in the South before the end of the Civil War stay there?

IN AMAZING FACT NO. 40, we saw that before the Civil War, the free black population in the South actually *outnumbered* that in the North by a substantial margin. Of the 488,070 free African-American people in the United States in 1860—11 percent of the total black population—according to the federal census, some 35,766 *more* lived in the slaveholding *South* than in the North, as analyzed in Ira Berlin's 1974 *Slaves Without Masters* and Eva Sheppard Wolf's 2006 *Race and Liberty in the New Nation*.[1] Just as remarkably, the vast majority of these free southern black people stayed put in the Confederate states even during the Civil War.

One of the most important reasons free blacks stayed in the South, Berlin suggests, was that they couldn't be sure things would be better for them in the North. In many cases they were right, especially in states that restricted the admission of free blacks, among them Ohio, Iowa, Indiana, and Illinois (the last two in their state constitutions).

Interestingly, an antebellum court case in Massachusetts, *Roberts v. Boston* (1849), upheld segregation in Boston's public schools. (It would be cited by the U.S. Supreme Court in its dreaded 1896 opinion reinforcing Jim Crow segregation, *Plessy v. Ferguson*.) Even though the Massachusetts decision was later overruled by legislative action, the point was made, writes Berlin: "In the North, blacks were despised and degraded as in the South."

But comparative dread was not the only reason that most free blacks remained in the South. At the top of the list was family unity. After all, when a slave family was split up, the free members often remained close, attempting to raise funds to buy the remaining members of the family. They built churches in their communities, where they worshipped with family members and friends who were still slaves, and they worked in proximity to them, too, sometimes even in the same fields and workshops. And while they "were not a revolutionary caste," according to Berlin, many did what they could to "[help] individual slaves to ease the burden of bondage or escape it altogether."

Another reason they stayed was economic opportunity. While most free blacks in the South remained tied to the land, a number, especially in cities, acquired skills that allowed them to earn money and own property as artisans and craftsmen. Over time some trades became so associated with free blacks that they were known as "nigger work," Berlin writes. On those trades free blacks had a virtual lock, in part because whites didn't want the work or because blacks were willing to accept cheaper wages for it (often to compete with slaves).

In 1860, Richmond, Virginia, for example, was home to 174 skilled free blacks, and of those, 19 percent were barbers, 16 percent were plaster-

"A Barber's Shop at Richmond, Virginia." Wood engraving of a painting by Eyre Crowe, *The Illustrated London News,* March 9, 1861.

crs, and another 16 percent were carpenters; others included blacksmiths, shoemakers, and bricklayers. In the same year, Charleston, South Carolina, had 404 skilled free black craftsmen, dominated by carpenters (33 percent). Working-class whites, especially immigrants, resented them, and some refused to work by their side. Of all the workplaces in the South, Berlin reminds us, "brothels were perhaps the most integrated."

Many white southerners found it impossible to reconcile the presence of free blacks with their defense of slavery as a positive good and pushed for "solutions" to their free black population "problem." But the more they did so, it seems, the more free blacks clung to home out of sheer defiance. "Terrified by the unknown," Berlin writes,

> free blacks resigned themselves to the familiar oppressions of their homeland. Frequently they pleaded with local officials for permission to remain where they had long resided, and sometimes they simply ignored the law and settled on worthless, abandoned land near their former master's plantation. Some even refused to leave the old homestead and adamantly claimed it as their rightful home despite the stunned objections of their former owners.

This does not mean they always stayed put. In fact, early on, Berlin shows, manumitted blacks often preferred changing their names and tried to move away to start new lives. They also "voted with their feet" within the South by migrating back and forth over bordering state lines depending on which government offered a friendlier climate. In a few remarkable cases, northern free blacks even moved *into* the South, including New Orleans, for economic opportunity.

But the pull blacks felt toward greater degrees of freedom was real—to the North, even all the way to Canada, and to the South, even to the swamps of Florida. Over time some of the South's most talented free blacks left for leadership opportunities outside the region, creating a brain drain. As Berlin writes,

> During the nineteenth century, the proportion of American free Negroes living in the South shrank steadily, and the center of the free Negro population slowly moved northward. More important, this outward migration stripped the free Negro caste of some of its most talented, ambitious, and aggressive members. Among the blacks born free

in the South who later rose to prominence in the North were Martin Delany, Daniel Payne, Robert Purvis, and David Walker.

Those who stayed were reminded constantly that whites would never be comfortable with their presence—or let go of the comparatively cheap labor supply. This push-pull continued through the antebellum period, so that every time state governments seemed about to legislate a final solution to the question of free blacks—deportation to the North; colonization in Africa, the Caribbean, or South America; or re-enslavement—the business community prevailed in retaining the status quo. (In many ways, this impasse anticipated today's immigration debate.) "The inability to subjugate free Negroes frustrated whites and incited harsher repression, but still the free Negroes remained," Berlin writes. "And they multiplied."

In the 1850s, as the sectional crisis intensified, so did whites' fury at their increasingly confident and politically conscious free black populations. But if Berlin's detailed account proves anything, it is that there was and would always be a huge gap between the laws as written on the books and those that operated on the ground. Not only were many whites lax in enforcing their states' black codes, but free blacks themselves were nimble and resistant. They continued to live where they wanted to live, and even as secession finally spilled over in 1860, a majority of them still called the South home.

42

How did the son of a former slave defy the color bar to become a wealthy fixture of European nightlife during the Jazz Age?

DURING HIS LIFETIME Frederick Bruce Thomas kept many secrets under his hat, but two of them stand out as most consequential. The first concerned the death of his father. Lewis Thomas, a former slave and landowner, had been swindled out of six hundred plus acres in Coahoma County, Mississippi, by a white neighbor. (The litigation would last years, befitting a Dickens tome.) In 1890 Lewis moved his family to Memphis, where he took work as a flagman for the railroad. A few months later, in October, he was hacked to death in bed by Frank Shelton, a vengeful black tenant who was angry over Lewis's interference in his domestic affairs—namely, that Lewis had helped Shelton's wife after he'd attacked her. Shelton's ax sliced Lewis's face and arm—and it also cleaved the life of his victim's seventeen-year-old son. Just a short time later Frederick Bruce Thomas, who'd only known life in the South, hopped on the rails (presumably on a Jim Crow car) and traveled first to Arkansas, then to St. Louis, Chicago, and Brooklyn—anywhere, it seemed, but home.

Thomas preferred living in cities and worked at a number of different service jobs, from flower delivery boy to waiter to head bellboy to personal valet of the white well-to-do. Those experiences were his education—and escape—and while he didn't mind telling people he was the son of slaves, he never mentioned his father's murder. A century later the historian Vladimir Alexandrov was able to connect the bloody drops while working in an archive for his book *The Black Russian*.[1]

In 1894 Thomas left the United States for good—he said to study music. He worked at jobs in the finest European hotels and restaurants, in London and Paris; in Ostend, Belgium, and Cannes, France; in Cologne, Berlin, Düsseldorf, and Leipzig, Germany; in Monte Carlo; in Milan, Venice, and Trieste, Italy; and in Vienna and Budapest. Then, in 1899, he crossed the border into Russia.

In Russia, Thomas quickly learned that being black was even more of a curiosity than in western Europe, and yet it was also a nonissue. That didn't mean every ethnic or religious group was safe in Moscow; Jews were viewed as a scourge, "the 'Negroes' of Russia," Alexandrov writes. But in a city of a million people, Thomas was one of only a dozen blacks. He gained influence and power as a black man in increasingly rarified white circles.

His résumé gave him the three things he needed most: opportunity, access, and know-how. While working in the most exclusive Moscow restaurant, Yar, he squirreled away his substantial tips until he could afford to become an owner himself, then bought a nightclub, Maxim. He had a talent for booking musical acts from western Europe, so that first Maxim, then a second club, Aquarium, became *the* spots in which to be seen (and, for pleasure, in which to disappear) during Russia's late imperial era. As Alexandrov writes, "unabashed luxury was the norm," and at Maxim, black performers visiting from the States remembered, everything was "gold and plush" so that "you would sink so deep in carpets that you would think that you would be going through to the cellar." By 1912 Thomas had made his first 150,000 rubles ($1 million today) from Maxim.

Still, as far away as Thomas was from old Jim Crow, he was never wholly removed. At a minimum, he read the papers, and so he knew in 1912 that America's black heavyweight champ, Jack Johnson, had defeated Jim "The Great White Hope" Jeffries in "the fight of the century." And he knew, just days later, that Johnson had then been arrested for taking up with a white woman. Thomas offered Johnson an escape to Russia by setting up a boxing tournament that would culminate at his garden club.

Johnson arrived months too late to fight, but the two men understood each other and might even have become business partners had the Great War not intervened. With Thomas's help, Johnson departed for Europe. Thomas remained in Moscow, his fate (and wealth) too tied to the Russian Empire to abandon.

During the war, Thomas did his part to support the war effort by hold-ing benefits for soldiers, but in 1917, protests by Russian soldiers and work-ers helped force the tsar's abdication (and later the Bolsheviks overthrew the Provisional Government that governed the country from Petrograd), laying the groundwork for the Soviet state. None of that mattered now. Not even Thomas's clubs' status as "the favorite place of Muscovites" could insulate him from the storm of revolution. To the followers of Lenin, he was just another tsarist "White Russian" whose properties needed to be nationalized.

Fleeing to Odessa, then to Constantinople, Thomas, at forty-seven, had to reinvent himself again—this time with only twenty-five dollars to his name. Adding to the pressure, he had his third wife and three children (a fourth was missing) to support. His second wife, Valentina Hoffman, and other children would soon be nipping at his heels for money all the way from western Europe.

Thomas became co-owner of two successful clubs in Constantinople. More than that, he was their front man "directeur-propriétaire" (as his business

Frederick Bruce Thomas,
the "Black Russian."

card stated) and a very different kind of sultan, the "Sultan of Jazz" (a title that would be coined by an American obituary writer). Whatever his virgin experience of jazz music had been, he gave his refugee city its first taste at his Anglo-American Garden Villa (the Stella Club) on August 31, 1919, with acts by "Mr. F. Miller and Mr. Tom." At his second club, again called Maxim, he hired Harry A. Carter and the Shimmie Orchestra to headline the first season in 1921–22. Others would follow.

Thomas could not possibly have heard jazz music firsthand in America (it didn't get going in Harlem until the 1920s), but he always had "a nose for innovation," Alexandrov writes. Most likely, he sampled jazz in Europe or by trying out musical acts passing through. Still, it is amazing, even astonishing, that a black American expat who'd left the United States in 1894—and had become a Russian citizen in 1914—was bringing America's greatest musical gift to the other side of the world and hosting black jazz bands in Constantinople *before* Louis Armstrong had even joined King Oliver's Creole Jazz Band or moved to New York City.

But then, Thomas had already done similar things for the tango in Russia, Alexandrov writes. And whatever obstacles he had to overcome as a Russian refugee, in Turkey, at least in Ottoman times, there was no word for "Negro." There were second acts, however (to riff off Thomas's Jazz Age contemporary F. Scott Fitzgerald). Actually, by then Thomas was on his third or fourth act. The U.S. consulate in Constantinople admitted that Thomas ran the "highest class cabaret" in the city, and he told those who visited his clubs "he was 'conservatively rated to be worth at least $250,000,'" which, Alexandrov notes, "would amount to $10 million today."

But to visiting Americans, including one southern white woman, Thomas would always be a "good, polite Negro," though one "rolling in wealth." Others couldn't help but oversexualize him in their gossip, despite Thomas's long record of protecting his dancers from abuse. For this reason and others, Constantinople would never equal Moscow for Thomas. While he certainly benefited from (and was part of) Turkey's increasing secularization in the 1920s, he always seemed to be fending off rumors or creditors insisting he owed them money.

No one in the consulate had known Thomas was an expatriate, as they discovered when he applied to renew his U.S. passport (his only ticket out, since Russia was no longer safe). If anything, American officials were too blinded by their own perceptions of Thomas—that whatever name he went by (English or Russian), and however rich he was, he was a black man with a white wife and "mulatto" children who would have been crazy to return to the United States under Jim Crow. As a result, when the Allies left and the Turkish Nationalists swept into Constantinople in 1923, Thomas was again on the verge of losing everything he'd built—this time to taxes, regulations, and a state-sponsored rival, the Yildiz Municipal Casino under Italian businessman Mario Serra. Thomas would start other ventures before it was all over, make other attempts to break through, like Villa Tom, another "Negro Jazz" club, but never again would he reach the heights of wealth and acclaim he'd enjoyed as the Black Russian.

One wonders what hearing jazz music on the border of East and West evoked in him—those evolving strains of the blues, the memories of his parents' church, the voices of those black singers who had been shaped for many more years under American-style racism. Or at least while the party lasted, for a few short years later, there would be no sounds of jazz or any music where Frederick Bruce Thomas ended up—a man without a country but with insurmountable debts. A genius of self-reinvention, the early Jazz Age's black Gatsby abroad, Thomas died in Constantinople in 1928 at the age of fifty-five. Under new ownership, his club Maxim would continue for another fifty years.

43

Which massacre resulted in a Supreme Court decision limiting the federal government's ability to protect black Americans from racial targeting?

THE LOUISIANA GUBERNATORIAL RACE in 1872 was nominally between a Republican and a Democrat. But what made the election close was a split within the Republican Party. One wing sought to advance the goals of Reconstruction, with the candidacy of William Pitt Kellogg. The other Republicans were so anxious to pull it back that they formed a "Fusionist" coalition with the Democrats. Their candidate was James W. Hadnot.

Suffice it to say the results of the election were disputed, with each side accusing the other of fraud while holding its own inaugural parade. Because the Reconstruction Republicans still controlled the federal courts, their candidate, Kellogg, was ordered in, with backup from federal troops that President Ulysses Grant deployed. But when the controversy failed to subside, even Kellogg waffled in appointing like-minded men to run the courthouse in Colfax, the seat of Grant Parish in central Louisiana.

Having none of it was William Ward, a black Civil War veteran, militia leader, and outspoken Radical Republican of Louisiana, soon to have his own seat in the state legislature. He warned Governor Kellogg about what caving in to his Fusionist rivals would mean to the black voters who'd helped put him in office. With pressure from Ward, Kellogg kept his commitments and in so doing triggered a chain of events in Colfax that would destroy its backwater anonymity, and with it, innumerable lives.

The first violent contest over the Grant Parish courthouse took place on April 1, 1873. Ward's white rival in Colfax, the Fusionist candidate Hadnot, had told one of his black laborers that he intended to lead a posse on the courthouse and hang Ward and the other Republican officeholders for what they'd taken. The black worker then told Ward, who raised a posse of his own.

Hadnot arrived at the courthouse with about fourteen men on the morning of April 1, but what he found was so formidable that he departed without a direct confrontation. Recognizing the threat that Hadnot and his men presented, members of Ward's band moved out to raid their homes, seizing weapons, food, and a horse. The acts that followed "may have been violent," the historian Charles Lane notes, "but they were not random." They were a proactive defensive strategy "aimed at people likeliest to organize another attack against the courthouse."[1] There were no fatalities.

Word of the raids spread through the town, and the following day, April 2, a shoot-out erupted between whites and blacks near Smithfield Quarters, not far from the courthouse. No one was hurt, but the brief fire-

Blacks gathering the dead and wounded in the aftermath of the Colfax Massacre. Wood engraving, *Harper's Weekly,* May 10, 1873.

fight only exacerbated the tensions in Colfax. Many blacks believed their best chance was to join forces with Ward's men at the courthouse. That evening 150 blacks camped out.

With sporadic fighting spreading over the following days, William Ward became convinced he needed the help of U.S. troops stationed in New Orleans, so he hatched a plan to send a written appeal to the governor. He enlisted the former slaveholder Willie Calhoun to deliver it. The only catch—Ward's white opponents intercepted Calhoun onboard ship, where they found the appeal hidden in his boot. Threatening Calhoun's life, they told him the only way he'd survive was if he went back to the courthouse and ordered Ward and his black defenders to disperse. When he did, Ward's men refused to back down; no friend could convince them to give up ground, especially in a courthouse so symbolic of their still new political rights.

Ward decided to travel to New Orleans himself, and on April 11 he and a group of fellow black Republicans departed with hopes of returning with federal reinforcements. They had no idea that the battle was about to begin.

By Easter Sunday, April 13, the armed whites of Grant Parish had mobilized. "Roughly half of the men were former Confederate soldiers," Lane writes. "Among their leaders were four former rebel officers, including Christopher Columbus Nash," the Fusionist ex-sheriff in town. "There were even three former Union soldiers." Twenty men decided not to ride all the way to the courthouse after David Paul, a member of the Ku Klux Klan, warned, "Boys, this is a struggle for white supremacy. There are one hundred and sixty-five of us to go into Colfax this morning. God only knows who will come out. Those who do will probably be prosecuted for treason, and the punishment for treason is death."[2] The 140 or so who stuck with it now knew what they were getting into, and they were willing to die rather than see black men control the future of Grant Parish.

Back at the courthouse, the black defenders, now without their leader, William Ward, dug a hasty trench and attempted to rig up some artillery, building a makeshift cannon out of steam pipes. Sensing trouble, the few remaining whites inside the courthouse fled, leaving approximately 150 black men to fight for the Republican cause.

At noon, the white riders galloped through town to the courthouse, where former sheriff Nash and the other members of the white mob set up their cannon and opened fire. The blacks in and around the courthouse met their volley. For two hours, the fighting continued without either side claiming the advantage until the whites relocated their cannon to an unguarded levee around the blacks' left flank. Outgunned, the black defenders inside the trenches retreated to the courthouse. Others fled, many of them captured or killed by the whites. The quickest way to smoke the rest of them out, ex-sheriff Nash decided, was to set the two sides' long-fought-over prize on fire, which his men did by hoisting kerosene-soaked cotton wads to the end of a bamboo fishing pole and forcing one of their black prisoners at gunpoint to take it inside. With the courthouse in flames, its black defenders surrendered with handkerchiefs waving, but the whites kept firing. Their new goal: kill every black person in sight.

As night fell, the whites of Colfax celebrated. Addressing the black prisoners who'd been caught fleeing during the battle, ex-sheriff Nash asked, "If we turn you loose, will you stop this damned foolishness?" But not even Nash could control the other whites now. "Have you no better sense than to send them old niggers home?" one in the mob asked. "[If you do, you] won't live to see two weeks."[3] At that Nash left the scene. William "Bill" Cruikshank, a white supremacist planter, and others told the remaining black prisoners they were going to march them out two by two to spend the night in a temporary prison at the local sugarhouse, but when they commenced on foot, the white riders moved in along the line, shooting their defenseless prisoners at point-blank range. Estimates vary, but according to Lane, anywhere from sixty-two to eighty-one blacks were killed between the initial fighting and the murder of prisoners in Colfax.

The Colfax Massacre received national attention, but the spin was mixed. As the massacre was rehashed in papers, the ensuing criminal case worked its way up to the U.S. Supreme Court. It served as a test case over the meaning of federal-state relations, following ratification of the post–Civil War amendments to the Constitution guaranteeing blacks equal protection and banning racial discrimination in voting.

In particular, the decision in *United States v. Cruikshank* (named for the leader of the death march) turned on the constitutionality of the 1870 Enforcement Act, which Congress designed to safeguard civil rights and root out the Klan. Instead of charging the white defendants of Colfax with plain old murder—a state crime—the government hurled them into federal court arguing that, under the Enforcement Act, they (like the Klan) had "unlawfully and feloniously [banded] together with the unlawful and felonious intent and purpose to injure, oppress, threaten and intimidate . . . citizens of the United States of African descent," to use the words of United States attorney J. R. Beckwith.[4] Today we call these hate crimes.

A total of ninety-seven whites were indicted for the Colfax Massacre, but only three were found guilty. Of course, they appealed, and early on, the outcome for black civil rights looked ominous when sitting U.S. Supreme Court justice Joseph Bradley, in reviewing the case at the circuit level, overturned the convictions for defects in the underlying charges. Backing Bradley up at the Supreme Court, the majority of justices, spoken for by Chief Justice Morrison Waite, ruled in *United States v. Cruikshank* in 1876 that racial animus had to be explicit—and explicitly alleged—in order to be actionable at law (a factor federal prosecutors still struggle with in weighing hate crime charges today). At the same time, the court held that the federal government had no role to play in prosecuting individuals for violating the civil rights of African Americans—that was the states' job.[5]

By court fiat, the only role of the federal government—after *Cruikshank* struck down key sections of the 1870 Enforcement Act—was to ensure that states did not violate blacks' civil rights. Private citizens like Bill Cruikshank only had to look to their state and local laws to figure out the consequences of targeting blacks, even lynching them, for now treason was off the table. This would be the blueprint for the next seventy-eight years (they hoped longer), until *Brown v. Board of Education*.

44

Which episode of racial violence destroyed the community known as the "Black Wall Street"?

IN TULSA, OKLAHOMA, a city of 100,000 people, "the Drexel Building was the only place downtown where we were allowed to use the restroom," Robert Fairchild, Sr., recalled, according to the Tulsa Reparations Coalition.[1] That was why nineteen-year-old Dick Rowland was in the building. His boss at the white shoeshine parlor on Main Street had arranged for black employees like Rowland to use the "colored restroom" on the top floor.

On Monday, May 30, 1921, Rowland entered the Drexel Building and took a chance by violating one of the unwritten rules of Jim Crow: he rode an elevator with a white girl—alone. Seventeen-year-old Sarah Page was the building's elevator operator. No one knows how the two greeted each other, or if they'd met before, but minutes later someone heard a woman scream. Rowland ran.

Perhaps he should've waited for a crowd to get onto the lift with him, because in the aftermath Page claimed Rowland had assaulted her. That wasn't true, Walter White, executive secretary of the NAACP, was quick to clarify in a piece he wrote for the *Nation* magazine, on June 29, 1921: "It was found afterwards that the boy had stepped by accident on her foot." To White, it was obvious—and so he wondered why it had never "occurred to the citizens of Tulsa that any sane person attempting criminally to assault a woman would have picked any place in the world rather than an open

National Guard troops attend to blacks injured during the Tulsa Race Riot, 1921.

elevator in a public building with scores of people within calling distance." But it was too late for cooler heads, or even facts, to prevail. "The story of the alleged assault was published Tuesday afternoon [a day after the incident] by the *Tulsa Tribune,* one of the two local newspapers," White added, and its headline and text were vicious.[2]

"Nab Negro for Attacking Girl in Elevator," the page-one story ran. The *Tribune* claimed Rowland had gone by the nickname "Diamond Dick" and that he'd "attacked [Page], scratching her hands and face and tearing her clothes." More menacing, the paper let the people of Tulsa know exactly where Rowland was after being "charged with attempting to assault the 17-year-old white elevator girl. . . . He will be tried in municipal court this afternoon on a state charge."[3]

Blacks made up 12 percent of Tulsa's population. Most resided north of the city in Greenwood, sometimes called the "Negro Wall Street of America" because so many prominent citizens there had seen their fortunes rise as a result of the oil boom. Greenwood blacks were unwelcome downtown, except when working, so they had established their own newspapers, theaters, cafés, stores, and professional offices.

Those in Tulsa who paid attention to the news were well aware that a year earlier a white man had been lynched out of the county jail. And that same year in Oklahoma City, a young African-American male, Claude Chandler, had been hanged from a tree after being dragged out of jail on charges of killing a police officer. Greenwood blacks feared Dick Rowland would be next, and so they gathered at the black-owned *Tulsa Star* to figure out what to do.

Twenty-five or so black men, including veterans of World War I, took the ride to Tulsa's downtown, where, encountering a growing white mob, they formed a line and marched, with arms, up the courthouse steps to offer the white police force help in protecting Rowland. The police refused their offer, just as they had refused whites' demands to release Rowland to their brand of ask-no-questions justice. On the roof, police riflemen stood at the ready. Below, "cries of 'Let us have the nigger' could be heard echoing off the walls," the historian Scott Ellsworth tells us.[4]

Even though the black visitors returned to their cars, whites in the mob were enraged by their audacity and rushed home to get their guns. Others made an unsuccessful attempt to supply themselves with ammunition from the National Guard Armory. By nine thirty p.m., two thousand whites were crowding the courthouse.

Back in Greenwood, black Tulsans canceled regular activities, while another round of men, this time about seventy-five, decided it was time to head down to the courthouse. With their guns at the ready, they wanted to make one thing clear: There was not going to be any lynching in Tulsa that night.

"Then it happened," Ellsworth writes.

As the black men were leaving the courthouse for the second time, a white man approached a tall African-American World War I veteran who was carrying an army-issue revolver. "Nigger," the white man said, "what are you doing with that pistol?" "I'm going to use it if I need to," replied the black veteran. "No, you give it to me." "Like hell I will." The white man tried to take the gun away from the veteran, and a shot rang out. America's worst race riot had begun.[5]

There would be no reconciliation the night of May 31 in Tulsa. After the courthouse gunfight, a dozen black and white men were dead or wounded. Outnumbered, the blacks who'd driven down from Greenwood retreated through the streets while scores of whites were deputized on the spot by the Tulsa Police Department, which now perceived the event as "a Negro uprising," according to the historian Alfred L. Brophy.[6] One white who was turned away, a bricklayer named Laurel Buck, was even told, "Get a gun, and get busy and try to get a nigger," according to Ellsworth.[7]

A black Tulsan was gunned down running out of an alley near Younkman's drugstore. Another was chased into a white movie theater, where, spotted in the projector's glow, he was shot in the head. Still another was shot on West Fourth and knifed to the point where a white doctor, seeing him "writhing," realized "it was an impossible situation to control, that I could be of no help."

Walter White tried to convey the terror that swept north to Greenwood into the next morning, June 1:

> The [white] mob, now numbering more than 10,000, made a mass attack on Little Africa. Machine-guns were brought into use; eight aeroplanes were employed to spy on the movements of the Negroes and according to some were used in bombing the colored section. All that was lacking to make the scene a replica of modern "Christian" warfare was poison gas. The colored men and women fought gamely in defense of their homes, but the odds were too great. According to the statements of onlookers, men in uniform, either home guards or ex-service men or both, carried cans of oil into Little Africa, and, after looting the homes, set fire to them.[8]

It continued when the Tulsa police and National Guard troops arrived in Greenwood on the morning of June 1 and imposed martial law. Still convinced blacks were to blame for the riot, the troops focused their efforts on detaining Greenwood's residents instead of shielding them from the terror. Estimates are that four thousand to six thousand Greenwood residents (almost half the population) were arrested and relocated to holding centers throughout the city, leaving their homes and businesses even more vulnerable to attack.

The last shots in the Tulsa Race Riot were fired sometime after noon on Tuesday, June 1. In the aftermath, twenty-six African Americans and ten whites were reported dead, but many who'd lived through it found the official count dubiously low. Eighty years later the Tulsa Race Riot Commission report determined that some 1,256 homes were burned in Greenwood, and while an exact count of those killed could not be established, even the best evidence pointed to between seventy-five and three hundred killed, with a ratio of three or four blacks to every white. Then there are the families that fled. The historian Aaron Myers puts that number at more than seven hundred.[9]

Shortly after the Tulsa Riot, a grand jury was convened to investigate the incident. Its findings were summed up in a headline published in the *Tulsa World:* "Grand Jury Blames Negroes for Inciting Race Rioting; Whites Clearly Exonerated," according to Brophy.[10] Whatever was lurking in Sarah Page's heart in September 1921, the most consequential elevator operator in Tulsa history was a no-show against Dick Rowland in court—and so his case was tossed. In an amazing turn of events, Rowland had survived the riot in jail and now was a free man once again.

Despite initial promises from Tulsa officials to rebuild Greenwood, blacks who had lost everything found no redress from the city or the courts. More than one hundred suits were filed in the years after the riot, but only two went to trial, Brophy reports, and both plaintiffs lost. Those who sought to rebuild found their progress slowed by a lack of funds and new zoning ordinances, while even those home and business owners who had insurance learned that their policies contained "riot exclusion" clauses. Because of the slow pace of progress, a thousand survivors spent the winter of 1921–22 living in tents.

45

How could integrating information
about the fight for civil rights into K–12
curricula better educate our children
and foster a real conversation on race?

IN 2010 TWELFTH-GRADERS were asked to identify the following quote on
the National Assessment of Educational Progress U.S. History Exam: "Separate educational facilities are inherently unequal." The twelve thousand
students tested didn't need to come up with the name *Brown v. Board of Education* (1954), mind you—they just had to know it had something to do with
segregation in the nation's schools. Yet a stunning 73 percent either skipped
it or received an "inappropriate" score. Only *2 percent* received full credit.

Brown v. Board of Education was not only a landmark U.S. Supreme Court
case for black people; it's arguably the most important case in American
legal history and one that, more than any other, affected *all* Americans by
making de jure segregation illegal, and integration the goal of our ever
more multicultural society.

In September 2011 the Southern Poverty Law Center (SPLC) issued
a report titled *Teaching the Movement: The State of Civil Rights Education in
the United States 2011.* Its conclusion was that the situation is "dismal." The
American school system is inexcusably treating the civil rights movement,
essentially, as if it never happened—part of a collective, general amnesia
about African-American history as a whole. As the SPLC report reveals,
where it really matters, where it counts most—in our nation's public
schools—far too many educators (and curriculum writers) view the movement "mainly as African-American or regional history."[1]

The SPLC, through its Teaching Tolerance project, reviewed all fifty states' standards for the school year 2011–12. It established a benchmark for the "generally accepted core knowledge" that every student should have about the civil rights movement, based on leading textbooks and historians. It scored each state with a letter grade, A through F, and compared them. Let's just say that the students who missed the *Brown* quote in 2010 weren't alone. A whopping thirty-five states received an F grade, which, according to the report, means they covered "less than 20 percent—or, in many cases none—of the recommended content." In fact, sixteen states required nothing "at all."

Only three states in the report earned an A grade—Alabama (70 percent), New York (65 percent), and Florida (64 percent). Three other states—Georgia, Illinois, and South Carolina— received B's. Six C's were handed out (to Lousiana, Maryland, Mississippi, Tennessee, Texas, and Virginia), and three D's (to Arizona, Arkansas, Massachusetts); D was also the grade Washington, D.C., the site of the 1963 march, received. Want an even big-

An integrated classroom in Washington, D.C., 1954.

Bayard Rustin (left) speaking to Cleveland Robinson,
co-organizer of the March on Washington for Jobs and
Freedom, August 7, 1963.

Court's ruling in *Morgan v. Virginia* (1946) that any state forcing segregation on buses crossing state lines would be in violation of the Commerce
Clause. It was a noble attempt, but Rustin soon found himself on a chain
gang in North Carolina.

In January 1953 Rustin, after delivering a speech in Pasadena, California, was arrested on "lewd conduct" and "vagrancy" charges, allegedly for
a sexual act involving two white men in an automobile. With the FBI's file
on Rustin expanding, FOR demanded his resignation. That left Rustin to
conclude, "I know now that for me sex must be sublimated if I am to live
with myself and in this world longer."[2]

In 1956, on the advice of labor leader and activist A. Philip Randolph,
Rustin traveled to Alabama to lend support to Dr. King and the Mont-

gomery Bus Boycott. While remaining out of the spotlight, Rustin played a critical role in introducing King to Gandhi's teachings while writing publicity materials and organizing carpools.

Rustin experienced one of the lowest points in his career in 1960, and the author of this crisis wasn't J. Edgar Hoover; it was another black leader. Representative Adam Clayton Powell, Jr. (D-NY), angry that Rustin and King were planning a march outside the Democratic National Convention in Los Angeles, warned King that if he did not drop Rustin, Powell would tell the press that King and Rustin were gay lovers. Powell had concocted the charge for his own malicious reasons, yet King, in one of his weaker moments, called off the march and put distance between himself and Rustin, who reluctantly resigned from the Southern Christian Leadership Conference. For that King "lost much moral credit . . . in the eyes of the young," James Baldwin wrote.[3] Fortunately, Rustin put the movement ahead of this vicious personal slight.

The idea for the 1963 march came from A. Philip Randolph, who wondered if younger activists were giving short shrift to economic issues as they pushed for desegregation in the South. In 1962 he recruited Rustin, and the two began making plans to commemorate the centennial of the signing of the Emancipation Proclamation.

"Birmingham changed everything," Rustin's biographer John D'Emilio writes. In May 1963 Birmingham police, under the notorious commissioner Bull Connor, turned fire hoses and attack dogs on children. The fallout forced the Kennedy administration to jump-start action on a civil rights bill, and suddenly "the outlook for a march on Washington" shifted. "King, who had not shown much interest in the earlier overtures from Rustin and Randolph, began to talk excitedly about a national mobilization, as if the idea were brand new."[4]

Rustin traveled to Alabama to meet with King and expanded the march's focus to "Jobs and Freedom." But Rustin's past again came into play when Roy Wilkins of the NAACP refused to allow Rustin to be the front man. "This march is of such importance that we must not put a person of his liabilities at the head," Wilkins said of Rustin.[5] As a result, Randolph agreed to serve as the march's director with Rustin as his deputy.

Their challenges were manifold: unite feuding civil rights leaders, fend off opposition from southern segregationists who opposed civil rights, counter opposition from northern liberals who advocated a more cautious approach, and figure out the practical logistics of the demonstration itself.

On the last point, Rustin later said, "We planned out precisely the number of toilets that would be needed for a quarter of a million people . . . how many doctors, how many first aid stations, what people should bring with them to eat in their lunches."[6]

The whole time, Rustin feared interference from the Washington police and the FBI. Then, three weeks before kickoff, Senator Strom Thurmond (D-SC) attacked Rustin personally. It didn't matter that Thurmond was hiding a daughter he had fathered with an African-American woman who was a maid; Rustin was a gay ex-Communist, and in 1963 reading from his FBI file made political hay.

Tensions in every direction persisted. John Lewis, one of the leaders of the Student Nonviolent Coordinating Committee (SNCC), had prepared a militant speech for the event, reading in part, "The time will come when we will not confine our marching in Washington. We will march through the South, through the Heart of Dixie, the way Sherman did. We shall pursue our own 'scorched earth' policy and burn Jim Crow to the ground—nonviolently."[7] To appease other speakers and refrain from alienating the Kennedy administration, Rustin and Randolph had to persuade Lewis to tamp it down.

The march itself, of course, turned out to be a tremendous success, including those glorious moments when the official estimate of 200,000 was announced. (Actually, there were as many as 300,000.)[8] Marian Anderson and Mahalia Jackson sang; John Lewis and Dr. King spoke; and Bayard Rustin read out the march's demands. Perhaps the most poignant statement of the power of nonviolence was that there were only four arrests, all of them of white people.[9]

The following year, ahead of launching the A. Philip Randolph Institute, Rustin found himself embroiled in Democratic politics at the 1964 convention in Atlantic City. When President Johnson made a deal to seat the state's conservative wing, Rustin cautioned delegates of the Mississippi Freedom Democratic Party to back down. "You're a traitor, Bayard!" Mendy Samstein of SNCC shouted at the convention.[10] Rustin tried articulating his views in a 1965 essay called "From Protest to Politics," but the damage was done.[11]

As memories of the march faded and the movement entered its more militant phase, Rustin's coziness with the Democratic Party power structure angered proponents of black power. He also alienated antiwar activists when he failed to call for the immediate withdrawal of troops from

Vietnam and when he cautioned Dr. King against attacking the war in a famous speech at Riverside Church. Increasingly, it seemed, Rustin took positions that put him at odds with a movement he had so fundamentally helped to shape.

Despite tensions with other black activists, Rustin remained engaged in the struggle for justice. When Dr. King was assassinated in Memphis, Rustin participated in the memorial march and demanded economic justice for sanitation workers. At the same time, he expanded his focus on international causes, including offering support to Israel, promoting free elections in Central America and Africa, and aiding refugees as vice-chairman of the International Rescue Committee.

During the 1980s Rustin opened up publicly about the sexuality he had "sublimated" since the 1950s. He worked to bring the AIDS crisis to the attention of the NAACP, once predicting, "Twenty-five, thirty years ago, the barometer of human rights in the United States were black people. That is no longer true. The barometer for judging the character of people in regard to human rights is now those who consider themselves gay, homosexual, lesbian."[12]

47

Did Martin Luther King, Jr., improvise in the "Dream" speech?

DR. KING BEGAN WORKING in earnest on his speech the night before the March on Washington with a small group of advisers in the lobby of the Willard Hotel. The resulting draft was, as Taylor Branch notes, "a mixture of truncated oratory and fresh composition" that was "politically sound but far from historic."[1]

When Dr. King took the stage the following day, the August heat was rapidly approaching unbearable, and the cavalcade of speeches, whatever their individual merits, was beginning to weary the audience. Still, the crowd anxiously anticipated the march's climax. A. Philip Randolph introduced him as "the moral leader of our nation . . . Dr. Martin Luther King, J-R." King approached the podium keenly aware that he was addressing not only the massive crowd gathered before him at the Lincoln Memorial but also the millions more watching live on TV.

The power of King's "I Have a Dream" speech came in part from the fact that he "framed this vision entirely within the hallowed symbols of Americanism: the Bible, the Declaration of Independence, the Constitution, the Emancipation Proclamation and the 'American Dream,'" as Adam Fairclough has pointed out.[2] But when he started talking that day, he had not planned to discuss any dreams.

After alluding to Lincoln and saying that "the Negro still is not free," King turned to the novel metaphor of the "promissory note"—that the Declaration of Independence was a check of sorts written to all Americans of all races

Participants in the March on Washington gathered at the National Mall, viewed from the Lincoln Memorial, August 28, 1963.

as a guarantee of their rights, but that so far, for "the Negro people," it had been "a bad check . . . which has come back marked 'insufficient funds.'"

In the following sections of the speech, King responded to critics who cautioned moderation ("gradualism," he named it) and those who called for armed militancy and racial separation. King stressed the need for action in "the fierce urgency of now" and argued for a nonviolent, biracial approach, reminding those demanding more radical action that "the marvelous new militancy which has engulfed the Negro community must not lead us to distrust all white people, for many of our white brothers, as evidenced by their presence here today, have come to realize that their destiny is tied up with our destiny. . . . We cannot walk alone." King then encouraged Americans to continue fighting for right over might, as "we are not satisfied, and we will not be satisfied until justice rolls down like waters and righteousness like a mighty stream."

Soon after delivering that now-famous line, King looked down at his prepared speech and reached this mouthful of a sentence: "And so today, let us go back to our communities as members of the international association for the advancement of creative dissatisfaction." He balked. Instead of reading it, he transformed his speech into a sermon.

He instructed the audience to "go back to Mississippi, go back to Alabama . . . South Carolina . . . Georgia . . . Louisiana . . . to the slums and ghettos of our Northern cities, knowing that somehow this situation can and will be changed. Let us not wallow in the valley of despair."

King speechwriter Clarence Jones saw King "push the text of his prepared remarks to one side" and realized what was happening. "I leaned over and said to the person next to me, 'These people out there today don't know it yet, but they're about ready to go to church.'"[3] Onstage that day the singer Mahalia Jackson, who had performed earlier, reportedly kept saying to King, as he spoke, "Tell 'em about the dream, Martin."[4] King never said if he heard her or not, but Julian Bond recently told me it would have been impossible not to, given their proximity on the stage and the resonance of Jackson's powerful voice.

In any case, *her* dream was fulfilled when King continued, "Even though we face the difficulties of today and tomorrow, I still have a dream. It is a dream deeply rooted in the American dream. I have a dream that one day this nation will rise up, live out the true meaning of its creed." In classic black preacher oratorical fashion, King turned to repetition, outlining the specifics of his dream, which emphasized interracial cooperation across the South. Poignantly, he exclaimed, "I have a dream that my four little children will one day live in a nation where they will not be judged by the color of their skin but by the content of their character. I have a dream today!"

Soon the speech reached its dramatic climax. King quoted the first verse of "My Country 'Tis of Thee" (the song Marian Anderson had opened with at the Lincoln Memorial in 1939; she was also there to sing the national anthem in 1963) and commanded, "Let freedom ring" in "New Hampshire . . . New York . . . Pennsylvania . . . Colorado," and "California," but also "from Stone Mountain of Georgia . . . from Lookout Mountain of Tennessee . . . from every hill and molehill of Mississippi, from every mountain side. Let freedom ring."

He saved his most dramatic exhortations for last: "When we allow freedom to ring—when we let it ring from every village and every hamlet, from every state and every city, we will be able to speed up that day when all of God's children, black men and white men, Jews and Gentiles, Protestants and Catholics, will be able to join hands and to sing in the words of the old Negro spiritual, 'Free at last, free at last, thank God Almighty, we are free at last.' "

Three months later King explained his decision to go off script: "I started out reading the speech . . . just all of a sudden—the audience response was wonderful that day—and all of a sudden this thing came to me that I have used—I'd used it many times before, that thing about 'I have a dream'—and I just felt that I wanted to use it here."[5]

The long-term importance of the march and the speech cannot be overstated. Look no further than the explosion of marches on Washington that have occurred in the years since. That such a wide variety of people and organizations have riffed upon the March on Washington by attempting to restage it is a testament to what King, Randolph, Rustin, Lewis, and the other leaders of the march achieved more than fifty years ago. It's such a testament that the singular focus on King's climactic speech (really, a few sound bites) has fostered an overly simple portrait of King himself. As the historian Vincent Harding argues, "Brother Martin spent a fair amount of time in jail, but his worst imprisonment may be how his own nation has frozen him in that moment in 1963."[6]

The freeze began taking hold after King's assassination in 1968, the historian Drew Hansen explains. Anxious that inner-city neighborhoods might burn, "politicians and the media [wanted] to influence the perceived direction of black protest" away from militancy and back toward the "good" civil rights movement of peaceful protest and visions of "all of God's children . . . able" (and *wanting*) "to join hands and sing."[7]

The emphasis on the "dream" part of the speech especially obscures King's later agenda. As Julian Bond once cautioned, most commemorations "focus almost entirely on Martin Luther King the dreamer, and not on Martin King the antiwar activist, not on Martin King the challenger of the economic order, not on Martin King the opponent of apartheid, not on the complete Martin Luther King."[8]

The speech also is too easily leveraged by political actors who surely would not have agreed with King's message during the 1960s. For example, many opponents of affirmative action believe that the speech supports their argument; as Ronald Reagan said in 1986, "We are committed to a society in which all men and women have equal opportunities to succeed, and so we oppose the use of quotas. We want a color-blind society. A society that, in the words of Dr. King, judges people not by the color of their skin but by the content of their character."[9] The estate of Dr. King even threatened to sue a group of supporters of Proposition 209, a 1996 California anti–affirmative action bill, when it used King's speech in its advertisements.

48

Which enslaved African managed to press his case for freedom all the way to the White House?

IN ABOUT 1762 Abd al-Rahman Ibrahima, an ethnic Fulani and a Muslim, was born into a prominent family in the city of Timbo, "seat of the Fulani emirs until its occupation by French troops in 1896," according to Britannica.com.[1] (Today Timbo is part of Guinea, in West Africa.) His father, Sori, was a leader of the Fulani people and fought to extend their influence in the Futa Jallon region (in west-central Guinea). In Timbo, Ibrahima was educated, taught to read and write Arabic.[2]

In 1788 Ibrahima led his own soldiers on a mission to open a trading route to the Atlantic coast of Africa—only to be surrounded by rivals, the Hebohs. " 'I will not run from a [Heboh],' " Ibrahima apparently said, staring down their rifles. The Hebohs captured him and recognized who he was based on his "clothes and ornaments." If they tried to ransom him, they knew, he might exact "vengeance."[3]

But he would be valuable to the Europeans as a slave, so they marched him one hundred miles to the Gambia River. As was commonly done to "African kings and princes . . . defeated in a war," the historian Terry Alford tells us, the Hebohs sold Ibrahima to Mandinka *slatees,* "black merchants," who then sold him to European slave traders.[4] The overwhelming majority of Africans sold into slavery to the New World were captured by other Africans and then sold to European merchants.

Despite his father Sori's efforts, including "burn[ing] the country," as Ibrahima later said, he was shipped across the ocean in the Middle Passage

Fac simile of the Moorish Prince's writing

Abduhl Rahhahman

Henry Inman. *Abduhl Rahhahman* (Abd-al-Rahman Ibrahima). 1828. Lithograph. Frontispiece, *Colonization and Journal of Freedom*, 1834.

to Dominica, then to New Orleans, and finally to Natchez, Mississippi, a distance of approximately five thousand miles.[5]

In Natchez, Ibrahima was purchased by Thomas Foster, a yeoman tobacco farmer who also raised cattle. Ibrahima tried to explain who he was, even telling Foster his father would pay a ransom for his release, but Foster ignored him. When Ibrahima tried running away, he found he had no viable means to escape back home. He was trapped.

Defiant and proud, Ibrahima soon proved himself of value to Foster as a laborer, and so in a strange twist, the warrior's son, once a leader of men, was promoted to slave overseer. His one resolve: he would not convert to Christianity. It didn't matter what they called him—even "Prince"—his name was Ibrahima, and he was and would remain a Muslim for life.

In 1807, Ibrahima met a white man at a Natchez market. It was the last year of the transatlantic slave trade to the United States (at least according to law) and the twentieth year of Ibrahima's enslavement. The white man was John Coates Cox, an Irish surgeon, who, incredibly, had fallen ill on a trip to West Africa many years earlier and had been taken to Ibrahima's father's house to recover.

Until his death in 1816, Cox worked to free Ibrahima, but Foster remained adamant: Ibrahima was too valuable to let go. But Ibrahima was determined as well. By this time, he had made other powerful friends, among them Andrew Marschalk, editor of the *Mississippi State Gazette*. Affected by Ibrahima's story, Marschalk pledged that if he wrote it down in a letter, Marschalk would forward it to the U.S. consul in Tunis, in North Africa, who happened to be his friend.

Several years passed before Ibrahima put pen to paper: perhaps he had a hard time expressing himself in writing, or perhaps he doubted anything would come of it. Whatever the reason, it was not until 1826 that he finally generated the letter. Honoring his pledge, Marschalk posted it with his own explanation of the plight of the "Prince."

Their letters reached the U.S. consul in Morocco in 1827, and once apprised, the sultan (perhaps impressed by Ibrahima's insertion of Koranic verses into his letter) reached out to U.S. secretary of state Henry Clay with an offer to pay for Ibrahima's release. Clay turned for support to U.S. president John Quincy Adams.

It's fascinating that Clay was a Kentucky slaveholder—and a renowned "compromiser" on slavery—while Adams was a Massachusetts antislavery man who would go on to make a dramatic argument for freedom in the 1841 *Amistad* case. The two were political bedfellows, however, and when it came to Ibrahima's case, they proceeded in lockstep. Whatever Clay's views were on the rights of slaveholders, he was an early supporter of the American Colonization Society (ACS). Founded in 1817, it was the conservative (and often racist) wing of American antislavery politics, an effort to rid the country—eventually—of its original sin and "solve" its race problem by sending freed slaves "back" to Africa. That Ibrahima had actually been born on that continent and wanted to return must have made him a poster child in ACS members' minds.

The Adams administration was prepared to grant the sultan of Morocco's request, but it would release only Ibrahima; his wife, Isabella, and their children would remain in bondage. As a halfway measure, Natchez citizens raised the funds needed to buy Isabella's freedom. Ibrahima's owner, Thomas Foster, agreed to let him go as long as he left the country; otherwise Ibrahima's presence could have an "improper influence" on his children still trapped in slavery.

To justify Ibrahima's transfer, whites in Mississippi like Cyrus Griffin, editor of the *Southern Galaxy,* spread the misinformation that he was a "moor," not a "negro." The distinction allowed them to portray Ibrahima as an exception—a mistake— and accept his release without upsetting the racial underpinnings of the slave system as a whole.

Ibrahima and Isabella probably traveled as freed people to Cincinnati in April 1828. From there, Ibrahima toured the United States telling his story and apparently met with President Adams at the White House.

While Adams's remarks to Ibrahima were not recorded, in his diary the president indicated Ibrahima's desire to clear up any confusion over his birthplace and to travel to Liberia, not Morocco. *Liberia?* That wasn't Ibrahima's home. Liberia was the colony that the American Colonization Society had helped set up six years earlier for free and freed African Americans.

But Ibrahima was being pragmatic. Whatever Liberia meant to the ACS, it was closer to Timbo than Morocco was, and to Ibrahima, those miles would have counted. (Present-day Liberia and Guinea are only 240 miles apart, while the distance from Morocco to Guinea is some 1,520 miles.)

The president and the "prince" also discussed Ibrahima's children. According to President Adams, Ibrahima "left at Natchez five sons and eight grandchildren—all in slavery; and he wishes that they might be all emancipated, and be sent with or to him." As important as they were to Ibrahima (the *living* legacy of his forty-year nightmare), there's no evidence that the matter went any further than conversation.

For the record, it was the U.S. government that paid for Ibrahima and Isabella's freedom, and it was the U.S. government that sent them to Liberia aboard the ship *Harriet,* which sailed on February 7, 1829. Before then, Ibrahima had collected signatures from anyone willing to donate money for the rest of his family's freedom, but at the time of his departure, promises remained promises.

On March 18 he and Isabella arrived in Liberia. Four months later, he died after a strain of diarrhea weakened his aging body. He was not yet seventy, not yet home to Timbo (though one of his last requests was to have his papers sent there).

Back in the United States, a sum of $3,500 was eventually raised as a result of Ibrahima's farewell tour. His former master, Thomas Foster, died within months of Ibrahima, whereupon Foster's children accepted the sum in exchange for freeing two of Ibrahima's children, Simon and Lee, as well as Simon's wife and children. The rest of Ibrahima's slave family, including seven additional children and many grandchildren, were parceled out to Foster's heirs.

49

Who was history's wealthiest person?

MANSA MUSA WAS EMPEROR of the West African kingdom of Mali in its golden years, between 1312 and 1337. He was worth $400 billion, which, incredibly, places him as the number one richest person in history, ahead of the Rothschild family ($350 billion), John D. Rockefeller ($340 billion), and Henry Ford ($199 billion).[1]

Mansa means "king of kings" or "emperor," and Musa's empire extended from the Atlantic Ocean to the Niger River. It was thought to contain the world's largest depositories of salt and gold. During a three-month stay in Cairo, Musa told a chronicler that he had become emperor only because his predecessor, Abubakari II, was convinced that new lands lay to the west across the Atlantic and set sail with an entourage of two thousand boats (and an additional thousand carrying water and supplies). They never returned, and no one knows the fate of the expedition.

We know about Mansa Musa from Arabic sources, inherited oral history, and perhaps most important, the seventeenth-century historian from Timbuktu Ibn al-Mukhtar. The founder of Musa's dynasty was Sundiata, who was either Musa's grandfather or great-uncle.[2]

In Mali, the *mansa* generally spoke publicly through an interlocutor called a *jeli*.[3] But Musa's *actions* spoke far louder. Everywhere he turned he saw—and seized upon—opportunities to build.

Musa, a devout Muslim, was told by his diviners to plan for an ambitious trans-Saharan journey that would take him to Mecca, the birthplace

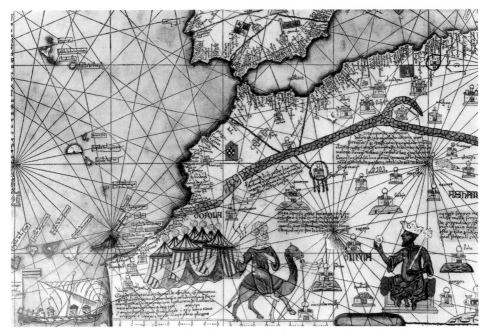

Mansa Musa, enthroned in his kingdom of Mali, from the *Catalan Atlas* of Abraham Cresques, 1375.

of Islam. He was joined on his pilgrimage by his senior wife, but this was anything but a second honeymoon. Accompanying the royal couple were sixty thousand porters in a caravan of eighty camels, each carrying three hundred pounds of gold. "Leading the host were 500 heralds, clad in Persian silk and bearing four-foot-long golden staffs glistening in the sun and nearly blinding anyone who looked at them," the historian David Tschanz writes. "Next came the royal guards some bearing spears and sword, others the flags of their empire." Also in tow was "a retinue of 12,000 of the king's personal slaves" and five hundred of his senior wife's maids.[4]

On the way to Mecca, Mali's king of kings made a three-month sojourn in Cairo, where he met with the sultan and, as a result, helped open key trading routes to North Africa. Great journeys were not uncommon among Mali's early rulers. In fact, while in Cairo, Musa told the sultan that tale about the mysterious disappearance of his former boss, Abubakari II, who may very well have been Columbus before Columbus. There to record the tale was Ibn Hajib, a district governor in Egypt. The Arab-Egyptian scholar Al-Umari translated Musa's story as follows:

> The ruler who preceded me believed it was possible to reach the extremity of the ocean that encircles the earth (meaning the Atlantic). He wanted to reach that (end) and was determined to pursue his plan. So he equipped two hundred boats full of men, and many others full of gold, water and provisions sufficient for several years. He ordered the captain not to return until they had reached the other end of the ocean, or until he had exhausted the provisions and water. So they set out on their journey. They were absent for a long period, and at last just one boat returned.
>
> When questioned the captain replied: "O Prince, we navigated for a long period, until we saw in the midst of the ocean a great river which flowing massively. My boat was the last one; others were ahead of me, and they were drowned in the great whirlpool and never came out again. I sailed back to escape this current." But the Sultan would not believe him. He ordered two thousand boats to be equipped for him and his men, and one thousand more for water and provisions. Then he conferred the regency on me for the term of his absence, and departed with his men, never to return nor to give a sign of life.[5]

The historian David Conrad qualifies the tale: "The clearly exaggerated numbers of ships (several hundred in the first expedition and 2,000 in the last) call into question the story's accuracy, but it offers an unusually detailed account of how one Malian ruler came to power."[6] Although no one knows for sure what happened to Abubakari II and his massive fleet, researchers in Mali, as reported by the BBC in 2000, think they made it as far as Brazil.

Musa, while in Egypt, was apparently so generous with his gold that he crashed the local market with it—for the next decade. By the time he returned home, he had barely any gold and had to borrow some at soaring interest rates. But he had brought back something else of value—actually, someone: the Andalusian architect and poet Abu Ishaq al-Sahili, who soon introduced domed palaces to the skyline of Mali.

During his twenty-five-year reign as king of kings in Mali, Musa launched diplomatic relations with Morocco. He underwrote students studying abroad. (You might call them Musa Scholars.) And last but not least, as a result of his famous pilgrimage, he spread the legend of Mali through the Islamic world to Europe, where before long his image began appearing on cartographers' maps. One from 1375 shows Musa on his throne admiring a golden nugget in one palm and clutching a golden scepter in the other. By then, he had been dead for almost forty years, but his legend as the "Lion of Mali" endured.

Musa was worth *$400 billion,* making him history's wealthiest person. But there's another reason he outranks many of the tycoons of history. As a historian of Africa once wrote, Musa "was [one of] the first to penetrate the iron curtain of colour prejudice . . . and to win for the true African a small measure of the respect which, even today, is often grudgingly granted him."[7]

50

Who was the first black poet
in the Western world?

JUAN DE SESSA LIVED ROUGHLY between 1518 and 1597. He claimed to
have been born in Ethiopia, in part to distinguish himself from the Moors
of North Africa, who were being persecuted. He was a slave in the home of
Don Luis Fernández de Córdoba, the Count de Cabra, in Spain.

His principal task as a slave, it seems, was to be the companion and
friend of Don Luis's son, Don Gonzalo Fernández de Córdoba, the third
duke of Sessa. Juan would claim, in a poem, that the two were breast-fed
with the same mother's milk. According to legend, Juan de Sessa was the
young duke's page and accompanied him to his Latin classes taught by
Pedro de Mota, held in the Cathedral of Granada, carrying his books to
class. Somehow the slave was able to study with his master and excelled
so much that he took the name "Juan Latino." His owner, the count, freed
him when he was a young man, but we are not sure when.

Latino was extraordinarily well educated, even compared to a white
Spaniard of his day. He received his first degree, the *bachillerato,* from the
University of Granada in 1546, then went on to earn two further degrees,
the *licenciatura* in 1556 and finally a master of arts in 1557. In 1566 Archbishop Pedro Guerrero appointed Latino as professor of Latin grammar at
the Cathedral of Granada, a position, it seems, that he held until his death,
although he is reported to have gone blind at some point. Juan Latino was
the first black person to become a faculty member at any European institution of higher learning.

He published two books of poetry. The first one, dated 1573 and entitled *Ad Catholicum,* "contains epigrams in praise of King Philip of Spain," writes the historian J. Mira Seo, as well as "poems on the relations between the Spanish Crown and Pope Pius V, and a hexameter epic in two [parts] on the battle of Lepanto, entitled *The Austriad.*" Latino's second book, *De translatione corporum regalium,* published in 1576, "consists of poems on the transfer of the Spanish royal family's remains from Granada to the monastery of El Escorial, and an autobiography of the poet in verse." Latino also published a pamphlet in 1585, but no copies have been found.[1]

The Austriad, Latino's most famous work, consists of two volumes of Latin poetry, 763 and 1,074 verses, respectively. It is a commemoration of

AD CATHOLICVM,
PARITER ET INVICTISSIMVM
PHILIPPVM DEI GRATIA HISPA-
niarum Regem , de fœliciſsima ſereniſsimi
Ferdinandi Principis natiuitate, epi -
grammatum liber.

DEQVE SANCTISSIMI PII
Quinti Romanæ Eccleſiæ Pontificis ſummi,
rebus, & affectibus erga Philippum
Regem Chriſtianiſsimum,
Liber vnus.
AVSTRIAS CARMEN, DE EX-
CELLENTISSIMI DOMINI. D. IOANNIS
ab Auſtria, Caroli Quinti filij, ac Philippi inuictiſsimi
fratris, re benè geſta, in victoria mirabili eiuſdem Phi
lippi aduerſus perfidos Turcas parta, Ad Illuſtriſ-
ſimum , pariter & Reuerendiſsimum. D.D.
Petrum à Deza Præſidem, ac pro Phi-
lippo militiæ præfectū . Per Ma-
giſtrum Ioannem Latinum
Garnatæ ſtudioſæ ado-
leſcentiæ modera-
torem. Libri
duo.
CVM REGIÆ MAIESTATIS PRIVILEGIO.
G A R N A T AE.
Ex officina *Hugonis de Mena.*
Anno. 1573.
Proſtant in ædibus Ioannis Diaz Bibliopolæ, in vico ſanctæ Mariæ.

Juan de Sessa (aka Juan Latino). *Ad Catholicum, Pariter et Invictissimum Philippum* . . . , 1573. Title page.

the naval Battle of Lepanto, in Greece, on October 7, 1571. During that battle the Holy League fleet (an alliance of Venice, Pope Pius V, and the Spanish king Philip II), with Don Juan of Austria as commander in chief and the Duke of Sessa by his side, defeated the Ottoman navy in a battle over the Venetian colony of Famagusta, in Cyprus, which was under attack by Turkish forces. It was hailed as a decisive victory for Christianity over the Muslims.

Shortly before Lepanto, the Moriscos had revolted. "The little Moors" were Muslims who had been forced to convert to Catholicism when Granada, the capital of Muslim Andalusia, fell to the Catholic monarchs Isabella and Ferdinand in 1492. (Muslim kingdoms had ruled the Iberian Peninsula—Spain and Portugal today—between 756 and 1492.) King Philip II issued a royal decree forbidding the Moriscos from using their language, their dress, their food, their festivals, and even the public baths (and from owning black slaves). When the Moriscos revolted, they were brutally crushed in the War of Alpujarras (1568–71). That war was conducted under the leadership of Don Juan of Austria, King Philip's illegitimate half brother, and Latino's friend and patron the Duke of Sessa. The duke enslaved the surviving Moriscos in the areas that had rebelled and expelled almost the entire Morisco population from Granada, relocating them to other parts of Spain. As the historian Baltasar Fra-Molinero remarks, "All of this was occurring as Juan Latino was writing his famous poem."[2]

Juan Latino was a part of a black community composed of slaves and former slaves in Granada. But even among the free black community, he was exceptional for how high he rose in social status, and for the unprecedented success of his academic career. His success was so rare, in fact, that his master and friend, the Duke of Sessa, is said to have frequently commented of him, "My black is as rare on this earth as the Phoenix." While Latino was one of three famous black men in Granada at the time, the other two were of mixed-race ancestry, including a Dominican priest, Father Christoval de Meneses, and a well-respected lawyer named Licenciado Ortiz, "the son of a knight of the [military] order of Santiago and a black mother," according to the historian Glyn Redworth.[3]

That there were free black men and women living in both Spain and Portugal in the sixteenth century is a testament to the fluidity of status that the Spanish Crown would later extend to Africans enslaved in the British colonies of Carolina and Georgia. Nevertheless, lest we romanticize black slavery in Spain, these three members of the Spanish elite in the mid-1500s were anomalies, although Spain—given its proximity to Africa and the fact that the Moors ruled it for more than eight centuries—was probably more mixed ethnically than any other country in Europe.

Although Juan Latino was quite well known in his hometown, he would be immortalized in Spanish literature by Miguel de Cervantes, author of the novel *Don Quixote,* the most famous work of all Spanish literature, published in 1605. Cervantes and Latino had a connection through the Battle of Lepanto. Unlike Latino, Cervantes actually fought at Lepanto. Sailing on board the *Marquesa,* he received three wounds from gunfire, one of which led to permanent paralysis of his left hand.

Cervantes cited Latino as an example of the old linguistic convention that he intended his novel to displace. Latino, for him, stood for Spanish poets who wrote in Latin, rather than in vernacular Spanish, which wasn't judged sophisticated or complex enough to be the language of great art. In one of his novel's epigraphs, a magus or wizard named "Urganda the Unknown" instructs Cervantes to avoid the Latinate diction of "el negro Juan Latino" and instead tell his tale in vernacular Spanish, which of course Cervantes did, just as Dante had done with the Italian vernacular in the early fourteenth century.[4]

Most fascinating to us, Juan Latino insisted on referring to his African ancestry and took obvious pride in his blackness. In his first book, he identifies himself as "an Aethiopian Christian," cleverly linking himself to the conversion of the Ethiopian eunuch by the disciple Philip, also the name of the king who led the Battle of Lepanto, as both Fra-Molinero and Seo point out.

This black man rose from race-based slavery and thrived, reaching the highest levels of Spanish academia and society, in what Seo rightly calls "the violently anti-Islamic environment of sixteenth-century Granada," when hundreds of thousands of black Africans were being purchased and shipped into perpetual slavery in the New World. How it could have happened is one of the most curious and fascinating episodes in black history during the European Renaissance.

51

Who was the founder of Chicago?

"THE FOUNDER OF the City of Chicago was Baptist Pointe de Saible, a Negro, in 1779," Joel Rogers claimed in *100 Amazing Facts About the Negro*. In Rogers's earlier comic book, *Your History,* he sketched out a bit more of the legend of Jean Baptiste Point du Sable (that's how most spell his name), including that he was from "Santo Domingo"; that he "built the first Cabin on the site of that now great metropolis Chicago"; that he "made a fortune trading with the Indians and selling his holdings to a Frenchman, named de Mai"; that he "retired to Peoria, IL in 1796 where he died"; and that he "was also probably the first civilized man to use" the name "Chicago," which, according to Rogers, derived "from the Indian word, Eschicagou."[1]

Two stories are at play here. One is the story of du Sable himself, whose life was fascinating and contradictory (at least what we know of it). The second is the story of how du Sable, the legend, was lost and recovered as an icon of black history.

The sparse historical record leaves many aspects of du Sable's life uncertain. Scholars believe he was born, as Rogers claimed, in Saint-Domingue before the Haitian Revolution (1791–1804) to a white Frenchman, a sailor, and an African-born black woman, possibly free. (A less common story suggests du Sable's parents were a white man and his black servant, both of whom emigrated from France to Canada.)

Du Sable's youth is similarly opaque. But we know that at some point he settled in North America, either by traveling north from New Orleans or entering from Canada—for him, a personal proto–Great Migration.

In 1779 du Sable appeared in the historical record for the first time when Arent Schuyler de Peyster, a British officer overseeing posts at Michilimackinac and Detroit, identified him in his journal as a "handsome negro, (well educated and settled in Eschecagou) but much in the French interest."[2] Du Sable was a successful trapper and trader nimble at negotiating the multilingual, multinational world of the Great Lakes region, with its population of Native Americans—the Potawatomi especially—as well as the French and Americans with whom the British were at war. He had taken a Native American wife, a Potawatomi woman named Kittahawa (later Catherine), and they had two children, with whom they lived in a cabin in the area of "Eschecagou" or "Eschikago," on the banks of what is now the Chicago River.

Encountering de Peyster, du Sable and his family found themselves detained by the British and were sent to Port Huron, near present-day

Erik Blome. *Jean-Baptiste Pointe DuSable*. 2009. This bronze bust sits prominently in Pioneer Square along the Magnificent Mile, Chicago.

Detroit.[3] With the Revolutionary War in full swing, the British sought control of the Great Lakes, which required the loyalty of that region's Native American population. Apparently one group of Native Americans, south of Port Huron, asked the British to replace their current French overseer with du Sable, who then managed their trading post and supplies.

Du Sable did not return to Eshecagou until after the peace, in 1784. There he continued trading while building a new home for his family (a forty-by-twenty-two-foot structure, impressive for that time and place) and furnishing it with luxurious French items and works of art. While the British had lost the Revolution, du Sable continued to rise.

In 1789 du Sable acquired an additional four hundred acres of land from the new American government. But a decade later he appears to have sold his stake and holdings for $1,200 and moved some three hundred miles southwest to St. Charles, Missouri, to live with his son.[4] Why he did so is a matter of speculation. Had his wife, Catherine, died? Had he been forced out? Or was it, as Shirley Graham Du Bois (wife of W.E.B.) speculated, because a white trader named John Kinzie—who would eventually be remembered as Chicago's founder—told du Sable, "You and your family can stay here," but "We're here now to get the Indians out"? Du Sable could never have gone along with such a mission, given his extensive network of Potawatomi friends, neighbors, and kin.[5]

Again, the record is dim, but regardless of whatever profits du Sable had made through his earlier land sales, he appears to have died in poverty in 1818, the same year his former home territory was admitted as a U.S. state and two years before the Missouri Compromise extended the free-slave line west, setting up a future Civil War.

In early histories of Chicago written by white men, du Sable received only a passing mention as a "negro" and "Indian trader" who sold his property to a French trader, who then sold it to John Kinzie. They give Kinzie the credit for upgrading du Sable's home into the "Kinzie Mansion," where his family lived until 1828—long enough, perhaps, to make them Chicago's first "permanent" European settlers.[6] Not surprisingly, the Kinzie family had a heavy hand in this narrative, including the assertion that Kinzie's daughter, Ellen Marion, was the "first white child" born there.[7]

When other writers acknowledged du Sable, it was usually as the punch line to a racist joke. "Not in jest, but in naive, sober earnest," the early historians Joseph Kirkland and John Moses related how "the Indians used to say that 'the first white man in Chicago was a nigger.' "[8] Far more impressive than this insulting and wrongheaded slur was the way future generations of black Chicagoans picked up the thread and turned it into a tapestry of pride.

First, though, the city had to attract a black population. During the Great Migration, that population *surged*. A city that had only 6,000 blacks in 1880 had, by World War I, its own "Black Belt" of more than 65,000.

In 1912, coinciding with the migration, a plaque commemorating du Sable appeared in downtown Chicago on the site of his former home, with "the concurrence of the Chicago Historical Society and the Society of the Daughters of the American Revolution."[9] A year later Dr. Milo Milton Quaife, a white historian at the Lewis Institute in Chicago, became the first to give du Sable a detailed treatment.[10] By the late 1920s, du Sable was making regular appearances in black history features, particularly during the Negro History Week (now Black History Month) launched by the great Carter G. Woodson and the Association for the Study of Negro Life and History in 1926.

Even the Harlem Renaissance poet Langston Hughes gave du Sable shout-outs in his "Week by Week" column in the *Chicago Defender,* referring to him as "the brownskin pioneer who founded the Windy City" and cleaning up the old racist joke to read, "The first white man in Chicago was a Negro" in the November 23, 1957, issue.

Whenever the broader white community left him out of the story, black Chicagoans were there to point it out. Amazingly, two hundred years after du Sable, a half-French, half-black Saint-Dominguan, established himself as paterfamilias of a half-Potawatomi family, his memory was claimed and kept alive by the African-American community of a "Great American City" on whose lands he had built his home without ever knowing that one day they would migrate there or why.

52

What's the real story of the legendary mixed-race slave trader Joel Rogers called "Mongo John"?

THE TRANSATLANTIC SLAVE TRADE, as the historian David Eltis writes, "was the largest long-distance coerced movement of people in history and, prior to the mid-nineteenth century, formed the major demographic well-spring for the re-peopling of the Americas following the collapse of the Amerindian population."[1] It was a system of capture and trade in black human beings that involved African elites, European merchants, and even a class of prosperous mulatto slave traders.

Some slaves were captured in wars that African leaders waged, some specifically for the purpose of generating bodies to be sold for the New World slave trade. A significant number of those shipped across the Atlantic began their horrific journey as by-products of these wars. Others were captured illicitly by African bandits and gangs. Still others were enslaved by judicial means. Overall, some 90 percent of all of the Africans destined for the nightmare of slavery in North and South America and the Caribbean began their journeys in one of these three ways, and one-third of the Africans enslaved were captured by other Africans.[2]

African elites brought their victims to the coast and sold them to slave traders who operated through a variety of trading places. Some were sold at a "factory," the residence of a European or African trading agent of a slaving company, established in strategic locations along the African coast. Some were sold at coastal forts, in Senegal, the Gambia, and Guinea-Bissau:

After Jean-Baptiste Debret. *Nègres Cangueiros*. Water carriers in the streets of Rio de Janeiro. Hand-colored print, nineteenth century.

"South of the latter (Guinea-Bissau) to the Gold Coast (Ghana), there was a large number of small, but fortified, trading posts."[3] From Ghana east to the Togo boundary today, there were about forty castles of varying size.

Farther east, from Little Popo in Dahomey (Benin) to Lagos, Nigeria, "the flow of slaves was controlled by African polities, and the Europeans had agents and storehouses under the protection of an African ruler," Eltis notes. "From the Niger Delta to Northern Angola, there were no permanent European posts at all, so each slave ship would negotiate with the African polity, and Europeans would not have had a permanent land-based presence, though the Congo River had a lot of European-controlled barracoons [enclosures to hold the enslaved] in the last 25 years of the trade." The exception was Luanda, in Angola, "the biggest trading site of all, which was Portuguese-controlled, as was Mozambique island," where there would be warehouses and holding yards.

Surprisingly, some of the largest traders in slaves were actually "mulattos," the offspring of European traders and the daughters of African rulers. They were connected to both the European merchants and the African elites by marriage, clientage, and trade alliances.

As Eltis explains, "From very soon after the start of the slave trade, there would have been traders on the coast with mixed African and European origins." The most prominent of a group of about half a dozen mulatto traders in Sierra Leone in the early nineteenth century was John Ormond, Jr.

Though his exact origins are a matter of debate, John Ormond, Sr., a white European, was likely born in Liverpool around 1750. At an early age, he "sailed to West Africa . . . as a cabin boy aboard a British slave ship," writes the historian Bruce Mouser.[4] George E. Brooks has Ormond Sr. landing in 1759 in Sierra Leone, where he worked for slavers on Bunce Island, a major trading post, before relocating to Boké along the Nunez River. Ormond Sr. broke off on his own in 1763, in order to capitalize on the market for buying and selling slaves from the Fula-Susu war near the Pongo River, where he eventually distinguished himself as "the most notorious slave trader of the late eighteenth century."[5]

Ormond Sr. bought low from his "African supplier[s]" and sold high to his European "ship[pers]"—what Eltis calls "the factor markup."[6] Ormond Sr. also earned a sales commission of 2 percent.[7]

With the nickname "Mongo John," or Chief John, Ormond Sr. was "renowned for his ruthlessness and his capricious and sadistic depravities," Brooks reveals. Yet at the same time, he ingratiated himself with the most powerful African families and political units. Not only was he aligned with Fula traders, Mouser explains, but he eventually "married the daughters of several Susu and Baga chiefs from the Bangalan and Fatala rivers, among them the daughter of the Susu paramount-chief of Bangalan."[8] By wedding the Susu chief's daughter, Ormond Sr.—a white man in an African world—replicated a pattern among other white Europeans.

In 1791, while still in his early forties, John Ormond, Sr., traveled to Iles de Los due to concerns for his health (and a recent jihad in Moria). While away, he left his son William in charge, a move that panicked his slaves in Baga. Would they be sold? Would their families be split apart? Their fears sparked a revolt, Mouser writes. Ormond's slaves destroyed his property, seized fifteen hundred of his slaves—and killed William. Not long after, fate—whether illness, a broken heart, or poisoning—took Sr.'s life as well.

After the headmen of Baga quelled the slaves' uprising, there was no obvious heir. John Ormond, Sr., was a white European without local siblings (only brothers in Britain). He did have wives, however, and the senior

one—the daughter of the "paramount chief," who fled "to her father's protection in Bangalan"—asserted her authority. She held Sr.'s estate together
until "the new Mongo" appeared to resume his father's trade "at the head
of the Pongo River."[9]

That "new Mongo" was John Ormond, Jr., who, at a young age, had
been sent by his father to England to receive an education. Because he died,
Sr.'s "agent in England refused to extend additional credit" to cover his
mulatto son's schooling, leaving Jr. a "poor boy . . . an outcast," recalled
Théophile Conneau, a contemporary business associate.[10]

After five years of impressed service in the British Royal Navy, John
Ormond, Jr., returned to West Africa in 1805. While the amount of property Sr. left remains unclear, his widow, the African chief's daughter,
turned over everything she had been safekeeping to Jr. after accepting him
as her son—and persuaded other family members to do the same. "Soon
thereafter," Mouser adds, Jr.'s mother intervened again in support of his
efforts to "bribe his opponent" to become the "elected chief" when "the
Susu chief of Bangalan died."

Adding to Jr.'s power was his leverage over "a large network of family
relatives"—relatives by blood, not just marriage like his European father—
including "a large number of wives and concubines."[11] Picking up where
his father had left off, Jr. charged an estimated factor markup of $25 to $30
per slave shipped out of Rio Pongo in 1826.[12] For every African bought
and sold from his factory into the wider transatlantic slave trade, Mongo
John the second, half African himself, took a cut. And when other factors
gave up or were seized after the British government banned the international slave trade in 1807, Ormond Jr. consolidated his power as head of a
coalition of slavers, making him one of the dominant factors in the Pongo
region.[13]

To be profitable, Ormond Jr.'s operation had to exploit a flow of embar-
kation and *dis*-embarkation points, origins in Africa and destinations in
the New World—the hallmarks of the transatlantic slave trade. Ormond
concentrated his operation mainly in Cuba, Brazil, and the French West
Indies, especially *after* the abolition of the slave trade (but not slavery itself)
in England in 1807 and the United States in 1808.

In 1814, Ormond provided most of the slaves onboard a Spanish slave
ship, *La Isabela,* bound for Havana.[14] When more than half of the crew

suaded Northup to journey farther south with them; arriving in Washington, D.C., on April 6, the trio lodged at Gadsby's Hotel. The next day the two men got Northup so drunk (he implied they drugged him) that, in the middle of the night, he was roused from his room by several men urging him to follow them to a doctor. Instead, when Northup came to, he found himself "in chains," at Williams's slave pen, with his money and free papers nowhere to be found. Attempting to plead his case to the notorious slave trader James H. Birch (also spelled "Burch"), Northup was beaten and told he was really a runaway slave from Georgia. Birch paid more than $600 for his "slave" (recollections varied: Birch later said $625; others recalled it was $650).

Shipped by Birch on the *Orleans* under the name Plat Hamilton (also spelled Platt), Northup arrived in New Orleans on May 24 and, after a bout of smallpox, was sold by Birch's associate, Theophilus Freeman, for $900. Northup was to spend his twelve years in slavery (actually it was 11 years, 8 months, and 26 days) in Louisiana's Bayou Boeuf region. He had three principal owners: the paternalistic planter William Prince Ford (1841–42), the belligerent carpenter John Tibaut (also spelled Tibeats; 1842–43), and the overseer-turned-small-cotton-planter Edwin Epps (1843–53).

Ford gave Northup the widest latitude, having him work at his mills. Twice Northup and Tibaut came to blows over work; the second time Northup came so close to choking Tibaut to death (Tibaut had come at him with an ax) that Northup fled into the Great Cocodrie Swamp. Edwin Epps, though prone to drink, was brutally efficient with the lash whenever Northup was late getting to the fields, inexact in his work (Northup had many skills; picking cotton wasn't one of them), unwilling to whip the other slaves as Epps's driver, or too high on his own talents as a fiddler after Epps purchased him a violin to placate his wife, Mary Epps.

In 1852 Epps hired a Canadian carpenter named Samuel Bass to work on his house. An opponent of slavery, Bass agreed to help Northup by mailing three letters on his behalf to various contacts in New York. Upon receiving theirs, the Saratoga shopkeepers William Perry and Cephas Parker notified Solomon's wife and attorney Henry Bliss Northup, a relative of Solomon's father's former master. With bipartisan support, including a petition and six affidavits, Henry Northup successfully petitioned New York governor Washington Hunt to appoint him an agent of rescue. On January 3, 1853, Henry Northup arrived at Epps's plantation with the sheriff of Avoyelles Parish, Louisiana. There was no need for questioning. A local attorney,

"Solomon in his Plantation
Suit." Frontispiece,
*Twelve Years a Slave:
Narrative of Solomon Northup,
a Citizen of New-York,
Kidnapped in Washington City
in 1841, and Rescued in 1853*
(Auburn, New York:
Derby and Miller, 1853).

John Pamplin Waddill, had connected Henry Northup to Bass, and Bass
had led him to the slave "Platt." The proof was in their embrace.

Traveling home, Henry and Solomon Northup stopped in Washington on January 17, 1853, to have the slave trader James Birch arrested on
kidnapping charges, but because Solomon had no right to testify against a
white man, Birch went free. Solomon Northup was reunited with his family in Glens Falls, New York, on January 21.

Over the next three months, he and his white editor, David Wilson,
an attorney from Whitehall, New York, wrote Northup's memoir, *Twelve
Years a Slave*. It was published on July 15, 1853, and sold 17,000 copies in the
first four months (almost 30,000 by January 1855). "While abolitionist jour-
nals had previously warned of slavery's dangers to free African-American
citizens and published brief accounts of kidnappings, Northup's narrative
was the first to document such a case in book-length detail," the historian
Brad S. Born writes.[2] With its emphasis on authenticity, *Twelve Years a Slave*
gave contemporary readers an up-close account of slavery in the South,
including the violent tactics that owners and overseers used to force slaves
to work, and the sexual advances and jealous cruelties that masters and
masters' wives inflicted on slave women.

Heroes of the Colored Race. 1881. Chromolithograph. Left to right: Blanche Kelso Bruce, Frederick Douglass, Hiram Revels.

their numbers, it should have been more. (Until the Seventeenth Amendment was ratified in 1913, state legislatures, not voters, decided who would represent them in the U.S. Senate.)

This was raw political power that the Republican Party was eager to embrace and that southern Democrats feared. (Remember, Abraham Lincoln had been dead only five years.) So by the time Revels reached the U.S. Senate on February 23, 1870—and so soon after Appomattox—he was showered with applause from the gallery but met resistance from the Democrats on the floor. Particularly galling to them was the fact that Revels was about to occupy a seat like the one that their former colleague Jefferson Davis had resigned en route to becoming president of the Confederacy in 1861. When Davis was still in the Senate, the Supreme Court's 1857 ruling in *Dred Scott v. Sanford* had gone out of its way to reject blacks' claims to U.S. citizenship—the critical third test that any incoming senator had had to pass.

The Democrats' strategy was to proceed as though nothing had happened between 1857 and the passage of the Civil Rights Act of 1866 and the ratification of the Fourteenth Amendment in 1868. (Both of those measures had clarified blacks' status as citizens, blunting *Dred Scott*'s force—the Fourteenth Amendment as a matter of constitutional law.) As a result, by the Democrats' calculus, Revels, despite having been born a free man in the South and having voted years before in Ohio, could claim to have been a U.S. citizen for only two—and at most four—years, well short of the constitutional command of nine. It was a rigid argument that twisted the Founders' original concern over allowing foreign agents into the Senate into a bar on all native-born blacks until 1875 or 1877, thus buying the Democrats more time to regain their historical advantages in the South.

So Senator-elect Revels, instead of taking the oath of office upon his arrival in Washington, had to suffer two more days of debate among his potential colleagues over his credentials and the reach of *Dred Scott.* While the Democrats' defense was constitutionally based, occasional slips indicated just what animus—at least for some—lurked behind it. As the historian Richard Primus writes, "Senator [Garrett] Davis [of Kentucky] asked rhetorically whether any of the Republicans present who claimed willingness to accept Revels as a colleague 'has made sedulous court to any one fair black swan, and offered to take her singing to the altar of Hymen.' "[2]

Fortunately for all future black elected officials, other Republicans in the caucus refused to play along. As Primus notes, "Senator Simon Cameron of Pennsylvania [asked his colleagues,] 'What do I care which preponderates? He [Revels] is a man [and] his race, when the country was in its peril, came to the rescue . . . I admit that it somewhat shocks my old prejudices, as it probably does the prejudices of many more here, that one of the despised race should come here to be my equal; but I look upon it as the act of God.' "

For Republicans, the more decisive act, as Cameron's backhanded comment indicates, was the Civil War. Before the country had spoken through the Civil Rights Act or Reconstruction Amendments, *Dred Scott* had in their view effectively been overturned by what Senator James Nye (R-NV) called "the mightiest uprising which the world has ever witnessed."

Charles Sumner (R-MA), a radical Republican senator, wasn't about to concede any ground to *Dred Scott,* which in his view had been "born a putrid corpse" as soon as it left the late Chief Justice Roger B. Taney's pen. "The time has passed for argument," Sumner thundered. "Nothing more need be said . . . 'All men are created equal' says the great Declaration; and now a great act attests this verity. Today we make the Declaration a reality. For a long time in word only, it now becomes a deed. For a long time a promise only, it now becomes a consummated achievement."[3]

Whatever the merits—or genuineness—of their various arguments, the Senate ended up voting on Revels along strict party lines: forty-eight Republicans favored swearing him in, while eight Democrats opposed. On February 25, 1870, *Senator* Revels pledged before Vice President Schuyler Colfax to uphold the Constitution.

As it turned out, Senator Revels served only thirteen months in office. He "introduced only one successful bill," the historian Eric Foner notes—"a measure relieving the political disabilities of former Confederate Brig. Gen. Arthur E. Reynolds."[4] There was a "striking absence of all bitterness" to the man, a writer to the *Washington Post* wrote on February 3, 1901, but this meant "his radicalism [was] of a milk and water type."[5]

Revels gave three notable speeches on the Senate floor: one called for amnesty for ex-Confederates, while the other two urged Georgia to seat its elected black legislators and opposed segregated schools in Washington, D.C. "Although his brief Senate term was relatively undistinguished," the historian Kenneth H. Williams argues, his "skill as an orator, honed through decades in the pulpit, earned favorable attention from the national press."[6]

In Revels's first address, on March 16, 1870, he appealed both for the freedmen's rights and for harmony between the black and white races:

> I maintain that the past record of my race is a true index of the feelings, which to say, animates them. They bear toward their former masters no revengeful thoughts, no hatreds, and no animosities. They aim not to elevate themselves by sacrificing one single interest of their white fellow-citizens. They ask but the rights which are theirs by God's universal law, and which are the natural outgrowth, the logical sequence of the condition in which the legislative enactments of this nation have placed them. They appeal to you and to me to see that they receive that protection which alone will enable them to pursue their daily avocations with success and enjoy the liberties of citizenship on the same footing with their white neighbors and friends.[7]

Such sentiments about reconciliation and forgiveness, about the lack of animus felt by the former slaves, demonstrate the grace of one willing to turn the other cheek but also help explain why Revels has been criticized for not doing more to stand up to the reawakening ex-Confederacy.

After leaving the Senate in March 1871 (he had been elected only to serve out the balance of one of Mississippi's unexpired Senate terms), Revels rededicated himself to the causes of education and religion, serving as president of Alcorn University. He died while attending a religious meeting in Aberdeen, Mississippi, on January 16, 1901.

55

Which black governor was almost a senator?

RECONSTRUCTION IN THE UNITED STATES lasted little more than a decade, from the dawn of emancipation in 1863 until the politically expedient withdrawal of federal troops from the former Confederate states in 1877. Former slaves and free blacks were a fledgling but strong voting presence in the deepest parts of the South. Mississippi sent its first black U.S. senator, Hiram Revels, to Washington in 1870, and its second, Blanche K. Bruce, in 1875. Already waiting there—but still unsworn after two years—was the first black senator Louisiana had sent: the state's former acting governor, P.B.S. Pinchback.

BLANCHE K. BRUCE (R-MS, 1875–81)

Blanche Kelso Bruce was a thirty-four-year-old former slave when he was elected senator from Mississippi in 1875. Born in Virginia to a black enslaved mother and a white plantation owner, he had been educated alongside the master's son.[1] He left home (which by then was Missouri) when the Civil War began and his former study-mate joined the Confederate Army. After a year at Oberlin College in Ohio, he worked as a steamship porter in St. Louis, then caught wind of the opportunities Reconstruction was about to bring black men with prospects who were willing to relocate to black-majority states in the Deep South.

Bruce soon established his base of power in Bolivar County, Mississippi. At one point, he served in three roles simultaneously: as tax assessor, sheriff, and county superintendent of education. These positions earned him white men's trust and, in the process, generated handsome fees in sup-

Gov. Pinckney B. Stewart
Pinchback, governor of
Louisiana, ca. 1870–80.

port of a lifestyle that included purchasing a white man's sprawling cotton plantation. Bruce's early sponsor in the Magnolia State was a Confederate-brigadier-turned-Republican, James Alcorn, who would go on to become governor and U.S. senator. In the 1874 gubernatorial election, Alcorn dangled promises of higher office, but Bruce backed Alcorn's rival, Adelbert Ames, a northern carpetbagger, who had offered Bruce a ticket to the U.S. Senate. In a black-majority state like Mississippi, it was vital for white Republicans to cut deals with power brokers like Bruce who could deliver votes.

P.B.S. PINCHBACK (R-LA)

The other black man walking up the Capitol steps at the start of the Forty-third Congress was Pinckney Benton Stewart Pinchback, a member of New Orleans's black social elite. Born in Georgia in 1837, Pinchback, like Bruce, was the son of a white plantation owner and a black slave mother. Pinchback moved to Cincinnati with his brother, Napoleon, in 1847. By the time he was twelve, he was supporting his family as a cabin boy, after his father had died and the white side of the family left the black side penniless and in fear of being re-enslaved.

As a ship steward on the Mississippi, Pinchback could have fooled most into thinking he was white. It wasn't until the outbreak of the Civil War that he embraced being a "race man," when, after a stint with the all-white First Louisiana Volunteers, he recruited black soldiers for the Corps d'Afrique and joined the Second Louisiana Native Guards (later, the Seventy-fourth U.S. Colored Infantry). Once there, he rose to captain, then resigned over discriminatory promotional practices and unequal pay. After lobbying for black schools in Alabama, Pinchback returned to Louisiana in time for the state's 1868 constitutional convention (a precondition for rejoining the Union). As a delegate, he "worked to create a state-supported public school system and wrote the provision guaranteeing racial equality in public transportation and licensed businesses," historian Caryn Neumann writes.[2]

Pinchback was serving as president pro tem of the Louisiana Senate when, in 1871, the state's first black lieutenant governor, Oliver Dunn, died. This left Pinchback to take his place. A year later his nemesis, Louisiana's white governor, Henry C. Warmouth, was impeached after a bitter election. In the fallout, Pinchback stepped in to serve as acting governor from December 9, 1872, to January 13, 1873. As W.E.B. Du Bois noted,[3] Pinchback was the *only* black governor of any state during Reconstruction and remained the only one in U.S. history until Douglas Wilder's election in Virginia in 1989.

THE ELECTION OF 1872

In 1872 Pinchback might have assumed he was making the right (pragmatic) choice to back President Grant's Republican slate, but when it came to verifying the returns, Pinchback's old enemy, Governor Warmouth (before his impeachment), insisted that his preferred candidate, the Democrat John McEnery, had won. Warmouth used the machinery of government to try to make it so, even though when Reconstruction began, according to Du Bois, blacks in Louisiana accounted for 82,907 of the state's 127,639 registered voters. For months—really, years—Louisiana was caught up in a bloody mess (the Colfax Massacre, see Amazing Fact no. 43). There were even two inaugurations. "Practically," Du Bois wrote, "so-called Reconstruction in Louisiana was a continuation of the Civil War."

President Grant certified William Pitt Kellogg as the state's duly elected governor, backing him up with military force. To represent them in the U.S. Senate, the Kellogg legislature chose a black man: P.B.S. Pinchback. If all had gone according to plan, Pinchback would have been sworn in on March 4, 1873, two years before Blanche K. Bruce. Instead, the U.S. Senate Committee on Privileges and Elections threw up a roadblock. As the opposition mounted, Pinchback found himself the poster child for an entire era of greed and corruption that Mark Twain famously termed the "Gilded Age." By the time Senator-elect Bruce of Mississippi arrived for his swearing-in at the Capitol on March 5, 1875, Senator-elect Pinchback of Louisiana had already been awaiting his for two years, without satisfaction.

What should have been a ceremonial day in the Senate ended with an extra session to debate, among other things, what to do with the "other" black senator-elect waiting in the wings. During the extra session, Pinchback's potential Senate colleagues again postponed his confirmation, in a close 33–30 vote. Curiously, Blanche K. Bruce voted with the majority, perhaps to stave off an outright rejection on his first day as a Senate freshman.

The curious case of P.B.S. Pinchback dragged on for another whole year in the Senate—three in all—until March 8, 1876, when the full Senate voted effectively to reject him, 32–29. Five Republicans went along with the Democrats, in a clear signal that Reconstruction was losing steam. And with the wheel quickly turning against colored men, what had been almost a blessing at the start of Reconstruction was now a curse.

The pairing of Bruce and Pinchback in the Senate wasn't to be, and on July 6, 1876, for his many troubles, plus mileage, the Senate voted 27–11 to compensate the former Louisiana governor more than $16,000.[4] The following year Pinchback gave up his Senate fight altogether.

With Pinchback out of the picture, Blanche K. Bruce completed his full term in the Senate, the first African American to do so. Bruce had voted for Pinchback in that crucial last vote, but he was cautious on most race matters. This was in part, his biographer Lawrence Graham writes, because of "fear of retribution" back home in Mississippi, itself a cauldron of racial violence as whites reasserted their authority in Reconstruction's aftermath.[5]

For all his legitimate fears of the violence in his home state, the lifestyle Bruce enjoyed in Washington must have made it hard for some in the race to stomach his suggestion to those suffering under the heel of white privilege and power: "My earnest advice to the colored people is to remain in and only in menial positions, large numbers served in the army. Some 370,000 blacks served overall, including "639 men [who] received commissions, a historical first," Williams adds.[2]

Of the 370,000 blacks who served in World War I, 200,000 shipped out overseas, but even in the theater of war, few saw combat. Most performed backbreaking labor in noncombat service units as part of the services of supply. The historian Adriane Lentz-Smith puts the number of combat troops at 42,000, only 11 percent of all blacks in the army.[3]

For one of the two black combat divisions, the Ninety-second, the Great War was a nightmare. Not only were they segregated, their leaders scapegoated them for the American Expeditionary Forces' failure at Meuse-Argonne in 1918, even though troops from both races had struggled during the campaign. In the aftermath, five black officers were court-martialed on trumped-up charges. The white Maj. J. N. Merrill of the 368th Infantry Regiment's First Battalion wrote his superior officer, "Without my presence or that of any other white officer right on the firing line I am absolutely positive that not a single colored officer would have advanced with his men. The cowardice showed by the men was abject."[4] Even though Secretary of War Newton Baker eventually commuted the officers' sentences, the damage was done: the Ninety-second was off the line.

In contrast, Gen. John J. Pershing, the commander of American Expeditionary Forces in Europe, assigned the Ninety-third Combat Division to the French Army. The Ninety-third consisted of the 369th, 370th, 371st, and 372nd infantry regiments. "With the French, the Harlem Hellfighters fought at Chateau-Thierry and Belleau Wood. All told they spent 191 days in combat, longer than any other American unit in the war," according to a resource for teachers on the National Archives website.[5] They gave no ground to the enemy, and none of their men were captured—although at least one came close.

Henry Lincoln Johnson was born in Alexandria, Virginia, in 1897. As a teenager, he moved to the North, eventually settling down with a job as a porter in Albany, New York. Johnson enlisted in the army on June 5, 1917.

Black soldiers of the 369th Infantry on shipboard in February 1919, returning to New York after the end of hostilities in France.

Needham Roberts hailed from Trenton, New Jersey. His father was a preacher and janitor. Roberts took odd jobs as a teenager and first attempted to enlist in the navy in 1916 but was turned down for being too young.

Both men landed in France with their regiment, the 369th, in early 1918. Their date with history came on the night of May 13–14. Roberts and Johnson were two men on a five-man observation team looking for signs of German advances. According to the historian Christopher Capozzola, the "remote listening post [was] sixty yards into the no-man's-land between the French and German forces that faced off along the banks of the Aisne River."[6]

In a dramatic letter to Johnson's wife, the 369th's white colonel, William Hayward, explained what happened:

At the beginning of the attack the Germans fired a volley of bullets and grenades and both of the boys were wounded, your husband three times and Roberts twice, then the Germans rushed the post, expecting to make an easy capture. In spite of their wounds, the two boys waited coolly and courageously and when the Germans were within striking distance opened fire, your husband with his rifle and Private Roberts from his helpless position on the ground with hand grenades. But the German raiding party came on in spite of their wounded and in a few seconds our boys were at grips with the terrible foe in a desperate hand to hand encounter in which the enemy outnumbered them ten to one.

The boys inflicted great loss on the enemy, but Roberts was overpowered and about to be carried away when your husband, who had used up all of the cartridges in the magazine of his rifle and had knocked one German down with the butt end of it, drew his bolo from his belt. A bolo is a short heavy weapon carried by the American soldier, with the edge of a razor, the weight of a cleaver and the point of a butcher knife. He rushed to the rescue of his former comrade, and fighting desperately, opened with his bolo the head of the German who was throttling Roberts and turned to the *boche* who had Roberts by the feet, plunging the bolo into the German's bowels. . . .

Henry laid about him right and left with his heavy knife, and Roberts released from the grasp of the scoundrels, began again to throw hand grenades and exploded them in their midst, and the Germans, doubtless thinking it was a host instead of two brave Colored boys fighting like tigers at bay, picked up their dead and wounded and slunk away, leaving many weapons and part of their shot riddled clothing, and leaving a trail of blood, which we followed at dawn near to their lines. . . . So it was in this way the Germans found the Black Americans. Both boys have received a citation of the French general commanding the splendid French division in which my regiment is now serving and will receive the croix de guerre cross of war.[7]

With his letter to Mrs. Johnson, Colonel Hayward enclosed the equivalent of fifty francs, half of what the French general overseeing the 369th, Henri Gouraud, had earmarked for "the family of the first one of my soldiers wounded in a fight with the enemy under heroic circumstances." The other half, Hayward told her, would go to Roberts's family. As valuable as that money was, perhaps the following sentiment he shared brought as much comfort: "I regret to say that he [Johnson] is in the hospital, seriously, but not dangerously wounded, the wounds having been received under such circumstances that every one of us in the regiment would be pleased and proud to trade places with him." It was a far cry from what the black men of the Ninety-second Division had experienced, and the level of sympathy and respect stands out when we recall that Colonel Hayward and Private Johnson wouldn't have been able to ride the same railroad car in the Jim Crow South.

The French conferred a number of military decorations on black American soldiers in World War I, and Roberts and Johnson were the first Americans of any race to receive the coveted Croix de Guerre. By war's end, members of the 369th, 371st, and 372nd regiments had also received it.

Many black veterans received a hero's welcome when they returned to the United States, at least from their own communities. In New York, the *Tribune* observed, "Racial lines were for the time displaced. The color of their [the 369th's] skin had nothing to do with the occasion. The blood they had shed in France was as red as any other."[8]

57

Who were the African Americans
in the Kennedy administration?

THE BRILLIANCE OF John Fitzgerald Kennedy's administration lay in his stagecraft. JFK may have personally opposed discrimination as a moral matter, but when it came to politics, he was a pragmatist who balanced his cautious legislative approach with placement of symbols of desegregation and diversity in and around the White House. To keep southern Democrats like Senator Richard Russell of Georgia in the fold, he appointed their judges in the South. At the same time, to keep black voters in the North on his side, he went out of his way to see that talented black professionals, especially black newspapermen, were hired to get the message out to their readers, so that they—and the message—would be clearly in view.

The success of JFK's public relations strategy rested on the abilities of his advisers. A few prominent blacks charted his segmented outreach efforts. While top Kennedy surrogates soft-pedaled his civil rights record in the South (few blacks could vote there anyway in 1960), these black strategists targeted specific messages to black voters. It was a "strategy of association," the historian Nick Bryant writes.[1] The key to their strategy was hiring black talent and a black press committed to showcasing it.

The man the Kennedy team recruited to lead the charge was the long-time former editor of the *Chicago Defender,* Louis E. Martin, whom the *Washington Post* once called " 'the godfather of black politics.' " Back in the 1930s and '40s, Martin, as editor of the *Michigan Chronicle,* had helped turn Detroit Democratic in support of FDR's New Deal. He helped found the National Newspaper Publishers Association in 1940 and was a "well-versed representative of the black protest tradition," with strong ties to labor, as the historian Alex Poinsett writes.[2] He would eventually advise three sitting presidents.

In joining the Kennedy campaign, he, along with black Washington attorneys Frank Reeves and Marjorie Lawson, customized JFK's image for their friends at leading black newspapers across the country. Their two-pronged attack was far more sophisticated than the advisers to Kennedy's opponent, Richard Nixon, had calculated. While Kennedy toned down his message in the mainstream white papers, Martin and company amplified his support of the Democrats' strong civil rights plank in a series of brilliant advertisements. The campaign issued photographs of JFK side by side with notable black figures, from Representative William Dawson of Chicago (his support was vital) to Virginia Battle, the African-American secretary whom Kennedy had recruited to his Senate campaign in 1952.

Along the way, Louis Martin (with others) had a hand in persuading candidate Kennedy to place a timely call to Coretta Scott King when her husband, Martin, was in jail. The call was "the icing on the cake," Louis Martin said. "But the cake was already made."[3] Louis Martin also induced

Kennedy White House associate press secretary Andrew T. Hatcher, a key advocate of a larger role for blacks in the federal government.

New York's black power broker, Representative Adam Clayton Powell of Harlem, to accept $50,000 in exchange for making pro-Kennedy speeches.

Kennedy, in a tight election, won 68 percent of the black vote. Soon afterward Martin became deputy chairman of the Democratic National Committee, but as Bryant writes, Martin was, with his "great savvy in public relations," Kennedy's "personal point man on civil rights." His other point man was Harris Wofford, chairman of the subcabinet group on civil rights.

On the eve of the inauguration in January 1961, Martin and Wofford lobbied the president-elect to at least include a nod to "human rights . . . at home and around the world" in the sterling speech Ted Sorensen famously helped draft. All through the campaign, Kennedy had stressed that his approach to civil rights would flow from executive—more than legislative—action, and now, with Martin's counsel in casting the players, he was ready to deliver.

"I am not going to promise a Cabinet post or any post to any race or ethnic group," JFK announced before the election. "That is racism at its worst."[4] But his "strategy of association" called for precisely that, and the black men Kennedy hired were indeed (to borrow from the late David Halberstam) "the best and brightest," finally given their shot to shine. In Kennedy's first six months in office, the White House appointed some forty-five black men (*and* women) to executive branch jobs.[5]

To Democratic Party field-workers, Louis Martin emphasized that JFK was helping black professionals shatter ceilings in the federal government. Unlike previous presidents, he said, Kennedy offered positions that weren't merely "advisory" but were "decision-makers." The names of these men, largely forgotten to us now, were illustrious at the time and continued to be added to the rolls throughout JFK's thousand days. The black press followed these appointments closely, and they gave Kennedy cover in deferring civil rights legislation during his first two years in office.

Louis Martin and Andrew Hatcher, associate White House press secretary, traveled around the country speaking to black organizations, to emphasize the point that the Kennedy administration was desegregating the federal government dramatically. It was about making perception reality, of translating a symbolic stance into a cultural shift, so that even if readers couldn't feel change, they could *see* it.

The administration, they pointed out, also pressed for the Washington Redskins to sign their first black player. It refused to address segregated audiences or join whites-only clubs. It invited black notables to White House dinners and thousands of black leaders for Lincoln's birthday. It photographed the president with leaders of independent African nations. It showed Andrew Hatcher in the frame at the president's first televised press conference. It had Hatcher's five-year old son, Avery, integrate Caroline Kennedy's White House kindergarten class.[6] To placate southern Democrats, President Kennedy may have been "singing Dixie," as he once told a reporter (according to Bryant), but in Martin and Hatcher's spin, he was humming civil rights.

The optics that Kennedy's black "Mad Men" created opened opportunities for men like Dr. King outside the White House. And when it came time for massaging the relationships, including in the lead-up to the 1961 Freedom Rides, it was the *other* Martin who brokered the secret meeting at the Mayflower Hotel between the Kennedy and King teams. Well-documented as the external crises were that forced the president's hand during the civil rights movement, Martin, Hatcher, and the others were *his* handpicked men.

58

When did African-American women hit their stride in professional achievement?

IN SURVEYING THE LANDSCAPE of recent African-American history, perhaps the most remarkable accomplishment has been the rise of black women. So extensive has this phenomenon been that this most recent period can be—perhaps *should* be—characterized as the era of the Black Woman, an era fueled by increased access to higher education, structural changes in the U.S. economy, and dynamic social attitudes and norms.

To take just one example: "Black women currently earn about two thirds of all African-American bachelor's degree awards, 70 percent of all master's degrees and more than 60 percent of all doctorates," according to the *Journal of Blacks in Higher Education,* which adds, "Black women also hold a majority of all African-American enrollments in law, medical and dental schools."[1]

In November 1968 Shirley Chisholm (1924–2005) became the first black woman ever elected to serve in the House of Representatives (D-NY). Four years later she would also mount the first campaign for the presidency by a black woman. That same year Barbara Jordan (1936–96) became the first black woman from the South to win election to Congress, in a seat now held by Representative Sheila Jackson Lee (D-TX). In 1977 Patricia Harris (1924–85) was confirmed as President Jimmy Carter's secretary of housing and urban development, the first African-American woman to be appointed to a cabinet post. Two years later Hazel Johnson (1927–2011) became the first African-American woman promoted to the rank of general in the U.S. Army, while in 1998 Lillian E. Fishburne (b. 1949) would become the first African-American woman promoted to the rank of rear admiral in the U.S. Navy.

In 1991 Sharon Pratt Kelly (b. 1944) won election as mayor of Washington, D.C., the first African-American woman to do so in any large U.S. city; and in 1992 Carol Moseley Braun (b. 1947) was elected to the Senate. Also in 1992, the astronaut Mae Jemison (b. 1956) became the first African-American woman in space, on the crew of the space shuttle *Endeavour.*

In the field of journalism, Bernadette Carey (b. 1939) was the first black female reporter at the *New York Times,* in 1965, covering fashion and society news. Three years later, Nancy Hicks (1946–2008) became the first to cover politics and current affairs for the *Times.* Charlayne Hunter-Gault (b. 1942), the first African-American woman reporter for *The New Yorker,* became the substitute anchor and reporter for the *MacNeil/Lehrer Report* in 1978. (She is also credited with persuading the *New York Times* to switch its usage from "Negro" to "black.") In 1994 Isabel Wilkerson (b. 1961), a former national correspondent and bureau chief at the *New York Times,* became the first black woman to receive the Pulitzer Prize for individual reporting.

Oprah Winfrey (b. 1954) at age nineteen became the first black woman (and the youngest person) to anchor the news at WTVF-TV in Nashville; she moved in 1984 from Baltimore to Chicago to host *AM Chicago. The Oprah Winfrey Show* launched a year later and was syndicated nationally a year after that, becoming the highest-rated TV talk show in history. In 1988 she created Harpo Studios, becoming only the third woman (after Mary Pickford and Lucille Ball) to own her own studio. And in 2008 she partnered with Discovery Communications to create the Oprah Winfrey Network (OWN). In 2003 she became the first African-American woman to appear on *Forbes*'s list of billionaires, and she is joined in the business world by an increasing number of remarkable leaders, including Ursula Burns (b. 1958), who, as chairman and CEO of Xerox, is the first African-American woman to head a Fortune 500 company.

There are few fields in this period, it seems, in which black women haven't either dominated or managed to shatter glass ceilings. In 2002 Serena Williams (b. 1981) won the first of seven ladies' singles titles at Wimbledon, and she and her sister Venus (b. 1980) won the ladies' doubles. That same year Halle Berry (b. 1966) became the first African-American woman to win an Oscar for best actress.

In 2005 Condoleezza Rice (b. 1954) succeeded Colin Powell as U.S. secretary of state. Four years later Susan Rice (b. 1964)—no relation—was confirmed as the U.S. ambassador to the United Nations. Each woman was the first African-American female to hold her respective position.

Perhaps the most symbolic event in this long (yet partial) list of honors accorded to African-American women was the awarding in 1999 of the Congressional Gold Medal to Rosa Parks (1913–2005), and the issuing in 2013 of a U.S. postage stamp in her honor. Making it all the more remarkable was the fact that the woman inhabiting the White House with her family when it was issued was the first African-American first lady. Michelle Obama (b. 1964) is not only one of the most popular women in the world today; she is using her influence to strengthen the family, support military families, and encourage all Americans to lead healthier lives.

Literature written by African-American women is fundamentally redefining the canon, an unprecedented achievement in black American history. Some scholars characterize the last four decades as the "woman's era" in the African-American literary tradition. It commenced with the publication in 1969 of Maya Angelou's (1928–2014) classic autobiography,

Recent Nobel laureate Toni Morrison, center, feted at the home of Maya Angelou, Winston-Salem, North Carolina, September 6, 1994.

I Know Why the Caged Bird Sings, which became an instant best seller and has remained extraordinarily popular in the four decades since.

The next year saw the publication of stunningly brilliant debut novels by Toni Morrison (b. 1931) and Alice Walker (b. 1944), *The Bluest Eye* and *The Third Life of Grange Copeland,* respectively, as well as the canon-defining anthology *The Black Woman,* edited by Toni Cade Bambara (1939–95). The publication of Morrison's *Sula* in 1973 signaled that a major author's talent was impressively evolving. That same year the National Black Feminist Organization was founded.

In many ways, 1975 was a hallmark year in the history of black women's writing. Gayl Jones (b. 1949), in her searching novel about slavery and rape, *Corregidora,* broke new ground in the ways in which black women narrate fictional versions of their history. The first formal dramatic critique of black male chauvinism and misogyny debuted in Berkeley under the curious title *For Colored Girls Who Have Considered Suicide When the Rainbow Is Enuf,* by Ntozake Shange (b. 1948); it took Broadway by storm the following year. In 1979, the year Octavia Butler (1947–2006) released in print her boldly experimental science-fiction, neo-slave narrative *Kindred*, Michele Wallace (b. 1952) published a searching critique of black sexism and misogyny, *Black Macho and the Myth of the Superwoman.* The book, which has been thought of as a sort of companion piece to Shange's play, generated a firestorm of angry reaction from black male writers and critics, including in a special issue of the *Black Scholar* magazine. But a subject that had long been treated as a taboo—intraracial sexism, especially in the civil rights movement and the black power era—had been opened to debate and would continue to be debated for the remainder of the century and beyond.

In one of the most important contributions to African-American canon formation, Alice Walker traced her line of formal descent from Zora Neale Hurston. In two essays published in *Ms.* magazine, "In Search of Our Mothers' Gardens" in 1974 and "In Search of Zora Neale Hurston" in 1975, she redefined the concept of African-American women's literary ancestry. Walker would go on in 1983 to win both the Pulitzer Prize and the National Book Award for her stunningly original novel *The Color Purple,* a formal signifying riff upon Hurston's *Their Eyes Were Watching God* (1937).

Even the first major film by Spike Lee (b. 1957), *She's Gotta Have It,* which won an award at the Cannes Film Festival in 1986, reflected the force of black women's literary and artistic movement through its depiction of the rigorous independence of protagonist Nola Darling, portrayed by actress Tracy Camilla Johns (b. 1963). In 1991 *Daughters of the Dust*—the first nationally released feature film directed by an African-American woman, Julie Dash (b. 1952)—did so as well.

But 1993 stands as the banner year in the history of black women's writing. On January 20 Maya Angelou gave a powerful reading of her poem "On the Pulse of Morning" at the first inauguration of President William Jefferson Clinton. Poet Rita Dove (b. 1952) became U.S. poet laureate. And on October 7, Toni Morrison became the first African American to win the Nobel Prize for Literature. Nine years later Suzan-Lori Parks (b. 1963) would become the first African-American woman to win the Pulitzer Prize for drama, for *Topdog/Underdog*.

This era of black women's writing, characterized by a remarkable degree of both creativity and productivity, has amounted to its own literary renaissance, one with perhaps more lasting implications than even the Harlem Renaissance of the 1920s.

59

Who were the black passengers on the doomed *Titanic* voyage?

WHEN THE *Titanic* went down on April 15, 1912, African Americans mourned the dead but didn't think any of their own were among them. With stunning immediacy, the forces of discrimination, decadence, and disaster gave rise to two tall tales: one about the great boxer Jack Johnson, and the other about a mythical character, "Shine," supposedly the lone black passenger, who miraculously survived by swimming halfway across the Atlantic. Once Johnson's and Shine's tall tales hit the streets of Harlem, they inspired dozens of toasts and songs. They were wildly popular throughout the black community, almost like a joyful ritual of racial revenge.

But no one black at the time realized an honest-to-God *fact:* that one lone dark passenger had, in fact, actually been in the dark icy waters, tending to his family before the white man's "ten million dollar floating palace [sank] to the bottom of the sea," as the *Philadelphia Tribune* put it five days later. His *name* was there under readers' noses as they pored over lists of the missing printed in every major newspaper: Joseph Laroche. It sounded French, but it belonged to a black man who'd been returning home to this side of the Atlantic.

Laroche's white wife (who was pregnant with their third child) and two daughters had arrived with the rescued in New York City, unsure of what to do next: Should they journey on to Haiti, the land of Laroche's birth, or return to the only home they had ever known, France? It would take more than eighty years for their story to be made known.

Mademoiselle Louise Laroche became an honorary member of the *Titanic* Historical Society at its founding in 1963, but it was not until the

1990s, when a young historian named Edward Kamuda persuaded the researcher Olivier Mendez to call her, that the story of her black father was told. (Mendez published it in the *Titanic Commutator* in 1995.) In her mid-eighties, Louise would have only three more years to live. In that time, another historian, Judith Geller, would reach out to her to add Laroche's story to her 1998 book, *Titanic: Women and Children First*.[1]

Joseph Laroche was born in Cap-Haïtien, Haiti, on May 26, 1886. A precocious student from a well-to-do family with a desire to study engineering, he journeyed to France at fifteen with the Lord Bishop of Haiti. They settled in Beauvais, in northern France. During a visit to one of the monsignor's friends outside Paris, Laroche met and fell in love with Juliette Lafargue, the white daughter of a wine seller and widower in Villejuif, who agreed to let them marry once Joseph graduated.

Joseph and Juliette wed in March 1908. The harder part was finding work. "Although France is a pretty country with beautiful scenery, marvelous cities and nice people," Mendez wrote, "racial prejudice at that time could prevent someone from employing a young dark-skinned man. Joseph did find work, but his employers made excuses that he was young and inexperienced and paid him poorly."[2]

Children followed: a daughter, Simonne, in February 1909 and a second daughter, Louise, premature and sickly, in July 1910. To provide for his growing family, Joseph resolved to return to Haiti, where, according to

The RMS *Titanic*. The passenger liner sunk with great loss of life in the North Atlantic on April 15, 1912.

Geller, his uncle had become president. (Geller doesn't name him, but others suggest it was Dessalines M. Cincinnatus Leconte.) When the Laroches discovered a third child was on the way in March 1912, they sped up their plans.

Joseph's mother in Haiti treated them to the tickets. They had initially planned to travel on the ship *La France,* scheduled to set sail from Le Havre on April 20, but when they found out about its family-unfriendly policies (children couldn't dine with their parents), they exchanged their tickets for second-class tickets on the RMS *Titanic,* a British vessel due to pick up passengers in Cherbourg on April 10.

To get to the *Titanic*—it was too big to dock—the Laroches, with 270 other passengers, took the ship *Nomadic* at Passe de l'Ouest. "If you could see this monster, our tender looked like a fly compared to her," Juliette wrote her father the next day. "The arrangements could not be more comfortable. We have two bunks in our cabin, and the two babies sleep on a sofa that converts into a bed. One is at the head, the other at the bottom."

That didn't mean *Titanic* was discrimination-free, Geller writes. One woman on board took the Laroche children for Japanese. Nevertheless, Juliette presented a sunny picture to her father. "The sea is very smooth, the weather is wonderful. If you could see how big this ship is! One can hardly find the way back to one's cabin in the number of corridors."

All that changed on the night of April 14, when the *Titanic* crashed into an Atlantic iceberg. In the panic, Mendez writes, "Joseph put everything valuable, money and jewels in his pockets. Unable to understand, Juliette let Joseph, who spoke English fluently, lead her to the lifeboats."

There were only sixteen lifeboats aboard the *Titanic,* so while Laroche ensured that his wife and children made it onto number ten, according to Geller, Joseph remained behind with the men. He would never be seen again.

His family was rescued by the *Carpathia* (a fact noted in the *New York Times* coverage on April 28, 1912), where, Geller notes, Juliette resorted to using dinner napkins for the girls' diapers. Arriving in New York City on April 18, they were taken to St. Vincent's Hospital, but while the staff could warm the Laroches' feet, they could not mend their hearts. Choosing against continuing on to Haiti, Juliette overcame what was surely a terrible fear of sailing again and took her girls back to France, aboard the *Chicago,* arriving in May 1912. That December, she gave birth to her and her late husband's third child, a son, whom she named Joseph Jr.

As World War I swept over France, Juliette's father was no longer able to support the family on his wine business alone, so heeding his advice, Juliette sued the White Star Line and in 1918 received a settlement of 150,000 francs, enough to open a small cloth-and-crafts business in the house. Two years later Joseph's mother visited from Haiti, Mendez writes, but apparently was so upset to discover that her grandchildren were decidedly French, she departed, never to see them again.

The world might have learned Joseph Laroche's story sooner, but in 1932 Juliette refused an interviewer's request. Her two girls never married. Of the three survivors, Simonne died first, in 1973. Juliette, by then paralyzed on one side, lived another seven years. Her grave, for posterity, says, "Juliette Laroche 1889–1980, wife of Joseph Laroche, lost at sea on RMS Titanic, April 15th 1912." In 1998 Louise followed them, the last French survivor of the *Titanic*. Joseph Jr., shielded in his mother's womb during the foundering, married in 1945, and he and his wife, Claudine, had three children before he died in 1987.

The facts were there all along but were not known overseas until the *Titanic* Historical Society published Mendez's account of Louise Laroche's story in 1995, followed by Geller's history three years later. Not long afterward a massive *Titanic* exhibit at the Chicago Museum of Science and Industry sparked a June 2000 article in *Ebony* magazine by Zondra Hughes, titled "What Happened to the Only Black Family on the *Titanic*?"

A woman reading it in a California salon was startled to notice the resemblance between Joseph Laroche, in a 1910 picture with his wife and children, and her own husband, Robert Richard. Richard's daughter, Marjorie Alberts, set out on her own genealogical search. Along the way, she learned the identity of Joseph's father (her ancestor, too), Henri Laroche, a cobbler in Haiti. "For me, the real love story is between Joseph and Juliette," said Alberts's cousin Christine LeBrun.[3] By the centennial of the *Titanic* disaster in 2012, there was a book of historical fiction based on Laroche's life, an opera, a play, and even talk of a screenplay.

"It is strange that nowhere in the copious 1912 press descriptions of the ship and the interviews with the survivors was the presence of a black family among the passengers ever mentioned," Geller writes, especially given "the keenness of the passengers and crew to take pot shots at other ethnic groups." Now, thanks to historians like her, it's out there, and black Americans are embracing their Haitian brother.

60

Which former slave became a deputy U.S. marshal and a renowned symbol of law and order in the Wild West?

BASS REEVES WAS BORN a slave in Crawford County, Alabama, most likely in July 1838.[1] His owner was William S. Reeves, a white war veteran and legislator who decamped to North Texas when Reeves was eight. William Reeves refused to teach young Bass to read the Bible, but he did let him learn the ways of the gun.

During the Civil War, Bass Reeves, in his early twenties, accompanied his owner's son, Col. George Reeves of the Eleventh Texas Cavalry Regiment, on the Confederate side (a fact Bass later used to put whites at ease). At some point, Bass fled into Indian Territory, where he became so immersed in Native American culture that he learned to speak Muscogee. In 1870, married with four kids, he moved to Van Buren, Arkansas, making his way as a farmhand, horse breeder, and territory scout and tracker. By the census of 1880, he and his wife, Jennie, had eight children between the ages of two and sixteen, with more to follow.

The turning point in Bass Reeves's life was the arrival of Judge Isaac C. Parker in Van Buren. Parker, a two-term U.S. congressman from Missouri, was tasked with overseeing the federal district court in western Arkansas. Its base was Fort Smith, a few miles from Reeves's house. Judge Parker's jurisdiction covered some 75,000 square miles, including the Indian Territory (present-day Oklahoma).

To police it, he ordered his marshal to hire two hundred deputies, though, according to a National Park Service historian, there were never more than forty to fifty deputies working at any given time. Bass Reeves was one of those men, and but for a couple of interruptions, he would serve for thirty-two years in a career that tracked—and in many ways enabled—the evolution of the western frontier from territory to statehood.

Judge Parker presided over the district court—known throughout the territory as "Hell on the Border"—from 1875 to 1896. It was open six days a week, and of the 13,500 cases that came before him, 8,500 ended up as convictions, including 79 hangings (of 30 whites, 26 Indians, and 23 blacks). Eighty-five percent of the crime in the district occurred in the Indian Territory, where Bass Reeves was an expert. During the Parker era, sixty-five deputy marshals were killed in the line of duty, while in his entire career, Reeves, despite numerous attempts on his life, suffered only one shot to the knee.

But how had African Americans gained a presence in the Indian Territory? Starting in the late eighteenth century, Native Americans in the South, like whites, had owned slaves.[2] When the U.S. government "removed" the five so-called civilized nations (Cherokee, Choctaw, Chickasaw, Creek, and Seminole) to the West in the 1830s, they took their slaves with them, so that "when the Civil War erupted in 1861, more than eight thousand blacks were enslaved in Indian Territory." In fact, one of the reasons the five tribes were called "civilized" was that they owned black slaves.

Enslaved people accounted for "14 percent of the population" of the Indian Territory. Not until after the Civil War did emancipation arrive for some of those slaves. In fact, as late as 1885, the governor of the Chickasaw was still protesting demands that they free their black slaves. A key distinction in the Indian Territory was between blacks who were native "Indian Freedmen" and those who had moved in from the United States as "State Negroes."

Judge Parker needed Reeves as a go-between in the territory, but more than that, he respected Reeves and in hiring him as a deputy signaled that he "would be in a position . . . to show the lawful as well as the lawless that a black man was the equal of any other law enforcement officer on the frontier."

Reeves's "outfit," in his travels, commonly featured a posse man, guard, and cook who manned the wagon (which would be filled with prisoners on the return trip to Fort Smith) while Reeves searched the perimeter on horseback. His favorite weapon was the Winchester rifle, but he also "wore [a pair of six-shooters] butts forward for a cross handed draw," wrote Charles W. Mooney in a Shawnee, Oklahoma, newspaper. Over the course of his career, Reeves estimated he'd made more than three thousand arrests, and it wasn't uncommon for him to haul seventeen people at a time over great distances to Judge Parker's court.

"Among the numerous deputy marshals that have ridden for the Paris (Texas), Fort Smith (Arkansas) and Indian Territory courts none have met with more hairbreadth escapes or have effected more hazardous arrests than Bass Reeves," D. C. Gideon related in 1901. "Several 'bad men' have gone to their long home for refusing to halt when commanded to by Bass." There were fourteen known Reeves killings, and probably more, since others may have gone underreported because of Reeves's race.

The Winchester was just one of Deputy Marshal Reeves's tools. He was also "a master of disguise," Charles Mooney wrote, and would wend his way into his targets' company dressed, for instance, as an indigent or a farmer before slapping the cuffs on. He profited from outlaws, collecting fees and rewards by outmanning and outsmarting them.

In one case, Reeves used even his illiteracy to his advantage by tricking two Texas outlaws into reading a letter for him just long enough for Reeves to throttle one, draw his gun on the other, and say, "Son of a bitch,

Bass Reeves, former slave and U.S. deputy marshal, served long and ably as a peace officer in the Indian Territory.

61

Who were the black people killed in the raid on Harpers Ferry?

FREE BLACK MEN PARTICIPATED in John Brown's famous raid on the arsenal at Harpers Ferry, Virginia, launched on October 16, 1859. But any discussion of them should begin with the most important one who *wasn't* there: Frederick Douglass. Douglass and Brown had met in Springfield, Massachusetts, a decade before. Though they couldn't have looked more different, Douglass, Brown, and their closest compatriots shared "black hearts" in their interracial alliances.[1] In Douglass's own words, Brown, "though a white gentleman," was "in sympathy, a black man, and . . . as deeply interested in our cause, as though his own soul had been pierced by the iron of slavery."[2]

Weeks before Brown was to launch his raid of liberation, he and Douglass rendezvoused for a historic war council at a quarry in southern Pennsylvania. He explained his reason for striking Harpers Ferry: it was home to one of the most productive federal arsenals in the country. "I want you for a special purpose," Brown said. "When I strike, the bees will begin to swarm, and I shall want you to help hive them."[3] But Douglass thought Brown's plot was implausible and refused to help.

In the aftermath, Douglass nonetheless drew suspicion for his suspected complicity in the planning of the raid. Investigators found a letter from Douglass in Brown's possession, and though it was two years old and silent on Harpers Ferry, the governor of Virginia enlisted the support of the Buchanan administration to track him down on charges of "murder, robbery, and inciting servile insurrection." Not until the following June, in 1860, did Virginia's governor "drop the charges against him," the historian John Stauffer writes. For a time, he had been "the most wanted man in America."[4]

RIP HEYWARD SHEPHERD

While abolitionists like Douglass were sympathetic to Brown's ultimate goal, they were skeptical of the mission itself, and so on the eve of the raid, he had been able to assemble a force of only twenty-two, including himself and five black men.

On the night of October 16, 1859, as they moved into Harpers Ferry (less than seventy miles west of Baltimore and Washington, D.C.), the people of the town had no idea what was about to happen.

Heyward Shepherd was a baggage master working the overnight shift at the train depot in Harpers Ferry. He must have heard the B&O express train out of Wheeling, Virginia (now West Virginia), slowing down on the Potomac Bridge—it was about to be ambushed by a group of Brown's raiders, including Brown's son, Oliver. The train's white conductor, Andrew Phelps, stepped out with four others to see what was going on. Once inside

The final moments of John Brown's raid at Harpers Ferry. Wood engraving, *Frank Leslie's Illustrated Newspaper,* November 5, 1859.

the covered portion of the railroad bridge, Phelps spotted the raiders' rifle ends. Then suddenly one of his men's lanterns was snuffed out, and Phelps heard a shout, "Stand and deliver!"

The next thing Phelps knew, "a tall black man staggered out from the covered bridge, crying, 'I am shot,'" as the historian Tony Horwitz writes. It was Shepherd. Horwitz notes the irony that "John Brown's campaign to liberate slaves had claimed as its first casualty a free black man, shot down while defying the orders of armed whites." In the dark, no one could be sure who had shot Shepherd, although just "hours after," one of Brown's men, Steward (or Stewart) Taylor, was discovered "by the bridge, pale and trembling [saying] he had shot a man and believed he had killed him."[5]

John Brown had had no intention of shooting anyone on the railroad or in the town. What he did want was to seize the arsenal's store of weapons and to spread the word to the slaves in the region that the day of emancipation—indeed, Armageddon—was at hand. He imagined that they would flee their plantations and become his black army. To this end, he even allowed Phelps's train to continue on its way to Baltimore in hopes the message would get out to the city's large free black population, whom he expected to rally to his side at Harpers Ferry. That decision backfired: the conductor's cable messages made it up the chain to the War Department and ultimately to President James Buchanan, who ordered in the marines under Col. Robert E. Lee. The rest, as they say, is history.

Sadly, we know little about Shepherd's life before the raid, other than that he was reportedly married, had several children, and owned property in the area. The historian Joseph Barry put Shepherd at forty-four and said he was "very black" and "uncommonly tall."[6]

Brown's Black Men

Long before Harpers Ferry, John Brown was accustomed to working with black men on unusually equal terms. Besides his friendship with Frederick Douglass, he had chosen to live near the free black community of Timbucto in the Adirondack Mountains of New York. He recruited five black men to join his raid, four free and one a fugitive slave. Among the free men was John A. Copeland, a twenty-three-year-old Oberlin College student who had once been imprisoned for helping to rescue a runaway slave, John

Price. A second free man was Copeland's uncle, Lewis S. Leary, a harness maker, also from Oberlin, whose wife eventually had a grandson we know as the poet Langston Hughes. Leary would be shot during the raid; Copeland, who saw it, apparently hid in rocks down by the river, only to be discovered by a group of white men who would have lynched him had not John Starry, the doctor who tended to Heyward Shepherd, intervened and had him jailed instead.

The third free black man—and the one whose situation was most tragic—was Dangerfield Newby. At about forty years old, he was the oldest of Brown's recruits, the son of a former slave and her master. His own wife and seven children were being held in slavery about fifty-three miles from Harpers Ferry in Brentsville, Virginia. He was on a mission to rescue them.[7]

The fourth black man in Brown's raid was Shields Green (aka "Emperor"). He was a fugitive slave who had left his son in South Carolina en route to Canada, then returned to the United States, where he was present at that historic war council between Frederick Douglass and John Brown. Green would pay for his decision to fight with his execution, alongside Copeland and two others, on December 16, 1859.[8]

The fifth and last of Brown's free black men was Osborne P. Anderson, the son of a free black father and a white mother who had moved from Pennsylvania to Canada for fear of being kidnapped by slave catchers following the passage of the Fugitive Slave Act of 1850. There, in 1858, Anderson attended the Chatham Conference, a secret constitutional convention to organize a government for the revolutionary black state that John Brown intended to form in southern Appalachia. Anderson was the sole survivor from Brown's main raiding party at Harpers Ferry, and once he made it back to Canada, he would write his account of the raid, *A Voice from Harper's Ferry*.[9]

In addition to these men and Shepherd, three slaves lost their lives during or after the Harpers Ferry raid, according to Horwitz: a coachman Jim (Washington), by drowning; Ben (Allstadt), in Charlestown prison; and Ben's mother, Ary, who had tended to him.

In every way, tactically, the raid was a failure. In all, seventeen raiders were captured or killed, including thirteen whites (Brown, plus his two sons, Oliver and Watson, among them) and the four black rebels (Newby, Leary, Green, and Copeland). Brown and his men killed five, four white men plus Shepherd (nine others were wounded), according to the Senate Select Committee Report.

John Brown was captured, tried, found guilty of treason, and executed by hanging in Charles Town, Virginia (now West Virginia), on December 2, 1859. His legend only grew, however, and by the time the Civil War erupted in 1861, his name lived on in song.

62

What myth of eternal youth in Africa inspired Europeans for centuries?

DATING ALL THE WAY BACK to the fifth century BCE, the fountain of youth was believed to be in Ethiopia. Back then, the First Persian Empire touched three continents, but Ethiopia resisted invasion. In his *History,* the first grand historical narrative (440 BCE), Herodotus recounted how the king of Ethiopia, protective of his lands, scoffed at the average life span of a Persian—eighty. "Most" of his people, "the long-lived Ethiopians . . . lived to be a hundred and twenty years old, while some even went beyond that age." When the king's visitors "showed wonder at the number of the years,

> he led them to a fountain, wherein when they had washed, they found their flesh all glossy and sleek, as if they had bathed in oil—and a scent came from the spring like that of violets. The water was so weak, they said, that nothing would float in it, neither wood, nor any lighter substance, but all went to the bottom. If the account of this fountain be true, it would be their constant use of the water from it which makes them so long-lived.[1]

In the twelfth century, the arrival in European courts of the so-called Letter of Prester John ignited a centuries-long search for a mysterious African king and his kingdom unrivaled in its geographic scope. The distinguished historian Malcolm Letts believed the story of Prester John had been transmitted orally well before his letter, so that when the letter arrived in Europe, witnesses were ready to believe it.[2]

By 1122 a representative from Prester John was said to have visited the pope from "India." ("India" often referred to the Horn of Africa.) Then, around 1157, Otto, Bishop of Freising in Germany, finished his *Historia de duabus civitatibus* (History of the Two Cities). A decade earlier, he wrote, he had observed a meeting between Pope Eugene III and Bishop Hugh of Jabala, Syria. In pressing for another crusade, the bishop had referred to "Presbyter Iohannes" as the Christian king who had scored a decisive vic-

EL PRESTE JUAN

EMPERADOR DE LOS ABISINIOS.

Pierre-Antoine Demachy. *El Preste Juan, Emperador de los Abisinios.* Color print, second half of the seventeenth century.

tory against his Persian, Median, and Assyrian rivals on the other side of the Tigris River. When "Presbyter Iohannes" had then tried to cross the Tigris into the Holy Land, his own horses had been stymied.

A letter attributed to Prester John landed on a Byzantine emperor's desk in 1165, then spread across Europe in an astonishing multitude of translations and reproductions in the mid- to late twelfth century. No scholar believes the "Letter of Prester John" was actually written by one of the kings of Ethiopia. The best current thinking is that it originated in western Europe and was, as Letts writes, a Latin tapestry of borrowed sources. But the myth of this African king was "irresistible," Letts concedes, because of its "miraculous powers" to conjure a distant world, cut off from Christian Europe. It soon "filled the early maps with monsters and fables, gave a new impulse to geographical discovery, brought fresh hope to Christendom and provided story-tellers with material which lasted for centuries."

The letter was addressed, without a date or return address, to the Byzantine emperor Manuel I Komnenos (1143–80), but it also reached Pope Alexander III and Frederick I. Its sender's full name was "Presbyter Johannes, *rex potentia et virtute dei et domini nostri Iesu Christi*."[3] The author made many fantastical boasts about his kingdom: it had peace without poverty, an abundance of wealth and precious stones, a sprawling palace, an invincible army, an array of ever-more-intriguing creatures, and a hierarchy in which seventy kings paid him tribute. "If indeed you can number the stars of heaven and sands of the sea," he wrote, "then you may calculate the extent of our dominion and power."

The letter was copied and recopied so many times and in so many languages that it eventually swelled to one hundred paragraphs with "various interpolations," making the original letter difficult to track down, Letts writes. And the more it was reprinted, the more it became "an early contribution to the literature of Utopias." By Letts's count, there were one hundred different manuscripts of the letter.

The legend of the Fountain of Youth in Ethiopia was blended into the Prester John letter as an interpolation, according to the historian Robert Silverberg, who reproduces a transcription from "a slightly later manuscript":

Whoever drinks of its water three times without having eaten will have no illness for thirty years; and when he has drunk of it, he will feel as

Kansas Colored Volunteer Infantry followed in August 1862 and distinguished itself in battle at Island Mound, Missouri, in October, two months before the Emancipation Proclamation went into effect. Each time the Lincoln administration withheld initial support, but change, out of military necessity, was clearly coming, whether the majority of whites wanted it or not.

Frederick Douglass penned editorials challenging the pervasive and paradoxical claims that black troops would prove cowardly or disloyal. "I am not so sure we could do much with the blacks," Lincoln himself told a group of antislavery ministers just nine days before issuing the preliminary Emancipation Proclamation. "If we were to arm them, I fear that in a few weeks the arms would be in the hands of the rebels." To neutralize such claims, Douglass invoked black soldiers' service in previous wars, as recorded in 1855 by the Boston African-American activist and historian William Cooper Nell.[3]

Douglass excerpted passages from Nell's book in *Douglass' Monthly* in August 1862 (the same month as the *second* Union defeat at Bull Run), including anecdotes of black soldiers at Bunker Hill, soldier slaves from Rhode Island, and the presence of one Prince Whipple, a general's aide, during the Crossing of the Delaware. "Colored men were good enough to fight under Washington," Douglass argued in a speech in Boston on February 5, 1862. "They are not good enough to fight under McClellan."

During the winter of 1862–63, the North grew increasingly dispirited by humiliating defeats it suffered at the hands of Confederate generals Lee, Jackson, and others. And as the prospect of a military draft loomed (and eventually came to pass in March 1863), even hardheaded racists had difficulty arguing that black men couldn't die just as well as white men.

The proclamation said:

> I, Abraham Lincoln, President of the United States, by virtue of the power in me vested as Commander-in-Chief, of the Army and Navy of the United States in time of actual armed rebellion against the authority and government of the United States, and as a fit and necessary war measure for suppressing said rebellion, do, on this first day of January, in the year of our Lord one thousand eight hundred and sixty-three . . . enjoin upon the people so declared to be free to abstain from all violence,

unless in necessary self-defence; and I recommend to them that, in all cases when allowed, they labor faithfully for reasonable wages.

And I further declare and make known, that such persons of suitable condition, will be received into the armed service of the United States to garrison forts, positions, stations, and other places, and to man vessels of all sorts in said service.

In other words, slaves could defend themselves if necessary and, if members of the armed services, shoot and kill white men on the other side. "A few years ago it was the custom, supported by public opinion, North and South, if a black man raised his hand against a white man, even in defence of his family or his life, it was considered a crime worthy of death," a jubilant Douglass told a crowd gathered at Shiloh Church in New York City a few months later. "Now, the government has given authority to these same black men to shoulder a musket, and go down and kill white rebels."[4]

As the mobilization began, Douglass transitioned from agitator to recruiter, working with Massachusetts governor John Andrew and his deputy, Maj. George Stearns, a white abolitionist who, like Douglass, had been a backer of John Brown. Their aim: to fill the ranks of the Fifty-fourth Massachusetts Regiment.

While Douglass and other black recruiters deserve credit for their efforts in the North, the majority of the 179,000 black soldiers who served in the Union Army came from the South. Their presence was indispensable, but it also made Confederate soldiers fight harder and more cruelly. The Confederate secretary of war and Congress authorized their men to treat black regiments as if the soldiers and their white officers were waging a slave insurrection no different from Nat Turner's or John Brown's. African-American soldiers' service was all the more remarkable given the discrimination they faced from their own side, including restrictions on the commissioning of black officers and requirements that they perform the hardest and most laborious of camp duties.

The War Department, acting on a technicality, moved to pay its black soldiers ten dollars a month (minus three for uniforms) while paying white soldiers thirteen without the deduction. Many who'd already enlisted refused to accept less than their fair share, but until the matter was addressed, their families suffered. At the urging of Major Stearns, Douglass took his grievances to Washington, where on August 10, 1863, he met with Secretary of War Stanton, then Lincoln.

But it wasn't until June 1864 that Congress finally corrected the unequal pay issue, making it retroactive to January 1, 1864. Though Douglass never gave Lincoln a complete pass for his "unsurpassed . . . devotion to the white race," as he put it, he credited the president for his personal and political growth. That growth included supporting at least limited voting rights for black men who had fought in the war, and for a few more "intelligent Negroes," as Lincoln curiously put it in the last speech he ever delivered, on April 11, 1865. Lincoln's change of heart about the right to vote was prompted, in large measure, by the bravery and battlefield successes of the same black soldiers whose courage and talent he had once doubted.

64

Which black man engaged a Founding Father in a debate about racial equality?

MUCH OF WHAT WE KNOW about Benjamin Banneker's life comes from a posthumous biography, *Banneker: The Afric-American Astronomer* (1884), written by his white neighbor and friend's daughter, Martha Ellicott Tyson.[1] In 1737 Robert Banneker, Benjamin's father, purchased one hundred acres of farmland in Oella, Maryland, in exchange for tobacco. As young Benjamin grew, his grandmother taught him to read the Bible. He also may have attended a small, integrated school under a Quaker's tutelage. Benjamin had an affinity for math and science, and on the farm he could apply it.

In 1753 a timely visitor arrived there: the trader Joseph Levi entrusted Benjamin with the care of his pocket watch (for reasons unclear). After taking the watch apart and reassembling it, Benjamin carved out his own timepiece—a clock—from wood and installed a striking mechanism with a penknife. It took him two years to perfect, but for the rest of his life, it worked.

Joel Rogers claimed that Banneker's was the "first striking clock in America," but Tyson never made such a claim, only that, given where he lived—a farm in colonial Maryland (she said "wilderness")—he had had no model from which to work. By the 1750s, clock-making already had a history in America: Thomas Nash of New Haven made one in the mid-1600s, as did Abel Cottey of Philadelphia around 1707.[2] While Banneker's may not have been the *first* clock in America, it's possible it was one of the *best*. As Tyson wrote, "It was considered from the regularity of its movements, and also from being the unassisted production of a black man, one of the curiosities of that wild region."

After Robert Banneker's death in 1759, Benjamin assumed responsibility for the family farm, a commitment that took time away from his study.[3] This began to change when Banneker struck up a friendship with a prominent Quaker family, the Ellicotts. During the upheaval of the American Revolution (1775–83), they allowed him to borrow their books and study the inner workings of their flour mill.

Banneker was taken with a tall case-clock that Joseph Ellicott had made: it had three dials for telling time, as well as devices for showing the moon phases, and it played twenty-four different musical tunes. Despite its beauty, Ellicott's clock did not work properly. Banneker was given permission to work on it. He fixed it in three months.[4]

Meanwhile, in New York City, President Washington had plans to

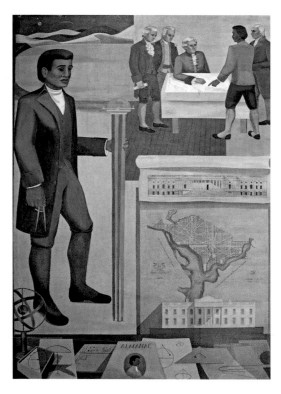

Benjamin Banneker—
architect, surveyor, scientist,
almanac compiler.

improve the seat of government. A compromise had been reached to situate the capital on public lands overlapping Maryland and Virginia. For surveying it, Washington commissioned Maj. Andrew Ellicott (Joseph's son), who took Banneker as his principal assistant. The two men began their journey there on February 7, 1791.

As with Banneker's clock, an amazing story swirls around those first surveys of what would become Washington, D.C. When the architect Pierre L'Enfant grew angry with the Washington administration, he withheld the only existing plan for the city. All would have been lost to history, runs the tale, had Banneker not miraculously re-created it from memory. According to historians at the Smithsonian, however, by the time L'Enfant abandoned the project, the Washington administration had drawn up its own plan based on L'Enfant's, without giving him credit.[5] Banneker may not have saved Washington the city from memory, but the fact that a largely self-taught black man worked as a surveyor's assistant for the Washington administration is astonishing, considering that four out of the first five U.S. presidents were slave owners.

After Ellicott and Banneker completed their work, Banneker returned to Maryland to pursue another dream: publishing an almanac. The primary purpose of an almanac back then was to provide readers (mainly farmers) with a calendar and compendium of astronomical information and weather predictions. Among the more popular almanacs in Banneker's America was Benjamin Franklin's *Poor Richard's Almanack,* launched in 1732.

Rejected by three different publishers, Banneker almost gave up until his idea attracted attention from Pennsylvania abolitionists, who saw in the project an opportunity to present a powerful argument against slavery in the form of a free and quite literate black man. Banneker's first almanac, published in 1792, was reviewed and approved by the scientist David Rittenhouse, the first director of the U.S. Mint.

In his 1781 *Notes on the State of Virginia* (in which he praised David Rittenhouse as a genius), Thomas Jefferson stated that "the blacks, whether originally a distinct race, or made distinct by time and circumstances, are inferior to the whites in the endowments both of body and mind." He went on to argue that "this unfortunate difference of color, and perhaps of faculty, is a powerful obstacle to the emancipation of these people."[6]

Despite his desire to be regarded for his scientific accomplishments, a perturbed Banneker could not avoid the raging debates over race and slavery. In August 1791 Banneker sent Jefferson an advance copy of his almanac, with a letter urging the then secretary of state to "embrace every opportunity, to eradicate that train of absurd and false ideas and opinion, which so generally prevails with respect to us." Banneker reminded the sage of Monticello of his authorship of the American creed, "We hold these truths to be self-evident, that all men are created equal," only to point out his contradictory actions: "detaining by fraud and violence so numerous a part of my brethren, under groaning captivity and cruel oppression," so "that you [Jefferson] should at the same time be found guilty of that most criminal act, which you professedly detested in others, with respect to yourselves." Banneker was no stranger to powerful white men, but these were incredibly direct words to put to the writer of the Declaration of Independence. He was accusing Jefferson of failing to live up to his own expressed ideals.

Jefferson responded noncommittally on August 30, 1791, writing, "No body wishes more than I do, to see such proofs as you exhibit, that nature has given to our black brethren talents equal to those of the other colors of men; and that the appearance of the want of them, is owing merely to the degraded condition of their existence, both in Africa and America."[7]

Jefferson promised to send Banneker's almanac to one of his contacts in Paris. Privately, however, in a separate letter, he gave a more negative assessment, confiding to his friend Joel Barlow in 1809, "We know he [Banneker] had spherical geometry enough to make almanacs, but not without the suspicion of aid from Ellicott, who was his neighbor and friend, and never missed an opportunity of puffing him. I have a long letter from Banneker, which shows him to have a mind of very common stature indeed."[8]

In a July 4, 1791, address attacking modern slaveholders, the white abolitionist and doctor George Buchanan listed Banneker, "the Maryland astronomer," as an example of why "Africans, whom you despise, whom you inhumanly treat as brutes, and whom you unlawfully subject to slavery, with the tyrannizing hands of Despots, are equally capable of improvements with yourselves."[9] Banneker, with his passion for experimentation, had become a data point in a much larger equation: freedom itself.

In his 1793 edition of the almanac, Banneker published his exchange with Jefferson. He continued publishing his almanacs until 1797, and in his old age, he worked out an arrangement with the Ellicott family to remain in his home and receive periodic cash payments in exchange for bequeathing his land to them after his death. He passed away on October 9, 1806.

———
65
———

How were Martin Luther King, Jr., and Nelson Mandela linked?

APARTHEID WAS A VIOLENT, degrading system of racial segregation that South Africa's white minority–run government implemented long before anyone had even heard of Martin Luther King, Jr. But the parallels between the struggle he eventually led in America in the 1960s and those of some 25 million black South Africans in the 1980s were unmistakable: de facto and de jure segregation as a legal and living reality in every imaginable sphere, including restrictions on black home ownership (whites owned 80 to 90 percent of the land), on access to schooling and jobs, and on the most fundamental human rights: whom a black person could love and marry, where he could travel, and how he could defend himself in and out of court. If anything, apartheid was even more extreme than Jim Crow, even though black South Africans accounted for 75 percent of the country's population.

The champion of their decades-old struggle was Nelson Mandela (1918–2013). In 1962 he was arrested, initially on charges of incitement and of leaving the country without a passport. At one point, in April 1963, Mandela and King were both in jail at the same time: Mandela, a lawyer, in Pretoria; and King, a Baptist preacher, in Birmingham. Both, too, were suspected of Communist ties, real or imagined.

But there were important differences as well. While King went free after ten days behind bars, in May 1963 Mandela was transferred to the prison on Robben Island, and the following year his original five-year sentence was extended to *life* on the additional charge of sabotage.

———

Just as King had his Coretta, Mandela had his Winnie. Mandela also had Bishop Desmond Tutu (b. 1931), the charismatic Anglican leader of the archdiocese of Johannesburg, a fellow black South African. For two weeks in January 1986, Bishop Tutu captured Americans' attention during a whirlwind twelve-city tour to raise awareness and funds for the cause.

Two years before, apartheid had rarely been front-page news in America; by 1986 it was becoming a lead story. The Free South Africa Movement had emerged to turn eyes (and feet) toward a direct appeal to U.S. institutions—corporations and universities alike—to divest their financial ties from South Africa. In September 1985 the Reagan administration had renewed limited sanctions on South Africa, but to movement leaders' special frustration, it had also aligned itself with corporate titans doing everything they could to lobby against stricter measures. Tutu's visit was perfectly timed for rallying the troops.

On January 8, Bishop Tutu arrived in the nation's capital. He seemed to take special delight in tweaking the Reagan administration for its reluctance, pointing out that while the administration was aggressively pushing sanctions on the leftist government in Nicaragua, it was also pursuing a policy of "constructive engagement" in South Africa. If only the U.S. president would be as consistent in opposing racial segregation abroad as he was in fighting Communism, Tutu declared, "Voila! . . . Apartheid would be over in next to no time."[1]

He visited the South African Embassy, site of a yearlong protest campaign against apartheid. Standing on an impromptu stage in the bitter cold, striking in his religious garb, he described the South African regime as "a vicious, immoral, un-Christian and totally evil system."[2] Applauding those present, he graciously took possession of a "truckload" of signatures expressing solidarity with his people. Twelve protesters (including the singers Peter, Paul and Mary) were arrested at the embassy that day, while D.C. mayor Marion Barry announced legislation to rename that portion of Washington Avenue "Nelson and Winnie Mandela Avenue."

Coretta Scott King may not have had the power to legislate U.S. policy on South Africa, but as head of the King Center in Atlanta, she could give Tutu a platform. She invited him to her late husband's church, Ebenezer Baptist, to preach and receive an award that would dramatically link King's memory to the Free South Africa Movement being waged two decades after his assassination.

Obviously aware of the approaching holiday, the bishop wrapped him-

Nelson Mandela at the time
of the Treason Trial, 1956. In
his autobiography, *Long Walk
to Freedom,* he titled this image
"Tense Times."

self in the King image. At a rally in Detroit on what would have been
Dr. King's fifty-seventh birthday, he stood with Rosa Parks. In New York
City, he preached at St. Mark's Church, citing King's final speech, saying that he too "had been to the mountain top and . . . seen the promised
land." In California, he addressed a throng of students in San Diego and
a fund-raiser of the Hollywood elite, including Sidney Poitier, who had
attended the March on Washington with King.[3]

At last the man, the memory, and the message came together on Martin
Luther King, Jr. Day weekend in Atlanta. That first national King holiday
wasn't a single-day celebration but *nine* days of events, including a half-
million-strong parade through the city's streets, a candlelight vigil, and a
conference specifically targeting South African apartheid. But it was at the
three-hour-long ecumenical service held on January 19 at Ebenezer Baptist
Church, the very church where Dr. King and his father had once ministered, that Tutu's anti-apartheid message was in fullest force.

When it was Tutu's turn to speak, he made clear that if nothing changed back home, he was prepared to lead a full-on protest that spring. He invoked images particularly poignant to those onstage and in the pews who had survived the civil rights movement's bloodiest moments. "Our people are peaceful to a fault," Tutu said. "We are stupid, for we keep going up against an intransigent government. They use tear gas, bullets, dogs and whips." Though Tutu had, like King, won a Nobel Peace Prize (in 1984), he was careful not to compare himself to the martyr in whose name all had gathered. "I do not belong in the same league with Dr. Martin Luther King Jr." For Vice President George H. W. Bush, captive on the Ebenezer stage with Tutu, he had these general words: "When we are free, we want to be able to say the leaders of the free world were on our side."

To Bush's great credit, he acted with remarkable dignity and class, and when his turn came, he spoke clearly. "In this sacred place, I call again for the end to apartheid," adding that he hoped that "South African leaders will be able to find the same moral courage" as Dr. King.[4] Coretta Scott King bestowed on Tutu the King Center's Nonviolent Peace Prize (an award that had first been given out in 1973, to Congressman Andrew Young), leaving little doubt about where she, the King family, or the King Center stood.

By the end of January 1986, shortly after Tutu's visit to the United States, the South African government, under President P. W. Botha, hinted at a new openness to the possibility of releasing Mandela. In remarks to the South African Parliament in Cape Town on January 31, Botha indicated a willingness to ease up, gradually, on certain apartheid measures. In response, Reagan State Department spokesman Bernard Kalb told the press, "We welcome the South African government's suggestion that it might release Nelson Mandela on humanitarian grounds, a step that could help break the stalemate in South Africa and lead to negotiations that so many have been hoping for."[5]

Behind the scenes, a cadre of leading American CEOs pressed the Botha government to make good on its offer. Reality was quickly setting in that the Free South Africa Movement wasn't going away anytime soon. U.S. companies were now facing the "twin pressures" of "unrest" in South Africa and "political harassment at home."[6] While only seven U.S. companies had divested in 1984, by February 1986 that number had risen to twenty-eight companies of note, not to mention the sixteen U.S. states and fifty-six cities that had passed divestment laws.

Most dramatically, in October 1986, Congress overrode President Reagan's veto of new and much tougher sanctions against the South African government. Moreover, U.S. banks refused to roll over $14 billion in loans to South Africa. The fate of apartheid was just about sealed. Four years later Nelson Mandela was released after twenty-seven years in prison. In 1994 he was elected president of the new South Africa.

Shortly after King's assassination in 1968, Coretta told Mike Wallace of *60 Minutes* that "unearned suffering was redemptive." Now, with the first Martin Luther King, Jr. Day on the books, a credit to her many years of lobbying, she saw that redemption bear fruit not only at home but an ocean away.

66

Did Lincoln really free the slaves?

THE EMANCIPATION PROCLAMATION, despite its enormous symbolic significance, did *not* abolish the institution of slavery in the United States. Rather, it "freed" any slave in the Confederate states who could manage to flee their plantation and make their way to Union lines. Historians estimate that as many as half a million black people managed to do so. To put this number into a bit of perspective, in 1860 there were about 3.9 million enslaved African Americans, which means that by the end of the Civil War, some 3.4 million black people remained in bondage, in spite of the Emancipation Proclamation. African Americans are free today because of the Thirteenth Amendment to the Constitution.

The Thirteenth Amendment was the high point of the American Civil War, fulfilling in the timeless book of law what President Abraham Lincoln had initiated only as a wartime measure in the Emancipation Proclamation two years before. As Lincoln himself would explain in his second inaugural address on March 4, 1865, the Thirteenth Amendment offered redemption for what many believed was the original sin of slavery. It is the only amendment in American history to be ratified with a president's signature on it.

The Thirteenth Amendment went well beyond the Emancipation Proclamation of 1863. It erased any lingering doubt that abolition would pass constitutional muster. (At the time, there was worry that the Supreme Court could strike down the Emancipation Proclamation as an abuse of executive power.) The amendment was to reach all the United States—not just the Confederacy—across generations, whereas the more modest

Abraham Lincoln during the Civil War in a photograph
by Anthony Berger, 1864.

Emancipation Proclamation, in Lincoln's telling, had been limited by perceptions that "it only aided those [slaves] who came into [Union] lines and
that it was inoperative as to those who did not give themselves up, or that it
would have no effect upon the children of the slaves born hereafter."

Unlike the Emancipation Proclamation, the words of the Thirteenth
Amendment were both sweeping and spare: "Neither Slavery nor involun-
tary servitude, except as a punishment for crime; whereof the party shall
have been duly convicted, shall exist within the United States, or any place
subject to their jurisdiction." Embracing it, Lincoln told those gathered
outside the White House to celebrate the signing of the amendment on
February 1, 1865, that "this amendment is a king's cure for all the evils. It
winds the whole thing up."

Remarkably, when the war began, the same President Lincoln had been
ready to sign an altogether different version of the Thirteenth Amendment. The earlier versions had little to do with the one that was finally
adopted. Though all addressed the issue of American slavery, they came

about at different times, in different Congresses, and under starkly different circumstances. The first was debated during the "secession winter" of 1860–61, those four months between Abraham Lincoln's election on November 6, 1860, and his inauguration on March 4, 1861.[1] During that time, seven states seceded, beginning with South Carolina on December 20 (Mississippi, Florida, Alabama, Georgia, Louisiana, and Texas followed). In Washington, D.C., members of Congress scrambled to find any shred of compromise in what appeared to be an uncompromising situation.

Today we have our various "gangs of six and eight" in Congress, but the secession winter Senate had its "Committee of Thirteen," organized on December 18, 1860 (just two days before South Carolina departed the Union), while Democratic president James Buchanan was still wringing his hands in the White House.[2] What came to be known as the "Crittenden Compromise" (for the committee member behind it, Senator John Crittenden of Kentucky) emerged in short order.[3] It was a package of proposals—a "grand bargain"—consisting of six constitutional amendments and four congressional regulations that aimed to revive and render permanent the old geographical boundary between free and slave territories in the Missouri Compromise of 1820, except this time that line would extend all the way to the Pacific Ocean, defying Lincoln's biblical maxim, "A house divided against itself cannot stand."

The Crittenden Compromise, responding to "serious and alarming dissensions" in the country, offered to make slavery of the "African race" explicitly and permanently part of the U.S. Constitution, so that no future Congress could ever undo it where it existed. Still, as compromises often go, it failed to attract support outside the political dead center. On the one hand, President Lincoln's Republican Party had campaigned for leaving slavery alone in the states where it already existed while blocking its extension further into the territories. So right away, the Republican members of the Committee voted against it.

On the other hand, the Crittenden Compromise stopped short of a full embrace of the *Dred Scott* decision. In his majority opinion for the Court in 1857, Chief Justice Roger B. Taney had ruled the Missouri Compromise unconstitutional as a violation of slave owners' property rights. The Crittenden Compromise would resurrect it. The two Deep Southerners on the committee didn't think the honorable John Crittenden had done nearly enough to protect their constituents' interests in the territories, so they refused to support his compromise, and it fell to defeat seven votes to six.[4]

As the winter rolled on, so did another potential thirteenth amendment—this time in the House. It was known as the Corwin Amendment, for Representative Thomas Corwin (R-OH), though as the historian Eric Foner points out, Lincoln's incoming secretary of state, William Seward, the former senator of New York, had "originally drafted" it.[5] The Corwin Amendment proposed a diluted version of the Crittenden pledge not to interfere with slavery in any state where it existed—essentially a reprint of the Republican Party platform of 1860: "No amendment shall be made to the Constitution which will authorize or give to Congress power to abolish or interfere, within any State, with the domestic institutions thereof, including that of persons held to labor or service by the laws of said State."

In other words, the Corwin Amendment would have been the anti–Thirteenth Amendment. Instead of abolishing slavery or even calling it out by name, it referred vaguely to "domestic institutions" and "persons held to labor or service," while attempting to close the door on any future amendment authorizing Congress to "abolish or interfere" with slavery in the states. While to us it reads like an outrageous sellout, it was, at the time, a perfect illustration of Republicans' calculating efforts to place responsibility for any pending war on the shoulders of secessionists while enticing those slaveholding states that had yet to depart to remain in the Union. And in his first inaugural address on March 4, 1861, President Lincoln suggested he was open to signing it.[6]

But the Confederacy wasn't buying. After all, the thinking ran, why should those southern states remain part of a federal government that had already proven shaky on the issue they held most dear? No, the Confederacy didn't want to be encumbered. And without any need for compromise with the Lincoln government, here's what the Confederate Constitution said on the matter, as adopted on March 11, 1861, just a week after Lincoln's first inaugural:

> Article IV. Sec. 2. (I) The citizens of each State shall be entitled to all the privileges and immunities of citizens in the several States; and shall have the right of transit and sojourn in any State of this Confederacy, with their slaves and other property; and the right of property in said slaves shall not be thereby impaired.

Once the Civil War begin in April 1861, four more slave states signed on: Virginia, Arkansas, Tennessee, and North Carolina.

The Corwin Amendment never really had a chance, as Eric Foner makes clear. In fact, after it moved through Congress and Lincoln sent it to the states on March 7, only three ended up ratifying it: Ohio, Maryland, and Illinois. Many Republicans opposed it, Foner explains, because it "violated [the] principle" that "the Constitution did not explicitly recognize property in slaves."[7] It was one thing to turn a blind eye to slavery in states where it existed; it was quite another to say explicitly that nothing could ever be done about it. The Corwin Amendment was one more desperate attempt by a failed Congress to rescue the Union as it was and without any loss of life.

Instead, the Civil War took its course, and in a nation reunited on the North's terms, the Thirteenth Amendment *as we know it* was ratified on December 6, 1865, even though Lincoln didn't live to see it. It had passed the Senate in April 1864, the House in January 1865, and the president's desk on February 1. When Representative George Julian (R-IN) tried to put the meaning of his vote down in words, he wrote, "I have felt, ever since the vote, as if I were in a new country."

67

How did Black History Month
come into being?

THE FOUNDER OF NEGRO HISTORY WEEK was Dr. Carter G. Woodson. Born to former slave parents in 1875, Woodson attended high school in West Virginia, graduated from the University of Chicago with his bachelor's and master's degrees, and went on to become, in 1912, the second African American, after W.E.B. Du Bois, to be awarded a doctorate in history from Harvard University.[1]

Harvard hadn't been a walk in the park. Woodson's professor Edward Channing had challenged him to prove Negroes had a history worth studying. Ever after, establishing the field of black history became Woodson's mission.

On September 9, 1915, in Chicago, he formed the Association for the Study of Negro Life and History (ASNLH). A year later he launched the *Journal of Negro History.* Eventually, he taught in the history departments at Howard University and West Virginia Collegiate Institute (later West Virginia State) before returning to Washington, D.C., to popularize black history full-time.

Having taught high school as well, Woodson recognized firsthand the disconnect between what elite scholars like Du Bois were generating at the university level and what teachers and students were working with in the poorest of segregated schools.[2] To turn the tide, Woodson first had to research the counternarrative of black history. The mission, as he wrote in 1922, was to "study this history, and study it with the understanding that we are not, after all, an inferior people, but simply a people who have been set back, a people whose progress has been impeded."[3]

Woodson recruited a brilliant team of black historians to the association. In his report for the year 1922–23, he announced that they were focusing specifically on the history of free blacks before the Civil War and of the Negro during Reconstruction. He reported progress on placing the *Journal of Negro History* "into libraries and schools," North and South. With support from the Carnegie Corporation and the Laura Spelman Rockefeller Memorial, he was building up his organization's strength.[4] The needle was moving.

But Woodson was still struggling to overcome the gap between what cutting-edge college and university research revealed and what was being taught in the nation's elementary and secondary schools. He had to find ways to stimulate demand for the association's research in order to reverse an epidemic of inadequacy and low self-esteem among the rising generation.

The research was badly needed. As an editorial in the *Chicago Defender* recounted, "A Chicago school-teacher was instructing a class of foreign children in the history of the Civil War. One Italian youngster asked her: 'What did the Negro do in that war? Didn't he fight for himself?' The teacher was abashed, scarcely able to account for this glaring omission in the records that the child had discovered."[5]

Without the association's research, the children of black sharecroppers and factory workers would have no way of knowing that "the greatest scholars of today are saying that there is no such thing as race in science and that there is nothing in anthropology or psychology to support such myths as the inferiority or superiority of races." But "these truths," Woodson warned "will have little bearing on the uplift of the Negro, if they are left in the state of academic discussion."[6]

The solution Woodson landed on was a public relations coup. The ASNLH "has selected the second week in February to inaugurate a celebration of negro history week, for observance in all parts of the United States," newspaper stories ran in January 1926. "The purpose of the celebration is to popularize the study of the history of the negro, and to obtain support for its promotion."[7]

When it launched, Negro History Week occurred on the second week of February "because the most important events of concern to the Negro took place at that time," Woodson explained: the birthdays of Abraham Lincoln (February 12), George Washington (February 22), and Frederick Douglass, who, not knowing his slave birthday, had taken February 14, Valentine's Day.[8]

Over the next two decades, Negro History Week caught on, thanks to support from black churches, clubs, and civic organizations. By 1933, Woodson's association was receiving a slew of invitations to speak at black and white schools deep in the heart of Texas and to create "wide awake courses dealing with every aspect of Negro life and history."[9]

The next move was to evolve from grassroots organizing to nationwide standardization. In 1948 the ASNLH prepared a new Negro History Kit, "designed for use in communities with few or no library facilities."[10] As part of the rollout, it offered a thirty-two-page "Negro History Pamphlet" at the low cost of two dollars and included six poems by Phillis Wheatley, Paul Laurence Dunbar, James Weldon Johnson, and Mavis B. Mixon; three orations by Frederick Douglass, Representative Robert Brown Elliott (R-SC), and Booker T. Washington; a list of plays; a program for each of the five school days of Negro History Week; bibliographical information for various student projects; and seventeen photos for display.

But over time Negro History Week did not seem to be advancing the goal of integrating the year-round curriculum. And Woodson's death at seventy-four in 1950 left a leadership vacuum at the head of the cause; the civil rights movement had not yet taken off. By the time the student movement came along in the late 1960s and '70s, the fallout from the King assas-

Carter Godwin Woodson, the "father of black history," seen here in 1915, when he founded the Association for the Study of Negro Life and History.

sination and the rise of the black power movement made Negro History Week feel like a relic of a second-class past—compartmentalized and co-opted.

By 1972 some balked at the term *Negro*. Others thought it was silly to include Lincoln's birthday when it didn't always fall in the same week as Douglass's. Mattie Evans of the Progressive Black Associates said, "We've moved to a point now where one week is not enough. We need to take the spotlight off the one week and put it on the year around." Joe Conner, vice-chairman of the Black Students Union at the University of Southern California, added, "Every day of our lives should be black and we shouldn't have to emphasize it one day."[11]

In 1976, America's bicentennial year, Negro History Week went national. The word *Negro* was changed to *Black,* and the week was stretched out to a month, with full support from President Gerald Ford. But in the years that followed, stories from the front lines of elementary, junior high, and high schools deepened skepticism among black historians. "Public authorities" in charge of school curricula around the country decided what was and wasn't taught. Woodson had intended Negro History Week to stimulate greater awareness and, from it, a greater lobbying effort of those same public authorities.

Until we achieve year-round integration of the American history curriculum in our schools, we should continue to leverage Black History Month to spotlight new research, and to measure our progress in fulfilling Woodson's noble vision. A good start would be to ask the same questions that Woodson put to his readers in 1938. During Negro History Week, he wrote, perhaps thinking back to the great emancipation anniversary in Chicago in 1915, "every Negro should ask the question as to whether his race is better off today than it was in 1865? We are free now we contend; but what is freedom?"[12]

68

What was the original color of the mythical beauty Andromeda?

IN GREEK MYTHOLOGY, Andromeda was the daughter of a king. She outraged Poseidon, the Olympian god, by claiming she was more beautiful than any creature on land or sea. (As the classicist Edith Hamilton wrote in her 1942 book *Mythology,* "an absolutely certain way in those days to draw down on one a wretched fate was to claim superiority in anything over any deity.")[1] So furious was Poseidon that he wanted to sink her father's entire kingdom, refraining only when the conniving seer Ammon persuaded him to settle for a single royal life instead—Andromeda's.

The princess is affixed with chains to a rocky cliff, to be devoured by a giant sea serpent rising up from the deep. For anyone who has seen the film *Clash of the Titans* (it has had two versions, in 1981 and 2010), the climactic scene is seared in the brain: the Greek hero Perseus, son of Zeus, rides in on winged feet to rescue her. Perseus found Andromeda's singular beauty so overpowering that he asked her father, Cepheus, for her hand in exchange for saving her life. Once she was promised to him, Perseus held up the decapitated head of Medusa, which he had in his bag, to turn the giant sea serpent to stone.

To convey Andromeda's virginal essence, the makers of the 1981 *Clash of the Titans* film cast Judi Bowker, and for the 2010 remake they cast Alexa Davalos. One actress is blond, the other brunette—and both are white. Their Andromedas appeared to satisfy Hollywood's idea of a perfect match for Perseus, and the films earnestly tried to evoke our inherited perceptions of ancient Greek culture with figures we might have seen in a Rubens painting or on the side of a vase at an art museum.

But while the myth of Perseus and Andromeda played out in the realm of the Greek gods, Andromeda's parents were the king and queen of *Ethiopia*. And Ethiopians were black.

The story of Perseus and Andromeda is at least as old as the fifth century BCE, when the playwrights Sophocles and Euripides drafted alternate versions to be performed in ancient Athens. While their manuscripts are lost to us today, we do know that Euripides' *Andromeda* (412 BCE) was set in Ethiopia.[2]

To be sure, Ethiopia wasn't the only option. They could have set Cepheus's kingdom in Asia, including present-day Israel and Syria.[3] And in book 7 of his *History* (440 BCE), the Greek historian Herodotus

Bernard Picart. *Perseus delivering Andromeda*. Engraving from *Tableaux du temple des muses* (Amsterdam, 1733).

located the kingdom in Persia, so named for one of the sons of Perseus and Andromeda.

Ethiopia might have made sense, however, because Perseus discovered Andromeda on his way home to Greece after killing Medusa and using her head to turn Atlas to stone. (The Atlas Mountains are located on the African continent, although across the Sahara in Algeria, Morocco, and Tunisia.) Ancient Greek writers used the name Ethiopia, which meant "burnt face," to describe any black person from Africa.

Among the ancient writers, Ovid, a Roman poet (43 BCE–CE 17), had doubts about the white virgin when he was updating the Greek myth for Latin audiences.[4] He authored a compendium of ancient myths, *The Metamorphoses,* and in his account of the legend there, he has Perseus associate Andromeda with her country, Ethiopia, and is stunned by her beauty.

The scholar Elizabeth McGrath points to a few telling indications in Ovid's other works. In the *Epistolae Heroidum* (Epistles of the Heroines), Ovid used the Latin word *fusca* to describe Andromeda, and *fusca,* according to McGrath, seems to suggest "black or brown." And he has Sappho explain to Phaon: "though I'm not pure white, Cepheus's dark / Andromeda / charmed Perseus with her native colour. / White doves often choose mates of different hue / and the parrot loves the black turtle dove."

In another work, *Ars Amatoria* (The Art of Love), Ovid says of the daughter of the Ethiopian king that Perseus found her among "the black Indians" (i, 53); that in terms of attraction, "Nor was Andromeda's colour any problem / to her wing-footed aerial lover" (ii, 643–44); and that in terms of clothing, "White suits dark girls; you looked so attractive in / white / Andromeda" (iii, 191–92).

The seventeenth-century Spanish painter Francisco Pacheco, says McGrath, wanted to paint Andromeda but first consulted the scholar Francisco de Rioja. He already had read of the "dark-skinned maiden Andromeda" in Petrarch's *Triumph of Love,* he wrote in *Arte de la Pintura* (1649), and "wanted to know / how it was that in Ethiopia the dark-skinned / maiden Andromeda / attracted him [Perseus] with her fine eyes and hair."

De Rioja looked at the evidence—from Apollodorus, Ovid, Pliny, Strabo, and Hyginus—and concluded that Andromeda was black. Recounting the argument, Pacheco concluded: "Now we see this story, explained most learnedly, goes contrary to the common practice of painting, which makes Andromeda pure white and most beautiful, although she was a native of Ethiopia. Still, the lies that painters multiply need not cause great wonder, even if they show their lack of knowledge; where they cannot be tolerated is in the stories and mysteries of our faith."

Wiser but not necessarily glad, Pacheco decided to write a sonnet about Andromeda instead of painting her. His sonnet reflected a transformation that had occurred between the writing of the Septuagint (Greek Old Testament), which had equated *black* with *beautiful,* and the Vulgate (Latin Bible), which in the fourth century inserted the word *but* between them. If black was the color of sin, the assumption ran, it could not be beautiful, and thus Perseus would have to have overlooked Andromeda's outward appearance to fall in love.

Western civilization, beginning with the ancient Greeks and Romans, was long assumed to be "of, by and for" white people, with black people playing only bit roles, as nemeses to be slain or servants to be summoned. Black people had no place in the great books of civilization, the argument went, because they were an "unfortunate race," a view that "prevailed in the civilized and enlightened portions of the world at the time of the Declaration of Independence, and when the Constitution of the United States was framed and adopted," as Chief Justice Roger Taney wrote in his 1857 *Dred Scott* majority opinion. Since blacks were absent from Western civilization's foundational texts, whites felt they had justification for enslaving them and, later, forcing them to attend segregated schools, where they would learn that they had no history worth studying, not a day, a week, or a month.

But as W.E.B. Du Bois wrote: "From out of the caves of evening that swing between the strong-limbed Earth and the tracery of stars, I summon Aristotle and Aurelius and what soul I will, and they come all graciously with no scorn nor condescension. So, wed with Truth, I dwell above the veil."[5] In summoning the best of Greek and Roman literature to himself, he was teaching African Americans trapped behind the color line to view themselves not as outsiders but as agents, whose ancestors had played pivotal roles in the birth of the civilization that was now oppressing them.

69

How often were enslaved Americans able to tell their stories?

SOLOMON NORTHUP PUBLISHED his memoir, *Twelve Years a Slave,* in 1853. The genre to which it belongs, the African-American slave narrative, was largely forgotten, devalued as literature or dismissed as valid historical evidence, until the first generation of black studies professors insisted on teaching it in the 1960s and '70s. Even then there were skeptics who felt that slave narratives had little to no literary value, and that if they were useful at all, it was for historical research.

It's important for modern audiences to know that Northup's memoir was a best seller in *his* day. In fact, the publisher of *Twelve Years a Slave* sold 10,000 copies within a month of its release in July 1853, and 30,000 copies in the first two years (see Amazing Fact no. 53). While these weren't *Uncle Tom's Cabin* numbers (Harriet Beecher Stowe's 1852 novel sold 300,000 copies in its first year alone), it dwarfed the sales of Walt Whitman's first edition of *Leaves of Grass* in 1855: 795.

Northup was far from the only author of a slave narrative. Olaudah Equiano (1789), Mary Prince (1831), Frederick Douglass (1845), and Harriet Jacobs (1861) are a few of the most famous. In 1946 the researcher Marion Wilson Starling put the total number of slave narratives at more than six thousand, but this tally included everything from broadsides to court records to some 2,500 oral histories recorded by the Federal Writers' Project during the Great Depression.[1] For years, scholars in the field estimated a smaller but still impressive number of *published* slave narratives at around one hundred.

Now, thanks to William L. Andrews and his colleagues at DocSouth,

Chiwetel Ejiofor as Solomon Northup, writing in an attempt to gain his freedom. Film still from *12 Years a Slave* (Fox Searchlight Pictures, 2013).

an online archive hosted by the University of North Carolina at Chapel Hill, we can put an exact number out there: 204.[2] From the height of the slave trade to the end of the Civil War in 1865, 102 known book-length slave narratives were written, while another 102 were written by former slaves *after* the war.

A slave narrative, according to Andrews, is more than an oral history or an unpublished interview, diary, or set of letters, and it is more substantial than a short essay or interview printed in a newspaper, magazine, or other periodical. With few exceptions, a slave narrative has to be (1) a "separately published autobiographical text," (2) "in English," and (3) "produced by slaves or former slaves."[3] Slave narratives may include "short autobiographies that were published as introductions to books." Also, to be clear, when Andrews says they must be "produced by slaves or former slaves," he means that every autobiography on his list involved the direct participation of its slave author, either by holding the pen or by dictating to an editor or amanuensis, usually a sympathetic white abolitionist with access to a printing press.

Slave narratives comprise a genre of literature with common voices, elements, experiences, and themes that, brick by brick, helped remove the impenetrable wall blocking outsiders' view of the harsh reality of American slavery. "The unity of black autobiography in the antebellum era is most apparent in the pervasive use of journey or quest motifs that symbolize multiple layers of spiritual evolution," Andrews writes.[4] With the exception of Northup's, antebellum slave narratives almost always move from birth in slavery (often beginning with the line "I was born . . .") to rebirth as a free man or woman.

It was something of a miracle for any slave to learn to read. As the film *12 Years a Slave* illustrates, even a free man trapped in slavery like Northup had to resort to crushed berries and dried leaves for his writing tools, and even then the risk of being caught, sold, and even killed for his efforts was omnipresent.

At the height of slavery, it was *against the law* for a slave to be taught to read. "If you teach that nigger . . . to read, there would be no keeping him. It would forever unfit him to be a slave," Douglass recalled his master warning. Of course, this only produced the opposite effect in Douglass and so many other slaves. "I now understood what had been to me a most perplexing difficulty—to wit, the white man's power to enslave the black man. It was a grand achievement, and I prized it highly. From that moment, I understood the pathway from slavery to freedom."[5]

For the American slave, literacy was the first, if metaphorical Underground Railroad, built by the slaves within the shadows of slavery; physical flight was the second. As Paul Berman writes, slave narrators "made a double escape—from bondage and from enforced illiteracy."[6] Writing a slave narrative was itself a traumatic act, as Andrews perceptively observes, because "reconstructing their past lives required many ex-slaves to undergo a disquieting psychic immersion into their former selves as slaves."[7] Often they began that reconstruction on the lecture circuit or in a church, where they related their harrowing tales, sometimes accompanied by demonstrations of visual proof of the torment they'd suffered on their own backs.

As propaganda in the fight against slavery, these first-person narratives were priceless. "Without the black spiritual autobiography's reclamation of the Afro-American's spiritual birthright," Andrews argues, "the fugitive slave narrative could not have made such a cogent case for black civil rights in the crisis years between 1830 and 1865."[8]

When giving a lecture, genius orators like Frederick Douglass had a built-in audience of abolitionists eager for a front-row seat on slavery, but authoring a memoir could potentially reach many more people, including those who were cautious but persuadable. Through their vivid first-person accounts, the slave narrators helped galvanize the antislavery movement with stories that spoke to the heart and heartache of the American project. The books and pamphlets they produced might be unpolished or rough, but as the Unitarian minister Theodore Parker argued, "All the original romance of Americans is in them, not in the white man's novel."[9]

Douglass and Jacobs stand at the summit of early-nineteenth-century African-American literature, and their genre comprises the foundation of the modern African-American literary canon. Try to imagine Ralph Ellison's great novel *Invisible Man* or Malcolm X's *Autobiography* without Douglass's *Narrative.* Ask how Alice Walker's *Color Purple,* Toni Morrison's *Beloved,* or Maya Angelou's *I Know Why the Caged Bird Sings* would read without the echoes of Jacobs. Our current writers are ever in conversation with them, riffing on and revising their works, because they are the black tradition's initial first-person accounts of the first leg of our ancestors' journey from slavery to freedom. Unlike African-American writers today, slave narrators had to walk a fine line between self-expression and the expectations of readers who were less interested in exploring their inner lives than in knowing the gruesome details about life on a southern plantation.

Now, thanks to John W. Blassingame, who in 1972 broke ground by writing a history of slavery from the slave's point of view (*The Slave Community*), and William L. Andrews, among many others, historians and literary scholars take the genre seriously. Students read slave narratives in high school and college. And while you can click through to any of the out-of-copyright narratives on DocSouth, you can also purchase beautiful editions (often with scholarly background materials) that can be placed on bookshelves next to the all-time greats of world literature, because they deserve to be there.

70

What started the black newspaper industry in America?

THE FIRST BLACK NEWSPAPER PUBLISHED in America was called *Freedom's Journal,* and its first issue rolled off the press in March 1827. The paper's founding editors were the free black men Samuel Cornish and John Russwurm. A mulatto born free in Delaware in 1795, Cornish was also a trained minister who had studied in Philadelphia, did missionary work with slaves in Maryland, and established the first black Presbyterian church in New York City. The historian David Brion Davis calls Cornish "the most important black journalist before Frederick Douglass."[1]

Russwurm was a Jamaican native, born free in 1799 to a white father and black mother. After moving with his father to Canada, then to Maine, he studied at Bowdoin College as a contemporary of Nathaniel Hawthorne and Henry Wadsworth Longfellow. In 1826 he became only the third African-American college graduate in this country. Briefly, he considered becoming a doctor and moving to the black nation of Haiti, or accepting an offer to work as a free black émigré for the American Colonization Society's new effort to repatriate freed slaves to Liberia.

Instead, Russwurm met Cornish in New York City, and the rest is history. In March 1827 Russwurm, Cornish, and other free black leaders met at the home of Boston Crummell, an ex-slave and the father of Alexander Crummell, the first African-American graduate of the University of Cambridge, future black missionary, scholar, and founder in 1897 of the American Negro Academy. There they conceived of creating a black newspaper. At that time, writes Davis, a number of pressing issues faced the black community. The Missouri Crisis of 1819–1821 had suddenly exposed slavery as a critically divisive issue that could threaten the very existence of the nation, reinforcing desires to repress and avoid the subject as much as possible. There was also an inevitable tendency to blame blacks for the country's most dangerous problem. The nature and future of antislavery was therefore much in doubt.

And many whites—as well as some blacks—believed that the only hope for the country's emancipated slaves was for them to be returned "home" to Africa; otherwise, they feared, both races would be dragged down in an unholy race war.

Freedom's Journal was deliberately initiated as a counterbalance to the white newspapers, which seemed to focus only on negative news stories about blacks that fit a racist frame.

During its first year, the paper was published in four pages with a total of sixteen columns. In March 1828 it expanded to eight pages and a total of twenty-four columns. As the historian Jacqueline Bacon notes, "Most original material appears to have been written by African Americans, although white authors occasionally contributed pieces written specifically for the newspaper. In addition, as was common practice at the time, articles were frequently reprinted from other periodicals."[2]

The paper's editors attempted to correct misrepresentations of black Americans. "To some extent," the historian Elizabeth McHenry writes, "Samuel Cornish and John Russwurm identified discrimination against the free black population as a problem [stemming from misunderstandings caused by] misleading representation. The majority press's erroneous and incomplete reports on free blacks led to inaccuracies about black people becoming lodged in the white imagination."[3] *Freedom's Journal* therefore sought to give a more accurate representation of black accomplishments.

The paper also focused on moral uplift. "In the columns of the paper," Bacon writes, "the editors and contributors promoted self-help efforts that would lead to moral improvement, advocating that African Americans seek educational advancement and economic self-sufficiency, observe decorum, serve as exemplars, and avoid vice."[4] Penelope Campbell lists

Front page of an early issue of *Freedom's Journal*,
March 30, 1827.

some of the topics the paper covered: "Weekly issues carried a variety of material: poetry, letters of explorers and others in Africa, information on the status of slaves in slaveholding states, legislation pending or passed in states that affected blacks, notices of job openings, and personal news such as marriages and obituaries."[5]

One of the paper's central concerns was education. *Freedom's Journal* contained articles and stories that could be read by people of all ages and literacy levels. The content could be varied. In one issue, McHenry writes, the paper's "Varieties" column "included instructions for the proper burial of corpses alongside a table outlining the consumption of wheat and other grains in the United Kingdom. Other 'newsworthy' items printed in the same column were titled 'A Polish Joke,' 'Rare Instances of Self-Devotion,' and 'Curious Love Letter.'" What the paper termed "useful knowledge" could come in a variety of forms, Bacon adds: "an article about a fund to assist New York City's poor with their fuel costs or a notice about the work of the African Dorcas Association, which collected clothing for children attending New York's African Free Schools, gave community members vital information."[6]

Although *Freedom's Journal* served an important role for African Americans in New York and beyond, it did not last long. Within six months of the first issue, Cornish resigned. Scholars have often pointed to the break between the two editors as resulting from their increasingly differing opinions on colonization. Cornish, Bacon writes, "was a member of the Haytian Emigration Society but became opposed to the idea of leaving the country after many emigrants to Haiti returned, dissatisfied, to the United States. In particular, he was strongly averse to African colonization."[7] But Russwurm came around to the idea of colonization because, as Davis observes, he "ultimately became convinced that the depth and immutability of white racism presented a permanent obstacle to slave emancipation—unless some way could be found to remove free blacks."

Still, Russwurm did not announce his public support for African colonization until 1829, two years after Cornish resigned. And even after leaving, Cornish remained involved with the paper as a "General Agent," "authorized to transact any business relating to it," as Bacon informs us.[8] By January 1828 Cornish had become the New York Manumission Society's General Visiting Agent for the African Free Schools.

The paper faced many problems. It was difficult to attract subscribers, and many subscribers did not pay their dues on time or at all. The paper initially alienated white readers by *opposing* colonization; then, when Russwurm began publishing articles *supporting* colonization, the paper lost black support. As Bacon writes, "Pieces opposing colonization continued to be published during 1828, but in smaller numbers, and by late 1828 the number of positive articles about Liberia and its settlers had increased."[9] Winston James adds, "What triggered this apparently sudden change of heart is not at all clear. No catalyst can be identified, and it does appear, as Russwurm himself wrote, to have been a decision arrived at after an accumulation of experience and observation, capped by careful study of the limited options available to African Americans."[10]

This growing support for colonization led Russwurm to end the paper and, eventually, to leave the country. In January 1829 he wrote to Ralph Gurley of the ACS—the man who had offered him the job after he graduated from Bowdoin—"I am on the eve of relinquishing the publication of *Freedom's Journal*, with my views on the subject of Colonization *materially* changed. . . . I am willing to be employed in the colony [of Liberia] in any business, for the performance of which you may deem me qualified."[11]

Russwurm made his support of colonization known in a *Freedom's Journal* editorial dated March 14, 1829: "Sensible then, as all are of the disadvantages under which we at present labour, can any consider it a mark of folly, for us to cast our eyes upon some other portion of the globe where *all* these inconveniences are removed where the Man of Colour freed from the fetters and prejudice, and degradation, under which he labours in this land, may walk forth in all the majesty of his creation—a new born creature— a *Free Man*!"

71

What percentage of white Americans have recent African ancestry?

ACCORDING TO A STUDY by the population geneticist Katarzyna "Kasia" Bryc, only about 5 percent of African Americans have at least 2 percent Native American ancestry, while the average African American has only 0.8 percent Native American ancestry. The average African American has a whopping 24 percent European ancestry, which explains why Great-grandma had those high cheekbones and that straight black hair.[1]

Although long suspected, what hasn't been confirmed until now is how many self-identified white women and men are walking around today with recent, hidden *African* ancestry in their families. Judged by the notorious one-drop rule of the Jim Crow era, they would have been legally black, yet many of them don't even know it. How many might sense it but aren't sure why? And how would they react if they did know? Southerners, in particular, have more than just Confederates in the attic. The proof and guide is their DNA.

Here's how Scott Hadly reported Kasia Bryc's findings: "About 4 percent of whites have at least 1 percent or more of African ancestry, known as 'hidden African ancestry.' "[2] That percentage is "relatively small," Hadly continues, but it "indicates that an individual with at least 1 percent African ancestry had an African ancestor within the last six generations, or in the last 200 years [meaning since the time of American slavery]. This data also suggests that individuals with mixed parentage at some point were absorbed into the white population," which is a very polite way of saying that they "passed."

How many ostensibly white Americans today would be classified as black under the one-drop rule? Judging by the last U.S. Census, *7,872,702.* To put that in context, that number is equal to roughly *20 percent,* or a fifth, of the total number of people identified as African American in the same census count.

In other words, there are a *lot* of white people with "hidden African ancestry," and they don't have to look too far back in time to find it. Yet paradoxically, their families were able to pass for white relatively quickly.

Also fascinating is what the researcher Kasia Bryc revealed about the frequency of "hidden African ancestry" on a state-by-state basis. "Southern states with the highest African American populations tended to have the highest percentages of hidden African ancestry," Hadly writes of Bryc's findings. "In South Carolina at least 13 percent of self-identified whites have 1 percent or more African ancestry, while in Louisiana the number is a little more than 12 percent. In Georgia and Alabama the number is about 9 percent. The differences perhaps point to different social and cultural histories within the south."

If we apply those percentages to the last federal census, that means 487,253, "white" people in Georgia, 385,156 "white" people in South Caro-

Theater orchestra with mixed-race audience.

lina, 328,186 in Louisiana, and 288,396 in Alabama are actually "black" according to the one-drop rule. And for the record, the states highlighted in Hadly's report were among the first to secede from the Union before the Civil War; they also had the highest slave populations recorded in the 1860 U.S. Census.

While the data points are fascinating, on a larger scale, Bryc's DNA research has the potential to round out the more common narrative we have of African Americans (such as First Lady Michelle Obama) discovering that they have white roots (and cousins) tracing back to a common slave-owning ancestor. Twenty-four percent of us do, and I'm no exception.

But, really, does any of this matter?

Of course it matters, because the more we learn about the black, white, and *browning* of our past, the more we can see how absurd, arbitrary, and grotesque the one-drop rule—which defined the color line in America for decades and decades during its most painful chapters—truly was. Back then, a white-enough black woman or man could pass for white; now, with Bryc's findings, we realize that, all along, there was a whole other layer in the color aristocracy that no one could see. To shop owners, hotel clerks, railroad conductors, and federal judges in those times, appearances were what mattered; in our time, thankfully, it is the truth that sets us free.

72

Who was the first American-born black person to draw crowds using sleight of hand—and voice?

RICHARD POTTER WAS BORN in Hopkinton, Massachusetts, in 1783, the last year of the American Revolution. Although the Commonwealth of Massachusetts would not officially outlaw the slave trade until 1788, emancipation was in the air and in the courts. The slaves Mum Bett (Elizabeth Freeman) and Quok Walker were suing for freedom under the state's new constitution, which stated, "All men are born free and equal, and have certain natural, essential, and unalienable rights."

Those rights didn't magically appear, and they could be stolen—a reality that Potter's mother, "Black Dinah," may have known firsthand. Dinah Swain was kidnapped during her childhood in Guinea. By her own account, she was poisoned by her captors with a lump of sugar dipped in rum. She was then brought to New England, where she became a slave of Sir Charles Henry Frankland, a tax collector for the Port of Boston.[1] Richard was born to Dinah fifteen years after Frankland died in England, leaving his wife—and later son Henry—to manage the family's Massachusetts estate. Richard's father was a local white man named George Stimpson, making Potter's surname a mystery.

One of six or possibly seven children, Potter appears to have received some schooling in Hopkinton before the age of ten. Some accounts state that he then sailed to Europe as a cabin boy and arrived in England, where he was enthralled by a Scottish magician and ventriloquist, John Rannie. Recent scholarship by the historian John Hodgson suggests that

Potter traveled to Europe around the age of sixteen and began his career as an acrobat there, but he did not meet John Rannie and his older brother James in Europe.[2]

Potter returned to North America around 1803 and was back in Boston by 1807. In the interim he had begun apprenticing with John and then James Rannie, and had acquired expertise as a magician and ventriloquist. The following year he married Sally Harris. They had two sons and a daughter; their first child, Henry, was killed in a wagon accident in 1816. When at home in Boston in those early years, Potter worked briefly for the family of the Rev. Daniel Oliver, and he honed his craft by entertaining the children around the fire.

In 1810 Rannie decided it was time to "hang up his cloak" and retire from public life to tend to the large tract of land he had acquired. When he did,

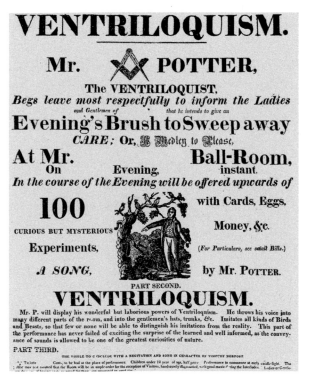

Richard Potter, the first American ventriloquist, seen here in whiteface on a playbill.

he left his former apprentice with a virtual lock on the U.S. market. Potter wasted little time staking out his claim.

Thankfully, a few broadsides for his engagements were preserved. One of these (ca. 1811), adorned with the Masonic symbol and a woodcut of a man communing with birds, previewed the show Potter would perform at a local ballroom. His stated purpose: "to give an Evening's Brush to Sweep away CARE." The first part of Potter's act would feature his magic, with "100 curious but mysterious experiments with cards, eggs, money, &c." In the second part of the show, the ad stated:

> Mr. P. will display his wonderful but laborious powers of Ventriloquism. He throws his voice into many different parts of the room, and into the gentlemen's hats, trunks, &c. Imitates all kinds of Birds and Beasts, so that few or none will be able to distinguish his imitations from the reality. This part of the performance has never failed of exciting the surprise of the learned and well informed, as the conveyance of sounds is allowed to be one of the greatest curiosities of nature.[3]

For a few years Potter also performed what was known as a "Man Salamander" act, in which he handled a red-hot bar of iron and immersed his feet in molten lead.

It's a wonder that Potter, throughout his career, seems to have steered clear of white America's fears that black magic lurked behind various slave revolts in their midst. For example, despite fears of a black conspiracy when a black man allegedly set fire to a Boston ship in 1817, Potter remained unscathed. Perhaps aware of his audiences' perceptions of otherness and identity, Potter, early in his career, advertised himself as "West Indian," and later passed as white when touring in the South. In the latter part of his career, some accounts identified him as "colored." This is one of the many important revelations in Hodgson's investigative biography.

Wherever Potter was, whatever he appeared to be, he exploited his otherness to add allure to his fame. In this way, he prefigured such black performers as the fugitive slave Henry Box Brown and the great African-American ventriloquist of the twentieth century John W. Cooper (1873–1966).

Richard Potter died at age fifty-two on September 20, 1835, exactly 145 years before the fictional Harry Potter was born (1980, if you do the math in J. K. Rowling's books), and 39 years before that other famous Harry, Houdini, was born in Budapest, Hungary. Potter was buried in Potter Place,

New Hampshire, under a headstone transcribed by the nineteenth-century black historian and abolitionist William Cooper Nell:

> In Memory of
> RICHARD POTTER,
> THE CELEBRATED VENTRILOQUIST,
> Who died
> Sept. 20, 1835
> Age 52 years.

73

Who was the first black actor to play the role of Shakespeare's tortured Moor?

FOR MORE THAN TWO CENTURIES following *Othello*'s 1604 launch in England, the title role, despite the description of "Moor," had been played by white actors, beginning with Richard Burbage,[1] whose death in 1619 happened to coincide with the arrival of the first African slaves in the English colony of Jamestown in the New World. Two centuries later the godfather of black stage actors, Ira Aldridge, the self-proclaimed "African Roscius" of the nineteenth century, a native of the New World, ventured to prove to theatrical audiences that a man who looked like Othello could also make the lines Shakespeare had written for him sing.

Ira Aldridge was born on July 24, 1807, in lower Manhattan, across the East River from the present-day St. Ann's theater in Brooklyn. His parents were Daniel Aldridge, a straw vendor and preacher, and his wife, Luranah. "Little is known about [his] early life," his biographer Bernth Lindfors tells us.[2]

Aldridge received a formal education at the African Free School in New York City (graduating in 1822) and took up acting at New York's African Theater, the nation's first black company, located at Mercer and Houston Streets. There, Alex Ross writes, "Aldridge played several roles and apparently took part in street fights that erupted in response to the venture."[3] When the African Theater closed for good in 1824, Aldridge slipped America for England, hoping he could find more work there than in his native land. The nineteenth century may have been witnessing a Shakespeare craze in the United States, but for an African-American actor seeking the main chance, the watchword might as well have been "go *east, young man.*"

As the historian Melissa Vickery-Bareford writes:

> Aldridge became a dresser to the English actor Henry Wallack, who was performing in New York. Henry Wallack's brother, James, then employed Aldridge as a personal attendant while on passage to Liverpool. . . . James Wallack had planned to sponsor Aldridge and make money off his engagements, but when Wallack told a reporter that Aldridge was his servant, the two went their separate ways.[4]

"I had the pleasure of Mr. Wallack's friendship whilst he performed in Chatham Street Theatre, New York, but I never was his servant,—*nor the servant of any man,*" Aldridge was to write in 1833.[5]

William Mulready. *The Black Tragedian Ira Aldridge as Othello.* Ca. 1826. Oil on panel. Baltimore, The Walters Art Museum.

On May 11, 1825, more than 220 years after *Othello*'s original premiere and
209 years after William Shakespeare died, seventeen-year-old Ira Aldridge
made his London debut playing Othello at the East End's Royalty Theatre.
For his first performance as the ill-fated general, Aldridge was described in
the *Public Ledger* as "a Gentleman of Colour, from the New York Theatre."[6]

Following his appearance at the Royalty, Aldridge took on the role
of Oroonoko in *The Revolt of Surinam* (based on the Thomas Southerne
play *Oroonoko*) at the Royal Coburg Theatre in London, in the fall of 1825.
Here was Aldridge, a free black man born in America, portraying a slave
in a play that exposed the institution's evils before the British government
took steps to abolish slavery throughout its empire in 1833 and nearly forty
years before his own country fought a civil war over the issue. Once again,
Aldridge's billing was "Tragedian of Colour, from the African Theatre,
New York."[7]

The *Sunday Monitor* was less than thrilled: "There is no end to dramatic
novelty. The days of Theatrical dogs, horses, and elephants have passed
away;—those of monkeys seem to be on the decline, and now for a more
monstrous exhibition than all the rest, we are to be treated with a *Black
Actor,* a right earnest *African Tragedian*." Yet once Aldridge proved himself
onstage, the *Monitor* changed its tune:

> Mr. Keene [a stage name Aldridge used] excited that gratification which
> should ever result from the belief, that a part of our species, whatever
> be the difference of hue, is advancing to that dignity which is man's sole
> prerogative; for we are convinced, that the sooty visitors of the African
> Theatre are not in so low a state of ignorance as is generally imagined, if
> they patronize and can appreciate the intellectual efforts of Mr. Keene.
> His performance throughout was marked by feeling, devoid of the least
> extravagance, a quick perception, and to which may be added, a degree
> of dignity.

At the Coburg, Aldridge also acted the part of Gambia in *The Ethiopian;
or, the Quadroon of the Mango Grove,* a version of Thomas Morton's *The Slave.*
"Audiences would come expecting one kind of show and he would give
them another," Lindfors writes. "Instead of making them laugh, he would
compel them to think. He would confront them with their own prejudices,

subverting by example their long-held belief in the inferiority and barbarism of Africans."[8]

Aldridge finished at the Coburg on November 26, 1825. When London was slow to offer him more promising roles, he toured the provinces, drawing great acclaim as the servant Mungo in *The Padlock,* beginning in 1827. He also began playing white characters, including the Dutch smuggler Dirk Hatteraick in Sir Walter Scott's *Guy Mannering,* Rob MacGregor in Scott's *Rob Roy,* and Shylock in Shakespeare's *The Merchant of Venice.*

Despite his successes, however, "a black actor in those days couldn't please everyone," Lindfors writes. Aldridge faced especially tough barbs from the London press. The controversy surrounding him came to a head in March 1833, when the renowned actor Edmund Kean collapsed (and later died) during a run of *Othello* at the Theatre Royal at Covent Garden. Grasping for a replacement, the theater manager tapped Aldridge. The press skewered the decision, with Aldridge's race at the forefront of the most severe attacks. In fact, before Aldridge even stepped onto the stage on April 10, the *Figaro in London* complained of "the introduction to the boards of Covent Garden theater, of that miserable nigger whom we found in the provinces imposing on the public by the name of the *African Roscius.*" The *Athenaeum* was horrified at the onstage intimacy between Aldridge as Othello and the white actress playing his wife, Desdemona, Ellen Tree: "In the name of propriety and decency, we protest against an interesting actress and lady-like girl, like Miss Ellen Tree, being subjected by the manager of the theater to the indignity of being pawed about by Mr. Henry Wallack's black servant."

Aldridge performed only two nights at Covent Garden. Lindfors argues that the primary reason for the short stay might have been that the box office was low for his performances, perhaps caused by negative publicity and a flu outbreak. Lindfors also wonders if the flu compromised Aldridge's own performance. Whatever the actual reason, the poisonous *Figaro in London* took credit for having "hunted the Nigger from the boards," as Ross notes.

Aldridge performed at smaller London theaters through June 1833, but it was clear that, as before, his future would be on the road. "After the Covent Garden setback," notes Ross, "Aldridge retreated to the provinces, and in Ireland, among other places, he became a full-on star, his popularity only heightened by stories of Londoners' disdain."

In the ensuing years, Aldridge variously performed with touring companies, started his own touring troupe, accepted engagements with local acting companies, and even devised his own solo show, which, says Ross, "mixed lectures on drama, recitations of Shakespeare, commentary on racism, and popular songs." Apparently, as part of his act, Aldridge borrowed from the American blackface performer Thomas Rice and was even known to don *whiteface* as entertainment.

74

Who was the patron saint of African slaves and their descendants?

SAINT BENEDICT OF PALERMO was born in San Fratello, Sicily, in 1524. His father, Cristoforo, was a devout Catholic known for teaching peasants to say the rosary; he also was a slave who helped manage his owner's lands. It is unclear whether Benedict's mother, Diana, was a free woman at the time of her son's birth. Cristoforo and Diana lived separately after their marriage to avoid the temptation of conceiving children who would be born into slavery, and upon learning this, Cristoforo's owner promised them he would free their first child.[1]

While most sources assume Benedict was born free or became free, his current biographer Giovanna Fiume is not certain, because contemporary Sicilians often referred to him as "Santu Scavuzzu," or "Saint Slave." Fiume also believes that whatever siblings Benedict had remained slaves.[2]

Sometime in the mid-1540s, Geronimo (or Girolamo) Lanza, a nobleman-turned-ascetic, invited Benedict to join his "irregular Franciscan community" of lay hermits traveling across Sicily.[3] Seeing Benedict taunted in the fields where he was tending oxen, Lanza is said to have warned Benedict's tormentors, "You are ridiculing this poor workman, but in a few years you will hear something of him."[4] Lanza and his followers eventually migrated to Monte Pellegrino, where, after Lanza's death, Benedict was elected superior.

Following the Council of Trent in 1562, Pope Pius IV mandated that hermits enter into monastic life. Benedict chose the Franciscan Reformed Minor Observantins at Santa Maria di Gesù near Palermo, Sicily. Because he did not take formal vows in the order, he remained a lay brother, serv-

Attributed to José Montes de Oca. *Saint Benedict of Palermo.*
Ca. 1734. Polychrome and gilt wood, glass. Minneapolis
Institute of Art.

ing as a cook in the monastery kitchen, where he was noted for his extreme
devotion to the poor and to the Franciscan virtues of wisdom, simplicity,
poverty, humility, charity, and obedience.

Joel Rogers recounts Benedict's wondrous deeds in the second volume
of his *World's Great Men of Color.* Benedict is said to have turned down
the advances of noblewomen and apparently wore a tunic of palm leaves
beneath his outer robe. He chose to live in a small cell dwelling with a char-
coal cross on the wall. He was illiterate, but he schooled his fellow Francis-
cans on the scriptures he had memorized; according to the hagiographers,
he cured the blind, washed the feet of the poor, and even hovered over an
altar. In this way, he became something of a celebrity, attracting numerous

visitors to the monastery—from the very rich to the very poor—seeking his consolation and aid, not least his prophetic and healing powers.

Benedict eventually was elected guardian of the friary in the late 1570s. "The more confused and mortified the Saint became," Carletti translates, "the more he vainly sought to fly this applause, the more did they cry aloud: Behold the Saint." Rather than cling to power, Benedict resumed his duties as cook after serving as the monastery's vicar and novice master.

He died on April 4, 1589, after several months of illness. If you believe Rogers, Benedict's last words were the Christ-like: "Into thy hands, O Lord, I commend my spirit." His feast day, April 4, is the day Martin Luther King, Jr., was assassinated in 1968.

For Rogers, the story of Benedict all but ends here; for later historians such as Giovanna Fiume, it was just beginning.

Just two years after he died, Benedict's body was moved from the monastery's common burial ground to its sacristy in 1591. In 1594, the first inquiry into Benedict's potential canonization came before the Archbishop of Palermo; ninety-seven witnesses testified. A key advocate was the merchant Giovan Domenico Rubbiano of Palermo, whose letters eventually reached King Philip III of Spain.

The Spanish king ordered Benedict's body moved again—this time from the sacristy of the monastery to the altar, enshrined in a silver coffin. In a letter Philip revealed his motivation: the transatlantic slave trade. "It has pleased the Lord to use this humble servant black of hue to assist the conversion of the Negro population of the Indies, which could not have happened except by divine decree," he wrote, according to Fiume. The church gave its permission to depict Benedict with shining rays and a crown on his head well before he was a saint. For church leaders, Benedict was something of a public relations coup: a Franciscan layman who looked like the African people they were trying to convert—and control.

Fiume argues that Benedict quickly became the standard for "the ideal slave," and his image "helped [Franciscan] missionaries in evangelizing the African slaves because he demonstrated the epitome of sanctity, centered on humility, obedience, and love between races and social classes."[5] As a contemporary Franciscan testified, "the slaves for their part endure their harsh conditions more patiently, infused as they are with the honor which they bestow on their saint, in whose company they hope to draw near to Paradise by way of the road of suffering."[6]

Fiume argues that imagery of Benedict cradling the Baby Jesus in his arms was used to promote harmony between whites and blacks in the New World, but with a clear hierarchy of one group over the other: It "hinted at the need for love—in such a condition of racial disproportion as there was in colonial plantations and mines—between master and slave; the same way the black monk loved the white child at whom he gazed so adoringly, in this same way would the black wet-nurse love the white baby for whom she cared."[7]

But to the black people who beheld his image, he was one of their own, and in this way he inspired empowerment that was at odds with their forced removal from Africa to Europe and the Americas. As early as 1609, the first confraternity in Benedict's honor formed in Lisbon, Portugal; it became one of many established on the Iberian Peninsula and in the New World. Just a few years later a crowd of slaves in Lisbon was seen processing behind a standard of Benedict. To them, he was their patron saint and protector. And so the momentum for canonization kept building, with further attempts in 1620 and 1625–26.

The relative ease of this process of conversion and identification reflected "syncretism," Fiume explains. The Catholic rosary and confraternities comfortably mapped onto preexisting African objects, such as the traditional Yoruba divining instrument, which became known as a "rosary of Ifa," the name of the system of Yoruba divination. A fusion of musical forms and rituals followed, with slaves and freemen adopting Benedict as their own, kneeling at his altar and hoisting statues of him on their shoulders during Holy Week processions. As one witness from Lima, Peru, explained, he liked to kneel at the altar of Benedict because "he was black like me." In turn, Fiume writes, these confraternities to Benedict instilled in "their members a feeling of pride and identity" and gave them "a base of resistance in the face of the more extreme forms of slavery and sometimes a screen for illicit or subversive activities and plans for escape."[8]

Once these confraternities took off, the Catholic Church had fewer options to reverse course—only to delay. As one Franciscan testified, " 'They [blacks] venerate this Saint [Benedict] so ardently that if this veneration were to be forbidden or repressed, this would cause widespread outrage and would arouse doubts about the other saints. The harm done [by removing his image from the altars] would outweigh the great goodness done by so many men who have preached and established the Catholic faith.' "[9] Among those harms was the prospect of slaves converting to the Protestant faiths of their English and Dutch neighbors.

Eventually, the elevation came. In 1713, with the transatlantic slave trade in full swing, the case for canonizing Benedict reopened "through the spread of the Latin American cult," Dell'Aira explains. Benedict was beatified on May 11, 1743. He was canonized "Saint Benedict" by Pope Pius VII on May 24, 1807 (the same year the British Parliament passed a law banning the slave trade), becoming the first black saint after the papal reforms of 1634 and eighty-one years *before* slavery was abolished in overwhelmingly black and Catholic Brazil.

75

Was a black slave to blame for the Salem witch trials?

THERE IS NO AIRTIGHT EVIDENCE of when Tituba was born, or where and when she died, and given the looseness of seventeenth-century spellings, we also see her variously referred to as "Tetaby, Titibe, Tittabe, Tittube, Titibe, Titiba, Tittuba, and Titaba," according to the historian Marilynne K. Roach.[1]

Another historian, Elaine Breslaw, conducted a rigorous investigation of Colonial documents, including census records, slave inventories, and even naming patterns, and concluded that Tituba was a member of the Arawak Indian tribe from present-day Guyana or Venezuela. She had been stolen into slavery and was eventually bought by Samuel Parris, a merchant in Barbados (and also a Harvard man, I must say) before he moved to Boston in 1680.[2]

Breslaw makes the most compelling scholarly case for Tituba's origins, but her theory isn't the only one. The scholar Peter Hoffer points to evidence that Tituba is a Yoruba name and suggests that she was of African origin. Joel Rogers used the catchall category of "West Indian Negro," and it was true that Tituba arrived in New England by way of the Caribbean.[3] But whether she was American Indian, African, or a fusion of the two or more remains a mystery.

What we do know is that by 1689, the then-*Reverend* Samuel Parris had moved again, this time from Boston to Salem to oversee the village church. Soon afterward Tituba appears to have married another of Parris's slaves, John Indian. Evidence of their union is lacking (really, we can only assume they were married because of prevailing religious norms in New England),

Film still with Tituba from *Maid of Salem* (Paramount Pictures, 1937).

but Parris's last will and testament suggests that the couple may have had a daughter named Violet.

In the winter of 1691–92, Tituba was accused of witchcraft. By then she was likely in her late twenties or early thirties. Parris's nine-year-old daughter, Elizabeth, and eleven-year-old niece, Abigail Williams, were suffering repeated episodes of falling down, shaking, and babbling. Speculation, even by their doctor, swirled around a supernatural source, perhaps a curse. (The culprit could very well have been, in Jess Blumberg's words, "fungus ergot, which can be found in rye, wheat and other cereal grasses," common in places like Salem.)[4]

In late February 1692, a neighbor of the Parrises, Mary Sibley, intervened. Seizing on the cure, she enlisted Tituba and John Indian to prepare an English folk recipe called a "witch-cake," consisting of rye meal and the bewitched girls' urine. The object of the cake was a test: once baked, it had to be served to a dog that, by digesting the grains and urine, would somehow draw the girls' tormentors out.

Breslaw says there is no evidence that Tituba the slave had any particular interest in, knowledge of, or skill in magic before she arrived in Salem and that the ritual she performed was based on English folk magic at Sibley's behest. Although it is possible that Sibley chose Tituba and John Indian as her helpers because whites generally associated Native Americans with magic, this wasn't based in reality. Contrary to Joel Rogers's claim, Tituba and her husband were not the originators of the hysteria in Salem.

Context matters. The people of Salem were stressed over competition for resources, as outsiders displaced by King William's War between England and France in the colonies were moving in. Add to that existing family rivalries, as well as Parris's own increasing unpopularity with his flock. While today we look to science to explain uncertainties, back then, as my colleague David Hall writes, "the people of seventeenth-century New England lived in an enchanted universe."[5]

With the hysteria spreading, Parris's daughter and niece accused Tituba of witchcraft. They left John Indian out of it, perhaps because Tituba, as the house slave, had greater supervision over them and this was a way of getting back at her. The girls, says Marilynne Roach,

> reported that Tituba's specter followed them and clawed at them when she was nowhere near them. When she was out of the room and out of their sight, Tituba learned, the girls knew where she was and what she was doing, leaving her to wonder if Goody Sibley's charm *had* opened the girls' eyes to the Invisible World. . . . Tituba herself was now in an even more precarious position than slavery alone could impose.[6]

After being questioned by Parris and others, Tituba was taken into custody with two white women the girls also had accused—Sarah Good and Sarah Osborne—and searched for marks. At a magistrate's hearing in Salem during the first week of March 1692, Good and Osborne denied the charges, leaving Tituba to blame.

At first Tituba, too, denied involvement in any devilish activities, but it quickly became clear that that was not what her inquisitors wanted to hear. So perhaps to regain control over a rapidly deteriorating situation, she flipped and told her judges a series of fabulous and ever-creepier stories filled with witch covens and evil spirits. One such spirit, she claimed, belonged to Sarah Osborne, who Tituba said had a way of transforming into a winged creature and then back into a woman. Tituba then spoke of a "tall man" and a "thing with a head like a woman and two legs and wings" who told her to "hurt the [Parris] children," even to "kill the children," before a black dog appeared and ordered her to "serve me," to which she replied, "I am afraid."

But that wasn't all. During the second day of the hearing, Tituba admitted further to making a pact with the devil, an admission said to have astonished—even terrified—onlookers. Through her testimony, she was not only able to fend off death, but also seemed to succeed in frightening those who were, without question, above her socially, politically, economically, and with respect to religion. To pull this off, Breslaw posits, Tituba wove her story together with a mix of European, Indian, and perhaps even West African folklore that she had absorbed.

As a result, "the court valued Tituba's voice, as the magistrates believed her and considered the other two to be liars," says Roach. But all three were sent to jail to await trial as Salem continued to spin out of control with accusations. Throughout their long and terrible ordeal, Good and Osborne clung to their claims of innocence. Osborne eventually died in prison, and Good was found guilty and hanged. Tituba, meanwhile, borrowed time by continuing her confessions. Some warned her not to admit spectral evidence into court. Those warnings went unheeded, however, until the fever finally broke in 1693 and a general pardon was granted to those still alive to receive it.

All told, in the Salem witch trials of 1692–93, some two hundred people were accused of practicing witchcraft. Twenty-eight were convicted, nineteen were hanged, and one (Giles Corey) was pressed to death. Four others died in prison. These numbers made Salem exceptional in Colonial New England, but not unique. In fact, by the historian Carol Karlsen's calculation, between 1620 and 1725, at least 344 New Englanders were suspected of witchcraft and brought to trial.[7] And before then there had been tens of thousands of victims in Europe.

Tituba, however, was not yet home free. Even though she had escaped indictment as a witch, inmates in Colonial New England were required to pay their prison costs. This was a problem for Tituba, who, as a slave, had no assets and, worse, an owner in Parris who refused to pay so as to keep her from returning to his home. As a result, Tituba was sold to a new owner who agreed to cover the charge: seven pounds. It's possible that John Indian was sold with her, though all the records show is that young Violet, likely Tituba's daughter, remained a Parris family slave.

Not long afterward the people of Salem realized that something terrible had transpired in their village—not the selling of Tituba, to be sure, but the hysteria. In 1694 Parris stepped forward as the first person to publicly apologize for his role. Later, the General Court in Boston declared January 14, 1697, as a fast day during which all were to repent for the trials' excesses. By then, however, Tituba had vanished from the historical record.

76

What's the truth about many African-American families having a Native American ancestor?

ACCORDING TO GENETICISTS Joanna Mountain and Kasia Bryc, the average African American is 73.2 percent sub-Saharan, 24 percent European, and only 0.8 percent Native American.[1] Most African Americans have quite a lot of European ancestry and very little Native American ancestry. And if this Native American DNA came from exactly one ancestor, it surfaced in our family trees quite a long time ago—on average, perhaps as many as eleven generations, or three hundred years, ago. (Since many of our African ancestors had not even arrived in the United States by then, this dating helps explain why most of us don't have much Native American ancestry.) The bottom line is that those high cheekbones and that straight black hair derive from our high proportion of *white ancestors* and not, for most of us at least, from our mythical Cherokee great-great-grandmother.

Despite these averages, however, some African Americans do have significant amounts of Native American ancestry, though not as much as their European ancestry, by quite a long shot. (This does not include black people of Hispanic origin; Hispanic Americans tend to have far more Native American ancestry than African Americans do.)

Again, here are the statistics. Whereas virtually all African Americans have a considerable amount of European ancestry in their genomes, only 22 percent carry more than 1 percent Native American ancestry, while more than 5 percent of African-American people carry at least 2 percent

Native American ancestry.[2] How do these percentages translate into ancestry? If you have 5 percent Native American ancestry in your admixture result, that means you had one Native American ancestor four to five generations back (120 to 150 years ago). If you have 2 percent Native American ancestry, you had one such ancestor on your family tree five to nine generations back (150 to 270 years ago). One percent of Native American ancestry means that this ancestor entered your bloodline six to ten generations back (180 to 300 years ago).

In order to mate enough to be statistically significant, a sufficient number of Native Americans and African Americans had to have been living near each other. But in only a few periods in American history—and only a few circumstances—could this have been possible, since the average slave and the average Native American never even crossed paths. According to Claudio Saunt of the University of Georgia, it's a matter of geography: "Most Indians did not live on the margins of the slave states."[3] This simple but telling historical fact makes it quite impossible for significant numbers of Native Americans to have interacted with significant numbers of African-American slaves.

One period in which they could have interacted, Saunt relates,

> was certainly before 1715. In that early period, by one estimate, fully one-third of all slaves in South Carolina were Indian, but of course the absolute numbers were small. Indian slavery declined rapidly after that period, so contact would have occurred only when fugitive slaves ended up in Indian country—which they did in small numbers—or when Indians went to the [British or Spanish] colonies to trade. [But] of course, the absolute numbers were small.

And according to the historian Ira Berlin, "The chances of mixing were greatest in the seventeenth and early-eighteenth century, especially before the American Revolution."[4]

The historian Eric Foner agrees that opportunities for mixing most likely would have occurred very early in American history: "Presumably, blacks and Native Americans would be in proximity to one another during the Colonial era—before Indians were pushed further inland. Some slaves escaped to find refuge with Indian tribes, especially the Seminoles." Foner points to seventeenth-century New England, Virginia, and upstate New York as places where mixing might have happened, because "many slaves

Sanford Ward Perryman, A Creek Delegate, in an albumen print taken in Washington, D.C., 1867.

were said to escape to Indian nations [located in these places] during the seventeenth and eighteenth centuries."[5]

Another historian, David Eltis, suggests "early-eighteenth-century South Carolina as a strong possibility with Indian slaves sold into the Caribbean (and New England earlier) as well as African slaves coming into Charleston (and New England) first from the Caribbean and, beginning in 1701, directly from the Gambia. There must have been Indians and Africans working on those early rice plantations together." Eltis points out that Katherine Hayes's recent book *Slavery Before Race* "has fascinating evidence of Indian and African slaves working together in 1660s and 1670s Long Island."[6]

All these historians pinpoint these few locales, home to a small number of Indians and Africans, within a very early American historical time frame, as places where black people and Native Americans lived close enough to form family bonds. They all also point to a much later period when mixing doubtless occurred—during and after the Trail of Tears, as we will discuss below.

This time frame, however, presents a problem for explaining Native American ancestry in blacks. By 1715 few Africans had arrived in North

77

Which pioneering play introduced mainstream American audiences to the dynamics undergirding the civil rights movement?

LORRAINE HANSBERRY'S *A Raisin in the Sun* is a play about a black Chicago family divided by money and competing dreams about how to spend it. Resonating on multiple levels for black America, it remains as relevant today as when it opened in 1959, five years after *Brown v. Board of Education,* four years after the Montgomery bus boycott, two years after the showdown between the federal government and racist segregationists at Central High School in Little Rock, four years before the civil rights movement reached its zenith during the great March on Washington, and at a moment when free, decolonized African nations were being born. That year, 1959, was pivotal in the movement's history, and *A Raisin in the Sun*—keenly aware of this larger political context—was its literary fulcrum, posing questions about the costs of antiblack racism and the small but crucial ways in which individual choices affect historical change.

A Raisin in the Sun is, at its core, a play about hard choices: Will Walter Lee Younger, Jr., a demoralized chauffeur, invest his father's money wisely, or will he throw it away by helping an associate buy a liquor store license? Will Walter's pregnant wife, Ruth, a domestic, keep their baby? Will Walter's sister, Beneatha, accept a marriage proposal from her Nigerian boyfriend, Joseph Asagai? Will Beneatha and Walter's sixty-year-old mother, Lena, with still-vivid memories of sharecroppers and former slaves, use her late husband's money to buy the family a home, or will she continue to suffer in the same cramped apartment as the gulf between her and her children widens? And at the drama's climax, will they manage to escape their plight, or will Walter Lee Jr. accept the wish of the "Welcome Committee" and clear out of their new, all-white neighborhood?

In 1959 enough African-American families courageously chose dignity and resistance in the face of racism to create the conditions that led to the March on Washington in 1963 and the Pettus Bridge Incident in 1965. During that period, young women like Beneatha Younger (the character closest in spirit to Lorraine Hansberry) emerged as agents of change. Today Hansberry can be seen as a pioneering role model for the many successful African-American women since the 1960s. As we learned in Amazing Fact no. 58: "Black women currently earn about two thirds of all African-American bachelor's degree awards, 70 percent of all master's degrees and more than 60 percent of all doctorates," according to the *Journal of Blacks in Higher Education*.[1]

The success of the play reflected the nature and pace of racial progress. *Raisin* was initially rejected by financiers, but after it launched on

Denzel Washington as Walter Younger and Sophie Okonedo as Ruth Younger in 2014, at the second Broadway revival of *A Raisin in the Sun*. The critically acclaimed play was originally staged in 1959.

Broadway in March 1959, it became the first Broadway play by an African-American writer about an African-American family to attract African-American theatergoers in droves. At age twenty-nine, Hansberry went on to become the youngest and first black playwright to win the New York Drama Critics Circle award for best play. Two years later a film version directed by Daniel Petrie (though not with Hansberry's screenplay) won an award at Cannes.

"Ghetto-itis," to quote Beneatha, was "acute" in the United States, and it remains today a reality for too many families, complicating euphoric feelings in observing the civil rights anniversaries. Tension lingers between dreams fulfilled and dreams deferred. As Mama Younger says, "Seem like God didn't see fit to give the black man nothing but dreams—but He did give us children to make them dreams seem worthwhile." Mama's reflection was echoed four years later at the Lincoln Memorial. His dream, Dr. King said, was "deeply rooted in the American Dream. . . . I have a dream that my four little children will one day live in a nation where they will not be judged by the color of their skin but by the content of their character." Too many children today are still doing their dreaming in schools that are legally but not actually integrated.

But *A Raisin in the Sun* was never a play about integration; Mama tells the family that she tried to buy a house in a black neighborhood but that the prices there were twice as high (even though it was much farther out of town). Nor is Hansberry's ending the all-too-easy one of triumph over despair, the stuff of romance or melodrama. In fact, *Raisin* is about *getting out* of trapped, claustrophobic lives, and *that* struggle is far from won.

In the face of despair, what can an artist do? This question consumed Lorraine Hansberry, a child of middle-class parents who believed their people's ultimate salvation was to come—had to come—from those struggling for survival in the working and lower classes. As James Baldwin said of his "sweet Lorraine," she "made no bones about asserting that art has a purpose, and that its purpose was action: that it contained the 'energy which could change things.'"[2]

What shines through the play is Hansberry's artistic and political honesty, especially about the diversity and divisions within black families and how African Americans speak to each other when white people aren't around. For example, Walter, in his exasperation, says, "'Cause we all tied up in a race of people that don't know how to do nothing but moan, pray and have babies!" And at another point he says, "I been married eleven years and I got a boy who sleeps in the living room—(*Very, very quietly*)—and all I got to give him is stories about how rich white people live."

Hansberry lifted a curtain onto a world "behind the veil," as W.E.B. Du Bois put it famously in 1903. Honesty, Brooks Atkinson wrote in his review of *Raisin* for the *New York Times,* was "Miss Hansberry's personal contribution to an explosive situation in which simple honesty is the most difficult thing in the world. And also the most illuminating."[3]

Hansberry's honesty was part of the broader naturalistic movement among writers of the 1940s and '50s, a style and approach made famous in the era's most popular black novel, Richard Wright's 1940 *Native Son.* Hansberry, like Wright, presented an unsentimental view of the hard asphalt of urban life in Chicago after the Great Migration, when parents suffered structural hardships and their children slept on couches in living rooms fending off roaches and rats. White audiences, seduced by Hansberry's seemingly straightforward morality tale, developed empathy for the Youngers, only to realize, when the white representative of the "Welcome Committee" arrives later in the play, that it is too late to turn away from the reality of the society they helped create.

A Raisin in the Sun is clearly a rewriting of Wright's naturalistic *Native Son,* self-consciously echoing scenes and characters in that great novel. It opens in a tenement apartment on Chicago's South Side, as an alarm clock shatters a night of fitful slumber. Both protagonists are chauffeurs to rich white businessmen. Both contain references to a "toothless rat," among many other repetitions. But Hansberry rejects Wright's bleak, even despairing assessment of the possibilities of progress for the American Negro in an unyieldingly racist capitalist economy circa 1940. Instead she asks us to contemplate another set of life choices for a working-class black man who feels trapped in a world that allows him to glimpse the possibilities of life yet denies him any way to realize those possibilities.

78

What role did Lord Mansfield's mixed-race great-niece, Dido Elizabeth Belle, play in his famous decision on slavery in England?

WHILE ON DUTY with the Royal Navy in the West Indies, John Lindsay, the son of Sir Alexander Lindsay and Emilia (Murray) Lindsay, daughter of the fifth Viscount Stormont, encountered Maria Belle, a black female slave on a Spanish ship. Whatever passed between them, Lindsay took Belle back to England, where their child, Dido Elizabeth Belle, was born. Very little is known about Dido's mother except that she was a slave, which, as a matter of law, meant that Dido was too. Dido's West Indian origin and her mother's name are provided by an entry in the baptismal record at St. George's Church in Bloomsbury, London, in 1766. By that point, she was about five years old.[1]

In 1764 Dido's father was knighted. Returning for duty in the West Indies, he looked to his family for help raising his mixed-race daughter. It was not just any family to which he turned, but that of his mother's brother, William Murray, and his wife, Elizabeth Finch, soon to become the First Earl and Lady of Mansfield. By historical coincidence, this Lord Mansfield also happened to be the lord chief justice of England and Wales, roughly the equivalent of being the chief justice of the U.S. Supreme Court.

By the end of the eighteenth century, England's black population was estimated at between 10,000 and 15,000. "Not all black people in the latter half of the 18th century were slaves or servants. Black people were part of English society working as sailors, tradespeople, businessmen and musicians. They married and had families."[2]

Formerly attributed to Johann Zoffany. *Dido Elizabeth Belle and Lady Elizabeth Murray.* 1779. Oil on canvas. London, Kenwood House.

Belle's fate would unfold at Kenwood House in Hampstead, London, the home of William Murray since 1754. Murray (aka Lord Mansfield) was John Lindsay's uncle, which made Belle his great-niece. They, childless, agreed to raise Belle. She was joined by her cousin Lady Elizabeth Murray (1760–1825), daughter of David Murray, another of Lord Mansfield's nephews, who would later become the Second Earl of Mansfield. Both had lost their mothers, but only Belle was a slave.

Belle's position with Elizabeth Murray seems to have been that of lady's companion rather than the more common position of lady's maid. A lady's companion usually came from the gentry class associated with manorial life and was considered approximately the social equal of her employer. Such companions usually lived in the family quarters and had no responsibility for heavier or more common housekeeping duties. There is certainly the possibility, however, that Belle was accepted as a full member of the family, at least in principle.

This last point we can see in the well-known painting of Belle and her cousin dating from about 1779. Although no longer attributed to the eminent artist Johann Zoffany, the work nevertheless presents a tantalizing view of the two young women, leaving more questions raised than answered. Elizabeth Murray's figure dominates the foreground and presents her in the upper-middle-class convention of the well-read lady. Belle, dressed in an exotic turban and carrying a platter of fruit, moves behind her, her finger raised enigmatically to her face.

By this point in British aristocratic portrait painting, the representation of sitters with fawning black servants was going out of fashion, reflecting a growing distaste for such self-aggrandizement if not for the institution of slavery itself. But even if Belle's station at Kenwood had been compromised by her race and illegitimate status, her role there seems to have been more like that of a member of the household than that of a servant.

According to the historian Steven Wise, "Sometimes she [Dido] acted as his [Mansfield's] amanuensis."[3] That is, she was a black ghostwriter to the most influential judge in all of Great Britain.

The most intriguing question is whether Dido, while still a child, influenced the most famous legal case ever to cross Lord Mansfield's desk, the case that would help make slavery illegal in England.

The slave James Somerset was purchased in America and brought to England by his master in 1769. Slipping his owner there, Somerset was baptized in London in 1771, "perhaps in the hope that this would liberate him," writes the historian Kathy Chater. Instead, Somerset's owner "had Somerset captured and put on board . . . a ship bound for Jamaica." But three sympathetic witnesses cried foul and, in an attempt to rescue Somerset, "obtained from Lord Mansfield, the Lord Chief Justice, a writ of habeas corpus, a legal test of the right to imprison someone." In February 1772, "the case came before the Court of King's Bench, the highest court of common law in England and Wales."[4]

Somerset's lawyers, who included leading English abolitionist Granville Sharp, argued that the laws of slavery elsewhere in the colonies shouldn't be forced on Mother England, which, through its common law, was moving toward liberty. The other side argued that however repugnant slavery was, no court should rob a man of his property when he was traveling outside the country. Mansfield hoped the parties would settle, but when they didn't, he was forced to decide. Recalling the drama, former Massachusetts governor Thomas Hutchinson wrote in his diary, "A Jamaica planter being asked what judgement his Ldship would give? 'No doubt' he answered 'He

[Somerset] will be set free, for Lord Mansfield keeps a Black in his house which governs him and the whole family.' "⁵ He was speaking of Belle.

On June 22, 1772, Lord Mansfield ruled that Somerset could not be forcibly removed from England, that there were limits on what could be done with a slave, and that a coercive sale outside England was beyond those limits. "Whatever inconveniences, therefore, may follow from the decision, I cannot say this case is allowed or approved by the law of England," Mansfield wrote, "and therefore the black must be discharged."

Although slavery in England and the kidnapping of slaves out of England continued after the Somerset decision (and Mansfield himself ruled in 1785 that "black slaves in Britain were not entitled to be paid for their labour"),⁶ antislavery advocates in America and Britain now had a short but powerful precedent that said slavery was in no way God's or nature's law but an evil institution that could exist only where it had the force of local, *man*-made laws. Of course, it would take the British Parliament until 1807 to pass the Abolition of the Slave Trade Act and until 1833 to pass the Slavery Abolition Act extending throughout the empire. But the long arc of emancipation was beginning to turn, and Mansfield was there as a source.

"Some speculated that Dido had . . . badgered him [Mansfield] into it," Steven Wise writes, "though it is hard to believe a child could accomplish this." Then again, Belle's presence in his household could have brought to life for him the principles of law and liberty he read about in the works of Cicero, Montesquieu, and Blackstone. "He did adore her," Wise writes. "By 1785, aged twenty-two, she was receiving an annual allowance greater than 30 pounds, twice the salary of Mansfield's first coachman, and nearly four times that of a kitchen maid," though "substantially less than the 100 pounds her cousin, Lady Elizabeth, was receiving." He cautions that "that could have been because Dido was illegitimate, not because she was a mulatto."

No one knows how Belle reacted to the whispers at Kenwood about the Somerset case. But it is hard to imagine that Mansfield's proximity and fondness for his mulatto great-niece didn't factor into his view of the slave James Somerset in his court.

79

Who was the first African-American writer to investigate and report the wrongdoings of a world leader?

THE FIRST WHISTLEBLOWER about Belgian atrocities in the Congo wasn't Joseph Conrad in his 1899 novel, *Heart of Darkness,* but George Washington Williams, an African American writing from the heart of King Leopold's "Congo Free State." Leopold tried to trash Williams for his shocking exposé, but to W.E.B. Du Bois, George Washington Williams was "the greatest historian of the race."[1]

Leopold of Belgium had learned about the Congo, lands "discovered" by Portuguese traders in the fifteenth century, by reading of the exploits of the notorious Henry Morton Stanley, a correspondent for the *New York Herald* who had served as a Confederate soldier during the Civil War. But he had made his own presumption, calling them a "magnifique gâteau africain."[2]

Leopold hired the opportunistic Stanley as his agent, charging him with gobbling up land through sham treaties with local Congolese chiefs. From 1878 to 1883 Stanley concluded about four hundred such "cloth and trinket" treaties.[3] But Leopold didn't want their lands for the Belgian government. He wanted them for his own personal empire, outside the empire.

By the time he was finished, Leopold had accumulated nearly *one million* square miles. He somehow persuaded the international community to sanction his "Congo Free State" under the guise that he was an antislavery man who only wanted to spread to the continent "new ideas of law, order, humanity and protection of the natives."[4] Actually, he had designs on the

George Washington
Williams—Civil War
veteran, historian, journalist,
legislator, civil rights
activist. Engraving.

Congo's ivory supply and, in a diabolical racket, persuaded the powers-
that-be to declare it a free trade zone under his control so he could tax other
trading companies while exempting his own. Remarkably, Leopold himself never visited the Congo, which Paul Vallely describes as "unmapped
jungle, 75 times the size of Belgium."[5]

The first in a chorus of voices to expose his depraved, monopolistic
rule was that of a black man. That would have been surprising to Leopold, especially since the man was George Washington Williams, whom
he knew. In 1889 Williams had interviewed Leopold for a news article and
had been "dazzled," writes the historian Adam Hochschild.[6] Williams had
reported that Leopold was "a pleasant and entertaining conversationalist"
who had modestly said, "What I do there [in the Congo] is done as a Christian duty to the poor African; and I do not wish to have one franc back of
all the money I have expended."[7] In Leopold's Congo, Williams had seen
hope for his own missionary plan to recruit dozens of American black men
to venture overseas to bring order to their ancestors' home continent.

Born in Pennsylvania in 1849, Williams had misrepresented his age in
order to be accepted into the Union Army in 1864. Part of the last campaign
of the Civil War, Williams and his fellow black soldiers helped shut down
Confederate general Robert E. Lee's escape route out of Virginia's Appomattox Court House. After bouncing around in the Mexican and U.S.

armies after the Civil War, Williams studied for a short time at Howard University. In 1874 he graduated from the Newton Theological Institution outside Boston.

In the ensuing years, he ministered to congregations, started two newspapers, apprenticed as a lawyer, wrote a play about slavery, and became the first black man to serve in the Ohio state legislature. He eventually earned the honorary title "colonel" for his efforts on behalf of black Union Army veterans (though he stretched the truth to make it seem as if he had earned that rank for his service in the war). He even almost became the first African-American U.S. minister to Haiti, until President Chester Arthur left office and rumors of Williams's personal debts caught up with him.

Williams made his greatest impact as a historian. Having honed his skills as a writer at Newton, he cranked out close to eleven hundred pages in his *History of the Negro Race in America, 1619–1880,* published in two volumes in 1882–83.[8] He was lauded for his innovative investigative skills, including conducting interviews, contacting generals for information, and soliciting church records and other documents to fill in the gaps others had left. To his curriculum vitae he added another volume in 1887, *A History of the Negro Troops in the War of the Rebellion, 1861–1865.*[9]

Williams learned of Leopold's "Congo Free State" at a White House meeting with President Arthur and Leopold's lobbyist, Henry Shelton Sanford. He developed a plan to go to the Congo, write propaganda on behalf of Leopold, and recruit other ambitious young black men to follow. Seeking backers, he was eventually sponsored by American railroad tycoon Collis P. Huntington, an investor in Leopold's Congo railroad. Once he hatched his plan, Williams made his pitch for recruits at a Virginia college, but with little to go on, his audience balked.

Williams decided to check things out for himself and report what he learned back home. What he discovered as he sailed around the continent and up the Congo River was the rotten, brutal hypocrisy at the heart of Leopold's "Free State." This was no revolution to exalt African men and women but an extractive pursuit in which black human life had exactly *zero* worth.

Williams kept track of what he saw, and by the time he reached Stanley Falls in mid-July 1890, he couldn't take it anymore. He felt compelled to blow the whistle, as a black man Hochschild describes as "doubly horrified" by what he saw and by the grievous disappointment he felt.

He composed a four-thousand-word letter that opened by addressing

Leopold as his "good and great friend." But it was a takedown. Williams wrote of "how thoroughly I have been disenchanted, disappointed and disheartened," so that "it is now my painful duty to make known to your Majesty in plain but respectful language."

Williams charged Leopold with deception (and intimidation) in getting the Congolese chiefs to trade away their lands in exchange for their own enslavement, exploitation, pillaging, and forced prostitution. He noted the king's failure to build an adequate hospital even for his own white officers in charge of the carnage. The culprits, he made clear, were both white and black, including the mercenaries that Leopold's men hired from surrounding regions to enforce his rule. The victims were the inhabitants of the Congo condemned to torture, suffering, and death if they did not bend to his will. Williams's expressed goal was to persuade the world community to put pressure on Leopold and investigate his crimes.

He followed up with letters to the U.S. secretary of state and a report to President Benjamin Harrison. He said he had even been offered slaves. His open letter, which was published as a pamphlet and made public, was nothing less than "a milestone in the literature of human rights and of investigative journalism," Hochschild argues.

Leopold's response was to smear Williams as a liar who had puffed himself up with the inflated title of "colonel"; who was in the pocket of those who wanted looser trade in the Congo, perhaps the Dutch; and who should be taken with a grain of salt given what his countrymen were doing to the American Indians in the West.

But by the following decade, a chorus of voices were speaking out against Leopold, including those of Mark Twain, Sir Arthur Conan Doyle, journalist E. D. Morel, and the British consul Roger Casement, whose 1904 government report, Vallely writes, "suggested that at least three million people had died" in the Congo.

But Williams was no longer alive to see this support. Tragically, he had died a year after writing his open letter to the king, having contracted tuberculosis in Egypt. And before that, as further damage to his reputation, he had become engaged to a white woman while separated from his wife and son back in the States. George Washington Williams died in Blackpool, England, on August 2, 1891, at forty-one. He was buried in an unmarked grave there until his biographer, the distinguished African-American historian John Hope Franklin, arranged for a headstone in 1975.

80

Who were the first notable African Americans who stepped into America's institutions of higher learning?

JOHN CHAVIS

The first black college student hailed not from the North but from the South. John Chavis was the child of free black North Carolinians and a Revolutionary War veteran. He first studied privately with John Witherspoon, the sixth president of Princeton University (then called the College of New Jersey, James Madison's alma mater) and a signer of the Declaration of Independence. When Witherspoon died in 1794, he continued his studies at Liberty Hall Academy in Lexington, Virginia, the future home, ironically, of Washington and Lee University, named for two slaveholders, President George Washington and Confederate general Robert E. Lee.

There is no official record of Chavis's graduation from Liberty Hall Academy in 1799, but it is inferred from the fact that he was granted a license to minister in the Presbyterian Church. The minutes of the Lexington Presbytery on October 19, 1799, attest that "John Chavis, a black man personally known to most members of the Presbytery and of unquestionably good favor, & a communicant in the Presbyterian Church was introduced and conversed with relative to his practical acquaintance with living religion & his call to preach the Everlasting Gospel."

Chavis went on to become a teacher and preacher and continued until fallout from Nat Turner's rebellion in 1831 robbed him of that right. The North Carolina legislature now perceived African-American ministers, as a class, as a threat. It didn't matter that Chavis had willingly taught white students by day (including two future governors) and blacks by night. Reverend Chavis tried to distinguish himself from Turner, but his finances took a severe hit.

For years little was said of Chavis at Washington and Lee University. Now there is a house on campus named after him on Lee Avenue, a counterweight to the chapel nearby where the popular Confederate general (later president of the college) is buried. The school claims Chavis as "the first African-American to receive a college education in the United States."

MARTIN FREEMAN

By the 1830s, Middlebury College in Vermont had "adopted a policy of racial exclusion."[1] But in 1849 it granted an exception to Martin Freeman, salutatorian of his class. A year later Freeman became "the first college-educated black professor in America" when he joined the faculty at the Allegheny Institute and Mission Church (the future black Avery College) in Pittsburgh.[2] (Charles L. Reason, with his appointment to teach at New York Central College in 1849, was "the first African American to teach at a mixed race institution of higher education in the U.S.")[3]

GEORGE B. VASHON

The abolitionist haven Oberlin College opened its doors in 1833 and soon became a magnet for black men and women. Its first black graduate was George B. Vashon, class of 1844, who after the Civil War became one of the founding professors at Howard University. Most of Howard's original faculty was white and would remain so for decades; Vashon, Rayford Logan tells us, was "the first Negro teacher" at "The Capstone of Negro Education."[4] It took abolitionist schools such as Oberlin, willing to buck the proslavery trend in the United States, to train black scholars who would, in turn, train rising generations at the nation's historically black colleges and universities.

LUCY STANTON DAY SESSIONS

Oberlin honored other barrier-breakers before the Civil War. In 1850 Lucy Stanton Day Sessions became the first black woman to earn a certificate in literature from Oberlin. At her graduation, she gave a speech titled "A Plea for the Oppressed," which was published in the *Oberlin Evangelist*. "Ye that advocate the great principles of Temperance, Peace, and Moral Reform will you not raise your voice in behalf of these stricken ones!—will you not plead the cause of the Slave?" she implored.[5] After the Civil War, Sessions answered the call of history by moving to Georgia to teach under the sponsorship of the Cleveland Freedman's Association. After another stint in Mississippi, she and her family were among the first African Americans to live in the City of Angels: Los Angeles.

MARY JANE PATTERSON

In 1862 Mary Jane Patterson became the first African-American woman to receive a bachelor's degree in the United States, also from Oberlin Col-

Mary Jane Patterson in a formal portrait taken during her school years at Oberlin College, 1862.

lege. She became a teacher and, after the Civil War, moved to Washington to serve "as the first black principal at the newly established Preparatory School for Negroes, later known as the M Street School and still later as Paul Laurence Dunbar High School."[6]

OUR HISTORICALLY BLACK COLLEGES AND UNIVERSITIES

The Civil War and the civil rights movement, two bursts one hundred years apart, each in its own way profoundly changed the equation for black students pursuing a higher education. But there were many peaks and valleys in between. Although the Freedmen's Bureau took seriously its charge to educate the former slaves after emancipation, by the close of the nineteenth century the former Confederate states had found every way to manipulate the promise of equal protection by establishing separate colleges and universities for black and white students.

The first of the nation's historically black colleges and universities, Cheyney University of Pennsylvania, had been founded way back in 1837, but most black colleges broke ground in the half century after the Civil War as training grounds for teachers and other black professionals. W.E.B. Du Bois may have graduated from Harvard with bachelor's and master's degrees in 1890 and 1891, and with his Ph.D. in 1895, but he was first trained at Fisk University in Nashville as a member of the class of 1888. And although Martin L. Kilson may have been the first black professor to take up tenure in the Faculty of Arts and Sciences at Harvard in 1969, he was trained at Lincoln University near Ambler, Pennsylvania, as a member of the class of 1953.

Until the dawn of affirmative action in the 1960s, such luminaries as Du Bois and Kilson were the exceptions to the rule at historically *white* colleges and universities. These aspirants broke barriers, even though so many of the nation's educational leaders had decided in the early 1890s to track black students for education in industry rather than in the liberal arts and sciences, as staunchly advocated by Booker T. Washington.

81

What was Freedom's Fort, and how does it relate to Memorial Day?

FORT MONROE (later known as Freedom's Fort) was a Union stronghold on the southern tip of the Virginia Peninsula, at the mouth of the James River.[1] Across the river, in Confederate territory, on the coast above Norfolk, lay Sewell's Point. There, in the spring of 1861, slaves were being forced to build battlements for the Confederate Army.

On the night of May 23, the day Virginia officially seceded from the Union, three slaves risked their lives in a daring escape to Fort Monroe, which beckoned them from across the waters. It was one of the most memorable nights of the war. Frank Baker, Shepard Mallory, and James Townsend rowed in the darkness, not knowing whether they would survive the crossing, be shot dead when they landed, be returned to their master, Confederate Colonel Charles K. Mallory, or be punished by seeing their families sold.

What they did know was that if they stayed at Sewell's Point, they would be transferred deeper into Dixie to the Carolinas, where still more battlements would have to be built to defend slavery using their labor.

By seeking refuge with the Union Army, Baker, Mallory, and Townsend unofficially ignited the movement of slaves emancipating themselves with their feet—the contraband movement—which would extend the aim of the war from maintaining the Union at all costs to also *freeing the slaves*. That last aim would be the ultimate revenge on the South's rebel government, formed on the bedrock notion that one person had the right to own another.

On the Union side, the unsuspecting general about to receive the trio was Benjamin F. Butler, Fort Monroe's new commander and a slippery

Massachusetts Democrat who, in the presidential election just a year before, had supported the pro-slavery candidate against Abraham Lincoln.

To the three rowers, the fort in the distance was laced with meaning. As Eric Foner writes, Fort Monroe "stood near the spot where twenty slaves had been landed from a Dutch ship in 1619, marking the beginning of slavery in England's North American colonies."[2] Completed in 1834, the fort was named for James Monroe, the nation's fifth president and the fourth Virginia slaveholder to occupy the White House. Covering sixty-three acres, with walls stretching over a mile around, Fort Monroe stood watch at Old Point Comfort near Hampton. As with so many of our early landmarks, slaves had helped build it. One of the officers formerly stationed there was Robert E. Lee.

But on the night of May 23, 1861, none of that history mattered. For Baker, Mallory, and Townsend, both the decision and the risks were personal. It had been a month since the firing on Fort Sumter, during which a small skirmish had erupted between the guns at Fort Monroe and Sewell's

Stampede among the Negroes in Virginia—their arrival at Fortress Monroe. Wood engraving, *Frank Leslie's Illustrated Newspaper,* June 8, 1861.

Point. The people of Virginia were euphoric, celebrating their so-called independence from the North. Up in Washington, President Lincoln had made clear in his first inaugural address that he would refrain from interfering with slavery where it existed. Still, the three men rowed on toward their best chance for avoiding slavery deeper in the South. Baker, Mallory, and Townsend: to me, they are the Shadrach, Meshach, and Abednego of the Civil War.

After the escaped slaves came ashore at Fort Monroe, General Butler learned that two of them had wives and families in nearby Hampton and that he was to be their judge and jury. Here was his problem: before the Civil War, runaway slaves had been called fugitive slaves, and according to federal law, Union officers were required to return them without question. But things were different now. Even though President Lincoln denied it, the Confederates insisted they were citizens of a new foreign country, independent of U.S. law. Butler, looking for every advantage against the feisty rebels, decided to hoist them on their own logic.

The next morning he rode out to meet Confederate major John B. Cary, who was acting as an agent for Colonel Mallory, the slaves' owner. Under a flag of truce, Cary insisted that Baker, Mallory, and Townsend be returned. Butler gave Cary his terms: if Mallory swore his allegiance to the Union, Butler would give his "property" back. Not surprisingly, Mallory refused the offer. In the face of such defiance, Butler declared Baker, Mallory, and Townsend "contraband of war," no different from other armaments lost from one foreign country to another in the heat of battle.

There was a certain logic to it. Why should Butler return to the Confederates any makers of armaments that would kill Union troops? With that, Foner writes, "Butler had introduced a new word into the political lexicon." Although being named "contraband" was far from obtaining a guarantee of freedom, it wasn't slavery either. Baker, Mallory, and Townsend had, with their escape, opened up a middle ground and, with it, the possibility for more.

Slaves like Baker, Mallory, and Townsend were not passive recipients bowing in the marble friezes of history—they were pivotal in their own emancipation. At once, they had hurt the Confederate cause and given Butler the opportunity to bolster the Union's. But the logic was not bulletproof, Foner cautions. Right away, he says, "Butler's legal reasoning broke down further as escaping slaves who had not labored for the Confederate military, including women and children, joined male fugitives." In fact, just a few days after Baker, Mallory, and Townsend arrived, forty-seven more runaway slaves knocked on the door of Freedom's Fort, including a three-month-old baby.

But what was the Union to do with the African Americans now that they were contraband? Send them to colonies in Africa or in Central America? Sell them back to owners to pay for war debts? Put them to work? Keep the able-bodied and discard the sick and old? Or keep the slaves owned by those active in the rebellion and reject those belonging to masters still loyal to the Union? As the parlor debate advanced, the slaves of the South kept advancing the issue, crossing rivers one at a time, wherever and whenever they saw bluecoats.

President Lincoln now had a humanitarian crisis on his hands: runaway slaves were the refugees of the Civil War. He drew the line up to, but not including, emancipation. Butler could have his "fugitive slave" law at Fort Monroe, but more activist generals like John Frémont in Missouri, who tried to emancipate runaway slaves outright, would be slapped down. Lincoln was buying time as word had spread among the slaves of the South that Freedom's Fort was an actual place, and that whatever a contraband was, it wasn't a slave!

By the end of July 1861, 850 slaves had escaped to Fort Monroe. Even if they couldn't vote (they weren't even citizens), they were voting with their feet. To deal with them, on August 6, 1861, Congress passed the first of two Confiscation Acts allowing military commanders to declare "all such property . . . to be lawful subject of prize and capture wherever found."[3] The slaves who kept rowing were forcing their hands.

But for the refugees, fleeing the Confederacy was only the first part of the battle. After all, Congress's order didn't *require* the bluecoats to welcome every ex-slave who came knocking. Given the strange concept of human contrabands, some soldiers exploited the ex-slaves, a few killed them outright, and some even profited from illegally trading them on the black market back to the enemy.

With their interim status as contraband, men like Baker, Mallory, and Townsend forced the issue of emancipation. Lincoln's official Emancipation Proclamation on January 1, 1863, pledged to enlist and *arm* black troops. "By the end of the Civil War," according to National Archives teacher training materials, "roughly 179,000 black men (10 percent of the Union Army) served as soldiers in the U.S. Army and another 19,000 served in the Navy."[4] And you can draw a straight line from them back to Baker,

Mallory, and Townsend's arrival at Freedom's Fort and forward from them to the first Memorial Day, which is why I believe strongly that it is time for us to claim the contraband of the Civil War as veterans of the struggle for freedom and as heroes to be honored on this and every future Memorial Day.

With this in mind, I was particularly moved when I read of an army chaplain who, observing the contrabands, described how African-American slaves "flocked in vast numbers—an army in themselves—to the camps of the Yankees." He compared their arrival to "the oncoming of cities."[5] We may never know all of their names, or how many died trying to escape, but the varied resting places of the contraband men and women of the Civil War are a virtual tomb of unknown soldiers who won an important moral and material victory that transformed the war.

As the *New York Times* put it on August 13, 1861, more than a year before Lincoln issued the preliminary Emancipation Proclamation, "We begin to see now the stupendous fatuity of Secessionism, which under the color of protecting Slavery by dissolving the Union, is causing Slavery to melt from the land as snows under a summer's sun."[6] I wish I knew more about what happened to Baker, Mallory, and Townsend after their fateful night rowing to Freedom's Fort at the start of the war, but for sure I know we are indebted to them for helping those "snows" of slavery to melt.

Ironically, after the Civil War ended, the Confederacy's president, Jefferson Davis, was imprisoned at Fort Monroe. The surrounding city of Hampton became the site of Hampton Normal and Agricultural Institute (later Hampton University), which trained the freedmen and gave rise to Booker T. Washington and other leaders. Today, Fort Monroe, or Freedom's Fort, offers visitors a chance to reflect on this powerful legacy. Other markers honoring the contraband of the Civil War include the first safe haven for runaway slaves in North Carolina—"the Hotel De'Afrique" along the Cape Hatteras National Seashore; the Freedmen's Colony of Roanoke Island, North Carolina; the Contraband Camp of Corinth, Mississippi; and Freedom Park in Helena, Arkansas.

Especially touching is the recently rediscovered Alexandria Contrabands and Freedmen Cemetery, where some 1,800 African Americans were interred in the Civil War years. A short distance from Arlington National Cemetery in Virginia, the Contrabands and Freedmen Cemetery originally included seventy-five black contrabands-turned-soldiers of that war until hundreds of their fellow African-American troops convalescing at a nearby hospital learned what was going on and demanded that they be moved. Their 1864 petition declared: "We are not contrabands, but soldiers of the U.S. Army. We are now sharing equally the dangers and hardships in this mighty contest, and should share the same privileges and rights of burial in every way with our fellow soldiers, who only differ from us in color."[7]

And do you know what? They were moved to Arlington National Cemetery, incidentally the former estate of Robert E. Lee, now an integrated cemetery where so many of the fallen soldiers of the United States rest today. If you're interested in visiting, the black soldiers of the Civil War are buried in sections 23 and 27. With them in section 27 are the graves of 3,800 Civil War contrabands, many of whom occupied "Freedman's Village" on the confiscated Lee estate at Arlington during and after the war. The veterans' graves (including those of three Medal of Honor recipients) "are marked with the Civil War shield and the letters U.S.C.T.," according to the official Arlington National Cemetery website, while the contrabands' "headstones [are] marked with the words 'Civilian' or 'Citizen.' "[8]

May we keep them and all the departed contrabands of the Civil War in our hearts today, especially Frank Baker, Shepard Mallory, and James Townsend, the heroes of Freedom's Fort, who, by rowing their way out of slavery at the start of the war, helped elevate the Civil War's meaning in advance of the first Memorial Day.

82

Which French general under Napoléon had African ancestry and was a forebear to two French literary greats?

THOMAS-ALEXANDRE DUMAS WAS BORN Thomas-Alexandre ("Alex" for short) Davy de la Pailleterie on March 25, 1762, in Jérémie, Saint-Domingue, a French colony occupying the west of Hispaniola in the Caribbean Sea (in the country that we know as Haiti today).[1] Alex's mother was a black slave, Marie Cessette Dumas. His father was the French nobleman Alexandre Antoine Davy, whose title was Marquis de la Pailleterie. The marquis (known as Antoine) had ventured to Saint-Domingue to live with his brother, Charles, a prosperous sugar planter. When the two brothers had a falling-out, Antoine fled to the countryside, taking three of Charles's slaves with him.

Antoine and Marie Cessette had four children, all of them, according to one contemporary, "mulattoes and mulatresses." Given the blending of his parents, Alex "had the unique perspective of being from the highest and lowest ranks of society at once."

In order to finance his trip back to France, Antoine ended up selling Marie Cessette and three of his four children into slavery. Antoine's favorite child, Alex, he eventually sold, too, at Port-au-Prince, but only "conditionally"; when Antoine assumed control of his family's château in Normandy, France, in 1775, he bought Alex (but not the others) back so that he could come and live with him.

In 1776 Alex Dumas found himself heading east across the Atlantic to the Old World. There, as a member of his father's household, he received

Olivier Pichat. *Général Thomas-Alexandre Dumas in Battle,* 1790s. Oil on canvas. Villers-Cotterêts, Musée Alexandre Dumas.

an excellent education and embraced the nobleman's lifestyle. Whatever domestic bliss prevailed, however, ended in 1786 when Alex's father, by then seventy-one, married his thirty-three-year-old housekeeper and, in doing so, cut back on his contributions to Alex's lifestyle.

With few apparent options, Alex decided to join the military, even though that meant starting at the bottom as a lowly private. If Alex's future son, Alexandre Dumas *père* (the label *père,* which means "father" in French, can be confusing, given that he was Alex's son), is to be believed, Antoine Davy was so appalled, he told Alex, "I don't intend for you to drag my name through the lowest ranks of the army." In response, a defiant Alex dropped his father's noble name in favor of his slave mother's name. Thenceforth, he would be known not as Alex Davy but as Alex Dumas.

Once in the army, Dumas joined a group of dragoons (light cavalry), which, according to Tom Reiss, "did the toughest and dirtiest jobs."

Dumas established himself as the "consummate warrior and a man of great conviction and moral courage . . . renowned for his strength, his swordsmanship, his bravery and his knack for pulling victory out of the toughest situations."

The French Revolution was a critical turning point. In the year of revolution, 1789, Dumas met his wife, Marie-Louise Labouret, while stationed with her family at Villers-Cotterêts. They married in 1792—the same year Dumas was promoted to corporal after leading a group of four dragoons to capture twelve Austrian raiders along the Belgian frontier.

The year 1792 was important for another reason as well: King Louis XVI was deposed, and France became a republic. As the country mobilized, new military units formed. Among them was La Légion noire (the Black Legion), a coalition of free and mixed-race blacks from the French colonies under the command of a mixed-race man, Joseph Boulogne, the Chevalier de Saint-Georges. Hearing of Corporal Dumas's daring, Saint-Georges tried to recruit him, but Dumas's notoriety had spread so far that he became the object of a fierce bidding war. Then Saint-Georges offered him the rank of lieutenant colonel—second in command. As the historian John G. Gallaher writes, "Almost overnight he was catapulted from a corporal leading patrols of five or six men on reconnaissance missions to commanding a legion that quickly reached battalion strength."[2] Yet Dumas continued to demonstrate his valor in battle and in 1793 was promoted again, this time to general of division in charge of 10,000 men.

By 1794 Dumas had risen to commander in chief, the equivalent of a four-star general today. The number of men under his command: 53,000.

In November 1796 Dumas traveled to Milan, Italy, where he formed a bond with Napoléon Bonaparte. Dumas served under Napoléon in two major campaigns, Italy in 1796–97 and Egypt in 1798–99.

Ideological differences created tensions between them, says Reiss: "Dumas saw himself as a fighter for world liberation, not world domination." Reiss also believes Napoléon was jealous of Dumas's towering size. It couldn't have made him (at five feet seven inches) happy when the chief medical officer of the French invasion of Egypt wrote that Dumas, standing over six feet tall, "look[ed] like a centaur," so that "when [the troops] saw him ride his horse over the trenches, going to ransom prisoners, all of them believed that he was the leader of the expedition"—*not* Napoléon.

The feeling was mutual. Dumas disliked Napoléon for advancing his own political agenda and criticized him for not doing more to keep his troops from exploiting local populations and his generals from whipping up a cult of personality around him. At the same time, Dumas was convinced that Napoléon was going out of his way to diminish Dumas's military accomplishments.

In battle, Dumas continued attracting attention for his courage. After he led small groups of soldiers against the Austrians in Italy, people started calling him *der schwarze Teufel,* "the black devil." Napoléon, too, was bedeviled by Dumas's battlefield prowess, even coining his own nickname for him, "the Horatius Cocles of the Tyrol," a reference to the man who had protected ancient Rome from the Barbarians.

In 1798 Napoléon launched his Egypt campaign. French soldiers soon found themselves fighting in a sweltering climate without sufficient supplies, or even water, for a cause many of them did not support or understand. In the field with them, Dumas only felt more resentful of Napoléon's ambition. He vented at a meeting with his fellow officers, but this time he went too far.

Unbeknownst to Dumas, Napoléon had an informant shadow the meeting, and when word traveled back, Napoléon accused Dumas of mutiny and sedition. He even threatened to shoot Dumas if it continued. Not one to back down, Dumas reiterated his desire to fight for his country and *not* for the selfish goals of one man. With that, he asked for a leave to return to France.

General Dumas departed Egypt in 1799—months after Napoléon's own unannounced exit. When his ship, the *Belle Maltaise,* sprung a leak, the crew of 120 men was forced to make an unplanned stopover in Italy. Thinking they would land among friends, they were sorry to discover that Taranto had fallen to the anti-French insurgency, the Holy Faith Army. In the confusion, Dumas was seized as a prisoner of war. Only when his wife persuaded French officials to intervene did the general gain his release—two years later.

During all this, Napoléon was *governing* France, having staged a coup to topple the Directory and made himself head of a three-member consulate. In his new role as first consul, Napoléon eroded much of the egalitarian spirit of the early French Revolution. In particular, new, more restrictive laws were passed to undermine free black people living within France, while the slave trade was reopened in its colonies. Further, Napoléon also ordered the capture or killing of any black Saint-Dominguan caught wearing the uniform of a military officer.

When Dumas's former soldiers asked Napoléon to provide assistance to the retired general (his finances were in disarray after his imprisonment), Napoléon scoffed, "I forbid you to ever speak to me of that man!" Not long afterward Dumas died of cancer.

Responsibility for General Dumas's legacy fell to his son, Alexandre Dumas *père* (1802–70), one of the most illustrious novelists in French—indeed, *world* literature and a man keenly aware of his own African ancestry. (His name, as I've said, can be confusing. Because Alex Dumas was really Thomas-Alexandre, his son was not a junior but became the senior Alexandre Dumas *père* to his own son, Alexandre Dumas *fils,* also a writer, who lived between 1824 and 1895.) Although the young Alexandre *père* was only three when his father died, the stories of General Dumas's accomplishments stayed with him his entire life and lent inspiration to his legendary stories.

83

Which famous nineteenth-century French author had African ancestry?

ALEXANDRE DUMAS *PÈRE* was born in Villers-Cotterêts, France, on July 24, 1802, to Thomas-Alexandre Dumas and Marie-Louise Labouret. He was one-quarter black. Dumas's godfather was supposed to have been Napoléon Bonaparte, but as Dumas told it, the arrangement was dropped after his father and the future French emperor became enemies. General Dumas died in 1806, yet through his absence, he loomed even larger in his son's mind. "I adored my father," Dumas is quoted as saying. "Perhaps, at so early an age, the feeling which today I call love was only a naïve astonishment at that Herculean stature and that gigantic strength I'd seen him display on so many occasions; perhaps it was nothing more than a childish pride and admiration. . . . But, in spite of all that, even today the memory of my father, in every detail of his body, in every feature of his face, is as present to me as if I had lost him yesterday."[1]

The general's death hurt in other ways, for despite his high military rank, his pension was withheld. Growing up in poverty, Dumas was convinced that the vengeful Napoléon had blocked his admission to any military school or civilian college.

Dumas's mother, a widow and single parent, "exercised little authority over [her son], rearing him with abundant affection but almost in spite of herself letting him do whatever he wished," the biographer Richard Stowe writes, so that "Dumas at seventeen or eighteen was as learned in the ways of the woods as he was little schooled."[2] The seeds of Dumas's

Alexandre Dumas, as
photographed by Nadar. 1855.
Salted paper photographic
print.

literary ambitions were planted around age sixteen, when he met Adolphe
de Leuven, the teenage son of a Swedish nobleman, on vacation in Villers-
Cotterêts. Dumas was captivated by de Leuven's tales of Parisian life.

Soon de Leuven and Dumas began collaborating on comedic plays, and
two years after Dumas moved to Paris, they achieved a modicum of success with 1825's *Hunting and Love*. Dumas greatly expanded his network
of mentors in Paris, and as a guest at the literary salon of French writer
Charles Nodier, he rubbed elbows with Alfred de Vigny, Victor Hugo, and
Alphonse de Lamartine.

The year 1829 saw the debut of Dumas's hit play *Henri III and His Court*
at the Comédie-Française in Paris. Its success enabled Dumas to continue
writing plays, and he staged them at a breakneck pace. "Between 1829 and
the end of 1851," Stowe writes, "only one year—1844—saw no new play
by [Dumas] on some Parisian stage. Several years saw four or five produced, and in April of 1839 he actually achieved three premieres within
fifteen days." Dumas's audience ballooned, and as the historian Jonathan
Edwards writes, "although some elite writers could fault his literary style,
they envied his popularity."[3]

Beginning in 1837, Dumas turned his attention to writing novels. The reasons were practical: his plays had begun to falter at the box office, and a lively market was developing for serial novels, whose authors (like Charles Dickens) were becoming wealthy and famous.

"Never in the whole course of French literature has there been anything comparable to Dumas's output between the years 1845 and 1855," the historian André Maurois argues. "Novels of from eight to ten volumes showered down without a break on the newspapers and bookshops." Even more remarkable is that "in this vast production there were few failures."[4]

In 1844 Dumas released *The Three Musketeers,* the first book in his successful d'Artagnan trilogy, which would also feature *Twenty Years After* and *The Viscount of Bragelonne.* But it was with *Musketeers* that Dumas achieved literary immortality. "Whatever liberties and mistakes may be ascribed to him," Stowe observes, "in this novel [Dumas] produced a convincing illusion of historical reality, bringing a remote period to life with exceptional immediacy and concreteness."

The year that saw *The Three Musketeers* also saw the serialization of Dumas's *The Count of Monte Cristo,* which was published in book form in 1846. In these famous works, Dumas turned not only to national history but also to family history, drawing on the experiences of Gen. Thomas-Alexandre Dumas.

The issue of race was never far from Dumas, although it was not a subject he usually broached himself. In his biography, Reiss points out that "the writer Dumas grew up in a very different world from that of his father—a world of rising, rather than diminishing, racism. His fellow novelist Balzac referred to him as 'that negro.'"

The attacks grew worse as Dumas became more successful, says Reiss: "critics launched an endless, damaging public attack on Dumas, mocking his African heritage." Shockingly, "one well-known caricature shows Dumas leaning over a hot stove on which he is boiling his white characters alive: his popping eyes glare demonically at a musketeer he is lifting to his impossibly huge lips, apparently about to sample the European's flesh." But Dumas's quick wit served him well. Most famously, he said to one of his critics, "My father was a mulatto, my grandfather was a Negro, and my great-grandfather a monkey. You see, sir, my family starts where yours ends."[5]

At the same time, Dumas faced criticism from African Americans who believed he did not do enough to uplift the race. Frederick Douglass loved *The Count of Monte Cristo* and Dumas's 1843 novel *Georges,* in which, according to Peter Carr, "Dumas examines colonialism through the eyes of a half-French mulatto in Mauritius."[6] But that didn't keep Douglass from accusing Dumas of not speaking out enough for the race. According to the Douglass biographer Waldo E. Martin, Jr., Douglass wrote, "We have nothing to thank Dumas for. Victor Hugo, the white man, could speak for us, but this brilliant colored man who could have let down sheets of fire upon the heads of tyrants and carried freedom to his enslaved people, had no word in behalf [of] liberty for the enslaved."[7] Douglass respected Dumas's talents but did not think he was a leader.

Dumas died in Puys, France, in 1870 and was buried in the family vault. In 2002 he was exhumed and reinterred in the hallowed Panthéon in Paris, with the likes of Voltaire, Rousseau, Hugo, Zola, the Curies, and Louverture. According to a report on the proceedings, "French President Jacques Chirac declared at the ceremony that he was not only paying tribute to one of the great French writers but repairing an injustice to all French men and women who have been victims of racism."[8]

84

Which Zulu king led his men to victory over British invaders and mounted warfare that killed a French "prince"?

CETSHWAYO KAMPANDE WAS BORN in emLambongwenya in South Africa around 1826. His uncle Shaka Zulu presided over the Zulu Kingdom from 1816 until his death in 1828. His father, Mpande kaSenzangakhona, was Shaka's half brother and became king of the Zulus in 1840, initially naming Cetshwayo his successor. Mpande, however, had twenty-nine wives and, as time passed, considered naming a different wife, Monase, as "chief wife," which would have made her son, Mbulazi, his heir. That wasn't all.[1] Mpande also was jealous that Cetshwayo was becoming more popular than he. When it came to choosing sides, most stood with Cetshwayo, and at the 1856 battle of Ndondakusuka, his side triumphed and his rival heir, Mbulazi, was killed.[2] From then on, Cetshwayo's father was a leader in name only, while Cetshwayo was regarded as the Zulus' true king. In 1872 it became official.

The British, already controlling nearby Natal, had intervened by recognizing Cetshwayo as heir to the throne. But the British weren't exactly honest brokers. They believed their endorsement had made Cetshwayo king and, thus, their puppet, to be removed if and when they saw fit. It didn't take long for conflicts to emerge. Cetshwayo resented the British for failing to defend the Zulus against the Dutch when the British annexed the Transvaal territory in 1877, and in response, the British began cataloging his offenses, including allowing Zulu raiders to cross the border into Natal.

Chief among Cetshwayo's opponents was the British high commissioner, Sir Bartle Frere, who thought the British had an obligation to "civilize" the blacks of southern Africa. Really, Frere hoped to forge a confederation of all the southern African territories and then be named governor over them. This, of course, meant ousting Cetshwayo.

In December 1878 the British gave him an ultimatum: Hand over his raiders, pay an indemnity of six hundred cattle, disband his military, and recognize Britain's authority—or face invasion. When Cetshwayo refused, the British had the pretext they needed to invade the Zulu kingdom.

The invasion began on January 11, 1879, when the British crossed the Tugela River at Rorke's Drift into northwest Zululand. (Another column of troops advanced along the Indian Ocean to the southeast.) The British had fewer than 2,000 troops but superior firepower. The Zulu weapon was the *assegai*—essentially a spear—but they had more men, perhaps as many

"Cetshwayo kaMpande." Image from G. T. Bettany,
The World's Inhabitants or, Mankind, Animals, and Plants
(London, 1888).

as 12,000.[3] Taking a defensive position, Cetshwayo ordered his warriors to stay on their side of the Natal border. But if attacked, he was ready.

The Battle of Isandlwana was joined on the morning of January 22, 1879, when the British, under the command of Lord Chelmsford, crossed over the Buffalo (Mzinyathi) River at Rorke's Drift. Dividing his army, Chelmsford foolishly left a third of his force behind at Isandlwana under Col. H. B. Pulleine. On the scene was Frank Bourne, a sergeant in the British Twenty-fourth Regiment, who later wrote:

> Lord Chelmsford learned that the enemy was in force ahead of the Camp, and he moved out on the morning of the twenty-second with nearly half his force to attack them. But as he advanced they disappeared, and in his absence his Camp was attacked and overwhelmed by four thousand Zulus. So swift was the disaster that the few survivors who got away could give no reliable account of it, but the evidence of the dead who were afterwards found and buried where they lay told the unvarying tale of groups of men fighting back to back until the last cartridge was fired. . . . Fully twelve hundred men were killed. And by half past one no white man was alive in Isandhlwana Camp.[4]

In *100 Amazing Facts About the Negro,* Joel Rogers claimed that Cetshwayo, "King of Zululand, South Africa, massacred an entire British army sent against him in 1879, and a few days later defeated and killed the Prince Napoléon, heir to the French throne."[5] Was he right? Although Cetshwayo's Zulu warriors did not kill every British soldier in sight, they came close. According to the historian John Laband, the British lost 52 officers, 727 white troops, and 471 black troops. But what about Rogers's other claim, that the heir to the French throne, Prince Napoléon, was "defeated and killed"? According to the historian Ian Knight, the prince was Louis-Napoléon Bonaparte, son of Napoléon III, who had risen to power in France in 1848 only to be chased by the Prussians into exile in England thirty years later. There Napoléon III's "young son—also called Louis—became the heir in exile to Bonapartist dreams of a restoration."[6] Joining the British military, the prince was allowed to go to the Zulu kingdom as an observer. Out on patrol away from the British camp there, he was killed by Zulu forces on June 1, 1879.

Prince Napoléon did indeed die in battle, but he was only an observer, so it was a stretch for Rogers to say that he had been "defeated." And while

Rogers chose to end his story with the Zulus on top, their triumph at Isandlwana was anything but a done deal.

Reports from the scene referred to Cetshwayo's forces at Isandlwana as that "overwhelming force of Zulus,"[7] while remarking that "the greatest gloom and consternation" had swept over "the Cape Colony" when news of the British defeat arrived.[8] Clamoring for a response, British newspapers argued that "the moral effect of [the Zulu] victory on the morale of the natives in the British colonies is likely to cause new risings, unless the prestige of the British force is recovered by a brilliant victory."[9]

Clearly, the Zulu king had attracted Europe's attention with his victory at Isandlwana. And the British response was swift. In fact, later that same day—January 22, 1879—another Zulu force under Cetshwayo's brother Dabulamanzi kaMpande was repulsed when it attacked the British camp at Rorke's Drift. The fight continued into the next day, but in the end, the approximately 120 British soldiers stationed at the depot there gunned down 500-plus Zulu warriors.

Frank Bourne, one of those British soldiers, recalled: "To show their fearlessness and their contempt for the red coats and small numbers, they [the Zulu warriors] tried to leap the parapet, and at times seized our bayonets, only to be shot down. Looking back, one cannot but admire their fanatical bravery."

As the Anglo-Zulu War rolled on, the British racked up one devastating victory after another. These included the Battle of Kambula on March 29 and at Gingindlovu on April 2, when, according to *Britannica,*

> more than 1,000 Zulu were killed. Chelmsford's troops then moved on Cetshwayo's royal villages at Ulundi, where on July 4, 1879, they inflicted a final defeat on Cetshwayo's surviving soldiers. Cetshwayo himself was captured in August, and the Zulu nation was at the mercy of the British government, which had not yet considered how to incorporate Zululand into its Southern Africa holdings.[10]

A prisoner of war, Cetshwayo was exiled to Cape Town and later transferred to a farm in the Cape Flats. Still, the Zulu king had allies, including the Anglican bishop of Natal, John William Colenso, who successfully argued for Cetshwayo's release. In 1882 Cetshwayo traveled to London to make his own appeal to the British authorities that he should be reinstalled as king. And he was, over a much smaller territory and under British supervision in January 1883. By then, however, a number of rival chiefs had enhanced their own power under the British, so that when Cetshwayo returned, they were ready to battle his still-loyal forces in a civil war.

Cetshwayo did not live to see how that war ended. He died on February 8, 1884. The cause is unclear, but many of his allies believed he had been poisoned. Cetshwayo was buried near the Nkandla Forest, and artifacts from the wagon that carried his body are displayed at the Ondini Museum near the former capital of the Zulu kingdom in Ulundi. King Cetshwayo was succeeded by his son Dinuzulu, but the rule of the independent Zulu kings was over.

85

Why was the summer of 1964 pivotal in the fight for civil rights?

SINCE THE COLLAPSE OF Reconstruction in 1876, for nearly one hundred years, a war had raged between advocates for full and equal black citizenship and the architects of the snares that had hampered black progress. During the summer of 1964, it wasn't clear whether the Civil Rights Act, which failed to provide badly needed voting rights protections, would begin to fulfill Dr. Martin Luther King, Jr.'s dream of a new American racial order. But the movement had grown younger, more radical, and more diverse. Freedom Summer's greatest legacy is the counterintuitive philosophy behind it: that after decades of a top-down organizing strategy, everyday people had learned to lead themselves.

Beginning in the 1950s, Mississippi branches of the NAACP led the way, with Amzie Moore, Aaron Henry, and Medgar Evers in the forefront. African Americans in Mississippi, or those who had jobs, were typically stuck working as sharecroppers or domestics, and they lived in a segregated society without any political power. In 1962, the historian Lisa Clayton Robinson notes, "only 6.7 percent of African Americans in the state were registered to vote, the lowest percentage in the country."[1] And as the 1955 murder of Emmett Till demonstrated, white violence was an omnipresent threat.

Organizers from the Student Nonviolent Coordinating Committee (SNCC) and the Congress of Racial Equality (CORE) started pouring into Mississippi in the early 1960s. Among the young new leaders, none played

Aaron Henry, chair of the Mississippi Freedom Democratic Party delegation, speaking before the Credentials Committee at the Democratic National Convention, Atlantic City, New Jersey, 1964.

a more pivotal role than the brilliant but soft-spoken visionary Bob Moses, whose task was to spearhead a voter registration drive. Moses may not be as well known to the wider society today as King is, but he should be. Without him, there would have been no Freedom Summer, and without Freedom Summer, there would have been no Voting Rights Act a year later. Moses had been well on his way to earning his Ph.D. at Harvard in the late 1950s when his mother died and his father was hospitalized. On leave, Moses was teaching math at the Horace Mann School in the Bronx when he began collaborating with civil rights leader Bayard Rustin, who encouraged him to take a more active role in the movement.

The arrival of activists such as Moses angered white Mississippians. But NAACP leaders also were upset, fearing the newcomers would take control of the local movement they had been building. To make peace, Moses helped to form a new group, the Council of Federated Organizations (COFO), which brought together SNCC, CORE, and the local NAACP branches, as well as the Southern Christian Leadership Conference (SCLC) and local community groups.

Determined to open a new front against Jim Crow in Mississippi, Moses and fellow COFO leader Dave Dennis hoped to recruit northern white college students to the crusade. The plan was to attract attention, as Dennis explained in 1974: "The death of a white college student would bring on more attention to what was going on than for a black college student getting it. That's cold, but that was also in another sense speaking the language of this country."[2]

The average northern volunteer, writes the historian John Dittmer, was "white, affluent, politically liberal, and enrolled at a prestigious university. Just how many volunteers worked in Mississippi is subject to conjecture, for COFO never compiled a final tally. . . . Probably no more than 650 students worked in Mississippi, and not all of those people worked all summer."[3] For the most part, as Doug McAdam writes, "the volunteers lived in communal 'Freedom Houses' or were housed by local black families who refused to be intimidated by segregationist threats of violence."[4]

Freedom Summer began with horrific, widespread violence. Activists Andrew Goodman, James Chaney, and Michael Schwerner disappeared on June 21 while investigating the burning of a church in Philadelphia, Mississippi. It wasn't until August 4 that their tortured, brutalized bodies were discovered buried in a dam—slain by Klansmen with the knowledge of local police officers. "In just the first two weeks of the summer project," writes the historian Charles Payne, "in addition to the [murders], there were at least seven bombings or fire-bombings of movement related businesses and four shootings and a larger number of serious beatings."[5]

COFO activism during Freedom Summer proceeded along two tracks: freedom schools and voter registration drives. Freedom schools were the brainchild of Howard University student and SNCC leader Charles Cobb, who interpreted their mission broadly. Students would learn about black history and the civil rights movement. Cobb had planned for the schools to host one thousand students, but as Payne writes, "somewhere between twenty-five hundred and three thousand students actually showed up, and their ages ranged from seven to seventy. . . . The number of schools was increased from twenty-five to forty-one." Black children and adults attended freedom schools knowing they ran the risk of white retaliation. "The morning after a bomb leveled the church serving as the McComb freedom school," Dittmer notes, "seventy-five students showed up for class on the lawn in front of the smoldering ruins."

During Freedom Summer, Moses and COFO hoped to build on the momentum steadily rising from within the community by establishing the Mississippi Freedom Democratic Party (MFDP) as an alternative to the state's whites-only Democratic Party. Their goal: to send a delegation to the Democratic National Convention in Atlantic City and try to convince the party's credentials committee "that blacks had been excluded from the 'regular' party and that the FDP was the only party in the state loyal to the national ticket," Dittmer explains.

But once there, they encountered a problem: President Lyndon B. Johnson, who was desperate not to lose white support in the South ahead of his general election against conservative Republican Barry Goldwater, opposed the MFDP's efforts. He even instructed the FBI to spy on the delegates. LBJ's point man in Atlantic City was his running mate, Senator Hubert Humphrey (D-MN), who presented a compromise plan by which the MFDP would receive two at-large seats while the others would be "welcomed as honored guests," according to Dittmer. In addition, the white delegates from the Democratic Party of Mississippi would be required to sign a loyalty oath.

Not surprisingly, the MFDP rejected the plan, and most of the white Mississippi delegation walked out. Then, after gaining their credential passes from sympathetic delegates from other states, MFDP members staged a protest sit-in on the convention floor. Again, Humphrey tried to get the delegates to compromise, but again the MFDP refused.

That fall Johnson won a full term in a landslide victory and a year later signed the Voting Rights Act of 1965, after more blood was spilled in Selma, Alabama. "The measure dramatically increased voter registration in the short term," the U.S. House of Representatives website states. "By 1969, 60 percent of all southern blacks were registered. Predictably, the bill's impact was most dramatic in the Deep South. In Mississippi, for instance, where less than 7 percent of African Americans qualified to vote in 1964, 59 percent were on voter rolls by 1968."[6]

Freedom Summer had left its mark. But the failure of the MFDP in Atlantic City left SNCC—and much of the rest of the civil rights movement—in crisis. "Never again were we lulled into believing that our task was exposing injustices so that the 'good' people of America could eliminate them," recalled SNCC activist Cleveland Sellers. "After Atlantic City, our struggle was not for civil rights, but for liberation."[7] Two summers later, at a nighttime rally in Greenwood, Mississippi, SNCC leader Stokely Carmichael would begin speaking the electrifying language of black power. A new era had begun.

86

Which civil rights warrior received numerous telephone calls from the U.S. president during the fight to pass the Civil Rights Act of 1964?

ON JULY 2, President Lyndon B. Johnson signed the 1964 Civil Rights Act into law at the White House. Dr. Martin Luther King, Jr., and a bevy of politicians crowded around him, taking in the historic moment, as significant as any in advancing American race relations since the end of the Civil War. But just as vital to the bill's success as King or Johnson was an African-American leader who was far less well known. His name was Clarence M. Mitchell, Jr., and he was the chief Washington lobbyist for the NAACP during this extraordinary heroic phase of the civil rights movement.[1]

Clarence M. Mitchell, Jr., was, in the words of author Todd Purdum, "born into genteel poverty in Baltimore in 1911, in a family that would total ten children." While attending Frederick Douglass High School in Baltimore, Mitchell had a number of jobs, including delivering ice and working as an overnight elevator operator. In 1932 he graduated from the "black Princeton," Lincoln University of Oxford, Pennsylvania. Returning to Baltimore, he worked as a reporter for the *Afro-American* newspaper, where he exposed the racism shot through the southern justice system, covering the infamous Scottsboro Boys case. While working at the *Baltimore Sun,*

Clarence M. Mitchell, Jr. speaks with President Lyndon B. Johnson just after the signing of the Civil Rights Act in the White House, April 11, 1968.

Mitchell witnessed the horrors of a lynching on Maryland's Eastern Shore that altered his trajectory. He testified to Congress about the lynching and from then on embraced "a life of public service and political activism."[2]

During World War II, Mitchell worked with the Negro Employment and Training Branch in the labor division of the U.S. Office of Production Management, where his career in the federal government began. After President Franklin D. Roosevelt agreed to establish the Fair Employment Practices Committee in exchange for an agreement by civil rights leaders to call off the first planned March on Washington, in 1941, Mitchell served as its associate director and then as director of field operations.

When the war ended, he found a new position at the NAACP, which saw its membership soar to 600,000. By 1950 Mitchell had become both director and chief lobbyist of its Washington bureau. He was in charge of battling Jim Crow in Congress. Much of Mitchell's activism would come through the Leadership Conference, which Denton L. Watson describes as "a coalition of civil rights, civic, labor, fraternal, and religious organizations that vastly extended the NAACP's political reach."[3]

As the 1950s rolled on, Mitchell played an active role in lobbying for the end of segregation in the military and for passage of the civil rights bills of

1957 and 1960, when Lyndon Johnson was Senate majority leader. Under LBJ, those bills were notoriously gutted on their way to becoming law, but in Mitchell's quiet way, the groundwork was being laid. As Purdum explains, Mitchell was able to win the support of conservatives and "to cultivate civil relationships with even some of the most implacable southern segregationists."

Entering the White House, President John F. Kennedy was reluctant to pursue a strong civil rights bill for fear it would alienate southern congressmen, whose support was vital to his other domestic and foreign policy initiatives. But the horror of the violence in Birmingham, Alabama, in spring 1963 forced his hand. On June 19 of that year, coincidentally the same day Medgar Evers was buried at Arlington National Cemetery, Kennedy sent to Congress the civil rights bill his brother, Attorney General Robert Kennedy, had drafted. The push was on, with Mitchell and other civil rights leaders keenly aware that southern congressmen would try to block the bill and that the Kennedy administration would water it down.

Mitchell's lack of faith in Kennedy motivated his participation in the March on Washington that August. All summer long Mitchell conducted meetings with representatives from federal and city agencies and organized church groups to pressure the government. Finally, he believed he had the votes in Congress to get a real civil rights bill passed and, in October 1963, told NAACP activists to "take off the lambskin gloves" and fight. Then suddenly, a month later, Kennedy was felled by an assassin's bullet in Dallas. Mitchell now had to contemplate bringing up the bill with a new head man in the White House: the old Senate majority leader LBJ.

Mitchell met with Johnson on January 21, 1964. Surprisingly, given his hatchet job on the 1957 and 1960 bills, Johnson, Purdum writes, "acknowledged that he would oppose any efforts to strengthen H.R. 7152 in the House . . . the new president also assured his visitors that he would not brook weakening the bill in the Senate, either. 'I don't care how long it takes,' Johnson said. . . . 'We are not going to have anything else hit the Senate floor until this bill is passed.'"

Emboldened, Mitchell accelerated his lobbying efforts, and he and Johnson were in constant contact during the deliberations over the bill.

All the way through the process, Mitchell understood that he had to keep the pressure on congressional leaders. To that end, he organized NAACP delegates from ten states to keep tabs on lawmakers and prod them to vote for the bill.

The bill passed the House, but not without some late excitement. On February 8, 1964, Representative Howard W. Smith (D-VA) announced an amendment that included women as a protected class in Title VII of the bill. Mitchell had opposed the insertion of a gender provision during the 1956 debates over the creation of the Federal Civil Rights Commission, but this time he thought it would strengthen the bill, even as many of his allies thought it could kill it. He was right. Smith's amendment passed, and the House approved the civil rights bill on February 10. Mitchell and his allies were elated.

Next up: the Senate, which, for a generation, had been dominated by senior members of the Democratic Party from the South. Mitchell and civil rights attorney Joseph L. Rauh, Jr., a founder of Americans for Democratic Action, often sat in on strategy sessions led by floor managers Hubert Humphrey (D-MN) and Thomas Kuchel (R-CA). "Humphrey was Mitchell's liaison with the President," Watson writes, "but Johnson still maintained regular contact with Mitchell by calling him at his home in Baltimore at night or early in the morning to discuss developments and to issue marching orders," insider to insider.

Mitchell's constant presence was important for keeping the senators on track. At one meeting, Humphrey stated that "we ought to get the hell off civil rights and onto something else." He wanted a compromise and a cloture vote. Mitchell saved the day, Watson says, responding: "Senator, blacks in this country have been patient for years, for decades, for centuries. We have had atrocities committed on us. I think the Senate and its leadership can be patient just long enough until we can get the two-thirds vote we need."

Mitchell remained at the center of the storm during the final stretch. On June 10 he watched as Senator Robert C. Byrd (D-WV) mounted an all-night filibuster against the bill, and he was in the Senate chamber when that body, with key Republican support, voted 71–29 to invoke cloture and cut off debate. When the vote on the bill itself was held June 19, a year after President Kennedy had sent his draft to Congress, the Senate voted "yea,"

73–27. The House then approved the Senate version by a vote of 290–130, and the Civil Rights Act of 1964 became law under President Johnson's signature on July 2.

Though King was standing behind Johnson, Clarence Mitchell was a major reason for the bill's success. Even if the cameras rarely found him, insiders in Washington knew who the NAACP's fixer was and how crucial he had been in the legislative battle to destroy Jim Crow. "Clarence Mitchell was the man in charge of this operation," Roy Wilkins told reporters after the Senate cloture vote, according to Watson. "He perfected and directed flawlessly a wonderful group of representatives of church, labor, and all facets of the community to make this possible."

87

What happened to Argentina's black population?

"IN 1587 THE FIRST SLAVES arrived in Buenos Aires from Brazil," writes the historian Erika Edwards:

> From 1580 to 1640, the main commercial activity for Buenos Aires was the slave trade. More than 70 percent of the value of all imports arriving in Buenos were enslaved Africans. Slaves came primarily from Brazil via the Portuguese slave trade from Angola and other Western states in Africa. Once arriving in Buenos Aires, they could be sent as far as Lima, Peru; slaves were provided to Mendoza, Tucuman, Salta Jujuy, Chile, Paraguay, and what is today Bolivia and southern Peru. Córdoba functioned primarily as a redistribution center for this slave transfer until 1610.[1]

It's difficult to pin down the exact number of African slaves who passed through Argentina, since so much of the trade involved illegal smuggling (due to shifting laws against the importation of slaves and traders' desire to avoid paying taxes). But the Trans-Atlantic Slave Trade Database suggests that between 1601 and 1866, an estimated 67,000 slaves disembarked at the Viceroyalty of Rio de la Plata (compared with the more than 3 million slaves in Brazil). La Plata, under Spanish dominion after 1776, was headquartered in Buenos Aires, Argentina's present-day capital city, and touched parts of present-day Uruguay, Paraguay, and Bolivia. After earlier European settlers had tried—and failed—to subjugate the native popula-

Pedro Figari. *Candombe*. 1920s–30s. Oil painting. Private collection.

tion in the region, trading in African slaves, legally or illegally, proved too lucrative to pass up. At various points, the French, Portuguese, and British were in on the action, with the latter two wielding the greatest influence. Even the Jesuit priests of Córdoba had a hard time saying no to slavery.

After 1789, many restrictions on trade for American subjects were lifted, Joy Elizondo writes: "Slaves then came from Portuguese factories in Angola ([the people] were called Congos, Angolas, Benguelas, and Luandas) and from Mozambique. Between 1750 and 1810 approximately 45,000 slaves were imported by both legal and illegal means." Their presence was key to the rise of Buenos Aires as an economic and political power, Elizondo adds. Amazingly, as a result, "by the late 1700s nearly 50 percent of the population in the interior of the country was black, and between 30 and 40 percent of the population of Buenos Aires was black or mulatto."[2]

But you would never know that today. In fact, many Argentinians themselves don't know it. Some even think their country managed to avoid the slave trade entirely, victims of a sort of cultural amnesia that finds the black presence in Argentina somehow inconvenient, something to be denied.

While Argentina was battling for independence from Spain between 1810 and 1816—a war in which Afro-Argentinian slaves were conscripted into the liberation army of General José de San Martín—the assembly of the United Provinces officially banned the importation of slaves. The year was 1813, but, as Elizondo is quick to point out, "the slave trade continued until a pact with Britain in 1840 effectively ended it."

There were slaves in Argentina until about 1853, when the "blackout" began.[3] "While a number of Latin American countries pursued policies of racial Whitening," Elizondo writes, "Argentina stands out for its 'success' in this area." Some blamed it on the nineteenth-century wars that country fought, in which the black population suffered heavy casualties after being put on the front lines. Others attributed it to assimilation through marriage. Still others pointed to the devastating and disproportionate effects of cholera and yellow fever on black people, as well as emigration out of the country to other South American locales.

Now, however, thanks to the trailblazing work of recent historians, we know there were more deliberate forces at play.

"It has been alleged," the historian Palash Ghosh writes,

> that the president of Argentina from 1868 to 1874, Domingo Faustino Sarmiento, sought to wipe out blacks from the country in a policy of covert genocide through extremely repressive policies (including possibly the forced recruitment of Africans into the army and by forcing blacks to remain in neighborhoods where disease would decimate them in the absence of adequate health care). Tellingly, Sarmiento wrote in his diary in 1848: "In the United States . . . 4 million are black, and within 20 years will be 8 [million]. . . . What is [to be] done with such blacks, hated by the white race? Slavery is a parasite that the vegetation of English colonization has left attached to leafy tree of freedom."

Consequently, Ghosh adds, "by 1895, there were reportedly so few blacks left in Argentina that the government did not even bother registering African-descended people in the national census."

To justify it, Elizondo continues, "intellectuals such as Domingo Faustino Sarmiento, Carlos Octavio Bunge, and José Ingenieros advanced theories of scientific racism." She adds: "Creole elites had written for years about plans to attract European immigrants to temper the 'degenerate' qualities of Argentina's diminishing black and decimated indigenous populations. By the second decade of the twentieth century, approximately one-third of the country's population was foreign-born." And today, in a population of 43 million, an astonishing 97 percent of Argentinians are (or at least claim to be) white.

Over the decades, some of black Argentina was replenished through new immigrant waves from Cape Verde, or internally, Elizondo writes, by "cabecitas negras (literally, little black heads)" migrating from the outskirts to the capital. But never again did the country's overall population reflect its early history.

"On a broader scale," Ghosh concludes, "the 'elimination' of blacks from the country's history and consciousness reflected the long-cherished desire of successive Argentine governments to imagine the country as an 'all-white' extension of Western Europe in Latin America."

88

Which event in black history took place in what is now Iraq?

LONG BEFORE the Trans-Atlantic Slave Trade brought African people to the New World, eastern trade routes carried them to the Arabian Peninsula, as the dean of the history of slavery, David Brion Davis of Yale University, posits.[1] Iraq wasn't called Iraq until after World War II; before that it was known generally as Mesopotamia, the land between the Tigris and Euphrates, and was part of a sprawling caliphate that stretched from southern Asia to North Africa and the Iberian Peninsula.

Slavery predates the written historical record and at critical turns was supported legally by the major religions of Judaism and Christianity. Islam followed. And as the teachings of the Koran spread from Mecca to the conquered lands of Africa and beyond, beginning in the seventh century, the lucrative slave trade expanded from Africa *back* to the Middle East.

Africans were not just slaves in Mesopotamia—some played key roles in the formation of Islam.[2] But over time, the enslavement of African men and women went hand in hand with the maturation of Islam, and the caliphate's reliance on foreign, non-Arabic-speaking slaves, black and white, intensified as the empire grew. Davis writes:

> The spectacular Arab conquests, like those of the earlier Romans, revolutionized geographic boundaries and produced an immense flow of slaves for employment as servants, soldiers, members of harems, eunuch chaperons, and bureaucrats. Thanks to such earlier innovations as the North Arabian saddle and camel caravans, Arabs, Berbers, and their converts made deep inroads into sub-Saharan Africa, thus tapping, through

purchase or capture, an unprecedented pool of slave labor. According to some scholarship, this importation of black slaves into Islamic lands from Spain to India constituted a continuous, large-scale migration—by caravan and sea over a period of more than twelve centuries, beginning in the 600s—that may have equaled in total numbers all the African slaves transported to the Western Hemisphere. One French scholar, Raymond Mauny, estimates that as many as fourteen million African slaves were exported to Muslim regions.

Zanj was a label used for black slaves, in particular those tasked with the hardest, plantation-style work.[3] Some identify the Zanj specifically as black slaves from East Africa, but it was a much looser term than that. (*Zanj,* an Arabic word, is often translated as "black.")

Key information on Zanj work sites within Mesopotamia comes to us by way of the ninth-century Arab historian al-Tabari, who remembered the Zanj as black slaves who were forced to undertake the massive field project to drain the salt marshes of Lower Mesopotamia. It was backbreak-

M. Brown, after W. A. Churchill. "A Slave Gang in Zanzibar." Wood engraving, *The Illustrated London News,* March 16, 1889.

ing work, and the men were underfed and stuffed into labor camps of 500 to 5,000. While most slaves in Islamic countries were domestic workers, the Zanj toiled at the bottom of society at the southern end of the Arabian Peninsula.

Over time, their presence reinforced Arabs' negative stereotypes of blacks in general, as Davis explains:

> Regardless of their continuing enslavement and purchase of white Christian infidels, medieval Arabs came to associate the most degrading forms of labor with black slaves—with the Zanj whom the medieval Arab writer Maqdisi described as "people of black color, flat noses, kinky hair, and little understanding or intelligence." In fact, the Arabic word for slave, *abd,* came in time to mean only a black slave and, in some regions, referred to any black person whether slave or free. Many Arab writers echoed the racial contempt typified by the famous fourteenth-century Tunisian historian Ibn Khaldun when he wrote that black people "are, as a whole submissive to slavery, because Negroes have little that is essentially human and have attributes that are quite similar to those of dumb animals."

According to the historian Alexandre Popovic, two Zanj insurrections failed under the Umayyad Caliphate. The first, in 689–90, was small and local, and the prisoners were beheaded. The other, in 694, led by the "Lion of the Zanj," took two military offenses to defeat. It was followed by two centuries of silence.

A confluence of factors made the year 869 ripe for another push for freedom. The central government was mired in divisions among Turkish military leaders, Arab lawmakers, and Persian civil servants. The empire also was increasingly spread thin defending its positions abroad, while internally, governors were becoming ever more independent. "All that was lacking," Popovic writes, "was a leader capable of stirring up the Zanj and lighting the fire."

Enter Ali bin Muhammad, the matchstick of the Zanj revolt. Muhammad was not Zanj himself, but of Arab or Persian descent. Little is known about his early life except that he was a poet who claimed to have a direct line to the Almighty with instructions to lead a great crusade. He also was clever enough to assure his followers that his family tree included connections to the Prophet Muhammad. According to Popovic, Ali bin Muhammad moved restlessly around the empire searching for a people to lead. He found them in the lower canal region of Mesopotamia in September 869.

What began as a local revolt escalated when the fearful word spread from Basra to the central government. Heading to the fray was Ali bin Muhammad, who established himself as leader by promising the Zanj freer, better lives. Muhammad wrapped his message in a strain of Islam at once stark and egalitarian. According to *Britannica,* "Ali's offers became even more attractive with his subsequent adoption of a Khārijite religious stance: anyone, even a black slave, could be elected caliph, and all non-Khārijites were infidels threatened by a holy war."[4]

Before long Muhammad became known ironically as the Master of the Zanj. His flag became the flag of the Zanj, and unlike future slaves who failed to show up for John Brown at Harpers Ferry, the Zanj rallied, wave after wave. They weren't interested in abolition but in taking their masters' places. That included enslaving others in their wake.

The Zanj formed a ragtag, relentless army. In the initial fighting, Popovic writes,

> a troop of four-thousand men attacked the rebels. The Zanj "army" was poorly equipped to fend them off with only three sabers in its arsenal. One rebel was seen dashing into battle carrying only his plate as a weapon. Nevertheless, the Zanj won another victory and put the enemy to flight. One member of the attacking force was killed; others died of thirst. On orders from Ali b. Muhammad, prisoners were beheaded. The Zanj carried away the severed heads on their own mules.

As the Zanj revolt spread, the port city of al-Uballa fell into their hands in 870. Then dramatically, in 871, Basra fell under their control, with the Zanj massacring most of the city's residents. By 873 the Master of the Zanj had consolidated an independent state in Lower Mesopotamia. According to the historian Kent Krause, Muhammad "controlled the canal region of southern Iraq. He built a capital in al-Mukhtara and set up an independent government that collected taxes and minted its own coins."[5]

But the empire retaliated. In 880 the Abbasid caliph's military brother, al-Muwaffaq, assembled a second army to crush the rebellion. They set out from al-Firk and built a city of their own from which to lay siege to the Zanj stronghold, al-Mukhtara. For two years, al-Muwaffaq's army, including his son Abu al-Abbas, tightened the grip.

The Zanj revolt ended for good in 883 for a variety of reasons: promises of amnesty, offers to the Zanj to join the other side, and, most consequentially, the death of Ali bin Muhammad (by suicide, by beheading, or in battle). Three years later other Zanj leaders were executed—their bodies crucified. All told, Krause estimates, "between 500,000 and 2.5 million people died during the fourteen-year war." No slave rebellion on American soil ever came close to matching the intensity or duration of the Zanj revolt.

89

Did black people engage in piracy during its heyday in the Americas?

DURING THE SEVENTEENTH CENTURY, three pirates named Diego "el Mulato" targeted Spanish colonial officials.[1] The first was Diego "el Mulato" Martín, an ex-slave from Havana active in the Gulf of Mexico in the 1630s. Apparently he was such a capable pirate that the Spanish granted him a royal commission to get him to fight on their side.

The second "el Mulato" was Diego de los Reyes (aka Diego Lucifer), although the historian Matthew Restall leaves open the possibility that the first two Diegos were the same person. Diego de los Reyes concentrated on the Yucatec coast. After he sacked Campeche and Bacalar in 1642, the Spanish Crown ordered "every possible remedy to be taken to capture the mulatto pirate."

The third "el Mulato," Diego Grillo, was another former Havana slave, but he set up at Tortuga, on Hispaniola, a hotbed of black piracy.[2] This Diego, too, raided a number of Spanish ships. His story did not end happily. In 1673 he was captured by Spaniards and executed.

Why did these three turn to piracy? Restall points to vengeance—Africans reacting to their lives as slaves—as well as the New World influences of the Spanish. One of Diego Lucifer's captives, Thomas Gage, an English Dominican clergyman, alluded to the same. The historian Kris E. Lane quotes Gage as saying,

> This mulatto, for some wrongs which had been offered unto him from some commanding Spaniards in Havana, ventured himself desperately

in a boat out to sea, where were some Holland ships waiting for a prize. With God's help getting unto them, he yielded himself to their mercy, which he esteemed far better than that of his own countrymen, promising to serve them faithfully against his own nation, which had most injuriously and wrongfully abused, yea, and whipped him in Havana, as I was afterwards informed.[3]

Was piracy a viable path to freedom for blacks? The historian W. Jeffrey Bolster argues, "Buccaneering tempted black seamen with visions of invincibility, with dreams of easy money and the idleness such freedom promised, and with the promise of a life unfettered by the racial and social ideology central to the plantation system."[4] Often black seamen joined with poor white sailors and servants to form their own pirate bands and embraced greater responsibility and authority than they'd known on land

Naomie Harris as the enchantress Tia Dalma in *Pirates of the Caribbean: At World's End* (Walt Disney Pictures, 2007).

as wage laborers or slaves. A black man, says Bolster, reportedly served as the notorious Captain William Kidd's quartermaster, charged with distributing the booty and even boarding captured ships.

It's important not to assume too much, however. While some slave pirates had the opportunity to make money, the lion's share went to their masters. In eighteenth-century Bermuda, the historian Arne Bialuschewski notes, "it was customary that privateering slaves obtained one third or half of one man's share, while their masters received the rest."[5]

The pirate life had other limits—and risks, as Bolster makes clear: "Unattached black men operating in the virtually all-male world of the 'Brotherhood of the Coast' realized those yearnings [for freedom] to a degree, but also found abuse and exploitation, as well as mortal combat and pursuit." It is easy to overstate the camaraderie black pirates felt with their white counterparts, when many slaves who joined pirate ships were put to hard labor, betrayed by their captains back into slavery, or returned to the ship whence they came.

Bialuschewski argues that it was "very unlikely that pirates ever freed African slaves and accepted them as equal shareholding members in their ventures."[6] To many white pirates, slaves were, in Bolster's words, "pawns, workers, objects of lust, or a source of ready cash."[7]

One case stands out above all the rest. Thanks to trial records and scholarship, we now have a fairly complete record of the exploits of a man named Thomas Wansley, who, though hardly typical, was a free African-American man arrested and convicted of piracy and murder.

"A New Orleans Negro," Joel Rogers writes in *Your History,* Wansley

> was one of the most ferocious and daring pirates of the nineteenth century. Together with his white partner, Gibbs, he robbed many ships, one of them with $54,000 cash and a cargo several times richer. Both also captured beautiful women and took them to their rendezvous, an islet, off the Cuban coast, defended with cannons, after killing the men, the plainer women and the children on the ships. Wansley was finally captured and brought to trial in New York City, where he and Gibbs were hanged in 1831.

Rogers, however, considerably overstates Wansley's history as a pirate. In fact, Wansley was involved in only one robbery, and it was aboard the ship on which he was already working.[8]

In 1830 Wansley joined the *Vineyard* as a steward and deckhand under Captain William Thornber and first mate William Roberts. From what we know, he was the first person to sign on as a crewman. While loading its cargo, he learned it was carrying some fifty thousand Mexican silver dollars. It was a bounty too great to resist, and Wansley began conspiring with other men on board to kill Thornber and Roberts, seize the treasure, and escape aboard a twelve- to fifteen-foot boat that was carried on the *Vineyard*'s deck. His chief co-conspirator was a white pirate named James Jeffers. Three additional white men—Henry Atwell (or Atwood), Aaron Church, and Robert Dawes—joined their plot, while two others, John Brownrigg and James Talbot, were apparently left unawares.

On Wednesday, November 24, 1830, when the *Vineyard* sailed through stormy conditions off Cape Hatteras, North Carolina, the would-be pirates put their plan into action. "I looked, feeling some curiosity to see how a man looked when he was being killed," Dawes recalled of watching Wansley creep up behind Captain Thornber with a heavy pump lever. Dawes saw Wansley "str[ike] the Captain . . . on the back of the neck" so that he "moved forward and fell, crying oh! murder [*sic*]." Wansley hit the captain again, leading Dawes to believe the man "was dead" before being tossed "overboard."[9]

Atwell, Church, and Jeffers took care of first mate William Roberts with a club, and when he attempted to flee, Jeffers grabbed him so one of the men could strike him with the pump lever Wansley had used to kill Captain Thornber. Roberts put up a better fight, so the men heaved him overboard alive. Dawes later said he imagined Roberts "sw[imming] after the ship as long as he could, shouting as loud as he was able."

As for the booty, all seven men on board divided it the following day. The crew then sailed north until they reached Long Island, where, boarding two smaller boats, they set the *Vineyard* on fire. One of the two smaller boats, weighed down by silver, disappeared, presumably drowning the men on board. The surviving boat carried Wansley, Gibbs, Jeffers, and Brownrigg. Catching on, they started dumping money from the boat until they reached shore with only "four or five thousand dollars," writes the historian Joseph Gibbs.

They landed near Pelican Beach on Barren Island in Jamaica Bay, New York (in present-day Brooklyn), and stayed the night with a man named Johnson. They buried the remaining treasure near his home. In such stories, there's almost always a catch. In this case, it was Brownrigg's apparent confession to Johnson. The police apprehended the white pirates, but Wansley took off into the woods. He was soon caught, wearing a money belt that contained 259 Mexican dollars.

When the men appeared in court, Dawes and Brownrigg formed a united front, testifying that they had had nothing to do with the crime. Brownrigg was let go, while the prosecutor used eighteen-year-old Dawes against Wansley and Jeffers. Wansley did not testify on his own behalf, and it took the jury only twenty minutes to find him guilty.

Yet, before he was sentenced, Wansley spoke out. "I have often understood that there is a great deal of difference in respect of color, and I have seen it in this court," he said. "Dawes and Brownrigg were as guilty as I am, and these witnesses have tried to fasten upon me greater guilt than is just; for their life has been given to them. You have taken the blacks from their own country, to bring them here to treat them ill—I have seen this." Whatever Wansley had seen, the judge didn't buy it. Wansley and Jeffers ended up on the gallows.

90

How did the shattering of the color barrier for Rhodes scholarships forever change the black arts movement?

ALAIN LEROY LOCKE WAS BORN in Philadelphia in 1885, the only son of a lawyer and teacher, both of whom had been born free. He attended Central High School and the Philadelphia School of Pedagogy en route to earning a bachelor's degree, magna cum laude, from Harvard University in 1907. Locke had entered Harvard as a member of the Class of 1908 but completed his undergraduate studies in only three years in order to take full advantage of the Rhodes scholarship he had been awarded in his junior year.

Now more than 110 years old, the Rhodes scholarship in Locke's day was still an infant phenomenon and lily white. The Rhodes Trust website states, "[Cecil] Rhodes's vision in founding the Scholarship was to develop outstanding leaders who would be motivated to fight 'the world's fight' and to 'esteem the performance of public duties as their highest aim,' and to promote international understanding and peace."[1]

That Locke, a black Harvard junior from Pennsylvania, was deemed by the selection committee to possess these attributes at a time when the color line in America was deepening everywhere was a testament to his brilliance and self-possession. The first white American Rhodes scholars had been elected just three years earlier, in 1904. What made Locke's election ironic was that it (like everyone else's) had been made possible by the charitable bequest of a recently deceased imperialist British businessman and political leader in South Africa.

Cecil Rhodes had agreed to change the qualification for his scholar-

Betsy Graves Reyneau.
Alain Leroy Locke.
1943–44. Oil on canvas.
Washington, D.C., Smithsonian
National Portrait Gallery.

ships from "white" to "civilized" only "under liberal pressure," according to *Britannica.*[2] It was easy for men like Rhodes to assume that "white" and "civilized" were synonymous. But there was Locke, just a few years later, and at the height of Jim Crow no less, ready to destroy Rhodes's racist logic. It would take decades before the second African-American Rhodes scholar would be chosen (the writer John Wideman, in 1963).

Here is how Locke described his experience:

For three years (1907–1910), I was in residence at Oxford University as a Rhodes scholar from my home state, Pennsylvania. There, after a futile struggle with the English pronunciation of the classics, I read for the research degree (B.Sc.) in philosophy.

For me, as for others, Oxford was a college education over again, though naturally a "de-luxe" version, which would have been a waste of time,—considering that I had to put in one and a half years more of post-graduate study at the University of Berlin, but for three reasons that may be of some interest;—first, one had a chance to balance one's

education in the scales of two standard systems,—instead of transfer-
ring my allegiance from scholarships to scholarship itself, as would have
been best, I temporarily abandoned formal education for the pursuit of
culture—yet fortunately, without money enough to collect blue china;
second, in the midst of a type of life that is a world-type simply because
it is so consistently itself, one had every facility for becoming really cos-
mopolitan—it was a rare experience in the company of many foreign
students to pay Englishmen the very high tribute of not even attempting to be like them, but to be more one's self, because of their example.[3]

In his 1910–11 stint at the University of Berlin, Locke

studied the works of Franz Brentano, Alexius Meinong, and C. F. von
Ehrenfels. Locke associated with other Rhodes scholars, including Horace M. Kallen, author of the concept of cultural pluralism; H. E. Alaily,
president of the Egyptian Society of England; Pa Ka Isaka Seme, a black
South African law student and eventual founder of the African National
Congress of South Africa; and Har Dayal from India—each concerned
with national liberation in their respective homelands. The formative
years of Locke's education and early career were the years just proceed-
ing and during World War I—years of nationalist uprising and wars
between the world's major nation-states.[4]

Spending time in Europe, away from the day-to-day intractability of
the color line, gave Locke a chance to question and consciously embrace his
blackness. He and the arts world would never be the same. That is what a
Rhodes scholarship meant to a black man in 1907.

In 1915, writes the historian Leonard Harris, "Locke began a lecture series
sponsored by the Social Science Club of the National Association for the
Advancement of Colored People, titled 'Race Contacts and Interracial
Relations: A Study of the Theory and Practice of Race.' Locke argued
against social Darwinism, which held that distinct races exist and are biologically determined to express peculiar cultural traits." Instead, "Locke
introduced a new way of thinking about social entities by conceiving of
race as a socially formed category."

While teaching at Howard, Locke returned to Harvard for his Ph.D. in philosophy, which he earned in 1918. That same year he wrote his landmark essay, "The Role of the Talented Tenth," a concept popularized (though not coined) by W.E.B. Du Bois (see Amazing Fact no. 20). Locke found his calling in the arts and, as a critic, raised his profile writing for Charles S. Johnson's *Opportunity* magazine in the early 1920s. Through Johnson, Locke served as master of ceremonies at a 1924 literary banquet at Manhattan's Civic Club. There Paul Kellogg, the editor of *Survey Graphic,* became so impressed with Locke that he invited him to edit a special issue of his popular mainstream magazine. As editor, Locke subtitled the issue "Harlem: Mecca of the New Negro." Published in March 1925, it was a success.

Afterward Locke strove to reach a wider audience by turning the essays into a book. *The New Negro: An Interpretation* (1925) became the crystalizing anthology of the Harlem Renaissance. In its preface, Locke captured the significance of the emerging black culture:

> The New Negro must be seen in the perspective of a New World, and especially of a New America. . . . America seeking a new spiritual expansion and artistic maturity, trying to found an American literature, a national art, and a national music implies a Negro-American culture seeking the same satisfactions and objectives. Separate as it may be in color and substance, the culture of the Negro is of a pattern integral with the times and with its cultural setting.

The New Negro became the Who's Who of the Harlem Renaissance. Its contributors in fiction included Jean Toomer and Zora Neale Hurston, among others. The poetry section included Countee Cullen, Claude McKay, James Weldon Johnson, Langston Hughes, Arna Bontemps, Anne Spencer, Angelina Grimké, and others. There were works of drama by Jessie Redmon Fauset, musical selections by Locke, McKay, and Hughes, and an essay on the new musical form called "jazz" by none other than our old friend "J. A. Rogers."[5]

Such leading lights of the Harlem Renaissance as Arthur Schomburg, Walter White, and Kelly Miller contributed essays. The anthropologist Melville Herskovits published an essay there, as did the noted collector Albert Barnes, on black art. The last word in *The New Negro* went to Du Bois; the title of his essay, "The Negro Mind Reaches Out," was a perfect description of Locke himself.

Locke went on to edit *Plays of Negro Life* (1927, with Montgomery Greg-

374 / HENRY LOUIS GATES, JR.

ory), *Four Negro Poets* (1927), *The Negro in Art: A Pictorial Record of the Negro Artist and of the Negro Theme in Art* (1940), and *When Peoples Meet: A Study in Race and Culture Contacts* (1942, with Bernhard J. Stern). Perhaps more important than Locke's literary accomplishments and philosophical writings was his influence on younger writers, especially Langston Hughes and Zora Neale Hurston.

Alain Locke died June 9, 1954, at age sixty-eight. Ralph Bunche, W.E.B. Du Bois, Walter White, Mordecai Johnson (president of Howard University), and other notables were among the 110 people who attended the Harlem funeral, presided over by Channing Tobias, chairman of the board of the NAACP.

91

Which black female poet owned a garden house that became a popular home-away-from-home down south for the leading lights of the Harlem Renaissance?

HARLEM WAS CELEBRATED in legend and song as the world's "black mecca," as Alain Locke put it, but the Harlem *Renaissance* had roots and branches extending far beyond Upper Manhattan. It was a state of mind that connected a community of artists all across the country, the descendants of both slaves and free black people. They searched for new forms of expression—for freedom itself—throughout the major industrial areas of the North, from Chicago and Detroit through Pittsburgh, Baltimore, and Boston, even (or especially) in Jim Crow's backyard, segregated Washington, D.C.

In the American South, ironically, segregation, by restricting hotels to whites, forced black travelers to look for "tourist homes"—rooming houses, bed-and-breakfasts, and friends-of-friends' homes all rolled into one. You never knew whom you were going to bump into in a tourist home, or what talented fellow boarders you might discover there.

On the road, shared circumstances and chance had a way of creating conditions for interconnectivity, enriching to any artist, but especially to those confined by color. Segregation-induced reading clubs, literary societies, and middle-class cultural salons and arts contests sponsored by the *Crisis* and *Opportunity* magazines were at one end of the spectrum. At the other were juke joints, speakeasies, and late-night integrated jazz clubs.

Anne Bethel Spencer photographed in her wedding dress,
1900.

From this fertile soil grew the full range of the arts of the Harlem
Renaissance, from the finest poetry and fiction to achievements in the plas-
tic and visual arts to gutbucket blues, verbal signifying street rituals, the
more refined classic blues, and the emerging art form of jazz.

The poetic branch of the Harlem Renaissance was tended by the movement's leading African-American female poet, Anne Spencer. Her enchant-
ing house and garden in Lynchburg, Virginia, now a landmark museum,
was black America's version of Monet's garden at Giverny. Anybody who
was anybody in the black arts and letters scene made a point of stopping
by to "smell the roses" of her handcrafted artistry. By offering generous
hospitality to the black writers lodging in her salonlike home, she encour-

aged and cultivated some of the Harlem Renaissance's most profound and enduring poetry.

Spencer was born Annie Bethel Scales Bannister in Henry County, Virginia, on February 6, 1882. She was only an infant when her parents moved to Martinsville, where her father, Joel Cephus Bannister, a saloon owner born into slavery, could practice his trade. When her parents separated a few years later, she was on the move again, this time to Bramwell, West Virginia, to join her mother, Sarah Scales, the daughter of a slave mother and a mysteriously unidentified white father. "Your mother was never young," Anne's husband, Edward A. Spencer, would one day tell their children. "She went from childhood to middle age."[1]

In 1893 Annie attended the Virginia Seminary (today, the historically black Virginia University of Lynchburg), in the foothills of the Blue Ridge Mountains. She was only eleven years old. After graduating in 1899, she taught for two years in West Virginia before marrying Edward Spencer in 1901. That year the Spencers settled in Lynchburg. During the Civil War, the town had served briefly as home to the state government after the fall of Richmond; the Spencer home would put it on the map for a far different reason.

At 1313 Pierce Street, Edward Spencer, a postal worker and all-around renaissance man, built his bride a Queen Anne–style home with a bountiful garden. That place was to be her sanctuary during her twenty-year career as a librarian and teacher at the local Dunbar High School and as the mother of three: Bethel Calloway Spencer, Alroy Sarah Spencer, and Chauncey Edward Spencer. The Spencers called their garden house Edankraal, "a blend of names and an Afrikaans word for dwelling or enclosure."[2] It became the doorway through which Anne Spencer hosted the fledgling black literary world.

Spencer had started writing poetry as a student at the Virginia Seminary, but it wasn't until leading writer James Weldon Johnson discovered her work while staying with the Spencers on a business trip for the NAACP that she received the encouragement she needed to share her musings with the world. Actually, Johnson had to lobby Spencer to release her poem "Before the Feast of Shushan" to him for publication in the *Crisis* in 1920.

92

When President Abraham Lincoln met with free black leaders in 1862, what did he propose?

WHILE PRESIDENT LINCOLN WAS WEIGHING emancipation, he also had a very different solution in mind for America's seemingly intractable race problem. During his first years in office, he was obsessed with persuading free blacks to lead an exodus of African Americans out of the country. This would enable the United States to wash away the original sin of slavery without its citizens having to live alongside those the country had enslaved. To sell his plan, the president convened a meeting with local black leaders in Washington. It was billed to them as a policy conversation, but Lincoln wasn't really eager to listen. He wanted to deliver a message about a mission, and they had been chosen to receive it.[1]

The chairman of the free black delegation was Edward M. Thomas, messenger to the House of Representatives and a respected cultural leader in Washington's black community. Joining him in the delegation were John F. Cook, Jr., a local school leader who had studied at Oberlin College; John T. Costin, who, like Thomas and Cook, was a Freemason; Cornelius Clark, a member of the influential Social, Civil, and Statistical Association in Washington (Cook and Thomas were also members); and Benjamin M. McCoy, a teacher and leader in the Asbury Methodist Episcopal Church in Washington.

Their steward was Lincoln's emigration commissioner, the white Methodist preacher James Mitchell, who had spread the word through the black churches of Washington that Father Abraham was interested in talking.

J. Waeschle. "Emancipation of the Slaves, Proclaimed on the
22d September 1862, by Abraham Lincoln, President of the
United States." Ca. 1862. Lithograph.

Although the congregation members were honored by the president's
request, they were also wary. By way of prayer and vigorous debate, they
counseled each other to refrain from acting with haste or from giving the
impression that such a select group of leaders could possibly represent the
black community as a whole. More important, they pledged to remain
steadfast against colonization when it came up.[2]

A stenographer was there to take down the president's words:

You and we are different races. We have between us a broader difference
than exists between almost any other two races. Whether it is right or
wrong I need not discuss, but this physical difference is a great disadvan-
tage to us both, as I think your race suffer very greatly, many of them

by living among us, while ours suffer from your presence. In a word we suffer on each side. If this is admitted, it affords a reason at least why we should be separated.[3]

As the free black leaders soon discovered, Lincoln's invitation to discuss policy was a pretext for a one-sided sales pitch.

"I do not propose to discuss this, but to present it as a fact with which we have to deal," Lincoln continued. "I cannot alter it if I would. It is a fact, about which we all think and feel alike, I and you."

Lincoln unloaded on the delegates, even blaming their people for the Civil War:

> See our present condition—the country engaged in war!—our white men cutting one another's throats, none knowing how far it will extend; and then consider what we know to be the truth. But for your race among us there could not be war, although many men engaged on either side do not care for you one way or the other. Nevertheless, I repeat, without the institution of Slavery and the colored race as a basis, the war could not have an existence.

This brought the president to colonization, and his purpose for inviting the delegates to the White House—to get them to accept his trial balloon.

> I suppose one of the principal difficulties in the way of colonization is that the free colored man cannot see that his comfort would be advanced by it. You may believe you can live in Washington or elsewhere in the United States the remainder of your life [as easily], perhaps more so than you can in any foreign country, and hence you may come to the conclusion that you have nothing to do with the idea of going to a foreign country. This is (I speak in no unkind sense) an extremely selfish view of the case.

Then he pivoted: "But you ought to do something to help those who are not so fortunate as yourselves."

In his mind, if these free men stepped forward to lead the emigration of black people out of the United States, that would make it easier for white slaveholders to free the rest. He explained:

If you could give a start to white people, you would open a wide door for many to be made free. If we deal with those who are not free at the beginning, and whose intellects are clouded by Slavery, we have very poor materials to start with. If intelligent colored men, such as are before me, would move in this matter, much might be accomplished. It is exceedingly important that we have men at the beginning capable of thinking as white men, and not those who have been systematically oppressed.

"There is much to encourage you," Lincoln continued. "For the sake of your race you should sacrifice something of your present comfort for the purpose of being as grand in that respect as the white people."

After reviewing the pros and cons of Africa, Lincoln pushed Central America as his destination of choice. After all, he said, Liberia was far from African Americans' birthplace in the United States, and even if they weren't all that fond of white people, he could understand wanting to be close to their forcibly adopted "motherland."

Here was the old Thomas Jefferson canard with a Central American twist. Despite years of forced interracial mixing on southern plantations, African Americans were somehow, in Lincoln's estimation, more physically suited for certain geographies—namely, hot places—than white people. Lincoln even had a specific industry in mind once the free black leaders and their families arrived in Central America: "rich coal mines."

What he didn't tell them was that, behind the scenes, he had already been moving the pieces into place for a specific landing at Chiriquí, today a province of Panama but then part of Colombia. The plan had the potential to relocate more than ten thousand free blacks to a colony the U.S. government would purchase.

On August 16, 1862, Edward Thomas, leader of the delegation, politely wrote Lincoln, "We were entirely hostile to the movement until all the advantages were so ably brought to our view by you and we believe that our friends and colaborers [*sic*] for our race in [Philadelphia, New York, and Boston] will when the subject is explained by us to them join heartily in sustaining such a movement."

But this note hardly reflected the views of the free black community. When news of the meeting reached African Americans, they responded with outrage and despair. In fact, a writer for the *Christian Recorder,* Cerebus (a pseudonym), was outraged that the black delegates had the gall to think they could represent anybody in the black community to the president of the United States: "We, for one, should like to know *who* gave *that committee* authority to act for us, the *fifteen thousand* residents of color in this District—and who requested them to represent the interests of the *two hundred and ten thousand* inhabitants of color in the Free States!"

Lincoln had lobbed a political bomb into the black community. Frederick Douglass lashed out at him for "assum[ing] the language and arguments of an itinerant colonization lecturer," while two of Douglass's sons voiced interest in joining the expedition to Chiriquí. Concludes the historian Eric Foner, "What Lincoln said on August 14 to the black delegation made the meeting one of the most controversial moments of his entire career."

Then, on September 22, after the Battle of Antietam, Lincoln surprised everyone by issuing his Preliminary Emancipation Proclamation. He also opened the door to the arming of black soldiers, a move he would ratify in the official Emancipation Proclamation on January 1, 1863. Events were moving so quickly that some, including Lincoln, sensed divine forces at play.

In the aftermath, schemers for removing blacks from the country continued to approach Lincoln, and Lincoln continued to listen. Even *after* making good on his ultimatum to the South in the final Emancipation Proclamation, he supported one black minister's Liberian plan while backing another venture to Île-à-Vache, off Haiti.

93

Which black justices broke the color barrier at the federal court level?

Judge William Henry Hastie (1904–76)

Born in Knoxville, Tennessee, and raised in Washington, D.C., Hastie graduated magna cum laude from Amherst College in 1925. After teaching for two years at the Manual Training and Industrial School for Colored Youth in New Jersey, he punched his ticket to Harvard Law School, where, following in the footsteps of civil rights crusader Charles Hamilton Houston, he became the second black law student to serve on the *Harvard Law Review*. Hastie graduated with a bachelor of laws degree in 1930 and earned a research doctorate in law in 1933, also from Harvard.

Later, balancing professorial duties at Howard University Law School with his work at Houston's firm, Hastie helped develop the pro-integration legal strategies that would culminate in the *Brown v. Board of Education* decision. Specifically, he galvanized the NAACP's legal struggle for equal pay for black teachers in North Carolina, hiring one of his former law students at Howard, Thurgood Marshall, to assist on the case.

While Hastie was serving as solicitor for the Interior Department during the administration of Franklin D. Roosevelt, he was nominated and confirmed, on March 19, 1937, to a federal district court judgeship in the U.S. Virgin Islands. The federal court system consists of federal district courts and federal appellate courts, up to the U.S. Supreme Court. Hence Hastie was the first black federal court judge.

In 1946 President Harry S. Truman tapped Hastie to become the first

Judge William H. Hastie, while dean of the Howard
University Law School and a civilian aide to the
U.S. secretary of war, ca. 1941.

black governor of the Virgin Islands. Then, in 1949, just one year after announcing the integration of America's armed forces, Truman again made history by promoting Hastie to a judgeship on the U.S. Court of Appeals for the Third Circuit, based in Philadelphia, with jurisdiction over Pennsylvania, Delaware, and New Jersey. Judge Hastie was confirmed by the U.S. Senate on July 19, 1950.

In his role as a federal appellate judge, Hastie was committed to free speech during the Cold War, privacy rights, and a strict wall between church and state. In 1968 he ascended to chief judge of the Third Circuit. He retired in 1971 and died at age seventy-one in 1976.

JUDGE CONSTANCE BAKER MOTLEY (1921–2005)

Born in New Haven, Connecticut, to immigrant parents from Nevis, West Indies, Motley had early exposure to civil rights work: her mother founded the New Haven chapter of the NAACP. As a college student, she first enrolled at Fisk University in Nashville, then transferred to New York

University, from which she graduated in 1943. Three years later she had a law degree from Columbia University.

At the NAACP Legal Defense and Educational Fund, Motley was mentored by Thurgood Marshall and ultimately became associate counsel and lead trial lawyer. It was Marshall who sent Motley to Georgia to direct the landmark desegregation case against the University of Georgia, which had refused to admit Hamilton Holmes and Charlayne Hunter.

On October 17, 1961, Motley argued her first case before the Supreme Court, *Hamilton v. Alabama,* winning an important 9–0 decision guaranteeing the right of criminal defendants to counsel at their arraignments. Supreme Court Justice William O. Douglas wrote of Motley that she "was equal to [Charles Hamilton] Houston in advocacy of cases" and that "the quality of [her] arguments would place her in the top ten of any group of advocates at the appellate level in this country."[1]

According to a 2007 congressional resolution recognizing her, Motley

was the only female attorney on the legal team that won the landmark desegregation case, *Brown v. Board of Education,* [and] she argued 10 major civil rights cases before the Supreme Court, winning all but one . . . *Swain v. Alabama,* a case in which the Court refused to proscribe race-based peremptory challenges in cases involving African-American defendants . . . which was later reversed in *Batson v. Kentucky* on grounds that had been largely asserted by Constance Baker Motley in the *Swain* case.[2]

In the mid-1970s, as a federal judge in New York, Motley refused to recuse herself from a Title VII gender discrimination case when defense counsel argued that she would be biased because she had been a *female* lawyer before becoming a judge. "If background or sex or race of each judge were, by definition, sufficient ground for removal," Motley explained, "no judge on this court could hear this case, or many others, by virtue of the fact that all of them were attorneys, of a sex, often with distinguished law firms or public service backgrounds."[3] Motley became chief judge of her district court in 1982 and reached senior status in 1986.

JUDGE A. LEON HIGGINBOTHAM, JR. (1928–98)

Aloyisus Leon Higginbotham was born in 1928 to a maid and a factory worker in Trenton, New Jersey. As an engineering student at Purdue University, he challenged the school's practice of housing black students in an unheated attic. The president brushed him off, and Higginbotham transferred to Antioch College. He graduated from Yale Law School with high honors in 1952, then moved to Philadelphia, where he become a partner in that city's first African-American law firm and served as an assistant district attorney and local NAACP chapter president.

Appointed by President Kennedy to the Federal Trade Commission in 1962, Higginbotham became the first African American to serve on any regulatory commission. After Kennedy's assassination, he served President Johnson as an adviser on race relations, and in 1964 Johnson appointed him as the first African-American judge to the U.S. District Court for the Eastern District of Pennsylvania. At thirty-six, Higginbotham was the youngest federal judge in more than thirty years. In 1977 President Jimmy Carter promoted him to the Third Circuit U.S. Court of Appeals—Judge Hastie's old court. There Higginbotham served as chief judge from 1990 to 1991, when he assumed senior status because of illness, and retired from the court in 1993.

An international mediator during the first free South African election in 1994, Higginbotham helped the newly elected government, headed by Nelson Mandela, draft its constitution. He was appointed by President Bill Clinton to the U.S. Commission on Civil Rights. (Clinton awarded him the Presidential Medal of Freedom in 1995.)

JUDGE SPOTTSWOOD W. ROBINSON III (1916–98)

Spottswood Robinson III was one of America's most sparkling legal minds, known especially for a rare combination of fastidiousness, courage, and painstaking attention to detail. A native of Richmond, Virginia, Robinson took after his father, Spottswood W. Robinson, Jr., a lawyer, professor, and real estate broker. At age twenty, Robinson left his studies at Virginia Union University for Howard Law School, from which he graduated in 1939 with the highest grade point average in school history. While a teacher at Howard, Robinson joined forces with civil rights crusaders whom Charles Hamilton Houston had trained. Among them were Oliver Hill and Martin Martin, who, with Robinson, made up the dream team known as the NAACP's Virginia State Conference.

"In his first case of great consequence in 1943," recalled Hill in 1999, "more than a decade before Rosa Parks, Spot[ts] defended a woman, Irene

Morgan, who refused to move to the 'colored' seats at the back of an interstate bus. This case, *Morgan v. Virginia,* ultimately ended with the U.S. Supreme Court declaring segregation laws in interstate transportation unconstitutional."[4]

In 1947 Robinson, at Thurgood Marshall's behest, concentrated on ending segregation in Virginia's public schools. Under threat of lynching, he crossed the state, met with black community groups, and with the Virginia NAACP, launched actions in seventy-five locations. By 1950, Robinson had become the NAACP's southeastern regional counsel, and in 1951 he and Hill filed suit against school segregation in Prince Edward County, Virginia. At the Supreme Court, their case was joined with four other school cases to form *Brown v. Board of Education.* As part of that legendary legal dream team, Robinson argued brilliantly that segregation violated the Equal Protection Clause of the Fourteenth Amendment of the U.S. Constitution.

Robinson went on to serve as dean of Howard Law and accepted President Kennedy's invitation to join the U.S. Commission on Civil Rights. In 1964 he answered the call of another president, LBJ, becoming the first black judge on the U.S. District Court for the District of Columbia. Two years later Robinson again broke ground under LBJ, this time as the first black justice to serve on the esteemed U.S. Court of Appeals for the District of Columbia Circuit. From 1981 to 1986, he led the circuit as chief judge, then took senior status in 1989.

94

Who buried the war dead from the Battle of Gettysburg?

AFTER THE BATTLE OF GETTYSBURG, the job of burying the bodies fell to African Americans who, having suffered personally as a result of the battle, formed burial details to aid in its commemoration. In his timeless Gettysburg Address, delivered at the soldiers' cemetery on November 19, 1863, President Abraham Lincoln set the scene, saying, "We have come to dedicate a portion of that field, as a final resting place for those who here gave their lives that that nation might live." What most people probably don't know is that the "we" in Lincoln's remarks included a bona fide American hero. His name was Basil Biggs, and his life and toil at Gettysburg were—and always will be—heroically bound to the battle that turned the tide in the war that transformed America from a slave nation into the land of the free.

Basil Biggs was born in 1820 in New Windsor, Maryland. His parents were William Biggs and Elizabeth Bayne (or Boyne), and there's good reason to believe, based on evidentiary clues and DNA testing, that William Biggs was a white man, descended from a Benjamin Biggs, who had had a white wife (not Elizabeth!) and white children.

Basil was nothing if not industrious. The historian Margaret Creighton notes that he "began working for others at the age of four."[1] The historian Allen Guelzo identifies him as "a free black teamster in Baltimore."[2]

In 1858 he moved his family from the slave state of Maryland to the free state of Pennsylvania—to a little town called Gettysburg. There, according to the 1860 census, 186 free black people lived, Guelzo says, "with another 1,500 scattered through Adams County."

The same census tracked Biggs's move upward socially. By then the family had $1,000 worth of property and enough room for a farmhand. Biggs, however, wasn't just a successful farmer. He also was a skilled veterinarian, hired to treat animals on farms, both in Maryland and in Pennsylvania. He "must have been very good with animals," the historian Gabor Boritt writes.[3]

But what had spurred Biggs to leave Maryland? He moved, Guelzo writes, "so that his children could take advantage of Pennsylvania's Free School Act." Whereas in Maryland, black people—*even free people of color*—were excluded from public school, in Pennsylvania they were allowed to attend even with whites—if there were no black schools available.

Gettysburg must also have appealed to him as a safe haven for his family, in a state famous for its long history of opposing slavery. But even so, the town's black families lived under "the threat of the fugitive hunters always hover[ing]," as Guelzo writes.

Biggs had made his move at a fateful moment. Two years after he settled in, the United States was on the brink of civil war. In June 1863, the Con-

"A Burial Party in Cold Harbor, Virginia—April 1865." Albumen silver print, as published in *Gardner's Photographic Sketchbook of the War.*

federate Army invaded Pennsylvania, and some of Gen. Robert E. Lee's rebels saw it as a tempting opportunity to reverse the flow of the Underground Railroad and send runaways, refugees, and free black people—whomever they found—back down south and straight into slavery.

Area blacks weren't taking any chances. Biggs secured his family along the Susquehanna River, Creighton writes, and managed to escape himself "on a borrowed horse" just as the Confederate cavalry were arriving.

During the three days of combat (July 1–3, 1863), the invading Confederate troops turned Basil's farm into a field hospital. It would become one of the busiest Confederate hospital stations during that devastating battle. As the fighting dragged on, desperate soldiers from both sides ransacked the countryside for food and shelter.

Afterward, Basil returned home to find his farm in ruins. He had lost everything, from livestock to crops to furniture. He also discovered that "forty-five dead Confederates were buried on the farm."[4] Basil realized there was a job to do that nobody else would want to do—exhuming bodies that had been hastily buried during and immediately after the battle, and ensuring that they were returned home or reburied in a more dignified way. In making the dead and their families whole, Biggs saw a way to make his own family whole.

A white Gettysburg resident, F. W. Biesecker, won the government contract to exhume the bodies of Union soldiers and rebury them in the Gettysburg (or Soldiers') National Cemetery. Biesecker's "bid," according to Creighton, was "a little over a dollar and a half per body." Once he got the contract, he found a black man to execute the job.

The actual work of digging up and transporting the cadavers was subcontracted to Basil Biggs, who hired several black men to tackle the monumental task. Thirteen-year-old Leander Warren, who helped carry the bodies from Gettysburg, later recalled, "Basil Biggs, colored, of Gettysburg, was given the contract for disinterring the bodies on the field. He had a crew of eight or ten negroes in his employ."[5]

Work began October 27, 1863. Biggs and his men dug up, transported, and reburied 3,354 corpses that littered the area. We'll never know the internal story of Biggs and his black burial detail, for even the most disturbing photographs, Creighton writes, fail to capture "what these men did with their emotions as they sorted through people—whether they grew inured to the dead and learned to work mechanically, or whether the smell and sight of humans turned from flesh to dust exacted a lasting psychological toll."

What we do know is that thanks to Biggs and his men, Lincoln was able to deliver his Gettysburg Address in front of orderly rows of graves in the new national cemetery. "By November 19, 1863, when Edward Everett and Abraham Lincoln spoke to the throngs at Gettysburg," writes Creighton, "Basil Biggs and company had reburied close to a thousand men"—a job that would stretch on "until the middle of March 1864." In other words, while it took President Lincoln little more than two minutes to orate what he had written, it took Biggs and his crew *four months* to finish their grisly task. A Gettysburg resident who witnessed their effort said, "Words would fail to describe . . . the grateful relief that this work has brought to many a sorrowing household!"

Basil and Mary Biggs used the money he earned to rebuild their lives, purchasing a new farm where his family could live and thrive. (Biggs was never reimbursed for the damages to his property. He had been awarded $1,356 on paper, but Congress never released the funds to repay him.)[6]

Basil Biggs is buried in Lincoln Cemetery alongside his wife. His June 13, 1906, obituary in the *Gettysburg Compiler* reveals his most impressive accomplishment of all. Before the Civil War, he had been a farmer, a veterinarian, *and* a conductor on the Underground Railroad. Historians, including Creighton, William Switala, and James Paradis, have helped us understand how Basil Biggs took part in this complex and dangerous operation.

Reportedly, he used the barn at the McPherson Farm, which he rented, to hide runaway slaves. The routes were treacherous and rife with slave catchers and informants. After all, Gettysburg was less than ten miles from the Mason-Dixon Line. To avoid notice, arrest, and possible death under the Fugitive Slave Act of 1850, Biggs would wait until night to bring the fugitives to the home of another free black man, Edward Mathews, in Yellow Hill. From there, the escaped slaves would flee to Canada—and freedom.

95

What did Malcolm X do at
Oxford University?

IN DECEMBER 1964, Malcolm X traveled to Oxford University to debate the assumptions of Western scholars while reminding them of the atrocities committed by their ancestors who set about "discovering" the New World and Africa in 1492. Malcolm hadn't attended college, but he was, without a doubt, a genius, self-taught in the prison system of Massachusetts in the late 1940s and early '50s (while he was still Malcolm Little). And he was fearless about bringing his anticolonial message to college campuses, like that of Oxford, that were courageous enough to invite him.[1]

Ironically, Malcolm X was invited to Oxford to defend the position that former U.S. presidential nominee Barry Goldwater had staked out in his acceptance speech at the 1964 Republican National Convention: "I would remind you that extremism in the defense of liberty is no vice. And let me remind you also that moderation in the pursuit of justice is no virtue."[2] But Malcolm surely knew that Senator Goldwater had said nothing new in those quickly famous lines, so he didn't waste any time referring to him during his debate.

Malcolm X's opponent was Humphry Berkeley, a Conservative member of Parliament, who ostensibly took the other side of the "extremism" argument. But he went so far as to accuse Malcolm of being a racist in the same league as the *pro*-apartheid forces in South Africa; he even poked fun at his name.

Exposing the hypocrisy of Berkeley's "moderate" position, Malcolm rebutted, "I have more respect for a man who lets me know where he stands, even if he's wrong, than the one who comes up like an angel and is nothing but a devil." Malcolm also cleverly explained,

[Humphry's] right, X is not my real name [laughter], but if you study history you'll find why no black man in the western hemisphere knows his real name. Some of his ancestors kidnapped our ancestors from Africa, and took us into the western hemisphere and sold us there. And our names were stripped from us and so today we don't know who we really are. I am one of those who admit it and so I just put X up there to keep from wearing his name.

Malcolm X on the campus of Oxford University, December 3, 1964. His participation in that year's Oxford Union gave voice to the disaffection of black people with the status quo.

The truth is, Malcolm's signature sentiment, "by any means necessary," harked back to the African-American abolitionist movement—specifically, to David Walker's 1829 *Appeal, in Four Articles; Together with a Preamble to the Coloured Citizens of the World, but in Particular, and Very Expressly, to Those of the United States of America,* in which he urged slaves to rise up against their masters and resist efforts to uproot African Americans from their American homeland.

For Malcolm, the stakes were not about resisting emigration but about forging an international alliance between victims of Jim Crow at home and victims of colonialism abroad, all of whom were now demanding equal rights and independence. As Malcolm spoke at Oxford, the civil rights movement in America was about to take a most dramatic turn toward voting rights in Selma, Alabama, and Malcolm was working out what lay beyond the bridge.

Malcolm X's debate performance flowed out of a much longer Anglo-American narrative of slavery to freedom, reaching back to the eighteenth-century African-British abolitionist author and lecturer Olaudah Equiano and the nineteenth-century African-American abolitionist Frederick Douglass. Douglass in particular, for twenty eventful months between 1845 and 1847, successfully leveraged the distance between Britain and the New World to indict American slavery. Inside Queen Victoria's realm, across England, Ireland, and Scotland, Douglass delivered more than three hundred antislavery speeches. Like Malcolm X, Douglass had cast off his slave master's name, both out of protest and in an attempt to mask his identity as a fugitive slave.

A century after emancipation, Malcolm X was a different kind of fugitive. Not only had he broken with the Nation of Islam and his leader and former mentor, Elijah Muhammad, but he also was viewed by many Americans (even inside the civil rights movement) as a violent extremist. After an intensive pilgrimage to Mecca in the spring of 1964, during which he embraced orthodox Islam and turned more fully to an international human rights perspective, Malcolm X seized on the Oxford Union invitation as a chance to correct the record. He was especially eager to turn the very brand of extremism that had been fixed on him *against* his accusers. The goal was to expose the blatant hypocrisy that had made racism and racial violence seem moderate, prudent, and measured compared with these people's resistance to their own oppression.

The change exploding outside the debate hall that night was dramatic.

Two days earlier the Johnson administration had met to discuss the bombing campaign in Vietnam, and early that very morning, at the University of California, Berkeley, eight hundred protesters taking part in the student Free Speech Movement had been arrested for a sit-in at an administration building. A week later the Rev. Martin Luther King, Jr., would receive the Nobel Peace Prize, and the Cuban revolutionary Che Guevara would address the UN General Assembly, while the U.S. Supreme Court weighed the impact of the 1964 Civil Rights Act on public accommodations. To the world of that moment, Malcolm X was delivering a message of the necessity of "extremism" in the name of international human rights.

Compared with King (whom Malcolm X fiercely criticized as being too "soft"),[3] Malcolm was less a prophet and more a prosecutor, exposing crimes that few in the media would admit to. That night in Oxford, Malcolm laid claim to "intelligently directed extremism," which he manifested with his jabbing finger, his confident laughter, his trim black suit, his narrow tie and starched white shirt, and those trademark professorial glasses. In a sense, Malcolm was the political face of an aesthetic triumvirate that included Muhammad Ali and Miles Davis, each of whom, in his own way, expounded and improvised upon resistance to the "castration of the black man."

Technically, according to the audience vote, Malcolm X lost the debate, though the students gave him "enthusiastic applause," the historian Stephen Tuck says. But that was really beside the point. Malcolm had taught an entire college course in one night. All these years later, listening to him turn Shakespeare and Patrick Henry to his advantage is all the more poignant because we know that, so very shortly after his hour of apotheosis, he would exit the world stage—gunned down in New York City by Nation of Islam assassins on February 21, 1965. Ironically and most tragically, the Oxford Union debate was one of the last gospels Malcolm X would ever preach.

96

Which black man made many of our favorite household products better?

INVENTING IS A COLLABORATIVE EXERCISE, as Walter Isaacson reminds us in his riveting book, *The Innovators: How a Group of Hackers, Geniuses, and Geeks Created the Digital Revolution,* so it's critical from the start not to overstate the role of any single inventor in an iterative, constantly evolving process of improvement.[1] That being said, among the team of geniuses behind the development of Crest products over the years was a black Ph.D.

Although Dr. Herbert C. Smitherman, Sr., didn't *invent* Crest tooth-paste, he *dramatically improved* the Crest formula. His distinguished career as an inventor at Procter & Gamble, the parent company of Crest, is impressive by itself. But it's even more impressive when set within the longer legacy of black inventors, stretching all the way back to slavery days.

Smitherman was born on March 23, 1937, the only child of a minister and his wife. He grew up in Birmingham, Alabama, just down the street from the Rev. Fred Shuttlesworth, Sr., long before the latter co-founded the Southern Christian Leadership Conference and marched against Jim Crow.[2]

Smitherman graduated from Tuskegee Institute in Alabama and earned his Ph.D. at Howard University in Washington, D.C. In 1966, just a year after the Voting Rights Act was passed, he became "the first African American hired by Procter and Gamble with a Ph.D. in science," according to a press release from the Cincinnati NAACP upon Smitherman's passing in 2010.[3] In 2011, a resolution adopted by the Cincinnati public schools to honor Smitherman's life listed products he had helped develop, including

The improvement of Crest toothpaste is just one of the numerous contributions of black scientists to the enhancement of modern life.

"Crest toothpaste, Safeguard soap, Folgers coffee, Bounce fabric softener, Biz detergent, and flavors for Crush soda."[4] Further, "patents for tartar-control toothpaste, detergent composition, and detergent manufacturing were featured in the 'America I AM: The African-American Imprint' exhibit at the Cincinnati Museum Center," which later went to the Harvey B. Gantt Center for African-American Arts + Culture in Charlotte, North Carolina.

Crest toothpaste was developed in the 1950s, before Smitherman joined P&G. But during his time at the company, he was a valuable member of the development team. The U.S. Patent and Trademark Office database contains two patents issued under his name. The first, Patent No. 5,015,467, was for combined anticalculus and antiplaque compositions:

> Tartrate monosuccinate and tartrate disuccinate compounds of the formulae . . . are used in combination with various polymers to provide anticalculus and antiplaque effects on teeth. Oral care compositions such as dentifrices, mouthwashes, and the like, are provided. Use of the tartate-succinates and polymers in combination with other oral car [*sic*] ingredients such as fluoride, pyrophosphate and antibacterials is also described.[5]

400 / HENRY LOUIS GATES, JR.

This patent was used in the development of many of our everyday brush-and-rinse routines and has been cited by thirty-three other patents, according to the database. In assigning his patent to the company (standard industry practice), Smitherman was fortifying the Crest product line for millions of consumers.

The other patent for Smitherman, dated 1973, was Patent No. 3,755,429, for "a process for preparing a water-soluble sulfonated reaction product having excellent detergent properties which uses alpha-olefins as the starting reactant."

In addition to improving products, Smitherman touched many lives. "Dr. Smitherman was involved in aggressively recruiting minority undergraduate, graduate, and Ph.D. science, chemistry, and chemical engineering students from schools around the nation," his obituary records. "Many P&G African American chemists and chemical engineers who joined the company during the 70's and 80's were hired as a result of that recruitment program." Such efforts earned him the nickname "the Jackie Robinson of Procter and Gamble."

According to his obituary, "Dr. Smitherman worked for Procter and Gamble for 29 years. After retiring, he was employed by Wilberforce University"— the historically black university where W.E.B. Du Bois once taught—"for four years as assistant Vice President of Academic Affairs and professor of chemistry." Smitherman, the NAACP release tells us, "then started a high school called Western Hills Design Technology to augment African American students in performing at the highest levels in math and science. After graduating several senior classes he transitioned to the [Cincinnati Public Schools] Board of Education to work directly for Superintendent Mary Ronan." Just like the slave-turned-inventor John P. Parker, Smitherman "lifted as he climbed."

97

Which twentieth-century black actor played roles of all races during a time when Hollywood had few roles for black actors?

MORE THAN ONE HUNDRED YEARS AGO, on July 24, 1914, Frank Silvera was born on the Caribbean island of Jamaica. His father, Alfred, was white and Jewish, and his mother, Gertrude, was black. By the time Frank was eight years old, his parents had separated. He and his brothers migrated with their mother to Boston, where she took up work as a seamstress and he enrolled in school, graduating from English High School in 1934.

Silvera enrolled at Northeastern University School of Law in Boston, but his heart belonged to the stage. In 1934, he appeared in his first show, *Potter's Field,* at Boston's Plymouth Theatre. He also belonged to the city's Federal Theatre.

During World War II Silvera served in the U.S. Navy, and afterward he moved to New York. In 1945 he made his Broadway debut as Joe in *Anna Lucasta,* which had been adapted for an all-black cast by the American Negro Theater in 1944. Silvera honed his craft as a member of the Actors Studio alongside fellow young guns Marlon Brando and Paul Newman.

Silvera's first television gig was *The Big Story* in 1949, and his first screen role was in the 1952 Audie Murphy western *The Cimarron Kid.* A host of other parts followed, including three more that year: Paulino in *The Fighter,* Victoriano Huerta in *Viva Zapata!,* and Arturo dos Santos in *The Miracle of Our Lady of Fatima.* It soon became obvious that with his "café-au-lait" skin (the *Chicago Defender*'s words) and gift for accents, Silvera could play anyone. He was, as the *New York Times* put it on June 12, 1970, a "man of many parts."

Silvera played Minarli in *Mutiny on the Bounty* (1952) and the cruel boss Vincent Rapallo in Stanley Kubrick's *Killer's Kiss* (1955). In 1960 he appeared on TV in *The Untouchables*. He spent four years on the McCarthy-era blacklist, surviving on stage work until his agent cleared his name.[1] He played the father to a slate of white actors in the 1955 play *Hatful of Rain*, then King Lear in Central Park. In 1963 he earned a Tony nomination for best actor as M. Duval in Alexandre Dumas's *The Lady of the Camelias*. Most people associated Silvera with Hispanic roles, and he appeared in a slew of westerns, from *Bat Masterson* (1959) to *Bonanza* (1961–64) to *The Appaloosa* (1966). He even played an "Arab leader" in TV's *The Rat Patrol* (1966). "I have played . . . more varied national characters than I can honestly number," Silvera told the *New York Amsterdam News* on September 10, 1966. "Strange business."

Frank Silvera as Diego (right) and Burt Lancaster as Constable Bob Valdez, in *Valdez Is Coming* (United Artists, 1971).

The civil rights movement ignited Silvera's passion for shining his light on blackness. "I marched in the March on Washington, and after it I saw the hitch," he told the *Washington Post* on June 13, 1970. "I knew what was happening to me as a Negro and how I could transcend it as a white man. I knew the suffering that oppression causes. I was on a compassion kick. I decided I had to do something about it."

What had inspired him was James Baldwin's first play, *The Amen Corner*. Published in 1954, the play tells the tale of a Harlem evangelist who has a far more complicated family life than her ministry lets on. "I staged a reading of 'The Amen Corner,' then called Baldwin and told him I'd like to produce it," Silvera told the *Los Angeles Times* on March 2, 1965. Baldwin's response: "You just hit me with a blockbuster, baby." Silvera's staging of the play led to the creation of the Theatre of Being, which he founded in Los Angeles with Vantile Whitfield.

While movement leaders were drawing camera crews to the South to convey what Jim Crow was *really* about, Silvera wanted the Theatre of Being to give L.A. audiences the fullest possible sense of authentic black life, to see their own humanity reflected back to them in the struggles of black people. It wasn't about "trying to assume whitedom," Silvera told the Associated Press on May 9, 1965, but about the black American being "complete in his own reality."

The Theatre of Being opened in Los Angeles on March 4, 1964, or as Silvera liked to put it, "March Forth," echoing the movement. "As far as I'm concerned, this past decade has been marked by three distinct turning points when it comes to the civil rights struggle," he told the *New Pittsburgh Courier* on June 27, 1970. "The first was the protest marches and sit-ins. The second was the dramatic, though unfortunate, occurrence of virtual revolts in our cities. But the third turning point will, in my humble opinion, be the most effective. It's the effect that television programming and advertising is having and will continue to have on all our people, black and white."

Silvera's prediction was that as opportunities for African Americans expanded in Hollywood, "whites [would] come to see black people essentially as other Americans who, though they look different, are basically the same as themselves: the fear and suspicion of Blackness will recede." At the same time, he prophesied, "black people will experience a growing sense of self-worth: they'll see themselves 'in the picture,' a part of the mainstream of American life. And isn't this what the whole thing is really about? Of course it is."

Into the Theatre of Being Silvera poured his money and compassion, born out of the experiences he had endured in his fifty years. As an actor, a producer, a director, and a teacher, he was the one pulling on the rope of rescue. "The Theatre of Being takes us back [to] B.C.," he told the Associated Press on May 9, 1965, "before the corruption of words, and gets at the meaning behind words. In that process reality emerges."

Silvera's production group was home to that emerging reality from 1964 to 1967, right in the heart of Hollywood, from the Robertson Playhouse to the Coronet to the Music Box. In addition to *The Amen Corner,* they staged *Blood Knot* (by South African playwright Athol Fugard), held a poetry night called *For My People* (a tribute to Margaret Walker's 1942 book of poetry, which won the Yale Series of Younger Poets award), and had an open house in 1966 at which Maya Angelou performed, three years before the world would know her as the author of *I Know Why the Caged Bird Sings.*

Like Lorraine Hansberry, Frank Silvera was a genius, "a deeply earnest, studious man, who talks more like a college professor than a thespian," the *Chicago Daily Defender* said on March 6, 1971. In the AP interview, Silvera said that he was struggling against "the world's infrangible obduracy," asserting that "the nightmare of hate that engulfs us is due to a disease of the mind like polio is a disease of the blood." For Silvera, the struggle was ongoing. "I've poured all my money into this," he told the AP, "but I can't stop now."

By the late 1960s, Silvera felt encouraged by the changes he was seeing in Hollywood with such TV shows as *Mod Squad* and *Ironside.* No longer was the industry slavishly appeasing the old "southern bloc" that had balked at even the most innocent casting moves, such as giving Ethel Waters a role in a gasoline commercial. Now there was a growing black middle class to market to as well, not to mention foreign audiences.

Sadly, just as Silvera was arriving at this crossroads of change, he was struck down entirely by accident. While trying to fix the garbage disposal at his home in Pasadena, he was electrocuted. It was June 11, 1970, a month shy of his fifty-sixth birthday.

"It was a terrible irony," the black writer and activist Julian Mayfield wrote in the *New York Times* on June 21, 1970, "that he, who cared so much about his people, was seldom offered a role as a black man, but played a long succession of Mexicans, Indians, Puerto Ricans, and Italians."

None of this had been lost on Silvera when he was alive. "I am the son of a Sephardic Jew from Spain, married to a native Jamaican wife with Scottish and Maroon blood. I wasn't considered Negro or white. Who am I in all this?" the *Washington Post* of June 13, 1970, quoted him as saying.

But those who knew him, who studied him, recognized the groundwork he had laid.

98

Who were the first black boxing champions?

BOXING WAS the most popular organized sport in eighteenth-century England. The sport also was popular in America but was comparatively underdeveloped.[1] So it's not surprising that the history of early black boxers takes us across the pond.

BILL RICHMOND

Bill "the Black Terror" Richmond was "the first black boxer of international repute," the historian David Dabydeen writes.[2] Richmond was born in 1763 to slave parents brought north by their master from Georgia. He so impressed Maj. Gen. Earl Percy during the British occupation of Revolutionary New York that he was sent to England to study and apprentice as a cabinetmaker. There, the historian Michael Krenn writes, "Richmond found his real calling as a prizefighter."[3]

Richmond made his bones fighting British soldiers bare-knuckled. In 1804 he overcame a third-round knockout and, in 1805, throttled two opponents, "Youssop the Jew" and Jack Holmes. This put him in a position to challenge the future heavyweight champ Tom Cribb. But Richmond was ten years older than Cribb, and ninety minutes into their October 1805 bout, it showed. Amazingly, Richmond continued fighting into his fifties, defeating the man who had KO'd him, George Maddox, and winning his last fight, against Jack Carter, in 1818. With his winnings, Richmond opened a tavern and trained other boxers. He died in 1829 and was elected to the International Boxing Hall of Fame in 1999.

Tom Molineaux

Tom Molineaux was born in Virginia in 1784. Like his father, Zachary, he was a slave and a fighter whose owner, according to David Dabydeen, was "a wealthy playboy who frequently used him in fights against other slaves." "In one particular event," Dabydeen writes, "Molineaux's master bet $100,000 that he would defeat another slave in a match and promised to grant him his freedom should he win. Molineaux won and left for England in 1803, where he met and subsequently trained under Bill Richmond."[4]

In Molineaux's first fight in England, he "punished his opponent so severely, that it was impossible to distinguish a single feature in his face," wrote sportswriter Pierce Egan.[5] Soon he, too, set his sights on Cribb, the English champ. Their first match, on December 18, 1810, at Copthall Common in Sussex, "was an especially trying one," Dabydeen writes, "as the weather was severe, and Cribb's supporters became rowdy following Molineaux's impending triumph." At one point, "they entered the boxing ring, attacking Molineaux and consequently breaking his finger." Somehow Molineaux "persevered and knocked Cribb out in the 28th round." But Cribb's seconds "claimed that Molineaux had lead bullets in his fists, causing more riotous behaviour from Cribb's supporters," Dabydeen says, adding that he lost only because he "slipped and hit his head on a ring post."

Not surprisingly, Molineaux challenged Cribb to a rematch, but on September 28, 1811, the black boxer again went home brokenhearted, and this time broken-jawed, too, with Cribb winning in eleven rounds. Descending into "the drink," Molineaux nevertheless continued to box— and even wrestle on tour—losing his last fight, against George Cooper, in 1815. Molineaux died in Ireland in 1818, "a wasted skeleton, a penniless beggar, a shell of his former self," writes the historian Al-Tony Gilmore.[6]

Jack Johnson

Jack Johnson was born in Galveston, Texas, on March 31, 1878. He was a book lover with a soft spot for Napoléon, but boxing represented his shot at the American dream. Just as he was leaving behind menial jobs for the ring, his government was hardening the color line against black men. But Johnson lived according to a simple maxim he legislated with his fists: "I am not a slave."[7]

John Arthur "Jack" Johnson, appearing on a photo postcard from Chicago, 1910.

Johnson traveled anywhere there was money to be made, and by 1902 he had notched twenty-seven wins against black *and* white opponents. The highlight of the year was his May 16 knockout of Jack Jeffries, brother of the reigning heavyweight champ, Jim Jeffries, whom Johnson longed to fight. But Jeffries, like Sullivan before him, refused any challenge that might result in a black man wearing the belt.

Still, Johnson kept coming. In 1903 he defeated black boxer Ed Martin to become "the colored heavyweight champion of the world," as Johnson's biographer Geoffrey Ward writes.[8] None of this mattered, though, to Jim Jeffries, who in 1905 retired to his California farm claiming there was no one left to fight.

Succeeding him was Tommy Burns, who vowed to uphold the white-champs-only rule. But public pressure—even from Edward VII, the king of England, not to mention an Australian promoter's willingness to meet Burns's demands for a $30,000 cut plus a slice of the film rights—weakened

Burns's resolve. The interracial title bout was set for December 26, 1908. In Australia, the beating Johnson put on Burns was so fierce that the camera crew stopped filming to avoid inflaming audiences with the black challenger's devastating last punch.

Many whites wouldn't accept the result, insisting that because Burns hadn't won his belt outright from the retired Jim Jeffries, Johnson was technically a pretender to the crown. And so, as Johnson later wrote, "the hunt for a 'white hope' began."[9] Really, it was a comical affair, with Johnson making easy prey of all comers, so that the only possible solution was for Jim Jeffries to get back in the ring.

On July 4, 1910, Jeffries was no match for Johnson, whose baffling style alternated from relaxed dancer to executioner in a split second and who, while handling Jeffries, even breaking his nose, smiled at the crowd despite the insults they spewed. Johnson, in the fifteenth round, belted Jeffries to the mat repeatedly until it was over.[10]

With the celebrity spotlight shining on Johnson as never before, his personal life became fodder for newspapers sniffing around for a scandal. There was no denying that "the Big Smoke" loved fast cars and fancy suits, and before settling in Chicago, he had rankled his neighbors by moving into an all-white section of Bakersfield, California. What really infuriated the white public, though, were Johnson's public displays of affection with white women such as Hattie McClay and Belle Schreiber.

In 1911 Johnson married a divorced white woman, Etta Duryea, despite mutual accusations of infidelity and an incident in which he likely gave her a serious beating out of jealousy. In 1912, a few months after Duryea committed suicide, Johnson was seen in public with another white woman, Lucille Cameron.

As a famous black man living in Chicago, widower to a white woman, with another young white woman on deck, Johnson embodied white America's worst nightmare—interracial sexual relations and violence. The first of these fears had, in part, led Congress to pass the Mann Act of 1910, prohibiting the transportation of women and girls across state lines for "immoral purposes." The break for prosecutors came when they found a willing complainant in Cameron's mother. The only problem was, after Johnson was arrested in October 1912, he and Lucille busted up an already flimsy case by getting married.

But the prosecutors weren't going to quit. The historian Luckett V. Davis describes what happened next: "A second Mann Act case was brought against Johnson; the key witness was Belle Schreiber, who had traveled with him as his companion for several years and had suffered ill treatment at his hands." At the trial in May 1913, Davis writes, "Johnson was found guilty and sentenced to a year in jail. With bond posted, he appealed, but soon afterward left the United States for England to avoid serving his sentence."[11] Perhaps the most telling statement of all came from the district attorney in Johnson's case, who, as filmmaker Ken Burns quoted, said afterward, "It was [Johnson's] misfortune to be the foremost example of the evil in permitting the intermarriage of whites and blacks."

On the lam in Europe, Johnson continued to box and got help along the way from Frederick Bruce Thomas, "the Sultan of Jazz." Eventually, though, the legal ordeal caught up with his game inside the ring, and, as Burns has said, he "los[t] his title in Havana in 1915 to a much younger white opponent [Jess Willard] after a grueling 26-round fight in 100-degree-plus heat." He remained a fugitive from the law until 1920, when, losing his protection in Mexico, he crossed back into the United States. From there he was ordered to Leavenworth prison, where he served until July 9, 1921. In 1946 Jack Johnson was killed in a car wreck after furiously leaving a North Carolina restaurant where he had had to "sit in the back," as Ward recounts.

99

Who were the key scholars responsible for the discipline of black history?

RAYFORD W. LOGAN (1897–1982)

Born a year after *Plessy v. Ferguson*'s infamous "separate but equal" decree, Rayford Whittingham Logan grew up hearing stories about his free black lineage dating to before the Civil War. His father toiled as a butler in the home of a prominent white family in Washington, D.C., that took an interest in Rayford's education. After graduating first in his class from Dunbar High School in 1913, Logan attended Williams College in Massachusetts, where, four years later, he emerged a member of Phi Beta Kappa, ready to defend his country in the Great War. A member of the U.S. Army's all-black 372nd Infantry Regiment, Logan took part in the battles of the Argonne in France in 1918 and was promoted from private to lieutenant.

After the war, he stayed in France for five years, lending key support to W.E.B. Du Bois's fledgling Pan-African Congress. He developed close ties to the diplomatic corps of Haiti, the New World's first independent black republic. Returning to the United States in 1924, he took up teaching duties at Virginia Union and Atlanta universities while assisting Carter G. Woodson in building the Association for the Study of Negro Life and History into a thriving research institution.

Somehow Logan also found time to earn a master's degree in history from Williams in 1929 and a Ph.D. in history from Harvard in 1936. His Harvard dissertation, published as a book in 1941, was titled *The Diplomatic Relations Between the United States and Haiti, 1776–1891*. It was ground-breaking, as Kenneth Janken writes: "In the 1920s and 1930s [Logan's] scholarship on Haiti and colonial Africa earned him national recognition not only in the black diaspora—he was awarded Haiti's Order of Honor and Merit in 1941 for his scholarship and advocacy—but also from influential, predominantly white organizations such as the Foreign Policy Association."[1]

After Harvard, Logan embarked on a distinguished teaching career at Howard University, serving as chairman of the history department from 1942 to 1964.[2] He played a critical role in the early years of World War II, organizing mass protests against barring black soldiers from the armed forces, while he also lobbied and assisted President Franklin D. Roosevelt in drafting an order forbidding the exclusion.

In an era of thunderous change, Logan was the quintessential scholar-activist, helping to launch voter registration drives and citizenship schools—activities that would later serve as a blueprint for Freedom Summer.

DOROTHY PORTER WESLEY (1905–95)

Dorothy Burnett (later Dorothy Porter Wesley), born in Warrenton, Virginia, graduated from New Jersey's Montclair High School in 1923 and collected teaching credentials from the Palmer Method of Business Writing and the Myrtilla Miner Normal School in Washington, D.C. While working in the library at Miner Teachers College in D.C., she was inspired by a role model, librarian Lula Allan, to switch career tracks. In 1931, a year after earning an A.B. at Howard, she became the first black woman to graduate with a B.S. from the Columbia University School of Library Service. There, with a Julius Rosenwald Fund scholarship, she also earned a master's degree, in 1932.

The historian Constance Porter Uzelac writes:

Porter Wesley devoted her life to the acquisition and collection of materials relating to the African and African American diaspora. She joined the library staff at Howard University in 1928, and in 1930 she [was] appointed to administer and organize a Library of Negro Life and History from a small collection of three thousand titles presented to Howard University in 1914 by Jesse Moorland. The doors opened in 1933 as the Moorland Foundation, and the collection grew to nearly 200,000 items by her [Porter Wesley's] retirement in 1973, when it became known as the Moorland-Spingarn Research Center.[3]

In addition, Porter Wesley served as a representative of the National Council of Negro Women and on the executive council of the Association for the Study of African American Life and History, and she was on the editorial board of the Black Abolitionist Papers and Beacon Press. In the early 1960s, as part of the African independence movement, the Ford Foundation asked her to help establish Nigeria's national library collection.

In 1994 President Bill Clinton bestowed the National Endowment for the Humanities Charles Frankel Prize on Dorothy Porter Wesley, hailing her as "a preeminent archivist of African Americana."

CHARLES H. WESLEY (1891–1987)

Dorothy Porter Wesley's second husband, Charles H. Wesley, was an outstanding historian in his own right. A native of Louisville, Kentucky, by age fourteen Wesley had completed college prep courses at Fisk University, where he sang with the Fisk Jubilee Singers and studied classics before graduating with honors in 1911. Wesley then traveled to Yale University on a graduate fellowship and earned a master's degree in history and economics two years later (with honors)—while waiting tables. After teaching and attending a year of law school at Howard, he studied French in Europe, then returned to Washington, D.C., to serve as a minister and presiding elder in the African Methodist Episcopal Church.

Wesley took a sabbatical from Howard to pursue his Ph.D. at Harvard. Two years after he graduated in 1925 (as Harvard's third black Ph.D. in history, behind Du Bois and Woodson), his sensational dissertation, *Negro Labor in the United States,* was published to rave reviews for soundly rejecting the then-dominant assumption that blacks were lazy and incapable of skilled work.

In all, Wesley wrote twelve books—including *The Collapse of the Confederacy* (1937). His interests were wide ranging, from black fraternal organizations to southern history and the history of slavery, both in the British Empire and in the United States. Among Wesley's many achievements, in 1930 he became the first African American to win a Guggenheim fellowship.

John Hope Franklin, pioneering scholar and dean of
African-American studies.

JOHN HOPE FRANKLIN (1915–2009)

Franklin earned his Ph.D. in history at Harvard in 1941, and in 1969 the
university offered him the first chairmanship of its nascent Afro-American
studies department—although it refused to offer him a joint appointment in the history department. For Franklin, this was a deep professional
insult, as it contradicted the central point of his scholarship: that African-
American history was not to be ghettoized as a separate field of study. The
fact that Franklin was later awarded an honorary degree from Harvard and
invited to speak "on behalf of the history profession" at the inauguration
of the school's first woman president, Drew Gilpin Faust, left little doubt
about who had been right.[4]

Born in 1915 in Rentiesville, Oklahoma, not long before the notorious Tulsa race riot, John Hope Franklin graduated as valedictorian of his
high school and magna cum laude from Fisk University in 1935. After his
graduate studies at Harvard, he taught at several historically black colleges
and universities, including Fisk, St. Augustine's College, North Carolina
College, and Howard.

From Slavery to Freedom (1947) remains Franklin's most influential book.
The first comprehensive and popular history of the black experience in

America, it was significantly updated and revised by the distinguished Harvard historian Evelyn Brooks Higginbotham in 2008. Of the twenty volumes Franklin wrote or edited, two others were particularly path-breaking: *The Militant South, 1800–1860* (1956) and *Reconstruction: After the Civil War* (1961). He also wrote the definitive biography of an earlier black historian, *George Washington Williams* (1985), and, as a mark of his dedication, arranged for a long overdue headstone for his subject in England.

JOHN W. BLASSINGAME, SR. (1940–2000)

Before Blassingame published his great work of scholarship, *The Slave Community* (1972), most historians were reluctant to use the testimony of slaves in their analyses of the institution of slavery. Now, thanks to "Blass," slave narratives, and the slave's point of view, are firmly fixed in the American historiographical canon.

Born and raised on the black side of the Jim Crow line in Covington and Social Circle, Georgia, Blassingame earned a bachelor's degree from Fort Valley College in 1960 and a master's degree, in 1961, from Howard, where he worked under the direction of Rayford W. Logan. Blassingame was one of the breakthrough generation that, because of affirmative action, integrated the nation's historically white colleges and universities in the latter half of the 1960s. He earned a Ph.D. in history from Yale in 1971 and taught at Carnegie-Mellon and the University of Maryland before returning to Yale, where he eventually chaired the African-American studies program.

Blassingame sacrificed his deepest reserves of energy to authenticating the primary documents of African-American history, as in his 1977 volume *Slave Testimony;* the six volumes of Frederick Douglass's papers that he edited from 1979 to 1999; and 1982's *Long Memory: The Black Experience in America* (with fellow historian Mary Frances Berry).

100

What are the most important facts to know about American slavery?

The Middle Passage

1. During the transatlantic slave trade (1525–1866), 12.5 million Africans were shipped to the New World. Of them, 10.7 million survived the dreaded Middle Passage, disembarking in North America, the Caribbean, and South America. Only about 388,000 were transported directly from Africa to North America.[1]

2. Children typically comprised 26 percent or more of a slave ship's human cargo. On average, the voyage took "just over two months," David Eltis writes, and because of "filthy conditions," "a range of epidemic pathogens," and "periodic breakouts of violent resistance," "between 12 and 13 percent of those embarked did not survive the voyage."[2]

American-Style Slavery

3. The importation of slaves into the United States was banned by Congress in 1808, yet by 1860 the nation's black population had jumped from 400,000 to 4.4 million, of which 3.9 million were slaves. The primary reason was *natural increase,* a distinguishing feature of American-style slavery. As Ronald Bailey tells us, "For each decade between 1790 and 1860, the slave population increased between 25 percent and 33 percent, averaging 28.7 percent over the period."[3]

4. In the United States, on average, a slave mother gave birth to nine or ten children. Yet in 1860, according to the Gilder Lehrman Institute of

"Workers Harvesting Cotton in Florida." Engraving from a children's text, *Royal Geographic Readers,* no. 5 (London, 1883).

American History, "less than 10 percent of the slave population was over 50 and only 3.5 percent was over 60."[4]

5. Speaking of "natural increase," in that same year, 1860, "fully 40 percent of the Southern free Negro population were classified as mulattoes, while only one slave in ten had some white ancestry," Ira Berlin tells us.[5] The obvious reason: masters were more likely to free slaves who looked like—and, in many cases, descended from—them.

6. Largely as a result of natural increase, the United States went from being a country that accounted for 6 percent of slaves imported to the New World to one that in 1860 held more than *60* percent of the hemisphere's slave population.[6]

THE SECOND MIDDLE PASSAGE

7. Between the end of the Revolutionary War and the start of the Civil War, a second Middle Passage occurred *within* the United States. In all,

according to Walter Johnson, "approximately one million enslaved people were relocated from the upper South to the lower South . . . two thirds of these through . . . the domestic slave trade."[7] In other words, two and a half times more African Americans were directly affected by the second Middle Passage than by the first one.

8. The reason was the cotton trade. Where it flourished—in Alabama, Mississippi, and Louisiana—the slave population skyrocketed, demanding that entire families be relocated there from plantations in the East and Upper South. According to Ira Berlin, "The territory of Mississippi—which encompassed lands that would eventually be part of Mississippi, Alabama, and Florida—contained some 3,000 slaves at the beginning of the nineteenth century. In 1860, well over 400,000 slaves lived in Mississippi alone."[8] In turn, "Southern slave prices more than tripled," Steven Deyle writes, rising from $500 in New Orleans in 1800 to $1,800 by 1860 (the equivalent of $30,000 in 2005).[9] Of the 3.2 million slaves working in the fifteen slave states in 1850, *1.8 million* worked in cotton.

WHO OWNED SLAVES, AND WHERE DID THEY LIVE?

9. In 1860, 75 percent of white families in the United States owned not a single slave, while 1 percent of families owned 40 or more. Just a *tenth* of 1 percent of Americans owned 100 or more slaves.[10]

10. That same year, 1860, 31 percent of all slaves in the United States were held on plantations of 40 or more slaves, while a majority (53 percent) were held on farms of between 7 and 39 slaves. [11]

11. Of the total African-American population in 1860, nearly 90 percent were slaves. And while blacks made up only 13 percent of the entire country, in the South one in three people was black.[12]

12. In 1860 slaves made up 57 percent of the population in South Carolina, the highest proportion of any state in the Union. Coming in second was Mississippi at 55 percent, followed by Louisiana at 47 percent, Alabama at 45 percent, and Florida and Georgia, both at 44 percent. Perhaps not surprisingly, these were the first six states to secede from the Union following Lincoln's election.

13. In absolute numbers, Virginia had the highest slave population of any state in the country in 1860: 490,865. A year later it also was home to the Confederate capital, Richmond.

14. As late as 1850, the state of New Jersey, as a result of its gradual emancipation policies, still reported some 236 slaves in the federal census. New York, also having adopted a gradual emancipation policy, in 1799, was home to slaves well into the antebellum era. According to Eric Foner, "In 1817, the [New York] legislature decreed that all slaves who had been living at the time of the 1799 act would be emancipated on July 4, 1827. On that day, nearly 3,000 persons still held as slaves in the state gained their freedom, and slavery in New York finally came to an end. But the 1817 law also allowed southern owners to bring slaves into the state for up to nine months without their becoming free. In 1841, the legislature repealed this provision and made it illegal to introduce a slave into the state. But," Foner writes, "many southern owners ignored the new law and local authorities did little to enforce it, so for years after abolition slaves could still be seen on [New York] city's streets."[13]

The Slave Labor Force

15. In the slave labor force, "a third of slave laborers were children and an eighth were elderly or crippled," according to the Gilder Lehrman Institute.[14]

16. Slaves didn't just work on farms. They were hired out in the trades, worked in factories and on piers, and manned sailing vessels. They had built between 9,000 and 10,000 miles of railroad tracks by the time the Civil War broke out.

European and Native American Slaves

17. According to Alan Gallay, "Over a million Europeans were held as slaves from the 1530s through the 1780s in Africa, and hundreds of thousands were kept as slaves by the Ottomans in eastern Europe and Asia. . . . In 1650, more English were enslaved in Africa than Africans enslaved in English colonies."[15]

18. "North American Europeans did enslave Indians during wars, especially in New England (the Pequot War, King Philip's War) and the Southeast (the Tuscarora War, the Yamasee War, the Natchez War, just to name a few)," Gallay explains. "In South Carolina, and to a lesser extent in North Carolina, Virginia, and Louisiana, Indian slavery was a central means by

which early colonists funded economic expansion." Remarkably, in the Southwest, "large-scale enslavement of American Indians persisted well into the nineteenth century."[16]

19. From the late eighteenth century on, Native Americans in the South, like whites, owned slaves. And in the 1830s, when the U.S. government "removed" the Five Nations to "Indian Territory" (now Oklahoma), they took their slaves with them, so that "when the Civil War erupted in 1861, more than eight thousand blacks were enslaved in Indian Territory."[17]

FREE BLACKS IN THE SOUTH

20. On the eve of the Civil War in 1860, there were a total of 488,070 free blacks living in the United States, about 10 percent of the entire black population. Of those, 226,152 lived in the North and 261,918 in the South.[18]

21. Maryland was the state with the largest population of free blacks in 1860—83,942—and the highest proportion of free versus enslaved blacks, with 49.1 percent free.

22. In 1860 free black people composed 18 percent of the population in Delaware, the highest percentage of any state in the Union (though the total number of free blacks there was only 19,829). Louisiana, by comparison, had almost as many free black people as Delaware did in 1860—18,647—but they made up only 3 percent of the state's population, while New York had more than both of these states combined—49,005 free black women and men—but they accounted for only *1 percent* of the Empire State's total population.

23. Free blacks in the South largely resided in cities—the bigger the better, because that was where the jobs were.

24. A majority of free blacks in the South were female (52.6 percent in 1860), because free black men had a greater tendency to move out of the region.

25. Free black people were older than the average slave, because they often had to wait to earn or buy their freedom, or be "dumped" by their owners as weak or infirm.

26. The vast majority of free black people lived in the Upper South (224,963 in 1860 versus 36,955 in the Lower South in 1860). They were on average darker-skinned and more rural than their Lower South counterparts.

EMANCIPATION

27. The Emancipation Proclamation did *not* abolish the institution of slavery in the United States. Rather, it "freed" slaves in the Confederate states who could manage to flee their plantation and make their way behind liberating Union lines.

28. Free African Americans were listed by name in the U.S. Census prior to the Civil War. Slaves' names were *not* recorded in the census until after the war, in 1870.

Acknowledgments

100 Amazing Facts required one *amazing* team of colleagues and friends, and I am profoundly grateful to those who took this journey of discovery with me at every stage. At Harvard, I am blessed to work with a talented, and dedicated, team of scholars in my role as director of the Hutchins Center for African & African American Research, which officially launched during the writing of my original series, published in the online magazine *The Root* between October 2012 and November 2014. The series, borrowing the retro title *100 Amazing Facts About the Negro,* took its inspiration from the legendary black journalist Joel A. Rogers's book of brief, provocative snapshots of the African and African-American past. I would especially like to thank our director of research, Kevin M. Burke, who supervised and conducted much of the research during my march to one hundred columns, and Sheldon Cheek, assistant director of our Image of the Black Archive & Library, whose expertise proved vital in bringing each column to life visually. I also am indebted to Robert Heinrich, Moira Hinderer, and Steven J. Niven for their valuable research support, and to the Hutchins Center's extraordinary executive director, Abby Wolf, and my invaluable assistant Amy Gosdanian, who make all good things possible.

This series wouldn't have had a home on the Web without my dear colleagues at TheRoot.com, with whom I have been blessed to work since co-founding the site in 2008 with my dear friend Donald E. Graham. That partnership has continued unabated through TheRoot.com's transition from the Washington Post Company to Univision. Most of all, I owe special thanks to Sheryl Huggins Salomon for her brilliant editorial support throughout the life of the column, and to the immensely talented Lyne Pitts and Donna Byrd, who have taught me much about journalism in the digital age.

Then there are those who helped me translate these columns into

424 / Acknowledgments

book form. I am particularly grateful to the visionary Erroll McDonald, vice president and executive editor at Penguin Random House, Nicholas Thomson, of Alfred A. Knopf Editorial, and again to Kevin Burke, Sheldon Cheek, Rob Heinrich, and Steven Niven. I also am fortunate to count on a dedicated literary team, which, for this project, included Paul Lucas, David Kuhn, Lauren Sharp, and my cherished friend Bennett Ashley.

There are too many friends of this project to list by name, but I would like to close by thanking my constant companions: my beloved partner, historian Marial Iglesias Utset, who lovingly critiqued every entry; my dear friends Larry Bobo and Marcy Morgan, Glenn Hutchins and Richard Cohen; my brilliant and beautiful daughters, Maggie and Liza; my wonderful son-in-law, Aaron Hatley; and my granddaughter, Eleanor Margaret Gates-Hatley, who was born two days before the last column in my series, Fact #100, went up online. Here is a fact: Ellie, it is you who are amazing—"L'dor va dor," from Pop-Pop.

Notes

1. WHICH JOURNALIST WAS AMONG THE FIRST TO BRING BLACK HISTORY FACTS TO THE MASSES?

1. J. A. Rogers, *100 Amazing Facts About the Negro: With Complete Proof: A Short Cut to the World History of the Negro* (New York: Helga M. Rogers, 1957).
2. Thabiti Asukile, "J. A. Rogers: The Scholarship of an Organic Intellectual," *Black Scholar* 36, nos. 2–3 (2006): 35–50.
3. Rogers, *100 Amazing Facts,* 7.
4. W. Burghardt Turner, "J. A. Rogers: Portrait of an Afro-American Historian," *Black Scholar: Journal of Black Studies and Research* 6, no. 5 (1975): 32–39.
5. Alain LeRoy Locke, *The New Negro: An Interpretation* (1925; reprint New York: Arno, 1968).
6. Thabiti Asukile, "Rogers, Joel Augustus," in *African American National Biography,* ed. Henry Louis Gates, Jr., and Evelyn Brooks Higginbotham, 8 vols. (New York: Oxford University Press, 2008), 6:673–74.

2. HOW MANY AFRICANS WERE TAKEN TO THE UNITED STATES DURING THE ENTIRE HISTORY OF THE SLAVE TRADE?

1. David Eltis and Martin Halbert, "The Trans-Atlantic Slave Trade Database Has Information on Almost 36,000 Slaving Voyages," Trans-Atlantic Slave Trade, http://www.slavevoyages.org.

3. WHO WAS THE FIRST AFRICAN TO ARRIVE IN AMERICA?

1. "African Americans at Jamestown," National Park Service, U.S. Department of the Interior, https://www.nps.gov/jame/learn/historyculture/african-americans-at-jamestown.htm.
2. Ricardo Alegria, *Juan Garrido: El Conquistador negro en las Antillas, Florida, Mexico y California* (San Juan: Centro de Estudios Avanzados de Puerto Rico y el Caribe, 1990), esp. p. 10; Jane Landers, *Black Society in Spanish Florida* (Urbana: University of Illinois Press, 1999), pp. 10–12.

5. WHO WAS THE FIRST BLACK PRESIDENT IN NORTH AMERICA?

1. Theodore G. Vincent, "The Contributions of Mexico's First Black Indian President, Vicente Guerrero," *Journal of Negro History* 86, no. 2 (Spring 2001): 148.

6. WHO WERE AFRICA'S FIRST AMBASSADORS TO EUROPE?

1. Linda M. Heywood and John K. Thornton, *Central Africans, Atlantic Creoles, and the Foundation of the Americas, 1585–1660* (New York: Cambridge University Press, 2007).

7. WHO WAS THE FIRST BLACK EXPLORER OF THE NORTH AMERICAN SOUTHWEST?

1. Robert Goodwin, *Crossing the Continent, 1527–1540: The Story of the First African-American Explorer of the American South* (New York: Harper, 2008).
2. Shirley Ann Wilson Moore, "Sweet Freedom's Plains: African Americans on the Overland Trails," National Park Service Report, January 31, 2012, p. 4; David Arias, *Spanish-Americans: Lives and Faces* (Victoria, BC: Trafford Publishing, 2005), p. 43.

8. WHICH SLAVE LITERALLY WROTE HIS WAY TO FREEDOM?

1. Allan D. Austin, "Jallo, Job ben Solomon," in *African American National Biography,* ed. Henry Louis Gates, Jr., and Evelyn Brooks Higginbotham, 8 vols. (New York: Oxford University Press, 2008), 4:483–5.
2. John Thornton, email to author.

9. WHAT WAS THE FIRST BLACK TOWN IN NORTH AMERICA?

1. Herman L. Bennett, *Africans in Colonial Mexico: Absolutism, Christianity, and Afro-Creole Consciousness, 1570–1640* (Bloomington: Indiana University Press, 2003), pp. 21–22.
2. Jane G. Landers, "*Cimarrón* and Citizen," in Jane G. Landers and Barry Robinson, eds., *Slaves, Subjects, and Subversives: Blacks in Colonial Latin America* (Albuquerque: University of New Mexico Press, 2006), p. 124.

10. WHO WAS GEORGE WASHINGTON'S RUNAWAY SLAVE?

1. Cassandra Pybus, "Harry Washington (1760s–1790s): A Founding Father's Slave," in *The Human Tradition in the Black Atlantic, 1500–2000,* ed. Beatriz G. Mamigonian and Karen Racine (Lanham, MD: Rowman & Littlefield, 2010), p. 102.
2. Quoted in Cassandra Pybus, *Epic Journeys of Freedom: Runaway Slaves of the American Revolution and Their Global Quest for Liberty* (Boston: Beacon Press, 2006), p. 9; Henry Wiencek, *An Imperfect God: George Washington, His Slaves, and the Creation of America* (New York: Farrar, Straus & Giroux, 2003).
3. "Washington's Revolution (Harry that is, not George)," Black Loyalists, http://www.blackloyalist.info/washington-s-revolution-harry-that-is-not-george/.

11. WHO WAS THE FIRST BLACK PERSON IN THE UNITED STATES TO LEAD A "BACK TO AFRICA" EFFORT?

1. Donald R. Wright, "Cuffee, Paul," in *African American National Biography,* ed. Henry Louis Gates, Jr., and Evelyn Brooks Higginbotham, 8 vols. (New York: Oxford University Press, 2008), 2:503–5.

12. WHO WAS THE FIRST BLACK PERSON TO SEE THE BABY JESUS?

1. Paul H. D. Kaplan, *The Rise of the Black Magus in Western Art* (Ann Arbor, MI: UMI Research Press, 1985), pp. 28, 119.

13. WHERE WAS THE FIRST BLACK TOWN IN WHAT IS NOW THE UNITED STATES?

1. John Huxtable Elliott, *Empires of the Atlantic World: Britain and Spain in America, 1492–1830* (New Haven: Yale University Press, 2006), p. 283.
2. Jane Landers, *Black Society in Spanish Florida* (Urbana: University of Illinois Press, 1999).

14. WHAT HAPPENED TO THE "FORTY ACRES AND A MULE"
THAT FORMER SLAVES WERE PROMISED?

1. Barton Myers, "Sherman's Field Order No. 15," *New Georgia Encyclopedia*, September 25, 2005.
2. *New York Daily Tribune,* February 13, 1865.
3. Eric Foner, *Reconstruction: America's Unfinished Revolution, 1863–1877* (New York: Harper & Row, 1988), p. 71.

15. WERE SLAVES ACTUALLY EATEN BY DOGS?

1. Frederick Douglass, *Narrative of the Life of Frederick Douglass, an American Slave* (Cambridge, MA: Belknap, 1960).
2. Lisa K. Winkler, "The Kentucky Derby's Forgotten Jockeys," *Smithsonian,* April 23, 2009, http://www.smithsonianmag.com/history/the-kentucky-derbys-forgotten-jockeys -128781428/.
3. David Doddington, "Slavery and Dogs in the Antebellum South," *Sniffing the Past,* February 23, 2012, https://sniffingthepast.wordpress.com/2012/02/23/slavery-and-dogs-in -the-antebellum-south/.
4. William J. Anderson, *Life and Narrative of William J. Anderson Twenty-four Years a Slave Or: The Dark Deeds of American Slavery Revealed . . .* (Chicago: Daily Tribune Book & Job Printing Office, 1857), p. 48.
5. Philippe R. Girard, *The Slaves Who Defeated Napoléon: Toussaint Louverture and the Haitian War of Independence, 1801–1804* (Tuscaloosa: University of Alabama Press, 2011), pp. 106, 242.
6. Aisha Harris, "Was There Really Mandingo Fighting, Like in *Django Unchained*?," *Slate,* December 24, 2012.

16. WHERE WAS THE FIRST UNDERGROUND RAILROAD?

1. Jane Landers, "Southern Passage: The Forgotten Route to Freedom in Florida," in *Passages to Freedom: The Underground Railroad in History and Memory,* ed. David W. Blight (Washington, DC: Smithsonian Books, 2001), pp. 117–32.

17. WHAT WAS THE SECOND MIDDLE PASSAGE?

1. Walter Johnson, *Soul by Soul: Life Inside the Antebellum Slave Market* (Cambridge, MA: Harvard University Press, 1999), p. 5.
2. Ronald Bailey, "The Other Side of Slavery: Black Labor, Cotton, and Textile Industrialization in Great Britain and the United States," *Agricultural History* 68, no. 2 (1994): 35–50.
3. Ira Berlin, *Generations of Captivity: A History of African American Slaves* (Cambridge, MA: Harvard University Press, 2003), p. 168.
4. Ira Berlin, *The Making of African America: Four Great Migrations* (New York: Viking, 2010).
5. Steven Deyle, *Carry Me Back: The Domestic Slave Trade in American Life* (New York: Oxford University Press, 2005), p. 56.

18. HOW MUCH DID THE COTTON INDUSTRY SHAPE AMERICAN HISTORY
AND THE LIVES OF ENSLAVED AFRICANS?

1. Steven Deyle, *Carry Me Back: The Domestic Slave Trade in American Life* (New York: Oxford University Press, 2005), p. 60.
2. Eugene R. Dattel, *Cotton and Race in the Making of America: The Human Costs of Economic Power* (Chicago: Ivan R. Dee, 2009), p. xi.
3. Gene Dattel, "Cotton, the Oil of the Nineteenth Century: Important Lessons of History," *The International Economy,* Winter 2010, p. 61.
4. Ronald Bailey, "The Other Side of Slavery: Black Labor, Cotton, and Textile Industrialization in Great Britain and the United States (Eli Whitney's Cotton Gin, 1793–1993: A Symposium)," *Business Information, News, and Reports,* n.p., March 22, 1994.

20. WHO ORIGINATED THE CONCEPT OF THE "TALENTED TENTH"
BLACK LEADERSHIP CLASS?

1. W.E.B. Du Bois, "The Talented Tenth," in *The Negro Problem: A Series of Articles by Representative Negroes of To-day* (New York, 1903).
2. Evelyn Brooks Higginbotham, *Righteous Discontent: The Women's Movement in the Black Baptist Church, 1880–1920* (Cambridge, MA: Harvard University Press, 1993).
3. Henry L. Morehouse, "The Talented Tenth," *American Missionary* 50, no. 6 (June 1896): 182–83.
4. "Lincoln on Slavery," National Parks Service, U.S. Department of the Interior, September 8, 2014.
5. Michael Burlingame, "Essay: 150 Years Later," National Public Radio, February 1, 2011.

21. WHO WAS THE FIRST AFRICAN-AMERICAN FIGHTER PILOT?

1. Caroline M. Fannin, "Bullard, Eugène Jacques," in *American National Biography,* ed. Mark Carnes (New York: Oxford University Press, 2005), supp. 2, pp. 53–54.
2. William Chivalette, "Corporal Eugene Jacques Bullard," March 14, 2016, http://www.au.af.mil/au/afri/aspj/apjinternational/apj-s/2005/3tri05/chivaletteeng.html.
3. Fannin, "Bullard, Eugène Jacques."

22. DID BLACK PEOPLE OWN SLAVES? IF SO, WHY?

1. John Hope Franklin, *From Slavery to Freedom: A History of Negro Americans* (New York: Alfred A. Knopf, 1974), p. 173.
2. Thomas J. Pressly, "'The Known World' of Free Black Slaveholders: A Research Note on the Scholarship of Carter G. Woodson," *Journal of African American History* 91, no. 1 (2006): 81–87.
3. Carter G. Woodson, "Free Negro Owners of Slaves in the United States in 1830," *Journal of Negro History* 9, no. 1 (1924): 41.
4. Richard Halliburton, Jr., "Free Black Owners of Slaves: A Reappraisal of the Woodson Thesis," *South Carolina Historical Magazine* 76, no. 3 (1975): 129–42.
5. John Hope Franklin, *The Free Negro in North Carolina, 1790–1860* (New York: Russell & Russell, 1969), pp. 159–61.
6. Loren Schweninger, *Black Property Owners in the South, 1790–1915* (Urbana: University of Illinois Press, 1990), p. 110.
7. Michael Johnson and James L. Roark, *Black Masters: A Free Family of Color in the Old South* (New York: W. W. Norton, 1986).
8. Larry Koger, *Black Slaveowners: Free Black Slave Masters in South Carolina, 1790–1860* (Columbia: University of South Carolina Press, 1985), p. 23.

9. Halliburton, "Free Black Owners." Halliburton's examples are drawn from Calvin Dill Wilson, "Black Masters: A Side-Light on Slavery," *North American Review* 181, no. 588 (November 1905): 685–98.

23. HOW DID HARRIET TUBMAN BECOME A LEGEND?

1. Milton C. Sernett, *Harriet Tubman: Myth, Memory, and History* (Durham, NC: Duke University Press, 2007), p. 11.
2. Catherine Clinton, *Harriet Tubman: The Road to Freedom* (New York: Little, Brown, 2004).
3. Jean M. Humez, *Harriet Tubman: The Life and the Life Stories* (Madison: University of Wisconsin Press, 2005).
4. Kate Clifford Larson, *Bound for the Promised Land: Harriet Tubman, Portrait of an American Hero* (New York: Ballantine, 2004), pp. 225–26.
5. Robert W. Taylor and Booker T. Washington, *Harriet Tubman: The Heroine in Ebony* (Boston: George H. Ellis, 1901).
6. Sarah H. Bradford, *Scenes in the Life of Harriet Tubman* (Freeport, NY: Books for Libraries Press, 1971).
7. W.E.B. Du Bois, *Economic Co-operation Among Negro Americans: Report of a Social Study Made by Atlanta University under the Patronage of the Carnegie Institution of Washington, D.C. . . .* (Atlanta, GA: Atlanta University Press, 1907).
8. Earl Conrad, *Harriet Tubman* (Washington, DC: Associated Publishers, 1943).
9. Quoted in Sernett, *Harriet Tubman,* p. 223.
10. Sernett, *Harriet Tubman,* p. 227.
11. Larson, *Bound for the Promised Land,* pp. xvii, 100.
12. David W. Blight, *Race and Reunion: The Civil War in American Memory* (Cambridge, MA: Harvard University Press, 2001), p. 332.

24. WHEN DID BLACK LITERATURE BEGIN TO ADDRESS AFRICAN-AMERICAN SEXUALITY?

1. Richard Wright, "Between Laughter and Tears," *New Masses,* October 5, 1937, http://people.virginia.edu/~sfr/enam358/wrightrev.html.
2. *Saturday Review of Literature* 17 (April 2, 1938); emphasis mine.
3. James Baldwin, "Alas, Poor Richard" (1961), in *The Price of the Ticket: Collected Nonfiction, 1948–1985* (New York: St. Martin's Press, 1985), p. 273.
4. Marilyn Nelson Waniek, "In the Space Where Sex Should Be: Toward a Definition of the Black Literary Tradition," *Studies in Black Literature* 6, no. 3 (1975): 7–13. Waniek's title echoes Baldwin's phrase.

25. IS MOST OF WHAT WE BELIEVE ABOUT THE UNDERGROUND RAILROAD TRUE?

1. Wilbur Henry Siebert, *The Underground Railroad from Slavery to Freedom: A Comprehensive History* (1898; reprint New York: Dover, 2006).
2. David W. Blight, *Passages to Freedom: The Underground Railroad in History and Memory* (Washington, DC: Smithsonian, 2004), p. 237.
3. Larry Gara, *The Liberty Line: The Legend of the Underground Railroad* (Lexington: University of Kentucky Press, 1961).
4. Blight, *Passages to Freedom,* p. 244.
5. Donald Yacavone to author.
6. Blight, *Passages to Freedom,* p. 243; John Hope Franklin and Loren Schweninger, *Runaway Slaves: Rebels on the Plantation* (New York: Oxford University Press, 2000), p. 282.

26. DID RUSSIA'S PETER THE GREAT ADOPT AN AFRICAN MAN AS HIS SON?

1. Catharine Theimer Nepomnyashchy and Ludmilla A. Trigos, "Introduction: Was Pushkin Black and Does It Matter?," in *Under the Sky of My Africa: Alexander Pushkin and Blackness,* ed. Catharine Theimer Nepomnyashchy, Nicole Svobodny, and Ludmilla A. Trigos (Evanston, IL: Northwestern University Press, 2006).
2. Ibid.
3. Ibid.
4. Ibid.
5. Ibid.
6. T. J. Binyon, *Pushkin: A Biography* (New York: Alfred A. Knopf, 2003), pp. 45–46.
7. N. K. Teletova, "On the Occasion of the Three Hundredth Anniversary of the Birth of Alexander Pushkin's Great-Grandfather," in Nepomnyashchy, Svobodny, and Trigos, *Under the Sky of My Africa,* p. 70.

27. WERE ALEXANDER PUSHKIN'S AFRICAN ROOTS IMPORTANT TO HIM?

1. Catharine Theimer Nepomnyashchy, Nicole Svobodny, and Ludmilla A. Trigos, eds., *Under the Sky of My Africa: Alexander Pushkin and Blackness* (Evanston, IL: Northwestern University Press, 2006).
2. Catharine Theimer Nepomnyashchy and Ludmilla A. Trigos, "Introduction: Was Pushkin Black and Does It Matter?," in *Under the Sky of My Africa.*
3. Ibid.
4. Marial Iglesias Utset to author.
5. Nepomnyashchy and Trigos, "Introduction."
6. J. Thomas Shaw, "Pushkin on His African Heritage: Publications During His Lifetime," in Nepomnyashchy, Svobodny, and Trigos, *Under the Sky of My Africa.*
7. Nepomnyashchy and Trigos, "Introduction."
8. John Greenleaf Whittier, *National Era,* February 11, 1847, https://news.google.com/newspapers?nid=K6kyChav4UkC&dat=18470211&printsec=frontpage&hl=en.

28. WAS JACKIE ROBINSON COURT-MARTIALED?

1. Arnold Rampersad, *Jackie Robinson: A Biography* (New York: Alfred A. Knopf, 1997), pp. 102–9.
2. Cornel West, "On Jackie Robinson," in *The Cornel West Reader* (New York: Basic, 1999), p. 536.

29. WHAT WERE THE LARGEST SLAVE REBELLIONS IN AMERICA?

1. Herbert Aptheker, *American Negro Slave Revolts* (New York: International Publishers, 1963).
2. Daniel Rasmussen, *American Uprising: The Untold Story of America's Largest Slave Revolt* (New York: Harper Perennial, 2011).

30. WHAT WERE THE BIGGEST ACTS OF BETRAYAL WITHIN THE ENSLAVED COMMUNITY?

1. Deborah Gray White, "Let My People Go," in *To Make Our World Anew: A History of African Americans,* ed. Robin D. G. Kelley and Earl Lewis, 2 vols. (New York: Oxford University Press, 2000), 1:196.
2. Ned Sublette, *The World That Made New Orleans: From Spanish Silver to Congo Square* (Chicago: Lawrence Hill Books, 2008), p. 112.

3. Henry Bibb, *Narrative of the Life and Adventures of Henry Bibb, an American Slave, Written by Himself,* docsouth.unc.edu/neh/bibb/menu.html.
4. Junius P. Rodriguez, ed., *Encyclopedia of Slave Resistance and Rebellion* (Santa Barbara, CA: Greenwood Press, 2006).
5. Mary Miley Theobald, "Slave Conspiracies in Colonial Virginia," Summer 2002, https://www.history.org/foundation/journal/summer02/revival.cfm. Theobald is quoting colonist Robert Beverley.
6. Herbert Aptheker, *American Negro Slave Revolts* (New York: International Publishers, 1963).
7. Rory T. Cornish, "Stono Rebellion," in Rodriguez, *Encyclopedia of Slave Resistance and Rebellion,* p. 489.
8. Peter Wood, *Black Majority: Negroes in Colonial South Carolina from 1670 Through the Stono Rebellion* (1974; reprint New York: W. W. Norton, 1996).
9. Vincent Harding, *There Is a River: The Black Struggle for Freedom in America* (San Diego: Harvest, 1981), p. 35.
10. Douglas R. Egerton, *Gabriel's Rebellion: The Virginia Slave Conspiracies of 1800 and 1802* (Chapel Hill: University of North Carolina Press, 1993).
11. Frederick Douglass, *My Bondage and My Freedom* (New York: Miller, Orton and Mulligan, 1855).
12. Frederick Douglass, *Narrative of the Life of Frederick Douglass, an American Slave* (Cambridge, MA: Belknap, 1960).
13. John H. Paynter, "The Fugitives of the Pearl—Part 1," *Journal of Negro History* 1, no. 3 (July 1916).
14. Harry Thomas, "Summary of *Slavery Days in Old Kentucky. A True Story of a Father Who Sold His Wife and Four Children. By One of the Children*" (1901), *Documenting the American South,* docsouth.unc.edu/neh/johnson/summary.html.
15. Manning Marable, *Malcolm X: A Life of Reinvention* (New York: Penguin, 2011).

31. WHAT IS ONE OF THE MOST NOVEL WAYS A SLAVE DEVISED TO ESCAPE BONDAGE?

1. Henry Box Brown, *Narrative of the Life of Henry Box Brown, Written by Himself,* ed. John Ernest (Chapel Hill: University of North Carolina Press, 2008).
2. Paul Finkelman and Richard Newman, "Brown, Henry 'Box,'" in *African American National Biography,* ed. Henry Louis Gates, Jr., and Evelyn Brooks Higginbotham, 8 vols. (New York: Oxford University Press, 2008), 2:611–12.
3. Jeffrey Ruggles, *The Unboxing of Henry Brown* (Richmond: Library of Virginia, 2003).
4. Richard Newman, introduction to *Narrative of the Life of Henry Box Brown, Written by Himself* (New York: Oxford University Press, 2002), p. xv. Historian John Ernest writes that the box was addressed to James H. Johnson at 131 Arch Street. John Ernest, ed., *Narrative of the Life of Henry Box Brown, Written by Himself* (Chapel Hill: University of North Carolina Press, 2008), p. 9. Some sources, following William Still's account, say it was addressed to William H. Johnson.
5. Hollis Robbins, "The Wild West Turns East: Audience, Fugitive Mail: The Deliverance of Henry 'Box' Brown and Antebellum Postal Politics," *American Studies International* 50, no. 1–2 (Spring–Summer 2009): 14.
6. William Still, *The Underground Railroad* (Philadelphia: Porter and Coates, 1872), pp. 81–86, excerpted at http://housedivided.dickinson.edu/ugrr/recollection_boxbrown.html; Newman, introduction to *Narrative,* xv.
7. Finkelman and Newman, "Brown, Henry 'Box'"; Paul Finkelman, "Brown, Henry 'Box,'" in *Encyclopedia of African American History, 1619–1895: From the Colonial Period to the Age of Frederick Douglass,* ed. Paul Finkelman (New York: Oxford University Press, 2006), pp. 206–8.

8. Finkelman and Newman, "Brown, Henry 'Box.'"
9. Martha J. Cutter, "Will the Real Henry 'Box' Brown Please Stand Up?" *Common-Place* 16, no. 1 (Fall 2015), http://common-place.org/book/will-the-real-henry-box-brown -please-stand-up/; Finkelman and Newman, "Brown, Henry 'Box.'"

32. WHO WAS THE FIRST BLACK HEAD OF STATE IN MODERN WESTERN HISTORY?

1. J. A. Rogers and John Henrik Clarke, *World's Great Men of Color* (New York: Touchstone, 1996).
2. Paul Kaplan to author.
3. John K. Brackett, "Race and Rulership: Alessandro de' Medici, First Medici Duke of Florence, 1529–1537," in *Black Africans in Renaissance Europe,* ed. T. F. Earle (Cambridge, UK: Cambridge University Press, 2005), p. 313.
4. Mario de Valdes, "A View on Race and the Art World," PBS, January 14, 2005, http://www.pbs.org/wgbh/pages/frontline/shows/secret/famous/mediciupdate.html.
5. Mario de Valdes, "Alessandro De Medici," PBS, http://www.pbs.org/wgbh/pages /frontline/shows/secret/famous/medici.html.
6. Ibid.

33. WERE THERE ANY SUCCESSFUL SLAVERY ESCAPES BY SEA?

1. Helen Boulware Moore and W. Marvin Dulaney, "Who Was Congressman Robert Smalls?," Robert Smalls: A Traveling Exhibition, http://www.robertsmalls.com/history .html.
2. James M. McPherson, *The Negro's Civil War: How American Blacks Felt and Acted During the War for the Union* (New York: Ballantine Books, 1991).
3. *Journal of the Constitutional Convention of the State of South Carolina* (Columbia, SC: Charles A. Calvo, Jr., 1895), p. 476.

34. HOW WAS BLACK SUPPORT ENLISTED FOR WORLD WAR II, WHEN THE ARMED SERVICES WERE SEGREGATED?

1. Franklin D. Roosevelt, Executive Order No. 8802, 3 C.F.R. (1941).
2. Ray Elliot, "Ray Elliot, 1939–1945: Two Wars to Win," First Person Oral Histories, http://www.americancenturies.mass.edu/centapp/oh/story.do?shortName=elliot 1939vv.
3. William F. Yurasko, "The *Pittsburgh Courier* During World War II: An Advocate for Freedom," http://www.yurasko.net/vv/courier.html.
4. Ibid.
5. Interview with Patrick Washburn, *The Black Press: Soldiers Without Swords,* PBS.org, http://www.pbs.org/blackpress/film/transcripts/washburn.html.
6. Ibid.
7. Clarence Taylor, "Patriotism Crosses the Color Line: African Americans in World War II," *History Now: The Journal of the Gilder Lehrman Institute,* http://www.gilder lehrman.org/history-by-era/world-war-ii/essays/patriotism-crosses-color-line-african -americans-world-war-ii.

35. HOW DID THE BLACK SAMBO MEMORABILIA THAT IS COLLECTED TODAY COME TO BE?

1. W.E.B. Du Bois, *Black Reconstruction: An Essay Toward a History of the Part Which Black Folk Played in the Attempt to Reconstruct Democracy in America, 1860–1880* (New York: Harcourt, Brace, 1935).

2. Barbara Johnson, *A World of Difference* (Baltimore: Johns Hopkins University Press, 1987).

3. Homi K. Bhabha, "The Other Question: The Stereotype and Colonial Discourse," in *Twentieth-Century Literary Theory: A Reader,* ed. K. M. Newton (Macmillan Education UK, 1997).

4. NAACP, *Thirty Years of Lynching in the United States, 1889–1918* (New Jersey: Lawbook Exchange, 2012).

5. W.E.B. Du Bois, *Darkwater: Voices from within the Veil* (1920; reprint New York: Schocken Books, 1969).

6. Thomas C. Holt, "Marking: Race, Race-making, and the Writing of History," *American Historical Review* 100, no. 1 (1995): 1–17.

7. W.E.B. Du Bois, *Dusk of Dawn* (1940; reprint New York: Oxford University Press, 2007), p. 148.

36. WHO WAS PLESSY IN THE *PLESSY V. FERGUSON* SUPREME COURT CASE?

1. Keith Weldon Medley, *We as Freemen: Plessy v. Ferguson* (Gretna, LA: Pelican, 2003).

2. Kenneth W. Mack, "Rethinking Civil Rights Lawyering and Politics in the Era Before Brown," *Yale Law Journal* 115, no. 2 (2005); Charles A. Lofgren, *The Plessy Case: A Legal-Historical Interpretation* (New York: Oxford University Press, 1987); Brook Thomas, *Plessy v. Ferguson: A Brief History with Documents* (Boston: Bedford, 1997); Medley, *We as Freemen;* Mark Elliott, *Color-Blind Justice: Albion Tourgée and the Quest for Racial Equality from the Civil War to Plessy v. Ferguson* (New York: Oxford University Press, 2006).

3. *Civil Rights Cases,* 109 U.S. 3 (1883). Thirteen years later Bradley dissented from the majority in *Plessy v. Ferguson,* 163 U.S. 537 (1896).

37. WHAT IS JUNETEENTH?

1. "From Texas; Important Orders by General Granger. Surrender of Senator Johnson of Arkansas. A Scattering of Rebel Officials," *New York Times,* July 6, 1865.

2. Leon F. Litwack, *Been in the Storm So Long: The Aftermath of Slavery* (New York: Alfred A. Knopf, 1979), p. 33.

3. Elizabeth Hayes Turner, "Juneteenth: Emancipation and Memory," in *Lone Star Pasts: Memory and History in Texas,* ed. Gregg Cantrell and Elizabeth Hayes Turner (College Station: Texas A&M University Press, 2007).

4. Quoted in Litwack, *Been in the Storm,* p. 185.

5. Quoted in Turner, "Juneteenth," p. 148.

6. Isabel Wilkerson, *The Warmth of Other Suns: The Epic Story of America's Great Migration* (New York: Random House, 2010).

7. Turner, "Juneteenth."

8. Ashley Luthern, "Juneteenth: A New Birth of Freedom," *Smithsonian,* June 19, 2009, http://www.smithsonianmag.com/smithsonian-institution/juneteenth-a-new-birth -of-freedom-9572263/.

38. WHO WAS THE FIRST BLACK AMERICAN WOMAN TO BE A SELF-MADE MILLIONAIRE?

1. A'Lelia Bundles, "Madam CJ Walker: Business Savvy to Philanthropy," IIP Digital, http://iipdigital.usembassy.gov/st/english/publication/2010/03/20100301151516amg nowo.9658778.html#axzz4C1wdeF60.

2. Anne E. Dwojeski, William Grundy, Erica Helms, Katherine Miller, and Nancy Koehn, "Madam C. J. Walker: Entrepreneur, Leader, and Philanthropist," *Harvard Business Review* (March 2007).

3. Ibid.
4. A'Lelia Perry Bundles, "Walker, Madam C. J. (Sarah Breedlove)," in *Black Women in America,* ed. Darlene Clark Hine, 3 vols. (New York: Oxford University Press, 2005), 3:308–13.
5. "Wealthiest Negress Dead," *New York Times,* May 26, 1919.

39. DID BLACK COMBATANTS FIGHT IN THE BATTLE OF GETTYSBURG?

1. Donald Yacavone to author.
2. John Heiser, Gettysburg National Military Park historian, interview by author.
3. Allen Guelzo, *Gettysburg: The Last Invasion* (New York: Alfred A. Knopf, 2013), pp. 385–86.
4. Margaret S. Creighton, *The Colors of Courage: Gettysburg's Forgotten History: Immigrants, Women, and African-Americans in the Civil War's Defining Battle* (New York: Basic Books, 2005).
5. Heiser interview with author.
6. Creighton, *The Colors of Courage,* p. 132.
7. Ibid.
8. James M. Paradis, *African Americans and the Gettysburg Campaign* (Lanham, MD: Scarecrow, 2005).
9. Creighton, *The Colors of Courage,* p. 139.
10. Ibid.
11. Paradis, *African Americans and the Gettysburg Campaign,* p. 89.

40. BEFORE EMANCIPATION, DIDN'T MOST FREE BLACKS LIVE IN THE NORTHERN HALF OF AMERICA?

1. Ira Berlin, *Slaves Without Masters: The Free Negro in the Antebellum South* (New York: Random House, 1974).
2. Eva Sheppard Wolf, *Race and Liberty in the New Nation: Emancipation in Virginia from the Revolution to Nat Turner's Rebellion* (Baton Rouge: Louisiana State University Press, 2006).

41. WHY DID FREE BLACK PEOPLE LIVING IN THE SOUTH BEFORE THE END OF THE CIVIL WAR STAY THERE?

1. Ira Berlin, *Slaves Without Masters: The Free Negro in the Antebellum South* (New York: Random House, 1974); Eva Sheppard Wolf, *Race and Liberty in the New Nation: Emancipation in Virginia from the Revolution to Nat Turner's Rebellion* (Baton Rouge: Louisiana State University Press, 2006).

42. HOW DID THE SON OF A FORMER SLAVE DEFY THE COLOR BAR TO BECOME A WEALTHY FIXTURE OF EUROPEAN NIGHTLIFE DURING THE JAZZ AGE?

1. Vladimir E. Alexandrov, *The Black Russian* (New York: Grove, 2014).

43. WHICH MASSACRE RESULTED IN A SUPREME COURT DECISION LIMITING THE FEDERAL GOVERNMENT'S ABILITY TO PROTECT BLACK AMERICANS FROM RACIAL TARGETING?

1. Charles Lane, *The Day Freedom Died: The Colfax Massacre, the Supreme Court, and the Betrayal of Reconstruction* (New York: Henry Holt, 2008), p. 74.
2. Ibid., pp. 90–91.

3. Ibid., pp. 104–5.
4. Quoted in Lawrence Goldstone, *Inherently Unequal: The Betrayal of Equal Rights by the Supreme Court, 1865–1903* (New York: Walker Publishing, 2011), p. 91.
5. *United States v. Cruikshank*, 92 U.S. 542 (1875).

44. WHICH EPISODE OF RACIAL VIOLENCE DESTROYED THE COMMUNITY KNOWN AS THE "BLACK WALL STREET"?

1. Tulsa Race Riot, http://thetulsaraceriot1921.weebly.com/participant-accounts.html.
2. "The Eruption of Tulsa: An NAACP Official Investigates the Tulsa Race Riot of 1921," *History Matters: US Survey Course on the Web,* http://historymatters.gmu.edu/d/5119/.
3. Scott Ellsworth, "The Tulsa Race Riot," in *Tulsa Race Riot: A Report by the Oklahoma Commission to Study the Tulsa Race Riot of 1921* (CreateSpace Independent Publishing Platform, 2001), p. 58.
4. Ibid., p. 60.
5. Ibid., p. 63.
6. Alfred L. Brophy, *Reconstructing the Dreamland: The Tulsa Race Riot of 1921, Race Reparations, and Reconciliation* (New York: Oxford Univesity Press, 2002), p. 38.
7. Ellsworth, "The Tulsa Race Riot," p. 159.
8. "The Eruption of Tulsa."
9. Aaron Myers, "Tulsa Riot of 1921," in *Africana: The Encyclopedia of the African and African American Experience,* 2nd ed., ed. Kwame Anthony Appiah and Henry Louis Gates, Jr., 5 vols. (New York: Oxford University Press, 2005), 5:235.
10. Brophy, *Reconstructing the Dreamland,* p. xix.

45. HOW COULD INTEGRATING INFORMATION ABOUT THE FIGHT FOR CIVIL RIGHTS INTO K–12 CURRICULA BETTER EDUCATE OUR CHILDREN AND FOSTER A REAL CONVERSATION ON RACE?

1. Https://www.splcenter.org/sites/default/files/d6_legacy_files/downloads/publication/TeachingtheMovement.pdf.
2. James McKinley, "Conservatives on Texas Panel Carry the Day on Curriculum Change," *New York Times*, March 12, 2010.

46. WHICH CIVIL RIGHTS LEADER AND GAY BARRIER-BREAKER WAS KEPT IN THE SHADOWS BY THE CIVIL RIGHTS MOVEMENT ESTABLISHMENT?

1. Jervis Anderson, *Bayard Rustin: Troubles I've Seen: A Biography* (New York: HarperCollins, 1997), p. 19.
2. Bayard Rustin, *Time on Two Crosses: The Collected Writings of Bayard Rustin,* ed. Devon W. Carbado (San Francisco: Cleis Press, 2003).
3. James Baldwin, "The Dangerous Road Before Martin Luther King," *Harper's,* February 1961.
4. John Emilio, *Lost Prophet: The Life and Times of Bayard Rustin* (New York: Free Press, 2003).
5. Ibid.
6. Quoted ibid.
7. Lauren Feeney, "Two Versions of John Lewis' Speech," Bill Moyers, July 24, 2013.
8. Ben Cosgrove, "The March on Washington: Photos From an Epic Civil Rights Event," *Time,* August 27, 2012, http://time.com/3730150/the-march-on-washington-power-to-the-people/.
9. Taylor Branch, *The King Years: Historic Moments in the Civil Rights Movement* (New York: Simon & Schuster, 2013).

10. Quoted ibid.
11. Bayard Rustin, "From Protest to Politics: The Future of the Civil Rights Movement," *Commentary*, February 1965.
12. "Ask the Filmmaker: *Brother Outsider: The Life of Bayard Rustin*," PBS, January 1, 2003.

47. DID MARTIN LUTHER KING, JR., IMPROVISE IN THE "DREAM" SPEECH?

1. Taylor Branch, *Parting the Waters: America in the King Years, 1954–1963* (New York: Simon & Schuster, 1988), p. 875.
2. Adam Fairclough, *Martin Luther King, Jr.* (Athens: University of Georgia Press, 1995), p. 91.
3. Clarence B. Jones and Stuart Connelly, *Behind the Dream: The Making of the Speech That Transformed a Nation* (New York: Palgrave Macmillan, 2011), p. 112.
4. Branch, *Parting the Waters,* p. 882.
5. David J. Garrow, *Bearing the Cross: Martin Luther King, Jr., and the Southern Christian Leadership Conference* (New York: William Morrow, 1986), p. 283.
6. Vincent Harding, "The Road to Redemption," *Other Side,* January–February 2003.
7. Drew D. Hansen, *The Dream: Martin Luther King, Jr., and the Speech That Inspired a Nation* (New York: Ecco, 2003).
8. Quoted in Robin Toner, "Saving a Dissenter from His Legend," *New York Times,* January 19, 1986.
9. "Reagan Quotes King Speech in Opposing Minority Quotas," *New York Times,* January 18, 1986.

48. WHICH ENSLAVED AFRICAN MANAGED TO PRESS HIS CASE FOR FREEDOM ALL THE WAY TO THE WHITE HOUSE?

1. "Fulani (people)," *Encyclopaedia Britannica* Online.
2. Terry Alford, *Prince Among Slaves* (New York: Harcourt Brace Jovanovich, 1977).
3. Ibid., pp. 22–23.
4. Ibid., pp. 2, 23.
5. Ibid., p. 23.

49. WHO WAS HISTORY'S WEALTHIEST PERSON?

1. Brian Warner, "The 25 Richest People Who Ever Lived—Inflation Adjusted," April 14, 2014, CelebrityNetWorth.com.
2. "Mūsā I of Mali," *Encyclopaedia Britannica* Online.
3. David Conrad, "Musa, Mansa," in *Dictionary of African Biography,* ed. Emmanuel Kwaku Akyeampong and Henry Louis Gates, Jr. (New York: Oxford University Press, 2012).
4. David W. Tschanz, "Lion of Mali: The Hajj of Mansa Musa," *Makzan* (May 2012).
5. Ibid.
6. Conrad, "Musa, Mansa."
7. Edward W. Bovill and Robin Hallett, *The Golden Trade of the Moors: West African Kingdoms in the Fourteenth Century*, 2nd ed. (Princeton, NJ: Markus Wiener, 1995), p. 91.

50. WHO WAS THE FIRST BLACK POET IN THE WESTERN WORLD?

1. J. Mira Seo, "Identifying Authority: Juan Latino, an Ex-Slave, Professor and Poet in Sixteenth-Century Granada," in *African Athena: New Agendas,* ed. Daniel Orrells, Gur-

minder K. Bhambra, and Tessa Roynon (New York: Oxford University Press, 2011), p. 259.

2. Baltasar Fra-Molinero to author.
3. Glyn Redworth, "Mythology with Attitude? A Black Christian's Defence of Negritude in Early Modern Europe," *Social History* 28, no. 1 (2003): 49–66.
4. V. B. Spratlin and Diego Ximénez de Encisco, *Juan Latino, Slave and Humanist* (New York: Spinner, 1938).

51. WHO WAS THE FOUNDER OF CHICAGO?

1. J. A. Rogers, *Your History: From the Beginning of Time to the Present* (Baltimore, MD: Black Classic, 1983).
2. Quoted in Sidney Kaplan and Emma Nogrady Kaplan, *The Black Presence in the Era of the American Revolution* (Amherst: University of Massachusetts Press, 1989), p. 164.
3. Richard C. Lindberg, "Du Sable, Jean Baptiste Pointe," in *African American National Biography,* ed. Henry Louis Gates, Jr., and Evelyn Brooks Higginbotham, 8 vols. (New York: Oxford University Press, 2008), 3:78–79.
4. Kaplan and Kaplan, *The Black Presence in the Era of the American Revolution,* p. 165.
5. Shirley Graham Du Bois, *Jean Baptiste Pointe du Sable: Founder of Chicago* (New York: Julian Messner, 1953).
6. J. Seymour Curry, *The Story of Old Fort Dearborn* (Chicago: A. C. McClurg, 1912).
7. Eleanor Lytle Kinzie Gordon, *John Kinzie, the Father of Chicago: A Sketch* (Savannah?, GA, ca.1910).
8. John Moses and Joseph Kirkland, *History of Chicago, Illinois* (Chicago and New York: Munsell, 1895).
9. "Business League to Pilgrimage to 1st House in Chicago," *Afro American,* August 1, 1924.
10. Milo Milton Quaife, *Chicago and the Old Northwest, 1673–1835: A Study of the Evolution of the Northwestern Frontier, Together with a History of Fort Dearborn* (Chicago: University of Chicago Press, 1913).

52. WHAT'S THE REAL STORY OF THE LEGENDARY MIXED-RACE SLAVE TRADER JOEL ROGERS CALLED "MONGO JOHN"?

1. David Eltis, "A Brief Overview of the Trans-Atlantic Slave Trade," Trans-Atlantic Slave Trade Database, January 1, 2007.
2. Linda M. Heywood and John K. Thornton, *Central Africans, Atlantic Creoles, and the Foundation of the Americas, 1585–1660* (New York: Cambridge University Press, 2007).
3. David Eltis to author.
4. Bruce L. Mouser, "Trade, Coasters, and Conflict in the Rio Pongo from 1780 to 1808," *Journal of African History* 14, no. 1 (1973): 45–64.
5. George E. Brooks, *Eurafricans in Western Africa: Commerce, Social Status, Gender, and Religious Observance from the Sixteenth to the Eighteenth Century* (Athens: Ohio University Press, 2003).
6. David Eltis, *Economic Growth and the Ending of the Transatlantic Slave Trade* (New York: Oxford University Press, 1987).
7. Stephen Behrendt, "Human Capital in the British Slave Trade," in *Liverpool and Trans-atlantic Slavery,* ed. David Richardson, Anthony Tibbles, and Suzanne Schwarz (Liverpool: Liverpool University Press, 2007).
8. Mouser, "Trade, Coasters, and Conflict."
9. Ibid.

10. Theodore Canot and Brantz Mayer, *Adventures of an African Slaver: Being a True Account of the Life of Captain Theodore Canot, Trader in Gold, Ivory & Slaves on the Coast of Guinea* (New York: A&C Boni, 1928).
11. Bruce Mouser, *American Colony on the Rio Pongo: The War of 1812, the Slave Trade, and the Proposed Settlement of African Americans, 1810–1830* (Trenton, NJ: Africa World Press, 2013).
12. Eltis, *Economic Growth.*
13. Bruce L. Mouser, "Landlords-Strangers: A Process of Accommodation and Assimilation," *International Journal of African Historical Studies* 8, no. 3 (1975): 425.
14. The material on Ormond and La Isabela comes from Marial Iglesias Utset and Jorge Felipe Gonzalez, "The Rebellion on the Schooner Isabela (1814): A Case Study of TransAtlantic Commercial Networks between Upper Guinea and Cuba," unpublished paper presented at "The Slave Trade to Cuba: New Research Perspectives" conference, Havana, Cuba, June 9–11, 2016.

53. HOW DID THE STORY OF SOLOMON NORTHUP, THE AUTHOR OF *TWELVE YEARS A SLAVE*, FIRST BECOME PUBLIC?

1. Solomon Northup, *12 Years a Slave,* ed. Henry Louis Gates, Jr. (New York: Penguin, 2013).
2. Brad S. Born, "Northup, Solomon," in *The Concise Oxford Companion to African American Literature,* ed. William L. Andrews (New York: Oxford University Press, 2001).
3. John W. Blassingame, "Using the Testimony of Ex-Slaves: Approaches and Problems," *Journal of Southern History* 41, no. 4 (1975): 473–92.

54. WHO WAS THE FIRST BLACK MAN TO SERVE IN THE U.S. SENATE?

1. W.E.B. Du Bois, *Black Reconstruction in America, 1860–1880,* ed. David L. Lewis (1935; reprint New York: Simon & Schuster, 1995).
2. Richard Primus, "The Riddle of Hiram Revels," *Harvard Law Review* (April 2006).
3. Quoted in Henry Louis Gates, Jr., *Life upon These Shores: Looking at African American History, 1513–2008* (New York: Alfred A. Knopf, 2011), p. 164.
4. Eric Foner, *Reconstruction: America's Unfinished Revolution, 1863–1877* (New York: Harper & Row, 1988), p. 450.
5. "Free Negro Senator," *Washington Post,* February 3, 1901.
6. Kenneth H. Williams, "Revels, Hiram Rhoades," in *American National Biography,* ed. John A. Garraty and Mark C. Carnes (New York: Oxford University Press, 1999), 18:368.
7. Stephen Middleton, *Black Congressmen During Reconstruction: A Documentary Sourcebook* (Westport, CT: Praeger, 2002), p. 323.

55. WHICH BLACK GOVERNOR WAS ALMOST A SENATOR?

1. Lawrence Graham, *The Senator and the Socialite: The True Story of America's First Black Dynasty* (New York: Harper Perennial, 2007).
2. Caryn Neumann, "Pinchback, P.B.S.," in *Encyclopedia of African American History 1619–1895: From the Colonial Period to the Age of Frederick Douglass,* ed. Paul Finkelman (New York: Oxford University Press, 2006), pp. 516–18.
3. W.E.B. Du Bois, *Black Reconstruction in America, 1860–1880,* ed. David L. Lewis (1935; reprint New York: Simon & Schuster, 1995).
4. "Pinchback's Pay," *Detroit Free Press,* September 22, 1876.
5. Graham, *The Senator and the Socialite.*
6. "Senator Bruce Talks," *Washington Post,* April 15, 1878.

56. WHICH REGIMENT OF BLACK SOLDIERS RETURNING AFTER WORLD WAR I
RECEIVED A HERO'S WELCOME IN NEW YORK CITY?

1. Chad Louis Williams, *Torchbearers of Democracy: African American Soldiers in the World War I Era* (Chapel Hill: University of North Carolina Press, 2010), p. 75.
2. Chad Louis Williams, "African Americans and World War I," Africana Age, http:// exhibitions.nypl.org/africanaage/essay-world-war-i.html.
3. Adriane Lentz-Smith, *Freedom Struggles: African Americans and World War I* (Cambridge, MA: Harvard University Press, 2009), p. 111.
4. Quoted in Williams, *Torchbearers.*
5. "Teaching with Documents: Photographs of the 369th Infantry and African Americans During World War I," National Archives and Records Administration, https://www .archives.gov/education/lessons/369th-infantry.
6. Christopher Capozzola, "Roberts, Needham," in *African American National Biography,* ed. Henry Louis Gates, Jr., and Evelyn Brooks Higginbotham, 8 vols. (New York: Oxford University Press, 2008), 6:627–28.
7. Quoted in *Chicago Defender,* June 22, 1918.
8. Williams, *Torchbearers;* "Throngs Pay Tribute to Heroic 15th," *New York Tribune,* February 18, 1919.

57. WHO WERE THE AFRICAN AMERICANS IN
THE KENNEDY ADMINISTRATION?

1. Nick Bryant, *The Bystander: John F. Kennedy and the Struggle for Black Equality* (New York: Basic Books, 2006), pp. 159–61.
2. Alex Poinsett, *Walking with Presidents: Louis Martin and the Rise of Black Political Power* (Lanham, MD: Madison Books, 1997), p. xiv.
3. Quoted in Bryant, *The Bystander,* p. 189.
4. Quoted ibid., p. 175.
5. "Kennedy Appointees," *New York Amsterdam News,* November 30, 1963.
6. *Baltimore Afro-American,* September 29, 1962.

58. WHEN DID AFRICAN-AMERICAN WOMEN HIT THEIR STRIDE
IN PROFESSIONAL ACHIEVEMENT?

1. "Black Women Students Far Outnumber Black Men at the Nation's Highest-Ranked Universities," *Journal of Blacks in Higher Education* 51 (Spring 2006): 26–28.

59. WHO WERE THE BLACK PASSENGERS ON THE DOOMED *TITANIC* VOYAGE?

1. Judith B. Geller, *Titanic: Women and Children First* (New York: W. W. Norton, 1998).
2. "The Titanic Historical Society: Miss Louise Laroche," http://www.titanichistorical society.org/people/louise-laroche.html.
3. Dawn Turner Trice, "Black Passengers Add Another Facet to Titanic Story," *Chicago Tribune,* April 10, 2012.

60. WHICH FORMER SLAVE BECAME A DEPUTY U.S. MARSHAL AND
A RENOWNED SYMBOL OF LAW AND ORDER IN THE WILD WEST?

1. Arthur T. Burton, *Black Gun, Silver Star: The Life and Legend of Frontier Marshal Bass Reeves* (Lincoln: University of Nebraska Press, 2006). Except where indicated, Burton's book is the source for this chapter.

2. "Slavery," Oklahoma Historical Society, OHS Division, http://www.okhistory.org/publications/enc/entry.php?entry=SL003.

61. WHO WERE THE BLACK PEOPLE KILLED IN THE RAID ON HARPERS FERRY?

1. John Stauffer, *The Black Hearts of Men: Radical Abolitionists and the Transformation of Race* (Cambridge, MA: Harvard University Press, 2004).
2. "Editorial Correspondence," *North Star,* February 11, 1848.
3. As recalled in Frederick Douglass, *Life and Times of Frederick Douglass: His Early Life as a Slave, His Escape from Bondage, and His Complete History* (1881; reprint New York: Collier Books, 1962).
4. John Stauffer, *Giants: The Parallel Lives of Frederick Douglass and Abraham Lincoln* (New York: Twelve, 2008).
5. Tony Horwitz, *Midnight Rising: John Brown and the Raid That Sparked the Civil War* (New York: Henry Holt, 2011), pp. 138–39.
6. Joseph Barry, *The Strange Story of Harper's Ferry, with Legends of the Surrounding Country* (Martinsburg, WV: Thompson Bros., 1903).
7. Philip J. Schwarz, *Migrants Against Slavery: Virginians and the Nation* (Charlottesville: University of Virginia Press, 2001).
8. Zoe Trodd, "Green, Shields," in *African American National Biography,* ed. Henry Louis Gates, Jr., and Evelyn Brooks Higginbotham, 8 vols. (New York: Oxford University Press, 2008), 3:613–14.
9. Steven J. Niven, "Anderson, Osborne Perry," in Gates and Higginbotham, *African American National Biography,* 1:136–38. See also Osborne P. Anderson, *A Voice from Harper's Ferry: A Narrative of Events at Harper's Ferry; with Incidents Prior and Subsequent to Its Capture by Captain Brown and His Men* (Boston: Printed for the Author, 1861).

62. WHAT MYTH OF ETERNAL YOUTH IN AFRICA INSPIRED EUROPEANS FOR CENTURIES?

1. Herodotus, *The History* (440 BCE), trans. George Rawlinson, *Internet Classics Archive,* http://classics.mit.edu/Herodotus/history.html.
2. Malcolm Letts, "Prester John: A Fourteenth-Century Manuscript at Cambridge," *Transactions of the Royal Historical Society* 29 (1947): 19.
3. Umberto Eco, *The Book of Legendary Lands,* trans. Alastair McEwen (New York: Rizzoli Ex Libris, 2013), pp. 101–2.
4. Robert Silverberg, *The Realm of Prester John* (Garden City, NY: Doubleday, 1972), p. 146.
5. C. F. Beckingham, "The Achievements of Prester John," in *Prester John, the Mongols, and the Ten Lost Tribes,* ed. C. F. Beckingham and B. Hamilton (Aldershot, Hamps., UK: Variorum, 1996), p. 17.
6. Cates Baldridge, *Prisoners of Prester John: The Portuguese Mission to Ethiopia in Search of the Mythical King, 1520–1526* (Jefferson, NC: McFarland, 2012).
7. Matteo Salvadore, "The Ethiopian Age of Exploration: Prester John's Discovery of Europe, 1306–1458," *Journal of World History* 21, no. 4 (2010): 593–627.

63. HOW DID BLACK SOLDIERS COME TO FIGHT IN THE AMERICAN CIVIL WAR?

1. Edna Greene Medford, "U.S. Colored Troops," Lincoln Forum at Gettysburg, November 17, 2013, http://www.c-span.org/video/?316199-3/us-colored-troops.

2. David W. Blight, "Douglass and the Meaning of the Black Soldier," in *Frederick Douglass' Civil War: Keeping Faith in Jubilee* (Baton Rouge: Louisiana State University Press, 1989), p. 148. This is the best short essay on the subject.
3. William Cooper Nell, *The Colored Patriots of the American Revolution* (1855; reprint New York: Arno, 1968).
4. Quoted in *Liberator,* May 22, 1863.

64. WHICH BLACK MAN ENGAGED A FOUNDING FATHER IN A DEBATE ABOUT RACIAL EQUALITY?

1. Martha Ellicott Tyson and Anne T. Kirk, *Banneker: The Afric-American Astronomer* (1884).
2. Carl William Drepperd, *American Clocks and Clockmakers* (Garden City, NY: Doubleday, 1947).
3. Aaron Myers, "Banneker, Benjamin," in *Africana: The Encyclopedia of the African and African American Experience,* 2nd ed., ed. Kwame Anthony Appiah and Henry Louis Gates, Jr., 3 vols. (New York: Oxford University Press, 2005), 1:356.
4. Charles Cerami, *Benjamin Banneker: Surveyor, Astronomer, Publisher, Patriot* (Hoboken, NJ: John Wiley & Sons, 2002).
5. Kenneth R. Fletcher, "A Brief History of Pierre L'Enfant and Washington, D.C.," April 30, 2008, http://www.smithsonianmag.com/arts-culture/a-brief-history-of-pierre-lenfant-and-washington-dc-39487784/?c=y&page=2.
6. Thomas Jefferson, *Notes on the State of Virginia,* ed. William Peden (Chapel Hill: University of North Carolina Press, 1955), pp. 143–44.
7. Thomas Jefferson, "Jefferson's Reply to Banneker," August 1791, PBS Online, http://www.pbs.org/wgbh/aia/part2/2h72t.html.
8. Quoted in Benjamin Quarles, *The Negro in the American Revolution* (Chapel Hill: University of North Carolina Press, 1961).
9. George Buchanan, "Oration Upon the Moral and Political Evil of Slavery," Maryland Society for Promoting the Abolition of Slavery, July 4, 1791.

65. HOW WERE MARTIN LUTHER KING, JR., AND NELSON MANDELA LINKED?

1. Elizabeth Kolbert, "Tutu, in New York, Calls for Economic Sanctions," *New York Times,* January 7, 1986.
2. Steven Ginsburg, "Tutu Joins Washington Rally," *Lodi News-Sentinel,* January 9, 1986.
3. "Before the Battle Was Won," Detroit Public Library, February 18, 2014, http://www.detroitpubliclibrary.org/blogs/coleman-young-mayoral-papers-project/battle-was-won; "U.S. Firms Must Pull Out," *New York Amsterdam News,* January 18, 1986; "Tutu's U.S. Visit Stirs New Anti-Apartheid Awareness," *Los Angeles Sentinel,* January 30, 1986.
4. "Tutu Praises U.S. Public's Role in Forcing Action Against Apartheid," *Los Angeles Times,* January 21, 1986; "An Outpouring of Tributes to King," *Washington Post,* January 21, 1986 (with Bush's quotes).
5. "Botha Outlines Apartheid Reforms; Blacks Unmoved," *Los Angeles Times,* February 1, 1986; Alan Cowell, "Pretoria Links Mandela's Fate to Soviet Dissidents," *New York Times,* January 31, 1986.
6. "Continuing Anti-Apartheid Protests Hastened Pace of Exits by U.S. Companies from South Africa," *Wall Street Journal,* February 27, 1986.

clopedia of Nonconformists, Alternative Lifestyles, and Radical Ideas in U.S. History (Armonk, NY: Sharpe Reference, 2009); personal correspondence with John Hodgson, October 9, 2016.

3. George Schindler, *Ventriloquism: Magic with Your Voice* (New York: Dover, 2011), p. 9.

73. WHO WAS THE FIRST BLACK ACTOR TO PLAY THE ROLE OF SHAKESPEARE'S TORTURED MOOR?

1. Amanda Mabillard, "The History of Othello, Shakespeare Online," August 10, 2008, http://www.shakespeare-online.com/plays/othello/stagehistoryothello.html.
2. Bernth Lindfors, *Ira Aldridge,* 2 vols. (Rochester, NY: University of Rochester Press, 2011). See also Bernth Lindfors, ed., *Ira Aldridge, the African Roscius* (Rochester, NY: University of Rochester Press, 2007).
3. Alex Ross, "Othello's Daughter: The Rich Legacy of Ira Aldridge, the Pioneering Black Shakespearean," *New Yorker,* July 29, 2013.
4. Melissa Vickery-Bareford, "Aldridge, Ira," in *African American National Biography,* ed. Henry Louis Gates, Jr., and Evelyn Brooks Higginbotham, 8 vols. (New York: Oxford University Press, 2008), 1:57.
5. Quoted in Lindfors, *Aldridge,* p. 37.
6. Quoted ibid, p. 65.
7. Quoted ibid, pp. 79–81.
8. Ibid., p. 92.

74. WHO WAS THE PATRON SAINT OF AFRICAN SLAVES AND THEIR DESCENDANTS?

1. Friar Jacques Allibert, *Life of St. Benedict Surnamed "The Moor,"* trans. Giuseppe Carletti (reprint Book On Demand, 2013).
2. Giovanna Fiume, "Benedict the Moor: From Sicily to the New World,"in *Saints and Their Cults in the Atlantic World*, ed. Margaret Cormack (Columbia: University of South Carolina Press, 2007), p. 17.
3. Alessandro Dell'Aira, "St. Benedict of San Fratello (Messina, Sicily): An Afro-Sicilian Hagionym on Three Continents," *Proceedings of the 23rd International Congress of Onomastic Sciences* (Toronto: York University, 2009).
4. Allibert, *Life of St. Benedict,* trans. Carletti.
5. Giovanna Fiume, "Benedict the Moor," in Carole Davies, *Encyclopedia of the African Diaspora: Origins, Experiences, and Culture* (Santa Barbara, CA: ABC-CLIO, 2008), p. 155.
6. Quoted in Fiume, *Saints and Their Cults,* p. 20.
7. Fiume, "Benedict the Moor," p. 156.
8. Fiume, *Saints and Their Cults,* p. 24.
9. Ibid., p. 20.

75. WAS A BLACK SLAVE TO BLAME FOR THE SALEM WITCH TRIALS?

1. Marilynne K. Roach, *Six Women of Salem: The Untold Story of the Accused and Their Accusers in the Salem Witch Trials* (Cambridge, MA: Da Capo Press, 2013), p. 67.
2. Elaine Breslaw, *Tituba, Reluctant Witch of Salem: Devilish Indians and Puritan Fantasies* (New York: NYU Press, 1996).
3. Peter Charles Hoffer, *The Salem Witchcraft Trials: A Legal History* (Lawrence: University Press of Kansas, 1997).
4. Jess Blumberg, "A Brief History of the Salem Witch Trials," Smithsonian.com, October 23, 2007, http://www.smithsonianmag.com/history/a-brief-history-of-the-salem-witch-trials-175162489/?no-ist.

5. David D. Hall, *Worlds of Wonder, Days of Judgment: Popular Religious Belief in Early New England* (1989; reprint New York: Alfred A. Knopf, 2013), p. 71.
6. Roach, *Six Women*, p. 103.
7. Carol F. Karlsen, *The Devil in the Shape of a Woman: Witchcraft in Colonial New England* (New York: W. W. Norton, 1987), p. 300.

76. WHAT'S THE TRUTH ABOUT MANY AFRICAN-AMERICAN FAMILIES HAVING A NATIVE AMERICAN ANCESTOR?

1. ScottH, "DNA USA," *23AndMe*, March 4, 2014; Katarzyna Bryc et al., "The Genetic Ancestry of African Americans, Latinos, and European Americans in the United States," *American Journal of Human Genetics* 96 (January 8, 2015): 42.
2. Bryc et al., "Genetic Ancestry," p. 42.
3. Claudio Saunt to author.
4. Ira Berlin to author.
5. Eric Foner to author.
6. David Eltis to author; Katherine Howlett Hayes, *Slavery Before Race: Europeans, Africans, and Indians on Long Island's Sylvester Manor Plantation, 1651–1821* (New York: New York University Press, 2013).
7. Personal correspondence. Barbara Krauthamer is the author of *Black Slaves, Indian Masters: Slavery, Emancipation, and Citizenship in the Native American South* (Chapel Hill: University of North Carolina Press, 2013).
8. Joseph C. G. Griffith Kennedy, *Preliminary Report on the Eighth Census* (Washington, DC: Government Printing Office), p. 11.

77. WHICH PIONEERING PLAY INTRODUCED MAINSTREAM AMERICAN AUDIENCES TO THE DYNAMICS UNDERGIRDING THE CIVIL RIGHTS MOVEMENT?

1. "Black Women Students Far Outnumber Black Men at the Nation's Highest-Ranked Universities," *Journal of Blacks in Higher Education* (2006), http://www.jbhe.com/news_views/51_gendergap_universities.html.
2. Lorraine Hansberry, *To Be Young, Gifted, and Black: Lorraine Hansberry in Her Own Words*, ed. Robert Nemiroff (Englewood Cliffs, NJ: Prentice-Hall, 1969), introduction by James Baldwin.
3. Brooks Atkinson, "The Theatre: 'A Raisin in the Sun'," *New York Times*, March 12, 1959, reprinted in *Readings on "A Raisin in the Sun*," ed. Lawrence Kappel (San Diego, CA: Greenhaven, 2001).

78. WHAT ROLE DID LORD MANSFIELD'S MIXED-RACE GREAT-NIECE, DIDO ELIZABETH BELLE, PLAY IN HIS FAMOUS DECISION ON SLAVERY IN ENGLAND?

1. Reyahn King, "Belle, Dido Elizabeth (1761?–1804)," *Oxford Dictionary of National Biography* (Oxford: Oxford University Press, 2004; online edition, October 2007). Other sources have her birth as 1763: see Leslie Primo, "Lindsay, Dido Elizabeth (Belle Lindsay)," in *The Oxford Companion to Black British History*, ed. David Dabydeen, John Gilmore, and Cecily Jones (New York: Oxford University Press, 2007); and "Inside Out: Abolition of the British Slave Trade special" BBC, January 22, 2008, http://www.bbc.co.uk/london/content/articles/2007/02/27/insideout_abolition_special_feature.shtml.
2. "Black Lives in England," Historic England, https://historicengland.org.uk/research/inclusive-heritage/the-slave-trade-and-abolition/sites-of-memory/black-lives-in-england/working-lives/.

3. Steven M. Wise, *Though the Heavens May Fall: The Landmark Trial That Led to the End of Human Slavery* (Cambridge, MA: Da Capo Press, 2005), p. 79.
4. Kathy Chater, "Somerset Case," in Dabydeen, Gilmore, and Jones,*The Oxford Companion to Black British History.*
5. Thomas Hutchinson, *The Diary and Letters of His Excellency Thomas Hutchinson, Esq.,* vol.2, ed. Peter Orlando Hutchinson (Boston: Houghton Mifflin, 1886), p. 276.
6. "Slave or Free," The National Archives: Black Presence, http://www.nationalarchives .gov.uk/pathways/blackhistory/rights/slave_free.htm.

79. WHO WAS THE FIRST AFRICAN-AMERICAN WRITER TO INVESTIGATE AND REPORT THE WRONGDOINGS OF A WORLD LEADER?

1. Quoted in John Hope Franklin, *George Washington Williams: A Biography* (Durham, NC: Duke University Press, 1998), p. 236.
2. Paul Vallely, "Forever in Chains: The Tragic History of the Congo," *The Independent,* July 27, 2006, http://www.independent.co.uk/news/world/africa/forever-in-chains-the -tragic-history-of-congo-6232383.html.
3. Ibid.
4. *Daily Telegraph* (1884), quoted ibid.
5. Ibid.
6. Adam Hochschild, *King Leopold's Ghost: A Story of Greed, Terror, and Heroism in Colonial Africa* (Boston: Houghton Mifflin, 1998), p. 106.
7. Quoted ibid.
8. George Washington Williams, *History of the Negro Race in America, 1619–1880: Negroes as Slaves, as Soldiers, and as Citizens* (1883; reprint Whitefish, MT: Kessinger, 2006).
9. George Washington Williams, *A History of the Negro Troops in the War of the Rebellion, 1861–1865* (1887; reprint New York: Negro Universities, 1969).

80. WHO WERE THE FIRST NOTABLE AFRICAN AMERICANS WHO STEPPED INTO AMERICA'S INSTITUTIONS OF HIGHER LEARNING?

1. Sholomo B. Levy, "Twilight, Alexander Lucius," in *African American National Biography,* ed. Henry Louis Gates, Jr., and Evelyn Brooks Higginbotham, 8 vols. (New York: Oxford University Press, 2008), 7:675–77.
2. Russell W. Irvine, "Freeman, Martin Henry," in *African American National Biography,* 2nd ed., ed. Henry Louis Gates, Jr., and Evelyn Higginbotham, 12 vols. (New York: Oxford University Press, 2013), 4:512–13.
3. "Key Events in Black Higher Education" (timeline), *Journal of Blacks in Higher Education* (2011), https://www.jbhe.com/chronology.
4. Rayford W. Logan, *Howard University: The First Hundred Years, 1867–1967* (New York: New York University Press, 1969), p. 5.
5. Allison Kellar, "Sessions, Lucy Stanton Day," in Gates and Higginbotham, *African American National Biography* (2008), 7:144.
6. Roland Baumann, "Mary Jane Patterson," in Gates and Higginbotham, *African American National Biography* (2008), 6:267–69.

81. WHAT WAS FREEDOM'S FORT, AND HOW DOES IT RELATE TO MEMORIAL DAY?

1. Drew Gilpin Faust, *This Republic of Suffering: Death and the American Civil War* (New York: Alfred A. Knopf, 2008).

2. Eric Foner, *The Fiery Trial: Abraham Lincoln and American Slavery* (New York: W. W. Norton, 2011).
3. "The First Confiscation Act," August 6, 1861, Freedmen & Southern Society Project, http://www.freedmen.umd.edu/conact1.htm.
4. "Document for May 22nd: War Department General Order 143," National Archives and Records Administration, http://www.archives.gov/historical-docs/todays-doc/index .html?dod-date=523%20In%20the.
5. Quoted in Eric Wills, "The Forgotten: The Contraband of America and the Road to Freedom," *Preservation,* May/June 2011, http://www.preservationnation.org/magazine /2011/may-june/the-forgotten.html.
6. "Government Policy on Slavery in the Seceded States," *New York Times,* August 13, 1861.
7. Quoted in Wills, "The Forgotten."
8. "Black History at Arlington National Cemetery," Arlington National Cemetery, http:// www.arlingtoncemetery.mil/Explore/Notable-Graves/Minorities/Black-History-at -ANC.

82. WHICH FRENCH GENERAL UNDER NAPOLÉON HAD AFRICAN ANCESTRY AND WAS A FOREBEAR TO TWO FRENCH LITERARY GREATS?

1. Tom Reiss, *The Black Count: Glory, Revolution, Betrayal, and the Real Count of Monte Cristo* (New York: Crown, 2012). Reiss's book is the basis for this chapter, including quotations, unless otherwise indicated.
2. John G. Gallaher, *General Alexandre Dumas: Soldier of the French Revolution* (Carbondale: Southern Illinois University Press, 1997), p. 20.

83. WHICH FAMOUS NINETEENTH-CENTURY FRENCH AUTHOR HAD AFRICAN ANCESTRY?

1. Tom Reiss, *The Black Count: Glory, Revolution, Betrayal, and the Real Count of Monte Cristo* (New York: Crown, 2012). Reiss's book is the source for this chapter, including quotations, unless otherwise indicated.
2. Richard S. Stowe, *Alexandre Dumas père* (Boston: Twayne, 1976), p. 20.
3. Jonathan Edwards, "Dumas, Alexandre, *Père,*" in *Africana: The Encyclopedia of the African and African American Experience,* 2nd ed., ed. Kwame Anthony Appiah and Henry Louis Gates, Jr., 5 vols. (New York: Oxford University Press, 2005), 2:463–64.
4. Andre Maurois, *Three Musketeers: A Study of the Dumas Family* (London: Cape, 1957), p. 182.
5. Joel Dreyfuss, "Depardieu Covers Alexandre Dumas," *Root,* February 21, 2010.
6. Peter Carr, "Dumas, Alexandre," in *Encyclopedia of African American History 1619–1895: From the Colonial Period to the Age of Frederick Douglass,* ed. Paul Finkelman (New York: Oxford University Press, 2006), p. 429.
7. Douglass quoted in Waldo E. Martin, *The Mind of Frederick Douglass* (Chapel Hill: University of North Carolina Press, 1984), p. 93.
8. "The Body of a Legendary Black Novelist Is Laid to Rest in the French Pantheon," *Journal of Blacks in Higher Education* 38 (January 31, 2003): 43.

84. WHICH ZULU KING LED HIS MEN TO VICTORY OVER BRITISH INVADERS AND MOUNTED WARFARE THAT KILLED A FRENCH "PRINCE"?

1. Michael R. Mahoney, "Cetshwayo ka Mpande," in *Dictionary of African Biography,* ed. Emmanuel Kwaku Akyeampong and Henry Louis Gates, Jr., 6 vols. (New York: Oxford University Press, 2012), 2:53–54.

2. John Laband, *Rope of Sand: The Rise and Fall of the Zulu Kingdom in the Nineteenth Century* (Johannesburg: Jonathan Ball, 1995).
3. Saul David, *Zulu: The Heroism and Tragedy of the Zulu War of 1879* (London: Viking, 2004).
4. Kris Wheatley, "Rorke's Drift 1879," Legacy of the Rorke's Drift Heroes, January 1, 2014, http://rorkesdriftvc-com/pdf/Legacy.pdf.
5. J. A. Rogers, *100 Amazing Facts About the Negro: With Complete Proof: A Short Cut to the World History of the Negro* (New York: H. M. Rogers, 1957).
6. Ian Knight and Ian Castle, *The Zulu War 1879* (Oxford: Osprey, 2004).
7. "The Zulu War," *The Cambrian,* February 14, 1879.
8. "The Zulu War, Later Details of the British Defeat," *Manchester Guardian,* February 17, 1879.
9. "The Zulu War, The Latest News," *South Wales Daily News,* February 17, 1879.
10. "Battles of Isandlwana and Rorke's Drift," *Encyclopaedia Britannica* Online.

85. WHY WAS THE SUMMER OF 1964 PIVOTAL IN THE FIGHT FOR CIVIL RIGHTS?

1. Lisa Clayton Robinson, "Freedom Summer," in *Africana: The Encyclopedia of the African and African American Experience,* 2nd ed., ed. Kwame Anthony Appiah and Henry Louis Gates, Jr., 5 vols. (New York: Oxford University Press, 2005), 2:714.
2. Quoted in Howell Raines, *My Soul Is Rested: Movement Days in the Deep South Remembered* (New York: G. P. Putnam, 1977), p. 274.
3. John Dittmer, *Local People: The Struggle for Civil Rights in Mississippi* (Urbana: University of Illinois Press, 1994), p. 244.
4. Doug McAdam, *Freedom Summer* (New York: Oxford University Press, 1988), p. 4.
5. Charles M. Payne, *I've Got the Light of Freedom: The Organizing Tradition and the Mississippi Freedom Struggle* (Berkeley: University of California Press, 1995).
6. "The Civil Rights Movement and the Second Reconstruction, 1945–1968," History Art and Archives, United States House of Representatives, http://history.house.gov/Exhibitions-and-Publications/BAIC/Historical-Essays/Keeping-the-Faith/Civil-Rights-Movement/.
7. Cleveland Sellers and Robert L. Terrell, *The River of No Return: The Autobiography of a Black Militant and the Life and Death of SNCC* (New York: William Morrow, 1973), p. 301.

86. WHICH CIVIL RIGHTS WARRIOR RECEIVED NUMEROUS TELEPHONE CALLS FROM THE U.S. PRESIDENT DURING THE FIGHT TO PASS THE CIVIL RIGHTS ACT OF 1964?

1. Todd S. Purdum, *An Idea Whose Time Has Come: Two Presidents, Two Parties, and the Battle for the Civil Rights Act of 1964* (New York: Henry Holt, 2014). Except where indicated, this chapter is based on Purdum's book.
2. "Clarence M. Mitchell Jr.," *Baltimore Sun,* February 9, 2007.
3. Denton L. Watson, *Lion in the Lobby: Clarence Mitchell, Jr.'s Struggle for the Passage of Civil Rights Laws* (New York: William Morrow, 1990).

87. WHAT HAPPENED TO ARGENTINA'S BLACK POPULATION?

1. Erika Edwards, "Slavery in Argentina," *Oxford Bibliographies,* May 29, 2014.
2. Joy Elizondo, "Argentina," in *Africana: The Encyclopedia of the African and African American Experience,* 2nd ed., ed. Kwame Anthony Appiah and Henry Louis Gates, Jr., 5 vols. (New York: Oxford University Press, 2005), 1:243.

3. Palash Ghosh, "Blackout: How Argentina 'Eliminated' Africans from Its History and Conscience," *International Business Times,* June 4, 2013.

88. WHICH EVENT IN BLACK HISTORY TOOK PLACE IN WHAT IS NOW IRAQ?

1. David Brion Davis, *Challenging the Boundaries of Slavery* (Cambridge, MA: Harvard University Press, 2003).
2. Leyla Keogh, "Middle East," in *Africana: The Encyclopedia of the African and African American Experience,* 2nd ed., ed. Kwame Anthony Appiah and Henry Louis Gates, Jr., 5 vols. (New York: Oxford University Press, 2005), 4:4–7.
3. Alexandre Popovic, *The Revolt of African Slaves in Iraq in the 3rd/9th Century* (Princeton, NJ: Markus Wiener, 1999).
4. "Zanj Rebellion (Abbasid History)," *Encyclopaedia Britannica* Online.
5. Kent Krause, "Zanj Rebellion," in Appiah and Gates, *Africana,* 5:500.

89. DID BLACK PEOPLE ENGAGE IN PIRACY DURING ITS HEYDAY IN THE AMERICAS?

1. Matthew Restall, "Black Conquistadors: Armed Africans in Early Spanish America," *Americas* 57, no. 2 (2000): 171–205. Except where indicated, Restall is the source for the three Diegos.
2. J. A. Rogers, *Your History: From the Beginning of Time to the Present* (Baltimore, MD: Black Classic, 1989).
3. Kris E. Lane, *Pillaging the Empire: Piracy in the Americas, 1500–1750* (Armonk, NY: M. E. Sharpe, 1998), p. 71.
4. W. Jeffrey Bolster, *Black Jacks: African American Seamen in the Age of Sail* (Cambridge, MA: Harvard University Press, 1997).
5. Arne Bialuschewski, "Pirates, Black Sailors and Seafaring Slaves in the Anglo-American Maritime World, 1716–1726," *Journal of Caribbean History* 45, no. 2 (2011): 143.
6. Arne Bialuschewski, "Black People under the Black Flag: Piracy and the Slave Trade on the West Coast of Africa, 1718–1723," *Slavery and Abolition* 29, no. 4 (2008): 461–75.
7. Bolster, *Black Jacks.*
8. Joseph Gibbs, *Dead Men Tell No Tales: The Lives and Legends of the Pirate Charles Gibbs* (Columbia: University of South Carolina Press, 2007), is the source of this information on Wansley.
9. *Trial and Sentence of Thomas J. Wansley and Charles Gibbs, for Murder and Piracy on Board the Brig Vineyard* (New York: Christian Brown, 1831).

90. HOW DID THE SHATTERING OF THE COLOR BARRIER FOR RHODES SCHOLARSHIPS FOREVER CHANGE THE BLACK ARTS MOVEMENT?

1. "About the Rhodes Scholarships," http://files.www.rhodesscholarshiptrust.com/china -additional-materials/Notes_to_Editors_-_FINAL_-_EN.pdf.
2. Christopher Montague Woodhouse, "Cecil Rhodes," *Encyclopaedia Britannica* Online.
3. Alain Locke, in Harvard Class of 1908 Secretary's Second Report, 1914.
4. Leonard Harris, "Locke, Alain Leroy," in *African American National Biography,* ed. Henry Louis Gates, Jr., and Evelyn Brooks Higginbotham, 8 vols. (New York: Oxford University Press, 2008), 5:287–89.
5. Alain LeRoy Locke, *The New Negro: An Interpretation* (1925; reprint New York: Arno, 1968).

91. WHICH BLACK FEMALE POET OWNED A GARDEN HOUSE THAT BECAME A POPULAR HOME-AWAY-FROM-HOME DOWN SOUTH FOR THE LEADING LIGHTS OF THE HARLEM RENAISSANCE?

1. Penelope Green, "The Life of a Poet Allergic to Endings," *New York Times,* February 5, 2014.
2. Adrian Higgins, "Where the Harlem Renaissance Blossomed in Virginia, with Poet Anne Spencer," *Washington Post,* July 28, 2014.
3. Barbara McCaskill, "Spencer, Anne," in *The Concise Oxford Companion to African American Literature,* ed. William L. Andrews (New York: Oxford University Press, 2001).
4. Dora Jean Ashe, "Spencer, Anne," in *African American National Biography,* ed. Henry Louis Gates, Jr., and Evelyn Brooks Higginbotham, 8 vols. (New York: Oxford University Press, 2008), 7:351–52.
5. "A Guide to the Papers of Anne Spencer and the Spencer Family," University of Virginia Library, Special Collections, http://ead.lib.virginia.edu/vivaxtf/view?docId=uva-sc%2Fviu04082.xml.
6. See J. Lee Greene, *Time's Unfading Garden: Anne Spencer's Life and Poetry* (Baton Rouge: Louisiana State University Press, 1977).

92. WHEN PRESIDENT ABRAHAM LINCOLN MET WITH FREE BLACK LEADERS IN 1862, WHAT DID HE PROPOSE?

1. Kate Masur, "The African American Delegation to Abraham Lincoln: A Reappraisal," *Civil War History* (June 2010).
2. Eric Foner, *The Fiery Trial: Abraham Lincoln and American Slavery* (New York: W. W. Norton, 2010).
3. "Address on Colonization of Negroes," *Collected Works of Abraham Lincoln,* http://quod.lib.umich.edu/l/lincoln/lincoln5/1:812?rgn=div1;view=fulltext.

93. WHICH BLACK JUSTICES BROKE THE COLOR BARRIER AT THE FEDERAL COURT LEVEL?

1. Quoted in Constance Baker Motley, *Equal Justice Under Law* (New York: Farrar, Straus & Giroux, 1999).
2. *Annals of Congress,* 110th Congress, 1st sess., 132.
3. *Blank v. Sullivan & Cromwell* , 418 F. Supp. 1, 4 (S.D.N.Y. 1975).
4. Oliver W. Hill, "In Memoriam: Spottswood W. Robinson, III," *Harvard Black Letters Law Journal* 15 (Spring 1999).

94. WHO BURIED THE WAR DEAD FROM THE BATTLE OF GETTYSBURG?

1. Margaret Creighton, *The Colors of Courage: Gettysburg's Forgotten History* (New York: Basic Books, 2006).
2. Allen Guelzo, *Gettysburg: The Last Invasion* (New York: Alfred A. Knopf, 2013).
3. Gabor Boritt, *The Gettysburg Gospel: The Lincoln Speech That Nobody Knows* (New York: Simon & Schuster, 2006), p. 6.
4. "Basil Biggs," *Pennsylvania Quest for Freedom,* http://www.paquestforfreedom.com/basil-biggs.
5. James M. Paradis, *African Americans and the Gettysburg Campaign* (Lanham, MD: Scarecrow, 2005), p. 58.
6. Pennsylvania Civil War Border Claims, Records of the Department of the Auditor General, Record Group 2, Pennsylvania State Archives, Harrisburg, Pennsylvania, reprinted on Ancestry.com.

95. WHAT DID MALCOLM X DO AT OXFORD UNIVERSITY?

1. Stephen G. N. Tuck, *The Night Malcolm X Spoke at the Oxford Union: A Transatlantic Story of Antiracist Protest* (Berkeley: University of California Press, 2014).
2. Barry Goldwater, Republican National Convention Acceptance Speech, July 1964.
3. Martin Luther King, Jr., *The Autobiography of Martin Luther King Jr.* (New York: Warner Books, 2001).

96. WHICH BLACK MAN MADE MANY OF OUR FAVORITE HOUSEHOLD PRODUCTS BETTER?

1. Walter Isaacson, *The Innovators: How a Group of Hackers, Geniuses, and Geeks Created the Digital Revolution* (New York: Simon & Schuster, 2014).
2. "Herbert Charles Smitherman Sr.," Greater Cincinnati Tristate Obituaries, https://www.tristateobits.com/obituary/Dr-Herbert-Charles-Smitherman-Sr—1286991593.
3. "The Cincinnati NAACP Mourns the Passing of Dr. Herbert C. Smitherman, Sr.," press release, October 9, 2010, http://www.ourownvoices.com/?p=6465.
4. "A Resolution Memorializing Dr. Herbert Smitherman Sr.," Board of Education, Cincinnati, Ohio, Special Meeting, March 21, 2011, pp. 216–17, http://www.cps-k12.org/sites/www.cps-k12.org/files/pdfs/boardminutes/2011Mar21SpecReg.pdf.
5. "Search for Patents," U.S. Patent and Trademark Office, http://www.uspto.gov/patents-application-process/search-patents.

97. WHICH TWENTIETH-CENTURY BLACK ACTOR PLAYED ROLES OF ALL RACES DURING A TIME WHEN HOLLYWOOD HAD FEW ROLES FOR BLACK ACTORS?

1. *Chicago Daily Defender,* March 6, 1971.

98. WHO WERE THE FIRST BLACK BOXING CHAMPIONS?

1. Elliott J. Gorn, *The Manly Art: Bare-knuckle Prize Fighting in America* (Ithaca: Cornell University Press, 1986).
2. David Dabydeen and Shivani Sivagurunathan, "Richmond, Bill," in *The Oxford Companion to Black British History,* ed. David Dabydeen, John Gilmore, and Cecily Jones (New York: Oxford University Press, 2007).
3. Michael L. Krenn, "Richmond, Bill," in *African American National Biography,* ed. Henry Louis Gates, Jr., and Evelyn Brooks Higginbotham, 8 vols. (New York: Oxford University Press, 2008), 6:591–92.
4. David Dabydeen and Shivani Sivagurunathan, "Molineaux, Tom," in Dabydeen, Gilmore, and Jones, *Oxford Companion to Black British History.*
5. Quoted in Paul Magriel, "Tom Molineaux," *Phylon (1940–1956)* 12, no. 4 (1951): 329–36.
6. Al-Tony Gilmore, "Molineaux, Tom," in *Africana: The Encyclopedia of the African and African American Experience,* 2nd ed., ed. Kwame Anthony Appiah and Henry Louis Gates, Jr., 5 vols. (New York: Oxford University Press, 2005), 4:50–51.
7. Quoted in Geoffrey C. Ward, *Unforgivable Blackness: The Rise and Fall of Jack Johnson* (New York: Alfred A. Knopf, 2004).
8. Ibid.
9. Quoted ibid.
10. Ken Burns and Keith David, *Unforgivable Blackness: The Rise and Fall of Jack Johnson* (documentary), released 2004.
11. Luckett V. Davis, "Johnson, Jack," in *American National Biography,* ed. John A. Garraty and Mark C. Carnes (New York: Oxford University Press, 1999), 12:83–85.

99. WHO WERE THE KEY SCHOLARS RESPONSIBLE FOR THE DISCIPLINE OF BLACK HISTORY?

1. Kenneth Robert Janken, "Logan, Rayford Whittingham," in *African American National Biography,* ed. Henry Louis Gates, Jr., and Evelyn Brooks Higginbotham, 8 vols. (New York: Oxford University Press, 2008), 5:297–98.
2. Michael R. Winston, "The Howard University Department of History," https://www.howard.edu/explore/history-dept.htm.
3. Constance Porter Uzelac, "Wesley, Dorothy Burnett Porter," in Gates and Higginbotham, *African American National Biography,* 8:212–13.
4. Henry Louis Gates, Jr., "Farewell, John Hope," *Journal of Blacks in Higher Education* (2009), http://www.jbhe.com/features/64_gatesonfranklin.html.

100. WHAT ARE THE MOST IMPORTANT FACTS TO KNOW ABOUT AMERICAN SLAVERY?

1. David Eltis and Martin Halbert, "The Trans-Atlantic Slave Trade Database Has Information on Almost 36,000 Slaving Voyages," Trans-Atlantic Slave Trade, http://www.slavevoyages.org.
2. Ibid.
3. Ronald Bailey, "The Other Side of Slavery: Black Labor, Cotton, and Textile Industrialization in Great Britain and the United States," *Agricultural History* 68, no. 2 (1994): 35–50.
4. The Gilder Lehrman Guide to Create Teaching: Slavery Fact Sheets, Gilder Lehrman Institute of American History, http://www.class.uh.edu/gl/slaveryfactsheet.htm.
5. Ira Berlin, *Slaves Without Masters: The Free Negro in the Antebellum South* (New York: Random House, 1974).
6. Steven Mintz, "American Slavery in Comparative Perspective," Gilder Lehrman Institute of American History. http://www.gilderlehrman.org/history-by-era/origins-slavery/resources/american-slavery-comparative-perspective.
7. Walter Johnson, *Soul by Soul: Life inside the Antebellum Slave Market* (Cambridge, MA: Harvard University Press, 1999).
8. Ira Berlin, *The Making of African America: Four Great Migrations* (New York: Viking, 2010).
9. Steven Deyle, *Carry Me Back: The Domestic Slave Trade in American Life* (New York: Oxford University Press, 2005).
10. "Slaves and Slaveholdings," Gilder Lehrman Institute of American History, http://www.gilderlehrman.org/history-by-era/slavery-and-anti-slavery/resources/slaves-and-slavehol.
11. Ibid.
12. The Gilder Lehrman Guide to Create Teaching: Slavery Fact Sheets.
13. Eric Foner, *Gateway to Freedom: The Hidden History of America's Fugitive Slaves* (New York: Oxford University Press, 2015), p. 44.
14. The Gilder Lehrman Guide to Create Teaching: Slavery Fact Sheets.
15. Alan Gallay, "Indian Slavery in the Americas," Gilder Lehrman Institute of American History, https://www.gilderlehrman.org/history-by-era/origins-slavery/essays/indian-slavery-americas.
16. Ibid.
17. "Slavery," Oklahoma Historical Society, OHS Division, http://www.okhistory.org/publications/enc/entry.php?entry=SL003.
18. Berlin, *Slaves Without Masters.*

Index

Page numbers in *italics* refer to illustrations.

Illustration Credits

AFP/Getty Images: 165

Alan King Engraving/Alamy: 417

Alexander Gardner/Library of
    Congress: 141

Anthony Berger/Library of Congress: 262

Anwar Vázquez/Wikimedia Commons: 24

Bettmann/Corbis UK Ltd.: 47, 91, 268, 319

Biblioteca Nacional, Madrid/
    akg-images: 11

Bibliothèque nationale, Paris/Bridgeman
    Art Library: 19

bpk Bildagentur für Kunst, Kultur
    und Geschichte, Berlin/Photo Scala,
    Florence: 13

Brady-Handy Photograph Collection,
    Library of Congress: 209

Bruno Arrigoni/akg-images: 333

Caiaimage/Martin Barraud/Getty
    Images: 284

Carol M. Highsmith/Library of
    Congress: 252

Central Press/Getty Images: 228

Charles "Teenie" Harris Archive/Carnegie
    Museum of Art/Getty Images: 113

© Christie's Images/Bridgeman Art
    Library: 21

Christie's Images Ltd./Superstock Ltd.: 357

Cincinnati Art Museum, Ohio, USA/
    Subscription Fund Purchase/Bridgeman
    Art Library: 74

From the collection of the Earl of
    Mansfield, Scone Palace, Perth/Scone
    Palace: 315

ddp USA/REX Shutterstock: 311

Design Pics Inc./REX Shutterstock: 342

Erik Blome: 191

Everett Collection/Alamy: 155, 237

Everett Collection Historical/
    Alamy: 352

Fine Art Museum, Rio de Janeiro/
    akg-images: 52

Gemäldegalerie Alte Meister, Dresden/
    akg-images: 32

Haversat Collection/David Haversat
    Magic: 287

H. B. Lindsley/Library of Congress: 66

Historic New Orleans Collection: 122

Hulton Archive/Getty Images: 160

Hulton Fine Art Collection/Getty
    Images: 49

The Hutchins Center, Harvard
    University: 4

Illustrated London News Ltd./Mary Evans
    Picture Library: 361

INTERFOTO/Sammlung Rauch/Mary
    Evans Picture Library: 146

John Reekie/Library of Congress: 391

John Webb/Art Archive: 183

Jon Brenneis/The LIFE Images Collection/
    Getty Images: 219

Jon Feingersh/Getty Images: 399

Keystone Pictures USA/Alamy: 395

Library of Congress: 8, 35, 38, 45, 55, 61, 85,
    99, 108, 119, 131, 327, 381, 408

Liszt Collection/Alamy: 338

The Metropolitan Museum of Art/
    Art Resource/Photo Scala,
    Florence: 26

Michel Zabe/AZA/INBA/Bridgeman Art
    Library: 15

A NOTE ABOUT THE AUTHOR

Henry Louis Gates, Jr., is an educator, scholar, writer, editor, and public intellectual. He received his undergraduate degree summa cum laude from Yale College and his Ph.D. from Cambridge University. He lives in Cambridge, Massachusetts.

A NOTE ON THE TYPE

This book was set in a version of the well-known Monotype face
Bembo. This letter was cut for the celebrated Venetian printer
Aldus Manutius by Francesco Griffo and first used in Pietro
Cardinal Bembo's *De Aetna* of 1495.

Composed by North Market Street Graphics,
Lancaster, Pennsylvania

Printed and bound by Toppan Leefung,
China

Designed by Cassandra J. Pappas